Handbook on Testing

HANDBOOK ON TESTING

Edited by **Ronna F. Dillon**

Greenwood Press
Westport, Connecticut • London

Library of Congress Cataloging-in-Publication Data

Handbook on testing / edited by Ronna F. Dillon.
    p. cm.
    Includes bibliographical references and index.
    ISBN 0–313–28984–0 (alk. paper)
    1. Educational tests and measurements—Handbooks, manuals, etc.
    2. Examinations—Handbooks, manuals, etc. I. Dillon, Ronna F.
    LB3051.H3199   1997
    371.26—dc21   96–47430

British Library Cataloguing in Publication Data is available.

Library of Congress Catalog Card Number: 96–47430
ISBN: 0–313–28984–0

First published in 1997

Greenwood Press, 88 Post Road West, Westport, CT 06881
An imprint of Greenwood Publishing Group, Inc.

Printed in the United States of America

The paper used in this book complies with the
Permanent Paper Standard issued by the National
Information Standards Organization (Z39.48–1984).

10 9 8 7 6 5 4 3 2 1

Copyright Acknowledgment

The editor and publisher are grateful to the following for granting permission to reprint from their material:

Excerpts from *Standards for Educational and Psychological Testing* copyright © 1985 by the American Psychological Association. Reprinted with permission. Further reproduction without the express written permission of the American Psychological Association is prohibited.

Contents

Illustrations

FIGURES

Preface

Accurate measurement of intellectual abilities is essential on theoretical as well as practical grounds. Data from tests of knowledge, skills, abilities, and other attributes provide information with respect to theories of intelligence, broadly defined. Similarly, test data provide information regarding the nature and course of developmental change. From an applied perspective, the results of testing yield information with respect to the efficacy of particular interventions.

Researchers in the field of testing have witnessed recent significant changes in test development and test administration procedures. The motivation for such advances lies in changes in conceptions of intelligence and ability as well as modifications in testing technologies. The *Handbook on Testing* contains important recent work in testing, including new undertakings on a range of test administration methods, types of abilities, and measures taken from tests. New work in intelligence testing is included. The mechanisms and use of dynamic assessment and learning tests also are considered. In addition, issues of test theory and standards are discussed. Several large-scale testing programs are reviewed, including predictor and criterion development work in the military, private sector employment testing, and testing for admission to medical school. The link between assessment and instruction is highlighted in several chapters, including coverage in special education testing. The features and scope of the *Handbook on Testing* make it an important reference volume.

Chapter authors provide discussions of the conceptual frameworks that guide

their work, of predictor development issues, existing needs in the testing literature, and of the manner in which their work addresses these limitations, unique
constraints, and opportunities in each testing environment as well as future directions.

1

A New Era in Testing

Ronna F. Dillon

Most testing seems, at some level, to be tied to researchers' or test developers' conceptions of intelligence, sometimes as an end and sometimes as a means toward some more practical end. In the former case, testing may be undertaken for the purpose of elucidating intellectual, attitudinal, or other attributes, thereby resulting in theoretical advances. In the latter respect, the outcomes of testing are used for purposes such as selection, classification, and performance assessment. In any event, changes in conceptions of intelligence underlie changes in mental testing. Finally, advances in testing are made possible by advances in test theory as well as changes in testing technologies.

Our new era in testing is guided by a theory of the domain of interest, by goals (i.e., the desired uses to which test results will be put), and by rules and standards—some new, some enduring. The credibility of a test, then, is determined in large measure by the extent to which the test is grounded in a theory of the domain and is developed in the context of the rules of measurement, abiding appropriate test standards. The usefulness of a given test not only derives from its predictive power but also comes from the diagnostic and prescriptive information it provides. Testing programs range in purpose from work designed to redefine intelligence, to work directed toward selection and classification of individuals with a wide range of competencies in a wide range of job environments, to other ability and achievement testing, to efforts focused on ascertaining specific training effectiveness.

The comments made in this chapter are designed to be relevant to a broad range of testing paradigms, a very large set of predictors, and a wide range of test milieus. The chapter is divided into two sections. The first section provides an overview framework for understanding testing approaches. The second section offers a set of issues that cut across testing approaches.

FRAMEWORK FOR UNDERSTANDING TESTING APPROACHES

Testing programs can be considered along four dimensions: abilities, methods, measures, and timing. Abilities range from fundamental perceptual processes to information-processing components and metacomponents, to knowledge, reasoning abilities, and school subject abilities, to personality, temperament, attitude, and motivational attributes, to interpersonal attributes. Methods of test administration include, among other procedures, computerized adaptive testing and dynamic testing. The measures taken from the tests include, among other measures, psychophysiological recording, behavioral assessment, and psychomotor activity. Tests can be given prior to employment for selection or prior to job selection, for the purposes of classification, or for job enhancement, such as for training, retention, or promotion. Figure 1.1 summarizes the types of abilities, measures taken from the tests, and methods of testing.

ISSUES IN THEORY, TEST DESIGN, AND TEST DEVELOPMENT

Model-Based Measurement

In the model-based version of test theory, item response theory, some well-known rules of measurement do not apply. Embretson (this volume) provides a set of ''new rules of measurement'' to guide test development practice. She contrasts these rules with the well-known rules that are based on classical test theory.

Conceptions of Intelligence

Lohman (this volume) reviews the impact of personal, religious, and scientific beliefs on theories and tests of human abilities. Historical changes in notions, such as the extent to which human nature is plastic or fixed and the extent of innate human equality, are considered in the context of education and other social reforms of the past century. Theories of intelligence differ also in the nature of the database on which the theory rests. Naglieri and Das (this volume) note that some researchers (e.g., Horn, 1985; Jensen, 1982) base their views on complex and extensive statistical methods to uncover mental structures, while other researchers (e.g., Gardner, 1983; Piaget, 1950) base their formulations on interpretations of psychological observations and experimental findings. Still other researchers base their theories on psychophysiological, neurophysiological, or information-processing paradigms (Lindsley, 1960; Luria, 1966; Pribram,

Figure 1.1
Testing Approaches Framework

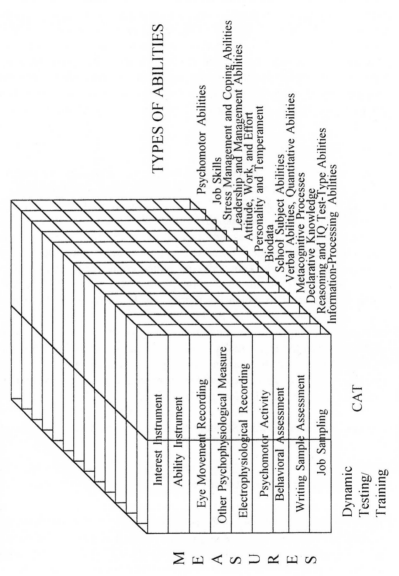

1971), sometimes coupled with other experimental manipulations (Dillon, 1985, 1986, 1989a, 1989b).

Naglieri and Das (this volume) note also that IQ tests, designed to meet the needs of applied psychologists, were developed in an essentially parallel manner to theoretical positions. Critical of the isolation of theoretical and applied psychology, Brody (1992) echoes a not-uncommon sentiment among intelligence researchers, that advances in the study of intelligence have not had a major impact on the development of intelligence tests. Theories differ also in their link to programs of remediation in general intellectual abilities or specific academic abilities (see Haywood & Tzuriel, 1992; Lochhead & Clements, 1979).

Specific Models

A specific example of research in the theory of intelligence comes from the PASS (planning, attention, simultaneous, successive) cognitive processing theory (Das, Kirby, & Jarman, 1979; Das, Naglieri, & Kirby, 1994; Naglieri & Das, this volume). In conceptualizing the theory (see Das [1972] for early work on the theory), central roles are given to the PASS processes, to the notions of interrelated interdependent functional systems, and to the influences of and influences on the base of knowledge on which cognitive processes are operating.

One of many important dimensions against which specific theories are evaluated is the extent to which the theory can be linked directly to instructional and remedial decisions. The PASS theory fares well in this regard. Bearing in mind that learning successes and failures may be due to many factors in addition to the nature of the individual's "PASS" abilities, the goal of PASS researchers is to provide a way to examine the cognitive characteristics of examinees to determine if these processes influence academic performance and to provide cognitive process-based training (Das, Mishra, & Pool, 1995). As an example of this work, the PASS Remedial Program (PREP; Das, Carlson, Davidson, & Longe, 1977) couples a PASS theoretical orientation with process-based training (Das et al., 1995).

Information-Processing Models

Componential researchers (Dillon, 1989a, 1992; Embretson & Schneider, 1989; Pellegrino & Glaser, 1980, 1982; Sternberg, 1977a, 1977b) conceptualize intelligence, in part, as the operation of a small number of elementary information processes, executed during complex IQ test–type tasks. The information-processing substrate is believed to be central to thinking and problem solving. The group of information-processing componential approaches to intelligence measurement diverges from traditional product-based intelligence measurement. In the language of the framework outlined in Figure 1.1, these techniques vary the measures taken from tests. Rather than solely using test scores as data, components researchers use measures of ongoing information-processing operations, in place of or in addition to other attribute measures, in models of intelligent performance. The models then are validated against the same sets of criteria against which traditional models have been validated. Two significant advantages emerged from this work. First, models comprised of information-processing components have been found to account for markedly greater variance in intelligent performance than do models comprised of test scores (e.g., Dillon, 1989a, 1992). Second, information-processing models are diagnostically and prescriptively useful. The models yield data about examinees' strengths and limitations in the information-processing components that underlie test scores. Component information reflects knowledge acquisition, performance, and meta-componential underpinnings of performance.

General versus Specific Abilities

In reviewing research on intelligence, Lohman (this volume) distinguishes general ability (g) theories from multiple ability theories (see also Ree & Carretta, this volume; Ree & Earles, 1991, 1994). Rather than advocating a particular perspective, Lohman considers constructing hierarchical models of ability organization. In this way, multiple differentiations of specialized abilities reside beneath g, and, as Gustafsson and Snow (this volume) note, the selection of ability constructs can be driven by theoretical or applied needs.

Ability Profiles

Gustafsson and Snow (this volume) and collaborators (Gustafsson & Balke, 1993; Gustafsson & Muthén, 1996; Gustafsson & Undheim, 1996) demonstrate the elegance and usefulness of hierarchical models of ability organization. Such models include both broad and narrow abilities. Hierarchical models make possible the description of patterns of performance in terms of profiles. Moreover, profile analysis can be extended to categorization into types, wherein contrasts between profiles are possible. Studies of the use of ability profiles for prediction as well as for diagnosis and prescription are ongoing. Researchers note that ability profiles can aid in diagnosing malfunctions in cognitive performance and in isolating specific learning difficulties. Moreover, they point out that ability profiles can play a role in research on multiple ability and aptitude dimensions. Finally, information derived from ability profiles should be useful in academic and career counseling.

Nature of Predictors

Another important point in understanding testing approaches concerns the nature of the predictor space. In this regard, the level of specificity of predictors, domains tapped, and the dependence on prior knowledge for successful completion of test items all are important factors.

Level of Specificity. In the past three decades, we have witnessed several cycles in prevailing views on test specificity. With respect to level of specificity of predictors, we have moved from measuring *g*-type phenomena, to linking predictors to specific job specifications, back again to general aptitudes that are independent of specific advantage or experience. In considering testing in the public sector, we see from comments made by Campbell and Kleinke (this volume) that linking predictors to specific job demands may become untenable in our current context, wherein the demands of specific jobs, and the need for the jobs themselves, change quickly.

Predictor Domains. Regarding the types of predictor domains, scientists have moved toward physiological and psychomotor measures, away from these domains, and back again. We have moved, also, toward tests of complex thinking and problem solving, away from such complex thinking skills toward simpler behavioral measures, and back again to complex cognitive processes. Also, current work reflects broadened conceptions of aptitude, wherein metacognitive phenomena, psychomotor predictors, and complex cognitive abilities such as flexibility and tacitly acquired knowledge are included in models of training or job performance (e.g., Dillon, 1989a, 1989b, 1992). Work by members of the Learning Abilities Measurement Program (LAMP) group at Armstrong Laboratory provides examples of some of this progress (e.g., Kyllonen, 1991, 1993, 1994; Tirre, 1995).

Tirre (this volume) considers predictor domain issues in predicting simulated and actual flight performance in Basic Flight Instruction Tutoring System (BFITS; Benton, Corriveau, Koonce, & Tirre, 1992) and the Semi-Automated Flight Evaluation System (SAFES; Benton, Baldwin, & Koonce, 1995) environments. Like work in my laboratory (e.g., Dillon & Larson, 1996; Dillon & Witick, 1996), the work of Kyllonen (1991, 1993, 1994), Tirre (1995), and others at Armstrong Laboratory (e.g., Ree & Earles, 1991, 1994) centers on the role of basic human abilities and learning rate for a range of pilot performance criteria. The work of Kyllonen, Tirre, and others at Armstrong Laboratory also includes consideration of the role of psychomotor measures in aviation performance, while work in my laboratory includes attention to the roles of cognitive flexibility and tacitly acquired knowledge in aviation performance. Moreover, my work posits a range of models for different proficiency levels (Dillon, 1996). Work in both settings also focuses on indices of situation awareness, such as location error, hazard detection, blindspot avoidance, and crash avoidance, to predict both simulated and actual flight performance.

Military testing scientists, Medical College Admission Test (MCAT) researchers, and private industry test developers point to the need to consider noncognitive factors in prediction models. Success in medical school, for example, may be related to factors such as motivation and maturity, while leadership and management processes may also play important roles in the success of military officers.

Interpersonal factors are receiving renewed attention. Borman and Motowidlo

(1993) distinguish task performance from contextual performance. They note that the latter processes, including assisting others and communicating effectively, are not job specific. As a consequence, Campbell and Kleinke (this volume) note that selection instruments designed to measure these constructs would be resilient to job changes.

Tirre (this volume) discusses predictor domain limitations that can plague testing efforts. First, he notes that the ability domain may not be sampled adequately. Second, abilities chosen may be too narrow in scope. Third, tests chosen may have inadequate stability. Fourth, tests may be constructed without adequate theoretical grounding, making revision problematic.

As noted earlier, the use of predictors that are relevant to specific job parameters may be ill-advised when one considers that the job likely will change quickly (Cascio, 1995). In addition, adverse impact considerations constrain the use of predictors that tap skills that will be the objects of job training. Clearly, differences between individuals in entry-level job competencies may not be related to those individuals' learning abilities during training or on the job.

Prior to the 1991 revision of the MCAT (Mitchell, Haynes, & Koenig, 1994), researchers faced an interesting problem. In attempting to maximize their scores on the MCAT, hopeful undergraduates gained as much exposure to science content as they could and, consequently, minimized their preparation in social sciences and humanities material. In contrast, there was a growing acknowledgment of the medical community's desire for physicians who were broadly prepared to address the human and social issues of medicine as well as possessing relevant domain-specific knowledge and skills and being literate in use of appropriate technologies. To address this need, the 1991 revision contains modified assessment formats, skill domains, and scoring procedures. The revised MCAT was developed to assess the following attributes: basic concepts in biology, chemistry, and physics; facility with problem solving and critical thinking; and communication and writing skills. Cognitive processes tapped by the test include comprehension, evaluation, application, incorporation of new information, flexibility in scientific reasoning, hypothesis testing, identification of components and relationships, identification of main ideas, reasoning using quantitative data, and seeking clarification. The writing sample was intended to measure the examinee's ability to develop a central idea, synthesize concepts and ideas, present ideas cohesively and logically, and write clearly.

Prior Knowledge. In terms of dependence on prior knowledge, certain assessments are aimed directly at specific prior knowledge, such as physical sciences or biological sciences knowledge. Other assessments, such as verbal reasoning, can, of course, be contaminated by specific knowledge requirements. With respect to the MCAT, researchers concluded that verbal reasoning task passages should be drawn from texts in humanities, social sciences, and natural sciences areas, but questions should not require specific subject matter knowledge. The Computerized Adaptive Testing–Armed Services Vocational Aptitude

Battery (CAT–ASVAB) coding speed test is another example of the importance of a highly general predictor domain.

Changes in predictor space configurations have been motivated by theoretical issues as well as practical concerns and the development of new technologies— an example of the latter being the availability of information-processing technologies (e.g., Dillon, 1989a, 1989b). Practical concerns such as improving test utility and reducing adverse impact have motivated other changes in test paradigms.

Curriculum-Based Assessment. Curriculum-Based Assessment (CBA) is being investigated as a potentially useful means of identifying and programming services for individuals with disabilities in the schools. The growing interest in CBA and support for its use in the classroom (McLoughlin & Lewis, 1990) come from its potential to link assessment, curriculum, and instruction. The CBA approach is curriculum based and behaviorally defined, it seeks to measure well-defined domains, and it permits assessment of minimal levels of proficiency. The CBA process (1) is based on clear behavioral tasks, (2) relates precisely to the components of the curriculum under instruction, and (3) focuses on and begins instruction at the student's knowledge and skill entry level (Howell & Morehead, 1987; Luftig, 1989). With respect to the limitations of Curriculum-Based Assessment, CBA tests typically are teacher made and, as such, are not designed to predict academic, social, or vocational performance. To bring about advances in assessment programs for students with disabilities, Miller and Miller (this volume) recommend that individuals concerned with testing be aided to reduce their reluctance to learn to employ new assessment tools, that students be evaluated with respect to skill mastery rather than class ranking or grades, and that both short- and long-term goal attainment be viewed as important.

Validating Models of Aptitude

A very important consideration in evaluating testing paradigms is establishing the grounding of the work in a model of intelligence. The work of scientists at the Association of American Medical Colleges (AAMC; Koenig & Wiley, this volume) points to the crucial role of such theoretical grounding in attempts to understand complex intelligent performance. By isolating the cognitive substrates of science, verbal reasoning, and writing, researchers have acknowledged the central role of mechanisms such as evaluation, application, incorporation of new information, flexibility in reasoning, hypothesis testing, identifying components and relationships, identifying main ideas, and seeking clarification in complex intelligent behavior.

The U.S. Air Force's LAMP work and the U.S. Army's Project A contributions in predictor development are discussed elsewhere (e.g., Maier, 1993; Martin, 1994). Waters (this volume) provides a historical overview of military testing research. Among important points to note from the military testing literature, differences in the predictor space as a function of the level of expertise of the learner is paramount. From work done in my laboratory with collegiate aviation students (i.e., student pilots), Jerry Larson and I (Dillon & Larson, 1996) demonstrate that different spatial and cognitive ability models predict performance at different "developmental" levels.

Psychometric Credibility

Clearly, the psychometric credibility of test instruments is central to the quality of research. Ekstrom, Elmore, and Schafer (this volume) discuss standards for educational and psychological tests and testing professionals.

Standardizability. Issues here concern standardizability of test procedures. Tests must be administered and scored in the same way for all examinees if meaningful interpretations are to be based on sets of test scores. Researchers at the AAMC addressed challenges with respect to standardization of scoring procedures when a direct writing assessment was included in the 1991 MCAT (see Koenig & Wiley, this volume). Understanding the test administration process for individuals with disabilities and for linguistic minority examinees also is essential (Eyde, Nester, Heaton, & Nelson, 1994).

Validity. Validity evidence may relate to the constructs being measured. In this case, changes over time or with intervention, group differences, and response patterns from correlational data are important sources of information. As Ekstrom et al. (this volume) note, validity evidence may relate to test content, including sampling and logical validity. Validity evidence also may derive from relations between test data and outside criteria, with different temporal relations between predictors and criteria. As in the case of using the MCAT to enhance prediction of success in medical school, researchers are often concerned with the extent to which a particular predictor test or battery increases usefulness of a selection protocol in identifying those apt to succeed in a particular setting. Interestingly, validity researchers have questioned whether all validity evidence might not be conceptualized more fruitfully as construct validity evidence (e.g., Messick, 1995).

As an example of validation work, relationships were examined among MCAT section scores as well as between MCAT scores and various concurrent criteria, including self-appraisal of academic skills, undergraduate grade-point average (GPA) in the sciences, and GPA in the nonsciences (Koenig & Wiley, this volume). In addition, the factor structure of the battery has been examined (Li & Mitchell, 1992). With writing assessment, because all prompts are designed to measure similar writing and cognitive skills, and subject matter is not germane to the assessment, assessment of the difficulty levels of test forms is of paramount importance.

GENERALIZATION. Test scores are said to possess generalizability when the scores derived from the tests have the same meaning across different populations. Generalization of validity involves using validity evidence obtained from one set of studies to justify the subsequent use of a test in a similar setting.

ADVERSE IMPACT. Issues related to adverse impact have posed challenges in military selection, pilot and air traffic controller selection, medical school and other college selection, as well as other selection and classification milieus. The issues center on the extent to which specific tests and/or test procedures have differential impact on specific groups of the population. The importance of adverse impact considerations is underscored when one considers that particular groups of examinees may perform poorly relative to other groups of equivalent relevant aptitude because of adverse impact of tests or test procedures, with such impact obscuring actual potential to succeed in training or on the job.

FAIRNESS. Test fairness implies the absence of group-related biases that would result in differential opportunities for examinees. The work of MCAT developers exemplifies precautions taken during form assembly to avoid bias. In developing multiple choice sections of the test, extra effort was exerted to recruit minority and women item writers. In addition, assessments of differential accessibility of test items were made throughout various regions of the country, and sensitivity reviews were undertaken. Finally, Differential Item Functioning (DIF) analyses were conducted, and items identified as functioning differentially were reviewed and revised.

Reliability. Reliability estimates are designed to measure the extent to which test scores are free of errors of measurement. Internal consistency, test-retest, and parallel forms coefficients are described below.

INTERNAL CONSISTENCY. Measures of internal consistency provide evidence of the extent to which test items tap a unidimensional attribute or construct. The most general measure of internal consistency is Cronbach *a*.

TEST-RETEST RELIABILITY. Test-retest coefficients provide measures of the consistency of examinees' responding to the same instrument on two different occasions. Test-retest reliability evidence is sought when stable traits, as opposed to more transient states, are being measured.

PARALLEL FORMS. Parallel forms reliability measures the extent to which examinees respond similarly to two different forms of a test, administered at the same point in time. Equivalence and stability are quantified by having examinees respond to two different forms of a test at two different times.

Nature of the Criteria

We need also to consider the criteria against which the paradigms are evaluated. Criteria vary from concurrent measures of intelligent performance to long-term prediction, such as success in medical school or success at the end of a lengthy course of technical training. Cascio (1995) advocates a change in focus from task-based job analysis to process-based analyses. The result of such a change could be an aggregation of tasks into job clusters, focusing on shared skill requirements.

The use of job-emulated criteria is increasing. For example, in the aviation work discussed by Tirre, BFITS has been used as a criterion, as are data from simulated flight scenarios and actual training aircraft. The latter criterion environments permit researchers to account for certain visual and vestibular aspects of flight that are not possible to emulate in simulated flight. As a result, some researchers (e.g., Tirre, 1995) believe that the ultimate validation of a pilot aptitude battery must be in a real airplane.

The SAFES device (Tirre, this volume) is being developed under Air Force contract. The device is designed to record in a real airplane flight performance data that are analagous to data that BFITS records in a simulator (Benton, Baldwin, & Koonce, 1995). Also, efforts such as SAFES could use the student's rate of flying skill acquisition as a criterion against which to validate an aptitude battery (Duke & Ree, 1996).

Tirre urges development of a rating scale—or other instruments—that captures and quantifies the flight instructor's assessment of the student's flying skills. Interestingly, such an assessment device has been developed in my laboratory (Dillon & Witick, 1996), as one of several criterion measures against which a model of aptitudes and learning abilities is validated. The work is designed to predict success in collegiate aviation training, thereby enhancing student pilot selection. With respect to Air Force pilot selection, Tirre notes that, ideally, the criterion for a validation study of a pilot selection battery would be the common factor underlying a set of criteria, such as learning rate, flight skills, and flight instructor's assessments. The ongoing collegiate aviation work in my laboratory quantifies such criterion measures, by measuring student performance in ground and flight courses, learning increments on simulated flight scenarios, and various weighted flight maneuvers from actual in-flight Federal Aviation Administration (FAA) check rides.

In addition to its efforts in predictor development, the work from the U.S. Army's Project A made a clear contribution to researchers' thinking about predictor/criterion relationships. Using the notion of the ''rolling predictor'' enabled researchers to integrate newly acquired information about learners' knowledge, skills, abilities, or other attributes with previous information to predict later performance. Attributes that were criterion measures at one point in time would serve as predictors at a later point. For example, the Armed Services Vocational Aptitude Battery (ASVAB) would be used to predict training performance, ASVAB and training performance together would be used to predict early job performance among soldiers, and performance during a soldier's second tour of duty would be predicted by the previous attributes plus performance during the first tour. Such an approach enabled researchers to validate a range of other predictors in addition to ASVAB.

Measures of training performance were the first criterion measures used in Project A. Measures for army-wide tasks and MOS-specific tasks were developed for selected Military Occupational Specialty groups. Criterion instruments used in Project A included hands-on, knowledge, rating, and administrative index scores, tapping the following constructs: core technical proficiency, general soldiering proficiency, effort and leadership, personal discipline, and physical fitness and military bearing. Researchers might consider the potential applicability of this model of performance for other occupations as well. The criterion work carried out in Project A provided links between training performance and job performance, and it provided researchers with a comprehensive framework for thinking about training and job performance and about the nature of aptitudes across occupations.

TEST ADMINISTRATION ISSUES

Several general guidelines are crucial to the integrity of tests and test administration procedures. As discussed earlier, issues of standardization of test administration procedures, reliability, and validity are central to the testing enterprise. Qualifications and training of test administrators also are important. Test security and a proper testing environment must be maintained. With respect to test scoring, we must maintain accuracy, timeliness, and confidentiality.

Method of Test Administration

Several important issues surround the most desirable method of test administration. Test users must consider the goals of testing (which, of course, are tied to one's definition of intelligence), the amount of time available for testing, available resources and technology, adaptability and readiness, and any needs particular to the group of individuals being tested.

Goals. The goals of the test administrator determine what to test and how to test. For example, one central goal is to assess as veridically as possible an individual's intellectual competence for the purpose of validating theories of intelligence. So the guiding view of intelligence determines the testing approach. If the researcher believes that intelligence is the ability to profit from experience, some type of test-train-test paradigm will be employed (Budoff, 1987; Feuerstein, Rand, & Hoffman, 1979). If a group of researchers believes that intelligence resides at the zone of proximal development—that is, at the intersection of the individual's unaided test performance and performance following intervention—then a paradigm such as the Graduated Prompting Assessment approach may be used (e.g., Campione, Brown, & Ferrera, 1982; Vygotsky, 1962, 1978). Here, intelligence is viewed as a developmental, dynamic structural capacity, wherein the extent to which competence is changed through training varies from one point in development to another point. If one believes that intelligence is elaborated thinking, then a testing-for-competence paradigm may be used. In this latter case, intelligence is activated by engaging examinees in test procedures that foster mediation and dual coding (see Dillon, 1996, this volume, for reviews and discussions of this work).

A second purpose of testing is to determine the extent to which an individual has profited from instruction or other experiences. Assessing program quality and instructional effectiveness is important, both to ensure that individuals are receiving appropriate services and to determine the best way to render those services.

A third major category of uses for tests is to aid selection, classification, training, promotion, and retention efforts. With respect to selection, tests are used to determine those individuals who have the greatest likelihood of succeeding during training or on the job. The substantial costs of training for many jobs, the often short time in which complex skills must be mastered in preparation for functioning on the job, and significant rates of attrition underscore the importance of effective testing programs. Classification efforts help test administrators determine those individuals who are best suited to particular training or jobs. Issues of retention and promotion also underscore the need for accurate testing of intellectual abilities. Testing for attainment of job standards and annual fitness for duty testing are important examples here (e.g., Campbell & Kleinke, this volume.).

A fourth purpose to which tests are put is to serve explicitly as tools to promote learning (e.g., Dempster, this volume). Research in this area demonstrates that the act of being tested often has an effect on what is measured. First, interest is in the *mechanism* by which such learning occurs. The retrieval hypothesis holds that retrieval processes play a major role in learning during testing, as evidenced by the finding that the memorability of newly learned material is enhanced more by further test trials than by additional study trials. In contrasting acquisition and forgetting, Dempster notes that further study increases the accessibility of information, while testing increases the resistance of information to forgetting because of the relatively greater demands that testing places on retrieval operations. A major point of this research is that testing may provide cognitive-processing benefits that are unavailable through other learning and study activities. It is not clear at this point what the relationship is between the type of classroom test administered and the amount and type of consequent learning. One might speculate that the type of test and resulting learning parallels the literature on teaching methods and learning. For example, one might expect test items that focus on factual information to affect fact learning, essay-type questions that focus on relations among facts to enhance the building of internal connections, and test items that require the examinee to build external connections to enhance rule learning.

Another important issue with respect to the role of tests in learning pertains to the *indirect* effects of tests on learning. For example, the act of taking a test subsequently may cause the learner to reprocess material that is not part of the test, due possibly to spatiotemporal or topical-semantic similarity between test questions and other affected material.

Time Available for Testing

Testing programs must yield the maximum amount of information about prospective trainees or employees in the most efficient manner possible. A factor that complicates such parsimonious testing is the need to assess an often extremely broad range of knowledge, skills, abilities, and other attributes underlying job performance. The current MCAT boasts a significant reduction in testing time over the previous version. Regardless of the purposes for testing, our testing time is at a premium because of the expense and lost work, study, or training time endured by examinees.

Resources and Technology Needed for Administration and Scoring

The military Computerized Adaptive Testing (CAT) development program has been a monumental undertaking in evaluating the relative validities of paper-and-pencil versus computerized adaptive testing of the ASVAB. Some of the challenges of this program are shared by other very large-scale testing programs, including the difficulty of becoming operational at different types of test sites. The costs associated with test and technology development are evaluated against any increases in validity and concomitant reductions in required testing time that may result. As Moreno, Segall, and Hetter (this volume) note, adaptive testing is designed to permit administration of relatively short tests that provide equally valid measurement across all ability levels. The computer-administered CAT-ASVAB program also exemplifies appropriate standardization of test administration procedures, item security, and maximum data scoring and recording accuracy.

The direct writing assessment on the MCAT exemplifies issues that are relevant to scoring writing samples. In the case of the MCAT, each essay is scored on a six-point scale by two raters. The two scores are summed to create a total score for each essay. Two essays are used, and their scores are combined. A final numeric score is converted to a letter grade for reporting. The work on the MCAT also underscores the need to monitor score use and test preparation practices.

Adaptability

Often, testing programs involve testing at different sites. In addition, differences in equipment and facilities often pose challenges. On a related matter, special considerations often arise when testing children. Frequently, procedures used with adult examinees are not appropriate for use with children.

Program Delivery

Numerous issues pertain to delivery of testing services. As examples of relevant issues, utility, implementation, and attrition are described below.

Utility. Important issues relate to test utility. Among these issues are ease of administration, costs associated with training test administrators, maintaining test sites and equipment, and preparing test materials.

Implementation. Often, test development and revision efforts take several years. Changing conceptions of the nature of intelligence, coupled with rapid changes in job demands, make careful operationalization, in as expedient a manner as appropriate, a potential goal in test development efforts. We also need to develop and use tests that have broad applicability.

Attrition. The need to minimize attrition will remain an important challenge in test development efforts. As the costs of training continue to rise, and as the specificity and technical demands of jobs at all levels continue to increase, it is important to remain vigilant in our efforts to reduce attrition. We should continue to pursue vigorously techniques that permit diagnosis of an examinee's potential to succeed in training or that enable optimal job classification, based on relevant knowledge, skills, abilities, and other attributes.

SUMMARY

Testing paradigms vary as a function of the knowledge, skills, abilities, and other attributes tested; the method of test administration; and the measures taken from the tests. In addition, testing activities differ in intended purpose. Some programs are designed to enhance selection, while other programs focus on job classification. Still other programs are used for training, promotion, and retention.

Abilities tested run the gamut: including information-processing components; reasoning and problem solving; metacognitive abilities; psychomotor abilities; verbal and quantitative abilities; personality and temperament dimensions; attitude, work, and effort dimensions; leadership and interpersonal abilities; stress management and coping dimensions; and technical expertise. Changes in conceptions of intelligence continue to be reflected in changes in predictor space configurations. The use of ability profiles addresses this disparity. In addition, changes in the manner in which various professions and associated professionals are viewed have motivated certain changes in predictor space configurations.

Variations in methods of test administration include dynamic assessment and computerized adaptive testing. Measures taken from the tests include eye movement recording, electrophysiological recording, psychomotor activity, behavioral assessment, writing assessment, and technical knowledge. The measures can be used in addition to, or in place of, paper-and-pencil and / or behavioral measures.

Significant changes continue to occur in conceptions of learner characteristics and the predictor space, methods of test administration, links between testing and intervention, tests, and testing technologies. In addition to providing the most accurate assessment possible for all examinees, testing time should be used judiciously. Moreover, models of the predictor space should move toward greater inclusiveness. Kyllonen (this volume) also conveys this sentiment, asserting that an advanced testing system for the twenty-first century must measure all relevant aptitude factors. Finally, we may do well to strive toward having tests "field ready" in as expedient a fashion as possible. Kyllonen (this volume) offers suggestions for incorporating all significant technology associated with abilities measurement, that is, computer delivery, item-generation technology, multidimensional adaptive technology, comprehensive cognitive abilities measurement, time-parameterized testing, and a latent factor–centered design.

In addition to providing valuable sources of information with respect to learners' knowledge, skills, abilities, and other attributes, the information from tests may be linked to intervention. Also, tests themselves may foster learning. That is, the act of taking a particular test may alter the attributes being tested. Changes in the field of testing seem certain to continue as the nature of jobs continues to change at an accelerated rate.

REFERENCES

Benton, C., Baldwin, T., & Koonce, J. (1995). *Implementation of a semi-automated flight evaluation system (SAFES) phase 2* (Annual Technical Report). Brooks Air Force Base, TX: Armstrong Laboratory—Human Resources Directorate.

Benton, C., Corriveau, P., Koonce, J. M., & Tirre, W. C. (1992). *Development of the basic flight instruction tutoring system (BFITS)* (AL-TP-1991-0060). Brooks Air Force Base, TX: Armstrong Laboratory—Human Resources Directorate.

Borman, W. C., & Motowidlo, S. J. (1993). Expanding the criterion domain to include elements of contextual performance. In N. Schmitt & W. C. Borman (Eds.), *Personnel selection in organizations* (pp. 71–98). San Francisco: Jossey-Bass.

Brody, N. (1992). *Intelligence* (2nd ed.). San Diego: Academic Press.

Budoff, M. (1987). The validity of learning potential assessment. In C. S. Lidz (Ed.), *Dynamic assessment: An interactional approach to evaluating learning potential* (pp. 52–81). New York: Guilford Press.

Campione, J. K., Brown, A. L., & Ferrera, R. A. (1982). Mental retardation and intelligence. In R. J. Sternberg (Ed.), *Handbook of human intelligence* (pp. 392–490). Cambridge, England: Cambridge University Press.

Cascio, W. F. (1995). Whither industrial and organizational psychology in a changing world of work? *American Psychologist, 50*, 928–939.

Das, J. P. (1972). Patterns of cognitive ability in nonretarded and retarded children. *American Journal of Mental Deficiency, 70*, 6–12.

Das, J. P., Carlson, J. S., Davidson, M. B., & Longe, K. (1977). *PASS: PASS remedial program*. Toronto: Hogrefe Publishing Company.

Das, J. P., Kirby, J. R., & Jarman, R. F. (1979). *Simultaneous and successive cognitive processes*. New York: Academic Press.

Das, J. P., Mishra, R. K., & Pool, J. (1995). An experiment on cognitive remediation of word-reading difficulty. *Journal of Learning Disabilities, 28*, 66–79.

Das, J. P., Naglieri, J. A., & Kirby, J. R. (1994). *Assessment of cognitive processes*. Needham Heights, MA: Allyn & Bacon.

Dillon, R. F. (1985). Eye movement analysis of information processing under different testing conditions. *Contemporary Educational Psychology, 10*, 387–395.

Dillon, R. F. (1986). Information processing and testing. *Educational Psychologist, 20*, 163–174.

Dillon, R. F. (1989a). Information processing and testing. In R. J. Sternberg (Ed.), *Advances in the psychology of human intelligence* (Vol. 5). Hillsdale, NJ: Erlbaum.

Dillon, R. F. (1989b). New approaches to aptitude testing. In R. F. Dillon & J. W. Pellegrino (Eds.), *Testing: Theoretical and applied perspectives*. New York: Praeger.

Dillon, R. F. (1992). Components and metacomponents of intelligence among navy and air force personnel. In *Proceedings of the 34th Annual Conference of the Military Testing Association*. San Diego: MTA.

Dillon, R. F. (1996). *Cognitive flexibility as a mechanism of dynamic assessment*. Unpublished manuscript.

Dillon, R. F., & Larson, G. E. (1996). *A cognitive model of flight performance*. Unpublished manuscript.

Dillon, R. F., & Witick, L. (1996). *Aviation performance: Modeling the criterion space* (SIU TR 96–002). Carbondale: Collegiate Aviation Program, Southern Illinois University.

Duke, A. P., & Ree, M. J. (1996). Better candidates fly fewer training hours: Another time testing pays off. *International Journal of Selection and Assessment, 4*, 115–121.

Embretson, S., & Schneider, L. M. (1989). Cognitive component models for psychometric analogies: Conceptually driven versus interactive process models. *Learning and Individual Differences, 1*, 155–178.

Eyde, L. D., Nester, M. A., Heaton, S. M., & Nelson, A. V. (1994). *Guide for administering written employment examinations to persons with disabilities*. Washington, DC: U.S. Office of Personnel Management.

Feuerstein, R., Rand, Y., & Hoffman, M. B. (1979). *Dynamic assessment of retarded performers*. Baltimore: University Park Press.

Gardner, H. (1983). *Frames of mind: The theory of multiple intelligences*. New York: Basic Books.

Gustafsson, J. -E., & Balke, G. (1993). General and specific abilities as predictors of school achievement. *Multivariate Behavioral Research, 28* (4), 403–434.

Gustafsson, J. -E., & Muthén, B. (1996). *The nature of the general factor in hierarchical models of the structure of cognitive abilities: Alternative models tested on data from regular and experimental military enlistment tests*. Unpublished manuscript, School of Education, UCLA.

Gustafsson, J. -E., & Undheim, J. O. (1996). Individual differences in cognitive functions. In D. C. Berliner & R. C. Calfee (Eds.), *The handbook of educational psychology* (pp. 186–242). New York: Macmillan.

Haywood, H. C., & Tzuriel, D. (1992). *Interactive assessment* New York: Springer-Verlag.

Horn, J. L. (1985). Remodeling old models of intelligence. In B. B. Wolman (Ed.), *Handbook of intelligence* (pp. 267–300). New York: Wiley.

Howell, K. W., & Morehead, M. K. (1987). *Curriculum based evaluation for special and remedial education*. Columbus, OH: Charles E. Merrill.

Jensen, A. R. (1982). Reaction time and psychometric g. In H. J. Eysenck (Ed.), *A model for intelligence*. Berlin: Springer-Verlag.

Kyllonen, P. C. (1991). Principles for creating a computerized test battery. *Intelligence, 15*, 1–15.

Kyllonen, P. C. (1993). Aptitude testing inspired by information processing: A test of the four-sources model. *Journal of General Psychology, 120*, 375–405.

Kyllonen, P. C. (1994). CAM: A theoretical framework for cognitive abilities measurement. In D. Detterman (Ed.), *Current topics in human intelligence: Vol. 4. Theories of intelligence* (pp. 307–359). Norwood, NJ: Ablex.

Li, W., & Mitchell, K. J. (1992). *Preliminary investigation of the 1991 Medical College Admission Test factor structure*. Paper presented at the annual meeting of the American Educational Research Association, San Francisco, CA.

Lindsley, D. B. (1960). Attention, consciousness, sleep, and wakefulness. In J. Field (Ed.), *Handbook of physiology*. Springfield: Thomas.

Lochhead, J., & Clements, J. (Eds.). (1979). *Cognitive process instruction: Research on teaching thinking skills*. Philadelphia: Franklin Institute Press.

Luftig, R. L. (1989). *Assessment of learners with special needs*. Boston, MA: Allyn and Bacon.

Luria, A. R. (1966). *Human brain and psychological processes*. New York: Harper & Row.

Maier, M. H. (1993). *Military aptitude testing: The past fifty years* (DMDC TR 93–007). Monterey, CA: Personnel Testing Division, Defense Manpower Data Center.

Martin, C. J. (1994). *Army alpha to navy theta*. Paper presented at the thirty-sixth annual conference of the International Military Testing Association, Rotterdam, The Netherlands.

McLoughlin, J. A., & Lewis, R. B. (1990). *Assessing special students* (3rd ed.). Columbus, OH: Merrill.

Messick, S. (1995). Validity of psychological assessment: Validity of inferences from person's responses and performances as scientific inquiry into score meaning. *American Psychologist, 50,* 741–749.

Mitchell, K. J., Haynes, R., & Koenig, J. (1994). Assessing the validity of the updated Medical College Admission Test. *Academic Medicine, 69,* 394–401.

Pellegrino, J. W., & Glaser, R. (1980). Components of inductive reasoning. In R. Snow, P. A. Federico, & W. Montague (Eds.), *Aptitude, learning, and instruction: Cognitive process analyses of aptitude* (Vol. 1). Hillsdale, NJ: Erlbaum.

Pellegrino, J. W., & Glaser, R. (1982). Analyzing aptitudes for learning: Inductive reasoning. In R. Glaser (Ed.), *Advances in instructional psychology* (Vol. 2). Hillsdale, NJ: Erlbaum.

Piaget, J. (1950). *The psychology of intelligence*. London: Routledge.

Pribram, K. H. (1971). *Languages of the brain: Experimental paradoxes and principles in neuropsychology*. Englewood Cliffs, NJ: Prentice-Hall.

Ree, M. J., & Earles, J. A. (1991). Predicting training success: Not much more than *g*. *Personnel Psychology, 44,* 407–444.

Ree, M. J., & Earles, J. A. (1994). The ubiquitous predictiveness of *g*. In C. Walker, M. Runsey, & J. Harris (Eds.), *Personnel selection and classification*. Hillsdale, NJ: Erlbaum.

Sternberg, R. J. (1977a). Component processes in analogical reasoning. *Psychological Review, 84,* 353–378.

Sternberg, R. J. (1977b). *Intelligence, information processing, and analogical reasoning: The componential analysis of human abilities*. Hillsdale, NJ: Erlbaum.

Tirre, W. C. (1995, March). *Dimensions and correlates of psychomotor abilities*. Paper presented at the Learning Abilities Measurement Program Mini-Conference on Human Perceptual-Motor Abilities, San Antonio, TX.

Vygotsky, L. S. (1962). *Language and thought*. (E. Haufmann & G. Vakar, Trans). Cambridge, MA: MIT Press. (Original work published 1934)

Vygotsky, L. S. (1978). *Mind in society: The development of higher psychological processes* (M. Cole, V. Hohn-Steiner, & E. Souerman, Eds. & Trans.). Cambridge, MA: Harvard University Press.

2

Measurement Principles for the New Generation of Tests: A Quiet Revolution

Susan E. Embretson

Educational and psychological testing has changed rapidly during the last decade. Although updating items and norms has always been routine in testing, the current generation of major test revisions is much more substantial. Testing has been fundamentally changed by the availability of microcomputers. Microcomputers have had obvious impact on test administration. Computers are used routinely to display items and record responses. Microcomputers also have had obvious impact on test interpretation. Increasingly, programs to score and interpret protocols are attractive features for many new tests.

Although much less obvious, microcomputers have also impacted the measurement principles that underlie the new generation of tests. That is, new measurement principles are required for adaptive testing, which is now feasible with computerized item presentation. In computerized adaptive tests (CATs), items are administered interactively, depending on the individual's responses. Items are optimally selected from an item bank to yield the most information about the individual's trait level. Items that are either too hard or too easy are not selected. With CATs, different individuals will receive different sets of items when their trait levels differ. In fact, in a group of individuals, CATs may result in administering each person a different test "form" with different average item difficulties. Classical test theory principles are inappropriate for equating scores under these conditions. New measurement principles—namely item response theory (IRT)—are required to equate scores from CATs.

The new measurement principles, however, are not only involved in CATs. In fact, many current tests apply IRT to solve measurement problems. For example, many individual ability tests, such as the Differential Ability Scales, the

Woodcock-Johnson Ability Tests, the Kaufman Adolescent Scales, and the Stanford-Binet, have all applied IRT in the recent versions of their tests. Further, several major group tests, including the computer adaptive form of the Armed Services Vocational Aptitude Battery (ASVAB), the computerized form of the Scholastic Aptitude Test (SAT), and the computerized Graduate Record Examination (GRE) are based on IRT.

Although IRT can be characterized as revolutionary in contemporary testing, the principles are not new. Lord and Novick's (1968) textbook contained coverage of IRT and showed how many classical test theory principles could be derived from it. Further, IRT is more theoretically plausible than classic test theory, since many paradoxes are resolved. In addition to the theoretical advantages, IRT also has many practical advantages (e.g., see Lord, 1980). Since Lord and Novick's (1968) classic book, IRT has become increasingly mainstream as a basis for test development.

The potential scope of application of IRT in testing is quite broad. A large family of diverse IRT models is now available to apply to diverse measurement tasks (see Hambleton & van der Linden, 1996). Although the early IRT models emphasized dichotomous item formats (e.g., the Rasch model), extensions to other item formats such as rating scales and partial credit scoring are now available. The newer IRT models for polytomous formats are particularly applicable to tests for personality traits, states, dispositions, or attitudes. Further, recently developed multidimensional IRT models can be applied to complex measurement goals. Traits that are operationalized by comparing a person's performance across subtasks or item subsets or even between different types of distractors can be measured with the newer multidimensional IRT models.

Despite the importance of IRT in the new generation of tests, many educators and psychologists are familiar with classical test theory rather than IRT. This is a serious problem because IRT is fundamentally different from classical test theory. Although many classical test theory principles may be derived from IRT, IRT may not be derived from classical test theory. Many "rules of thumb" from classical test theory no longer apply. Old rules from classical test theory must be revised, generalized, or even abandoned when IRT is applied.

Thus, IRT defines new rules of measurement. Although a short chapter that provides a clear overview of IRT would be ideal, such a chapter seems impossible at this point. IRT is statistically much more difficult than classical test theory and involves qualitatively different concepts. Instead, this chapter seeks to illustrate how deeply IRT differs from classical test theory, which hopefully will motivate the reader to pursue more advanced treatments of IRT.

A COMPARISON OF MEASUREMENT RULES

Embretson (1995) contrasted several old "rules" of measurement with the new rules from IRT. Several old rules follow directly from the principles of

Table 2.1
Some "Rules" of Measurement

The Old Rules

Rule 1. The standard error of measurement applies to all scores in a particular population.

Rule 2. Longer tests are more reliable than shorter tests.

Rule 3. Comparing test scores across multiple forms depends on test parallelism or test equating.

Rule 4. Meaningful scale scores are obtained by comparisons of position in a score distribution.

Rule 5. Interval scale properties are achieved by selecting items that yield normal raw score distributions.

The New Rules

Rule 1. The standard error of measurement differs across scores (or response patterns) but generalizes across populations.

Rule 2. Shorter tests can be more reliable than longer tests.

Rule 3. Comparing scores across multiple forms is optimal when test difficulty levels vary between persons.

Rule 4. Meaningful scale scores are obtained by comparisons of distances from various items.

Rule 5. Interval scale properties are achieved by justifiable measurement models, not score distributions.

classical test theory or its common extension. Other old rules are implicit in many applied test development procedures. In contrast, the new rules reflect principles from IRT. More recently, Embretson and Reise (in press) broadened the rule set to include measurement principles that are relevant to research on individual differences.

Table 2.1 presents five old rules that represent common knowledge or practice among psychologists. The old rules are followed by five corresponding new rules, which obviously conflict with the old rules.

Although the five old rules have guided the development of many published educational and psychological tests, there are some significant exceptions—for example, tests developed by large-scale testing corporations (e.g., Educational Testing Service [ETS], American College Test [ACT]) in which non-IRT procedures have been developed to circumvent the limitations of some old rules. That is, nonlinear test equating (see Holland & Rubin, 1982) was developed to counter Old Rule 3. However, these techniques are not well known outside large-scale testing programs; hence, they are not routinely applied in the development of many tests. Thus, the old rules characterize substantial practice in test development.

Rule 1: The Standard Error of Measurement

Old Rule 1. The standard error of measurement applies to all scores in a particular population.

New Rule 1. The standard error of measurement differs across scores (or response patterns) but generalizes across populations.

The standard error of measurement, in classical test theory, is computed as from the reliability and standard deviation for a target group (i.e., $SE_{Msmt} = (1 - r_{tt})\ \frac{1}{2}\sigma$). Confidence intervals are constructed for individual scores under the routine assumption that measurement error is distributed normally and equally for all score levels. The confidence intervals can guide score interpretations in several ways; for example, differences between two scores are not interpretable unless they fall outside the confidence interval bands.

To illustrate the old rule, item response data were simulated for 3,000 examinees on a 30-item test with a normal difficulty range. The examinees were sampled from a population with a standard normal ability distribution trait score (see Embretson, 1995). In the upper panel of Figure 2.1, classical true scores (shown as standard scores) are regressed on raw test scores. A 67 percent confidence interval, using a standard error of .32 (e.g., from internal consistency reliability), is shown by the dotted lines.

Two important points about the old rule may be gleaned from the upper panel of Figure 2.1. First, the estimated true score is a standard score that is derived as a *linear* transformation of raw score, as noted by the linear regression. Second, the confidence interval bands are also represented as straight lines for all scores since the same interval applies to each score. In classical test theory, both the transformation of raw score to true score and the standard error apply to a particular population because their estimation depends on population statistics. That is, the standard score conversion requires estimating the raw score mean and standard deviation for a population, while the standard error requires estimating both the variance and reliability.

New Rule 1 conflicts with both aspects of Old Rule 1. First, the standard error of measurement does not apply to all scores, as it differs between score levels. Second, the standard error of measurement does not depend on population true and error variances and so generalizes across populations.

To illustrate the differences, trait scores were estimated using the Rasch IRT model. Item difficulties were specified for a 30-item normal range test. At each possible raw score, consistent response patterns were specified to simulate examinee responses. Marginal maximum likelihood estimates of the trait score, and its standard error, were obtained for each raw score with the one parameter logistic IRT model (i.e., the Rasch model). In a large normal population of simulated examinees that was appropriate for the normal range test (see Em-

Figure 2.1
Regression of True Score on Raw Score

Classical Test Theory

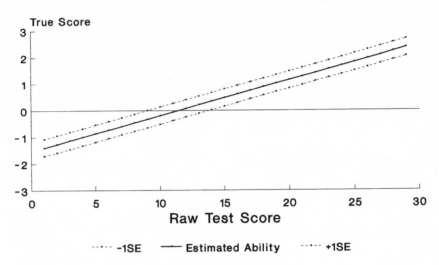

Item Response Theory

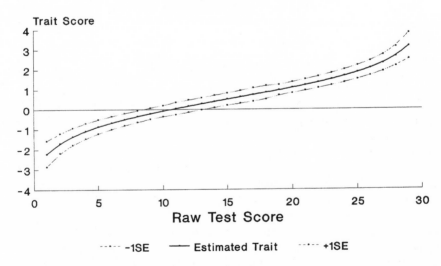

bretson, 1995), the average standard error, across examinees, was .32, the same as the uniform standard error shown in the first analysis.

In the lower panel of Figure 2.1, IRT trait score scores are regressed on raw scores. The lower panel differs from the upper panel of Figure 2.1 in two important ways: First, the relationship between trait score and raw score is nonlinear; second, the confidence interval band becomes increasingly wide for extreme scores. Unlike classical test theory, neither the estimation of trait score nor its corresponding standard error depends on population statistics. In IRT models, trait scores are estimated separately for each score or response pattern, controlling for the characteristics (e.g., difficulty) of the items that were administered. Standard errors are smallest when the items are optimally appropriate for a particular trait score level and item discriminations are high.

Rule 2: Test Length and Reliability

Old Rule 2. Longer tests are more reliable than shorter tests.
New Rule 2. Shorter tests can be more reliable than longer tests.

This rule is represented by an equation in classical test theory—namely, the Spearman-Brown prophesy formula. Specifically, if a test is lengthened by a factor of n parallel parts, true variance increases more rapidly than error variance (Guilford [1954] presents the classic proof). If r_{tt} is the reliability of the original test, then reliability of the lengthened test r_{nn} may be anticipated as follows:

$$r_{nn} = \frac{n\, r_{tt}}{1 + (n - 1)\, r_{tt}} \tag{2.1a}$$

Equation (2.1) may also be applied to shortened tests. That is, if a test with a reliability of .86 is shortened to two thirds of the original length (n = .667), then the anticipated reliability of the shorter test is .80. The upper panel of Figure 2.2 shows the effect of doubling, tripling, and so on, a test with an initial reliability of .70.

The new rule counters the old rule by asserting that short tests can be more reliable. The lower panel of Figure 2.2 shows the standard error of measurement at various levels of trait score for 30 item tests drawn from the same item bank in a simulation study (Embretson, 1995). Item discriminations were held constant so that test differences in measurement error do not arise from differences in item quality. The standard errors were computed from the difference between the true generating trait score and the estimated trait score for each simulated examinee. For the test with a normal item difficulty range, Figure 2.2 shows that the standard errors are largest for the extreme scores. A composite reliability (see Andrich, 1982) may be computed for the group by comparing the averaged squared standard errors, σ_θ^2, to the trait score variance, σ^2, as follows:

Figure 2.2
Two Versions of Measurement Error

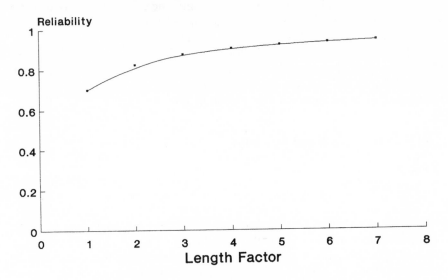

Test Reliability and Test Length
Classical Test Theory

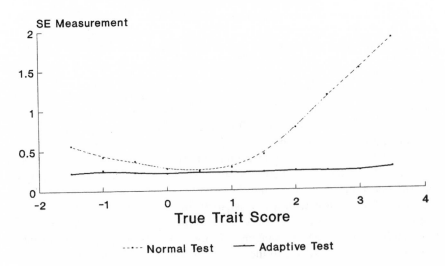

Measurement Error by Trait
Simulation Results

$$r'_{tt} = 1 - \frac{\Sigma_i \sigma_{\Theta_i}^2}{\sigma^2} \qquad\qquad (2.1b)$$

Obviously, the smaller the standard error at each trait score level, the higher the reliability.

The dotted line shows the standard error for an adaptive test of 30 items, in which the item difficulty level is optimally selected for a particular trait score. In the adaptive test, different items are administered. Notice how the standard error is nearly constant over trait scores, due to the optimal selection of items. Most important, notice that measurement error is smaller at all trait score levels. Thus, a more reliable "test" has been developed at the same length but with no differences in item quality. Now, if less than 30 adaptive items were administered, the standard errors would increase. However, notice that for extreme trait scores, adaptive test length could be reduced substantially because the adaptive test yields far less error than the normal range test. Thus, as a composite across trait levels, the shorter (adaptive) test can be more reliable than the longer normal range test.

In fairness to classical test theory, it should be noted that an assumption underlying the Spearman-Brown prophecy formula is that the test is lengthened with parallel parts. An adaptive test, by its nature, fails to meet this assumption. However, the point made here is that the old rule about test length and reliability conflicts sharply with current practice in adaptive testing, which is based on the new rule from IRT.

Rule 3: Interchangeable Test Forms

Old Rule 3. Comparing test scores across multiple forms depends on test parallelism or test equating.

New Rule 3. Comparing test scores across multiple forms is optimal when test difficulty levels vary between persons.

In Gulliksen's (1950) exposition of classical test theory, strict conditions for test parallelism were defined, which included the equality of means, variances, and covariances across test forms. If test forms meet Gulliksen's statistical conditions for parallelism, then scores may be regarded as comparable across forms.

More recently, substantial effort has been devoted to procedures for test equating (see Holland & Rubin, 1982) rather than to developing further statistical tests for evaluating test parallelism, as developed by Gulliksen (1950) and his students. Comparable scores between test forms are established by techniques such as linear equating and equipercentile equating, in conjunction with designs such as random groups or common anchor items (see Angoff, 1982, for a summary of several such methods). Although the methods provide equating for test forms that have different means, variances, and even reliabilities, equating error is influenced by differences between the test forms, especially in test difficulty level (see Peterson, Marco, & Steward, 1982). Thus, although scores can be linked between test forms, equating error can be problematic. Test forms with high reliabilities and similar score distributions will be most adequately equated.

To show the adverse effect of test difficulty differences on equating scores, consider the regression of scores from an easy test on scores from a hard test for the same group. The upper panel of Figure 2.3 shows a linear equating of observed test scores from two 30-item test forms that differ substantially in item difficulty. These scores were generated from a simulation study with 3,000 cases in which the other item properties were constant (i.e., item discriminations, guessing, and so forth), but item difficulties varied substantially.

These data have two problems for any equating. First, equating error will be substantial because the variance of easy test scores, given a particular hard test score, is sometimes quite large. For example, for a hard test score of zero, examinees are observed with scores ranging from 0 to 20 on the easy test. The hard test simply does not have the floor to distinguish these examinees, and so equating is not very satisfactory. Second, a nonlinear regression is needed to fully describe score correspondence. The upper panel of Figure 2.3 shows that easy test scores are underestimated at some score levels, overestimated at others. The low ceiling of the easy test compresses high scores, while the high floor of the hard test compresses low scores. The correlation between test scores is .817, which yields an expected true score correlation for either test of .903 (i.e., .817 ½).

The lower panel of Figure 2.3 shows the same data with trait score estimates obtained from adaptive tests in which test items are selected to be optimal for a particular trait score. Trait scores were estimated from the adaptive tests using the Rasch IRT model, which controls for the item difficulty differences between tests. Since these are simulated data, the estimated trait scores from the adaptive tests could be plotted by true trait score, which is known. The lower panel of Figure 2.3 shows little error in estimating true trait score from the adaptive test forms. Most important, better estimation of trait score is obtained by nonparallel test forms. That is, each adaptive test is a separate test form that differs substantially, and deliberately, in difficulty level from other forms. The correlation of estimated trait score with true trait score is .970, which is substantially higher than the expectation given from the upper panel of Figure 2.3.

Rule 4: Establishing Meaningful Scale Scores

Old Rule 4. Meaningful scale scores are obtained by comparisons of position in a score distribution.

New Rule 4. Meaningful scale scores are obtained by comparisons of distances from various items.

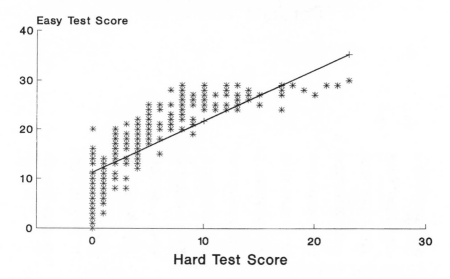

Equating Test Scores
Simulation Results

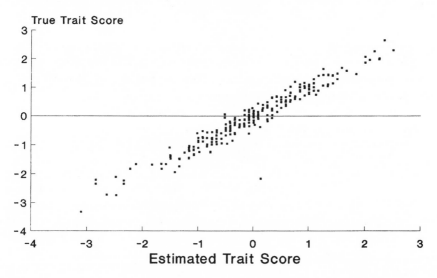

Adaptive Test and Trait Score
(r=.97)

Figure 2.4
Common Scale Measurement of Item Difficulty and Trait Scores

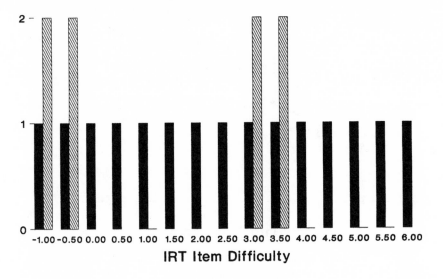

Common Scale Measurement for
Persons and Items

IRT Item Difficulty

In measurement theory, giving meaning to a test score requires specifying a comparison. A comparison has two features that must be specified: (1) the standard to which a score is compared and (2) the numerical basis of the comparison (order, difference, ratio, etc.).

The comparison standard for tests that stem from classical test theory is a relevant group of persons, namely, the norm group. The numerical basis of the comparison is order (i.e., position in the distribution). Standard scores are obtained by linear transformations of raw scores so that scores may be readily compared to positions in a normally distributed population of persons. Thus, meaning is determined by a norm-referenced standard, and the numerical basis is order. Of course, as has been argued by proponents of criterion-referenced testing, norm-referenced scores have no meaning for what the person actually can do. That is, scores are not anchored to the items.

In IRT models, trait score scores are compared to items since persons and items are placed on a common scale. The difficulty of items is located on a continuum, ranging often from −3 to +3. The black bars in Figure 2.4 indicate the difficulty levels (IRT Rasch model values) of 10 items. A person's trait score, as estimated in the Rasch model, may also be located on this same scale. Trait scores for four persons are shown by the gray bars in Figure 2.4. The difference between trait score and item difficulty has direct meaning for performance. If trait score equals item difficulty, then the person's probability of failing equals the probability of passing. A large positive difference between trait score and item difficulty means that the person is very likely to pass the item. For example, for Person 3, with $\theta_3 = 3.0$, the probability for passing items at an item difficulty level of 3.0 is .50. However, Person 3 has a probability of greater than .50 of passing all items that fall below 3.0.

Thus, in IRT models, meaning is given by comparing the difference of the person and the item on a common continuum. Trait scores may be interpreted with direct reference to the items. If these items are further structured by type, substantive meaning can be given by comparisons to the items.

It should be noted that IRT scaling of ability does not preclude linear transformations to standard scores, so that norm-referenced meaning also may be obtained. The meaning of ability for item performance may be retained as well if item difficulties are transformed by a corresponding linear transformation.

Rule 5: Establishing Scale Properties

Old Rule 5. Interval scale properties are achieved by selecting items that yield normal raw score distributions.

New Rule 5. Interval scale properties are achieved by justifiable measurement models, not score distributions.

Although most test developers probably would not explicate Old Rule 5, it is at least implicit in routine test development procedures. For many psychological tests, items are selected to yield normal distributions in a target population. For some tests, if normal distributions are not achieved, scores are transformed by a monotonic function or by a normalizing procedure to obtain a normal distribution. Both transformations are nonlinear.

The relationship between score distributions and scale levels may be considered by revisiting the upper panel of Figure 2.3, where easy test scores were regressed on hard test scores. The relationship was nonlinear because scores were compressed on opposite ends of the continuum for the two tests. Scale compression has two effects. First, the true score distance between adjacent scores varies between the two tests. Thus, interval scale measurement is not achieved. Second, tests with scale compression have skewed score distributions in the target population.

Jones (1971) points out that the classical methods to develop normally distributed trait score scores will achieve interval scale measurement under certain assumptions. Specifically, these assumptions are that true scores (1) have interval scale properties and (2) are normally distributed in the population. Only linear transformations preserve score intervals as well as distribution shapes (see Davison & Sharma, 1990, for the latter). Thus, if raw score scores are normally distributed, then only a linear transformation, such as a standard score conversion, will preserve score intervals to appropriately estimate true score. Notice, however, that scale properties are tied to a specific population. If the test is applied to a person from another population, can the interval scale properties still be justified? If not, then scale properties are population specific.

For the Rasch model, several papers (e.g., Fischer, 1995; Roskam & Jansen, 1984) show how interval or even ratio scale properties are achieved. The Rasch model also has been linked to fundamental measurement (see Andrich, 1988) due to the simple additivity of the parameters. A basic tenet of fundamental measurement is additive decomposition (see Michel, 1990), in that two parameters are additively related to a third variable. The trait score scale given by the Rasch model is an additive decomposition because the individual encounter of a person with an item is predicted by the difference between a trait score and an item difficulty.

According to the principle of additive decomposition, interval scale properties hold if the laws of numbers apply. Specifically, the same performance differences must be observed when trait scores have the same interscore distance, regardless of their overall positions on the trait score continuum. Suppose, for example, that the distance between Person 1 and Person 2 equals the distance between Person 3 and Person 4. Now, these intervals are justifiable if the same performance differential exists between the two pairs of persons. It can be shown that the equal distances between the two pairs of scores have equal meaning for performance differences when measured as log odds (see Embretson, 1995). The demonstration applies to any level on the trait score scale and to any item that is used in the performance comparison.

UNDERSTANDING THE NEW RULES

The purpose of this section is to build some intuitions about how IRT models accomplish some of the new rules. Specifically, New Rule 1 to New Rule 3 will be considered. New Rule 4 and New Rule 5 are elaborated sufficiently above.

Model-Based Measurement versus Classical Test Theory

Classical test theory has a limited model; the target of the model is total score, which is predicted from true score plus error, as shown below:

$$X_{score} = X_{true} + X_{error} \tag{2.2}$$

The prototypic observed score is the simple sum of item responses. However, since no provision for possibly varying item parameters is included in equation (2.2), it is assumed implicitly that X_{true} applies to items on a specific test or to items on a test with equivalent item properties. Thus, if more than one set of items may reasonably measure the same trait, the generality of true score depends on test parallelism, such as elaborated by Gulliksen (1950), or on test equating.

For the most simple IRT model, the Rasch (1960) model, the log odds for item solving may be predicted from equation (2.2), as shown above. The Rasch model also can predict the simple probability that person j passes item i, $P(X_{ij})$, from a logistic function as follows:

$$P(X_{ij} = 1 | \theta_j, b_i) = \frac{\exp(\theta_j - b_i)}{1 + \exp(\theta_j - b_i)} \qquad (2.3)$$

where θ_j is the trait score for person j, and b_i is the difficulty of item i. Notice that the meaning of trait scores, unlike true scores in (2.2), is not restricted to a particular set of items. Equation (2.3) applies to any item for which difficulty is known.

Estimation of Trait Scores and Item Properties

In IRT, trait scores are estimated in the context of a model [e.g., equation (2.3)] for each person's response pattern, controlling for the characteristics of the items. Suppose that five items with known difficulties (i.e., $-2, -1, 0, 1, 2$) were administered and that a person obtained the following response pattern (1,1,1,1,0) on the five items, respectively.

Estimates for trait scores from (2.3) are typically obtained by the maximum likelihood method, in which the estimated trait score for person j maximizes the likelihood of his or her response pattern, given the item difficulties. If the trait score were known for person j, then a probability could be calculated for each item P_{ij} from (2.3) and then multiplied to give the probability of the observed response pattern, L_j. That is,

$$L_{ij} = P_{1j}P_{2j}P_{3j}P_{4j}(1 - P_{5j}) \qquad (2.4)$$

Under the maximum likelihood method, numerical analysis methods are applied to find the trait score that yields the highest likelihood for person j. To summarize, trait scores are derived by maximizing the likelihood of a person's observed response pattern in the context of a model, controlling for item difficulty.

New Rule 3, which concerns the interchangeability of trait scores from tests of different difficulties, is explained by estimating trait score in the context of a model that controls for item difficulties. Trait score estimates may be obtained from a person's response pattern to any set of items, given the item difficulties. Equated item properties for different tests are unnecessary because the properties of the specific test items are included in the model. The meaning of the response patterns for estimating trait scores is adjusted accordingly.

Measurement Error in IRT

In psychological testing, traits are measured by responses of persons to items. Measurement error depends on the appropriateness of the items for the particular persons who are measured. To draw an analogy, suppose that athletic ability is measured by the number of hurdles that can be cleared. If two persons clear the same number of hurdles, like classical test theory, the Rasch IRT model would place them at the same ability. However, the persons may differ substantially in athletic ability if the height of the hurdles is not appropriate for distinguishing their abilities.

Now, low hurdles are relatively useless for distinguishing between two highly athletic persons. They clear them all easily. However, a small range of hurdles that are located right at their jumping threshold (so that they are as likely to clear as to miss) are useful for distinguishing their abilities. Similarly, only very low hurdles are really useful in distinguishing between persons with low ability. If the hurdles are too high, they are likely to miss them all. Thus, the hurdles that provide the most information about a person's ability are those at his or her threshold (i.e., as likely to hit as to miss). Or, conversely, measurement error is lowest when the hurdles fall at the person's threshold.

Figure 2.5 contains another illustration of the relationship of test appropriateness and test difficulty. Figure 2.5. shows the common scale locations of two persons and 10 items for two tests that vary in difficulty. Test 1 is more appropriate for Person 1 because the item difficulties vary less from his or her trait score. Test 2, which has higher levels of item difficulty, is more appropriate for Person 2.

The degree of measurement error is inversely related to the number of appropriate items that a person receives. The most appropriate items are those items at the person's threshold, where the person's chance of passing, P_{ij}, equals .50. Specifically, for the Rasch model, the standard error for person j depends on the probability of passing items as follows:

$$SE_{\theta j} = 1/[\Sigma_i P_i (1-P_i)]^{1/2} \tag{2.5}$$

Consider the two tests and two persons shown in Figure 2.5. Test 1 yields a small measurement error for Person 1 because items are distributed around his or her trait score. The trait score of Person 2 exceeds all but one item, however, so passing the items provides less useful information. Test 2, however, is more useful for Person 2 than for Person 1, since now items surround the trait score.

New Rule 1 and New Rule 2 both may be explained by the effects of item appropriateness on measurement error. That is, New Rule 1, different standard errors for measurement for different scores, follows directly from equation (2.5). If a test contains fixed item content, then different probabilities (P_{ij}'s) will be computed for different trait score levels. Further, the population generalizability

Figure 2.5
Common Scale Locations of Items and Persons for Two Tests

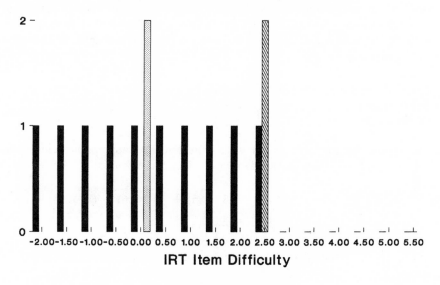

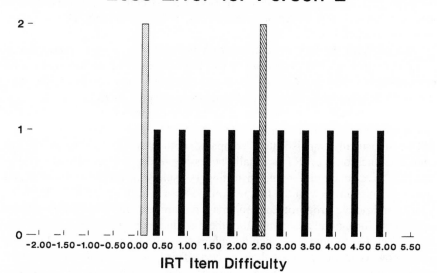

of New Rule 1 follows from (2.5) also because the standard error of measurement is computed for individual scores, not for populations.

New Rule 2, shorter tests can be more reliable than longer tests, follows also from equation (2.5). If the probabilities are relatively extreme that a person passes the items, then the standard errors will be large. For example, suppose that administering five items that are too easy yields high P_{ij}'s for a person $(.9, .8, .9, .7, .9)$, which are then used to compute the standard error of measurement as follows:

$$
\begin{aligned}
SE_{\theta j} = 1/[(.9 \times .1) + (.8 \times .2) + (.9 \times .1) + (.7 \times .3) \\
+ (.9 \times .1)]^{\frac{1}{2}} = 1.25.
\end{aligned} \tag{2.6}
$$

Now suppose that the same person was administered five appropriate items, with P_{ij}'s $(.5, .5, .4, .5, .6)$. Then the standard error of measurement is

$$
\begin{aligned}
SE_{\theta j} = 1/[(.5 \times .5) + (.5 \times .5) + (.4 \times .6) + (.5 \times .5) \\
+ (.6 \times .4)]^{\frac{1}{2}} = .90.
\end{aligned} \tag{2.7}
$$

Thus, a smaller standard error is found for a shorter test.

NEW MEASUREMENT PRINCIPLES AND TESTING EXPERTS

As noted in the introduction, IRT is now an important part of testing. As shown throughout the chapter, the principles of IRT are qualitatively different from the principles of classical test theory. Yet, as compared to classical test theory, relatively few educators, researchers, and practitioners have a strong background in IRT.

What explains the lack of foundation in IRT? Clearly, item response theory is not new. IRT is often traced to Lord's (1952) monograph on item regression or to Rasch's (1960) book. Since Lord and Novick's (1968) textbook introduction to IRT, other textbooks routinely include a chapter on IRT.

Several influences have contributed to the persistence of classical test theory as the only measurement principles that many testing researchers know. First, IRT is statistically sophisticated, compared with classical test theory. A full course devoted only to IRT is usually necessary to develop an adequate understanding. A chapter in a book on testing is usually insufficient. Second, and obviously interactive with the first reason, courses in IRT were not available for a large and active group of contemporary researchers. IRT was rarely offered as a course for individuals completing their graduate programs prior to the mid-1970s. Yet due to population demographics (i.e., the baby boomers), this large group now is at the peak of their careers. Third, it is difficult to learn IRT outside a course context. Although many new developments are readily learned by keeping abreast of the literature, IRT is unlikely to be learned this way. Learning IRT outside a graduate course environment would be comparable to learning statistics on one's own. The available textbooks are difficult to read unless part of a course, and the principles are not mastered without working through examples.

Certainly the new generation of testing experts can and should learn IRT as part of regular graduate coursework. In educational graduate programs, for example, IRT courses are often available. In psychology graduate programs, in which the measurement curriculum has been much weaker than in education in recent years, IRT is making some inroads. But perhaps even the "old" generation of testing experts will learn IRT principles. Perhaps a new generation of IRT textbooks, IRT workshops, and user-friendly IRT computer programs will provide the needed incentives.

REFERENCES

Andrich, D. (1982). An index of person separation in latent trait theory, the traditional KR 20 index and the Guttman scale response pattern. *Educational Research and Perspectives, 9*, 95–104.

Andrich, D. (1988). *Rasch models for measurement.* Newbury Park, CA: Sage Publishers.

Angoff, W. (1982). Summary and derivation of equating methods used at ETS. In P. Holland, & D. Rubin (Eds.), *Test equating.* New York: Academic Press.

Davison, M., & Sharma, A. R. (1990). Parametric statistics and levels of measurement: Factorial designs and multiple regression. *Psychological Bulletin, 107*, 394–400.

Embretson, S. E. (1995, August). *The new rules of measurement.* Paper presented at the annual meeting of the American Psychological Association, New York.

Embretson, S. E., & Reise, S. R. (in press). *Item response theory for psychologists.* Hillsdale, NJ: Erlbaum.

Fischer, G. (1995). Derivations of the Rasch model. In G. Fischer & I. Molenaar (Eds.), *Rasch models: Foundations, recent developments, and applications.* New York: Springer-Verlag.

Guilford, J. P. (1954). *Psychometric methods.* New York: McGraw-Hill.

Gulliksen, H. (1950), *Theory of mental tests.* New York: Wiley.

Hambleton, R. K., & van der Linden, W. (1996). *Handbook of modern item response theory.* New York: Springer-Verlag.

Holland, P., & Rubin, D. (1982). *Test equating.* New York: Academic Press.

Jones, L. V. (1971). The nature of measurement. In R. L. Thorndike (Ed.), *Educational Measurement.* Washington, D.C.: American Council on Education.

Lord, F. (1952). A theory of test scores. *Psychometric Monographs*, no. 1.

Lord, F. (1980). *Applications of item response theory to practical testing problems.* Hillsdale, NJ: Erlbaum.

Lord, F., & Novick, M. (1968). *Statistical theories of mental tests.* New York: Addison-Wesley.

Michel, J. (1990). *An introduction to the logic of psychological measurement.* Hillsdale, NJ: Erlbaum.

Peterson, N., Marco, G., & Steward, E. (1982). A test of the adequacy of linear score equating models. In P. Holland, & D. Rubin (Eds.), *Test equating*. New York: Academic Press.

Rasch, G. (1960). *Probabilistic models for some intelligence and attainment tests*. Copenhagen: Danish Institute of Educational Research. (Expanded edition, 1980. Chicago: University of Chicago Press)

Roskam, E., & Jansen, P. G. W. (1984). A new derivation of the Rasch model. In G. Fischer, & I. Molenaar (Eds.), *Rasch models: Foundations, recent developments, and applications*. New York: Springer-Verlag.

3

Standards for Educational and Psychological Tests and Testing Professionals

Ruth B. Ekstrom, Patricia B. Elmore,
and William D. Schafer

INTRODUCTION

Test standards have several purposes. They guide the actions of test developers by helping to ensure the quality of the test instruments. They also guide the actions of those who administer, score, and interpret tests and make decisions based on test results and help ensure appropriate treatment of test takers. And they have implications for the training of measurement professionals and other test users. In this chapter, we discuss test standards from three perspectives: (1) standards related to the characteristics of the test instrument itself; (2) standards intended to guide test users; and (3) standards related to the professional qualifications and training of test users.

The chapter focuses on standards for educational and psychological tests. It omits any extensive discussion of test standards as they relate to employment testing. Neither does it discuss standards for tests that are primarily of a physiological nature, such as those employed in neurological examinations or tests of vision, hearing, and so on. Finally, this chapter focuses on test standards as they exist in the United States; other countries also have test standards. These omissions are not intended as indications that test standards are less important in these areas. They simply reflect the authors' area of expertise.

Test standards are not a static thing, as is evident from the following brief history of such standards in the United States. New standards are being created and revisions are taking place. For example, the 1985 *Standards for Educational and Psychological Testing*, which are the fourth in a series, were being revised while this chapter was being written. The authors of this chapter used test standards that were in print at the time of this writing. Therefore, this chapter does not reflect changes that are being contemplated in various test standards. We will, however, discuss some of the issues being debated during the revision process.

The word *standard* is defined as "something established by authority, custom, or general consent as a model or example" (*Webster's Ninth New Collegiate Dictionary*). In keeping with this definition, test standards can be best thought of as goals to which test developers and test users aspire. In some cases, different emphasis is placed on different statements of standards. For example, in the 1985 *Standards for Educational and Psychological Testing*, standards are categorized as primary, secondary, or conditional. Primary standards are "those that should be met by all tests before their operational use and in all testing uses, unless a sound professional reason is available to show why it is not necessary, or technically feasible, to do so" (p. 2). Secondary standards are "desirable as goals but are likely to be beyond reasonable expectation in many situations" (p. 3). When the importance of standards varies with the particular application, the standard is described as conditional.

History of Test Standards

A major step in the development of test standards in the United States occurred in 1954 when the *Technical Recommendations for Psychological Tests and Diagnostic Techniques* was published by the American Psychological Association (APA). These standards were directed primarily toward test publishers' reporting of information about tests, stating that "a test manual should carry information sufficient to enable any qualified user to make sound judgments regarding the usefulness and interpretation of the test" (p. 2). Sections of the standards dealt with dissemination of information, interpretation, validity, reliability, administration, and scales and norms. These standards were revised in 1966, this time with the American Educational Research Association (AERA) and the National Council on Measurement in Education (NCME) joining APA in the venture that produced a volume entitled *Standards for Educational and Psychological Tests and Manuals*. The content emphasis remained very much the same as in 1954.

By the time these three organizations published the 1974 *Standards for Educational and Psychological Tests*, the focus for test standards had expanded beyond technical information to be supplied by test developers. A new section on standards for test use included material relevant to the qualifications of test users and addressed test user concerns. Novick (1981) attributes the emergence of concerns regarding test use to the 1970 publication of the Equal Employment Opportunity Commission (EEOC) *Guidelines on Employee Selection Procedures*. Changing social concerns over standardized testing also contributed to this broader view of test standards (see, e.g., Haney, 1981).

In another response to concerns about test use, the American Personnel and

Guidance Association (now the American Counseling Association [ACA]) and the Association for Measurement and Evaluation in Guidance (now the Association for Assessment in Counseling [AAC]) published *Responsibilities of Users of Standardized Tests* in 1978. A revised version was published in 1989 by the American Association for Counseling and Development (AACD) (now the American Counseling Association [ACA]) and the Association for Measurement and Evaluation in Counseling and Development (AMECD) (now the Association for Assessment in Counseling [AAC]). These standards include material on test decisions, qualifications of test users, test selection, test administration, test scoring, test interpretation, and communicating test results.

By 1980 there was recognition that the 1974 *Standards* were becoming outdated "because of new problems and issues involving testing and related fields, new and emerging uses of tests, and growing social concerns of the role of testing in achieving social goals" *Standards*, 1985, p. v). There was growing awareness of other participants in the testing process, especially the test taker, as well as awareness that test users may have divided loyalties (Novick, 1981). It is no surprise, then, to find that the 1985 *Standards for Educational and Psychological Testing* included major new sections on test use and contained, for the first time, a section on protecting the rights of test takers. In addition, professional organizations whose members are extensively involved in assessment began to address issues of test use, either in their ethical guidelines (such as APA, 1992; or American Counseling Association [ACA], 1995) or in other statements (National Council on Measurement in Education [NCME], 1995).

Both professional organizations and state governments became involved in setting standards regarding the kinds of education and training that would prepare individuals in occupations requiring the use and interpretation of tests. As of June 1994, 41 states and the District of Columbia had counselor credentialing laws. All 50 states and the District had licensure for psychologists. Most states require that educational support services personnel meet specified professional preparation standards. A recent survey found that all 50 states and the District of Columbia have certification requirements for school counselors, and all except Hawaii and Michigan have certification requirements for school psychologists (National Association of State Directors of Teacher Education and Certification, 1991, p. H-3). Professional preparation standards may require that those seeking to enter the field take certain courses, satisfactorily complete an approved educational program, and/or pass a certification/licensing examination. The considerable variation in these credentialing activities has led for calls for more control, either by the measurement profession (see, e.g., Loesch, 1983) or by government.

Test publishers also have become concerned that test users have appropriate qualifications. In 1985 the Joint Committee on Testing Practices (JCTP) was formed by several professional organizations as the result of a meeting of professional association representatives with 23 test publishers. (See Fremer, Diamond, & Camara, 1989, for a brief history of JCTP.) One of JCTP's goals was to promote quality assurance in testing by working with test publishers and with major test user groups. As part of this effort, JCTP has developed a test user qualifications system (Eyde, Moreland, Robertson, Primoff, & Most, 1988).

There has been concern in recent years that the general public also needs to have a better understanding of testing, especially testing in the schools. A recent government report stated that "one of the major problems with professional *Standards* is that most of the principal interpreters of educational test results (such as policymakers, school administrators, teachers, and journalists) are unaware of them and are untrained in appropriate test use and interpretation" (U.S. Congress, Office of Technology Assessment, 1992, p. 68). Anticipating such concerns, the Joint Committee on Testing Practices prepared the *Code of Fair Testing Practices in Education*. The *Code* describes the responsibilities of test developers and test users. It is "intended to be consistent with the relevant parts of the *Standards for Educational and Psychological Testing* . . . [and is] meant to be understood by the general public" (*Code*, 1988, p. 2).

For another perspective on the history of test standards in the United States, see Haney and Madaus (1991).

STANDARDS RELATED TO THE CHARACTERISTICS OF TEST INSTRUMENTS

The three sets of test standards that address the characteristics of test instruments are the *Standards for Educational and Psychological Testing* (1985), the *Code of Fair Testing Practices in Education* (1988), and the *Code of Professional Responsibilities in Educational Measurement* (NCME, 1995). The *Code of Fair Testing Practices in Education* was written to be consistent with the *Standards for Educational and Psychological Testing*, understood by the general public, and relevant to only educational tests. The *Code of Professional Responsibilities in Educational Measurement* describes the responsibilities of professionals working in assessment-related activities consistent with the technical test characteristics established by the *Code of Fair Testing Practices in Education* and the *Standards for Educational and Psychological Testing*. Since neither the *Code of Fair Testing Practices in Education* nor the *Code of Professional Responsibilities in Educational Measurement* added new principles over and above those in the *Standards*, this section will focus on the *Standards for Educational and Psychological Testing*.

The *Standards for Educational and Psychological Testing* is organized into four major parts and 16 chapters. Part I, "Technical Standards for Test Construction and Evaluation," specifically relates to characteristics of the test instruments. It is divided into 5 chapters including (1) validity; (2) reliability and errors of measurement; (3) test development and revision; (4) scaling, norming, score comparability, and equating; and (5) test publication: technical manuals and user's guides. This section of the chapter will be similarly organized.

Validity

The validity section begins by saying, "Validity is the most important consideration in test evaluation. The concept refers to the appropriateness, meaningfulness, and usefulness of the specific inferences made from test scores. Test validation is the process of accumulating evidence to support such inferences" (*Standards*, 1985, p. 9). Some psychometricians may disagree with the first sentence, since the square root of the reliability coefficient determines the upper limit of validity. They would argue that reliability should be assessed before validity studies are conducted.

A favorite definition of validity is: "The validity of a test concerns what the test measures and how well it does so" (Anastasi, 1988, p. 139). Descriptions of validity evidence always return to what characteristic(s) or construct(s) the test measures and how accurate that measurement is.

Validity evidence has traditionally been grouped into categories and discussed as construct-related, content-related, and criterion-related evidence of validity. Constructs are defined as "theoretical constructions about the nature of human behavior" (*Standards*, 1985, p. 9). Examples of constructs include abilities (verbal, spatial, problem solving, and quantitative) and personality characteristics (anxiety, impulsivity, and self-esteem). Methods of obtaining construct-related validity evidence include group differences, change after time or intervention, correlations such as in the multitrait-multimethod technique, and factor analysis, among others. Subcategories of construct-related validity evidence include convergent and discriminant validity evidence obtained using the multitrait-multimethod technique and factorial validity evidence using factor analysis.

Content-related validity evidence "demonstrates the degree to which the sample of items, tasks, or questions on a test are representative of some defined universe or domain of content" (*Standards*, 1985, p. 10). Subcategories of content validity include sampling and logical validity that require expert judgments to determine if the test content is representative of the universe it was designed to measure. It is further specified that "inferences about content are linked to test construction" (*Standards*, 1985, p. 11).

The third form of validity evidence is referred to as criterion related. This form of validity evidence is often classified into predictive and concurrent. When concerned about evidence of concurrent validity, the test and criterion are obtained simultaneously, whereas with predictive validity, the criterion is collected some time after the predictor measure. Criterion-related validity studies require a criterion that is reliable, appropriate for the situation, and free from bias and contamination.

There are some common characteristics of all validation studies. Validation is a continuing, never-ending process. The results of one study will not establish the validity of a test. The use of a test may be validated in a particular situation, using a specific sample of test takers and using a particular method of obtaining validity evidence. In most instances, researchers are compelled to obtain validity evidence for each use of a test. Validity generalization is a method of using validity evidence obtained from prior studies to support the use of a test in a new situation. Generalization of validity includes qualitative information such as literature review and quantitative techniques such as meta-analysis. Of course, the important issue is the transportability of validity evidence to a specific new situation.

The topics of differential prediction, selection bias, and fairness are a part of validity. *Differential prediction* refers to the situation in which different regression equations may be obtained for different groups of test takers. *Selection bias* occurs when different regression equations occur for different groups and the decisions for individual group members are systematically different from decisions based on pooled groups. *Fairness* is a nontechnical term that has different meanings in different social and political contexts.

There are 25 standards related to validity with 17 (68 percent) classified as primary, 3 (12 percent) as secondary, and 5 (20 percent) as conditional. Seven of the 25 validity standards relate to general validity concerns, 2 to content-related validity evidence, 3 to construct-related validity evidence, 8 to criterion-related validity evidence, and 5 to differential prediction and selection bias.

Reliability and Errors of Measurement

Reliability is defined in the *Standards* as "the degree to which test scores are free from errors of measurement" (*Standards*, 1985, p. 19). Test takers may perform differently from one occasion to another on the same instrument or from one form of an instrument to another form of the same instrument for reasons related to the purpose of measurement or for other reasons related to the individual such as fatigue or test anxiety. "Differences between scores from one form to another or from one occasion to another may be attributable to what is commonly called errors of measurement" (*Standards*, 1985, p. 19). Sources of measurement error include test items, forms, administrations, and other measurement facets.

The three main types of reliability coefficients are test-retest (stability), parallel forms (equivalence), and internal consistency. Test-retest reliability refers to the consistency of examinees responding to the same instrument at two different administrations with a time lapse between administrations. It is a measure of stability of responding over time and may be influenced by carryover effects such as memory and practice if the time span between the two tests is short. Test-retest reliability evidence is most appropriate when the test measures a stable trait that is not particularly affected by carryover effects.

Parallel forms reliability refers to the consistency of examinees responding to two different test forms administered at the same time. It is a measure of the equivalence of test content. A reliability coefficient measuring equivalence and stability refers to the consistency of examinees responding to two different test forms administered at two different times. Measures of equivalence and equivalence and stability are appropriate when different test forms measuring the same content are needed, as is usual for standardized test administrations.

Internal consistency reliability coefficients include split-half, Cronbach α and Kuder-Richardson 20 and 21. All of these measures of internal consistency provide evidence of unidimensionality of the trait or construct measured by the test. The most general is Cronbach α, and it is usually assessed when a measure of similarity or consistency of item content is appropriate.

The previous comments are relevant for both norm-referenced measurement when a person's test performance is interpreted relative to others taking the test and criterion-referenced measurement when a person's test performance is interpreted relative to a standard. However, the computation formulas are quite different for criterion-referenced reliability coefficients due to the customary lack of variability in the individuals' responses on the test.

"It is essential, therefore, that the method used to estimate reliability takes into account those sources of error of greatest concern for a particular use and interpretation of a test. Not all sources of error are expected to be relevant for a given test" (*Standards*, 1985, p. 19).

There are 12 standards related to reliability with 8 (66.6 percent) classified as primary, 2 (16.6 percent) as secondary, and 2 (16.6 percent) as conditional. The standards require that samples of examinees used to assess reliability be described in detail and that subgroups for whom the test is recommended also be described when their reliabilities differ or are expected to differ. Reliability estimates should be clearly reported in terms of the type and method of analysis. The effect of restriction of range and the speeded nature of the test need to be taken into account when deciding on the type of reliability evidence and the method of computation. Other standards deal with cut scores, adaptive testing, and multiple judges for scoring items.

Test Development and Revision

Chapter 3 of the *Standards* deals with test development issues such as test specification, item construction, sensitivity analysis, item tryout and item analysis, methods of scoring, and test-taking strategies used by examinees. There are 25 standards related to test development and revision with 12 (48 percent) classified as primary, 5 (20 percent) as secondary, 7 (28 percent) as conditional, and 1 (4 percent) as unclassified.

The elemental aspects of test development include the importance of test specifications, domain definitions, and their relationship to instructional materials; selection of the type and content of items to minimize the effect of examinees' ethnic, age, cultural, and gender groups or particular item selection procedures using criterion scores or item response theory; test scoring and score reporting; directions for test administration including computer administration; and when to revise or withdraw a test from operation use.

Many of the other standards in chapter 3 deal with construction of particular types of instruments like personality tests, interest inventories, and adaptive tests; instruments with a speed component; instruments where performance may improve with practice, coaching, or instruction; and instruments with an unusual response mode.

Additional concerns in test construction and revision include the effect of examinee test-taking strategies on test performance and information required when constructing a short form of a test.

It should be obvious from the discussion so far of chapters 1 through 3 of the *Standards for Educational and Psychological Testing* that all the chapters dealing with the technical characteristics of a test are very interrelated and that issues affecting reliability and validity also affect test construction and revision as well as the next two chapters on scaling, norming, and equating and the contents of the technical manual.

Scaling, Norming, Score Comparability, and Equating

In order to discuss chapter 4 of the *Standards for Educational and Psychological Testing*, it is first necessary to define the terms *equating, score comparability, scaling,* and *norming* with regard to tests. Two forms of a test are defined as equated when it would be a matter of indifference to anyone taking the test or using the test results which test form was taken (Lord, 1977). For tests to be equated, they must measure the same trait and be equally reliable. When tests cannot be equated in the strict sense, the scores on the tests can be scaled to achieve comparability. Equated scores are interchangeable, whereas scaled scores are similar or comparable. The term score scale refers to the method of reporting test scores including raw scores and transformed scores such as percentile ranks, normalized scores, and standard scores, among others. "Norms provide a basis for interpreting the test performance of a person or group in relation to a defined population of persons or groups" (*Standards*, 1985, p. 31). Norms are usually reported in terms of derived scales.

There are nine standards related to scaling, norming, score comparability, and equating with four (44.4 percent) classified as primary, two (22.2 percent) as secondary, and three (33.3 percent) as conditional. Scales used for reporting test scores should be consistent with the intended purposes of the test and described clearly in the test manual to facilitate accurate interpretation. Norms should refer to clearly defined groups, and norming studies should be described in sufficient detail for evaluation of appropriateness for individuals as well as groups.

When scores on different forms of a test are to be used interchangeably, details of the equating method, design, and statistical analysis should be provided and the characteristics of the anchor test provided when appropriate. When content specifications change from an earlier version of a test or when test specifications change, test users should be informed that scores are not equivalent. Periodic checks are required to maintain a common scale for a test over time.

Test Publication: Technical Manuals and User's Guides

Chapter 5 continues the discussion of essential elements of a technical manual that was begun in chapter 4.

The test manuals produced by the test publisher should provide sufficient information for a qualified user or reviewer of a test to evaluate the technical characteristics of the test for the intended purposes or applications. The manuals should communicate information to many different groups from highly qualified to minimally trained users. Test documentation should be complete, accurate, and clear in order to reduce the likelihood of misuse or misinterpretation of test scores.

There are 11 standards related to the technical and user's manuals with 7 (63.6 percent) classified as primary, 1 (9.1 percent) as secondary, and 3 (27.3 percent) as conditional. Promotional materials for a test should be accurate. The test manuals should be available at the same time as publication of the test and revised, amended, or supplemented as necessary; and additional information should be provided by the publisher on request.

The test manuals should provide the information necessary for proper test use and interpretation. The manuals should describe the rationale and uses for the test, cite a representative set of studies concerning test use, and clearly report relationships between test scores and criteria. To enhance test interpretation, the manual should specify the qualifications required to administer and interpret the test, the degree to which results from different response methods like test book-lets and answer sheets are interchangeable, and when appropriate, the validity of self or automated test interpretation.

STANDARDS RELATED TO TEST USE

As indicated earlier in this chapter, test standards are increasingly speaking to issues of test use, specifying expected professional actions and ethical be-haviors. It is not enough to have an instrument that meets test development standards and a test administrator who has taken the recommended courses. The test user is now expected to exercise professional judgment and to reach deci-sions about how a given instrument is related to the entire assessment situation. Moreover, the test user is expected to be flexible in this decision making, giving careful attention to the context in which the test is employed and to the impact that the results may have on the test taker. As the 1985 *Standards* point out, the greater the potential impact, the greater the need to satisfy relevant standards. This results in test users being faced with a variety of difficult challenges, often requiring careful thought about the ethical standards of their profession. Indeed, many groups now address test use issues within their ethical standards or guide-lines for professional behavior.

Changes between the 1974 and the 1985 revisions of *Standards for Educa-tional and Psychological Testing* make it clear how much emphasis is now being placed on test use. While most of the 1974 edition was devoted to technical standards for tests, with only one section on test use, the 1985 revision devoted three of its four parts to test use topics. Part II of the 1985 *Standards* is the major section on test use; after providing 13 general principles of test use, test use standards for a variety of settings—clinical testing, educational testing and psychological testing in the schools, test use in counseling, employment testing, professional and occupational certification and licensing, and program evaluation—are provided. Part III covers test use applications involving linguistic minorities and people with disabilities. Part IV includes standards for test administration, scoring and reporting procedures, and standards for protecting the rights of test takers.

The 1985 *Standards* and other test standards give major attention to the behavior of test users in five areas: (1) test selection; (2) test administration and scoring; (3) test interpretation, communication of results, and related decision making; (4) responsibilities to test takers; and (5) professional ethics.

Test Selection

There are two major problems in test selection: (1) choosing a test that will provide appropriate (valid) information for the situation in which it will be used and (2) choosing a test that will be appropriate for the individual(s) being assessed. These concerns are expressed in various ways in different test standards.

The 1985 *Standards* state, as the first general principle of test use: "Test users should evaluate the available written documentation on the validity and reliability of the test for the specific use intended" (p. 41). The *Code of Fair Testing Practices* (1988) states: "Test users should select tests that meet the purpose for which they are to be used and that are appropriate for the intended population" (p. 2). *Responsibilities of Users of Standardized Tests* (AACD/AMECD, 1989) states: "The selection of tests should be guided by information obtained from a careful analysis of the characteristics of the population to be tested; the knowledge, skills, abilities, or attitudes to be assessed; the purposes for testing; and the eventual use and interpretation of the test scores" (Section IV). And the *Code of Professional Responsibilities in Educational Measurement* (NCME, 1995) states: "Those who select assessment products and services for use in educational settings, or help others to do so, have important professional responsibilities to make sure that the assessments are appropriate for the intended use" (p. 5). In the last three documents, the more general statements are supplemented by a number of behavioral statements. Guidelines for computerized-adaptive tests (American Council on Education [ACE], 1995) also emphasize the need for these instruments to be appropriate for the purpose of the test, appropriate for the construct being measured, and appropriate to support the test purposes and to measure the examinee population.

The test selection process requires that the test publisher provide the test user with sufficient information for good decision making. Critical reviews of published tests, whether in volumes such as the *Buros Mental Measurement Yearbooks* or in professional journals, provide the test selector with objective evaluations that go beyond the test publisher's data and claims. Test selection also requires that test users have professional preparation that will enable them to understand the technical information being presented and to make wise decisions. This preparation should include familiarity with the standards for the evaluation of tests. Finally, the test selection process requires that test users have a comprehensive knowledge of the assessment situation.

The second part of test selection, ensuring that the test is appropriate for those who will be assessed, also requires that the test user have detailed knowledge of the testing situation. The test selector must determine appropriateness in relation to age, gender, educational, and experiential background. This is an essential part of test fairness and is addressed in the *Code of Fair Testing Practices in Education* (1988), which states, "Test users should select tests that have been developed in ways that attempt to make them as fair as possible for test takers of different races, gender, ethnic backgrounds, or handicapping conditions" (p. 3). In addition, the test selector must determine if the test-taking population includes language minorities or individuals with disabilities. If so, how will the test be appropriate for these individuals, or must it be modified for administration? Does the test publisher provide information about such modifications and about appropriate test use and interpretation for these populations? Section III of the 1985 *Standards* is currently the most detailed source on testing linguistic minorities and individuals with disabilities. Because test users must comply with the Americans with Disabilities Act of 1992, guidelines for employment testing (Eyde, Nester, Heaton, & Nelson, 1994) and for credentialing examinations (Council on Licensure, Enforcement, and Regulation, 1996) have been developed.

Test Administration and Scoring

This area of test user behavior has received extensive attention. It is covered in detail in the 1985 *Standards, Responsibilities of Users of Standardized Tests* (1989), and the *Code of Professional Responsibilities in Educational Measurement* (1995). All emphasize that standardized test administrations are crucial for good test interpretation and for comparisons of performance. The need for accurate test scoring is evident.

Several common themes run through standards for test administration. Test takers should be given proper orientation prior to the testing. The test administrator should be properly qualified and know how to conduct the assessment. The test administrator must protect the security of the test materials and remove opportunities for individuals to obtain test scores by fraudulent means. The testing environment should be free from distractions. The testing must follow standardized procedures, but necessary modifications should be made for administration of tests to individuals with disabilities or to linguistic minorities.

There is considerable disagreement about whether or not test modifications should be documented or if the scores earned under modified conditions should be "flagged." The 1985 *Standards* indicate that, in school situations not involving admissions and in clinical or counseling settings, modifications should be documented. Without such documentation, questions may arise about the validity of test scores or about how to interpret scores from a modified administration. But individuals with disabilities may feel that their privacy is being violated if their test score is flagged as having been administered under modified conditions. Responsibility to demonstrate the validity of a test administered under modified conditions appears to rest with the test user. "When a test user makes a substantial change in test format, mode of administration, instructions, language, or content, the user should revalidate the use of the test for the changed conditions or have a rationale supporting the claim that additional validation is not necessary or possible" (*Standards*, 1985, p. 41). Just what constitutes a "substantial change" is unclear. Mahaffey (1992) has suggested that accommodations be classified by the impact the accommodation may have on the testing process.

Modifying tests for individuals with disabilities is a complex problem. One source of assistance is the U.S. Office of Personnel Management guide for the administration of employment examinations to persons with disabilities (Eyde, Nester, Heaton, & Nelson, 1994). Test administration procedures for individuals who are deaf or hard of hearing, who are blind, who have motor impairments, and who have specific learning disabilities and attention deficit/hyperactivity disorder are described in detail.

Guidelines have also been developed for the administration of computer-based and computerized-adaptive tests (ACE, 1995; APA, 1986). These include ensuring that the items presented on the display screen are legible and free from glare, that the computer equipment is working properly, and that the test taker is provided proper training in the use of the computer and monitored to determine if assistance is needed.

Standards related to test scoring emphasize accuracy, timeliness, and confidentiality. Many of the scoring standards apply primarily to test-scoring services associated with group testing in large-scale programs rather than to the individual testing done by counselors and psychologists. Test takers should be informed about scoring procedures. Accuracy should be insured through rescoring, screening of results, and other quality-assurance checks. Test takers should be able to verify the accuracy of the scoring. When errors are found, corrected scores should be provided as quickly as possible. The confidentiality of individually identifiable information must be protected as prescribed by law. When test scores are maintained on individuals, in data files or in individual records, there should be a set of policy guidelines specifying how long the scores are to be retained, who will have access to them, and how they may be used over time. The 1985 *Standards* recommend that when test data about a person are retained, both the test protocol and any written report should be preserved.

Test Interpretation, Communication of Results, and Related Decision Making

Typically, test scores are presented as numerical information. But the numbers alone communicate very little. The numerical scores must be interpreted, often by consulting test norms and other information provided by the test developer. It is this interpretation, not simply the number, that must be communicated to the test taker and to those who will make decisions based on the test information.

As stated in the *Responsibilities of Users of Standardized Tests* (AACD/ AMECD, 1989), test interpretation encompasses all the ways that meaning is assigned to scores. It requires detailed knowledge of the test, the test taker, and the purposes of the assessment. Most test standards emphasize careful study of the test manual, with emphasis on the validity of the test for the intended use. Interpretation of a test must also stem from knowledge of any theories on which the test is based.

Test interpretation and related decision making are closely related to test validity. "Indeed, validity is broadly defined as nothing less than an evaluative summary of both the evidence for and the actual—as well as potential—consequences of score interpretation and use" (Messick, 1995b, p. 742). Validity can be considered to cover both the theory and the evidence that support inferences and decisions based on test scores. It is these inferences and decisions that must be validated, not the test instrument. Each type of use for any given test must be validated. This may require data collection and analysis by the test user. Indeed, validation should be viewed as a joint responsibility of the test developer and the test user.

Interpretative problems may occur if the content of the test is not a comprehensive sample of the construct being assessed (exhibits "construct underrepresentation"). Interpretative problems also may occur if the test contains material that is not related to the construct being assessed. Interpreting the results from a mathematics achievement test that consists only of word problems as an indication of mathematical ability, without giving any consideration to the limited definition of the construct or to the extent that the scores might be affected by reading ability or proficiency in English, is an example of the kind of interpretative error that arises from test invalidity.

A critical issue in score interpretation, as well as in validity, is generalizability. The test user must know if the scores have the same meaning across different populations. It is for this reason that test users are cautioned not to use tests unless they have been normed on a population similar to the one to be assessed. A test of aggressiveness that has been normed on army recruits is not likely to be useful in assessing a nursing home population. Generalizability problems can also arise in situations where the number of assessment tasks is limited, especially in performance assessments (see Linn, 1994; Messick, 1994). This is related to test reliability.

The error of measurement is one way of describing the reliability of a test.

It allows the test interpreter to present the range within which an individual's "true score" is likely to fall. Interpretations can be seriously flawed when test users place heavy reliance on cut-scores without giving proper attention to test reliability or the error of measurement.

Clear and accurate communication of test results is a critical part of assessment. The nature of the communication may vary for the assessment of individuals and the assessment of groups. The information may be communicated in a face-to-face situation by an individual psychologist or counselor, or it may be done using printed material from testing programs, such as those used in admission to colleges and to graduate and professional schools. Regardless of how the communication is carried out, it is important that the individual who took the test and the individuals who will use the test results understand what the scores mean. Proper interpretations should be communicated in a manner appropriate to the audience. Cautions should be taken to avoid likely misinterpretations. Guidelines have been developed for the reporting of assessment results (Aschbacher & Herman, 1991). While these guidelines were intended primarily for use in state reports of the results from large-scale assessments, they are relevant for many other types of score reporting.

Explaining the limitations of the assessment is an important part of communicating test results. The score recipient should know about circumstances that could have affected results. It is also important to stress to score recipients that test information should not be used alone for decision making.

One of the most important questions in test interpretation is "whether or not the test user has accurately described the extent to which the score supports any decision made or action taken" (*Standards*, 1985, p. 41). According to these standards, test users should have a sound technical and professional basis for their decisions.

It is important to inform all those involved in an assessment how decisions based on that assessment may affect them. When there is political use of test information, with group scores released to the public, efforts should be made to minimize uses that may be adverse to the interests of those being tested.

Responsibilities to Test Takers

Concerns about the test developer's and test user's responsibilities to the test taker are relatively recent. They appear to have arisen from a general concern with the protection of consumers and from criticisms of testing. One of the first references to test takers' rights appeared in a 1981 article by Melvin Novick, which stated, "Because the examinee is the least powerful participant in the testing and decision-making process, some strengthening of this position would seem necessary" (Novick, 1981, p. 1036).

The 1985 joint *Standards*, which were developed under Novick's chairmanship, were the first to contain a section on protecting the rights of test takers. This section stresses obtaining informed consent prior to testing, providing an interpretation of test results in a form that test takers can understand, confidentiality of and access to test scores, and issues of test security, including the cancellation of scores when there may have been irregularities.

The 1988 *Code of Fair Testing Practices in Education* also included a section on informing test takers. It recommends providing (1) information so that decisions can be made about whether or not an optional test should be taken; (2) information about test content, format, and test-taking strategies; (3) information about rights regarding retesting and obtaining copies of the test and completed answer sheet; and (4) information about how to register complaints and have problems resolved.

A recent government report concluded that most professional groups now agree that test takers should be provided with basic information about

Content covered by the test and type of question formats;

The kind of preparation the test taker should have and appropriate test-taking strategies to use (e.g., should they guess or not?);

The uses to which the test data will be put;

The persons who will have access to test scores and the circumstances under which test scores will be released to anyone beyond those who have such access;

The length of time test scores will be kept on record;

Available options for retesting, rescoring or cancelling scores; and

The procedures test takers and their parents or guardians may use to register complaints and have problems resolved. (U.S. Congress, Office of Technology Assessment, 1992, p. 70)

A working group of the Joint Committee on Testing Practices is currently developing a statement regarding the rights and responsibilities of test takers. This statement builds on the work cited above.

Professional Ethics

Because "the ultimate responsibility for appropriate test use lies with the user" (*Standards*, 1985, p. 3), ethical standards for and training of test users take on primary importance. For this reason, many professional organizations include in their codes of ethics not only general material on professional conduct but, also, ethical standards specific to testing and assessment (see, e.g., ACA, 1995; APA, 1992; American School Counselor Association [ASCA], 1992; National Association of School Psychologists [NASP], 1992).

There is not, at present, a code of ethics for all measurement professionals. Schmeiser (1992) has pointed out that the ethical considerations in the 1985 *Standards* are not comprehensive in scope and has asked, "Should the measurement profession consider developing a separate, more comprehensive code of ethics?" She provides examples of the kinds of ethical standards that might be prepared for measurement professionals, covering work in test development, test administration, and test research.

Even without such a code, certain commonalities are evident in the existing professional standards and codes of ethics. A basic part of professional ethics, as articulated in all of these documents, is the issue of professional competence. In this respect, these ethical codes relate to the professional training standards discussed below. For example, the APA *Ethical Principles of Psychologists and Code of Conduct* begins with the following statement: "Psychologists strive to maintain high standards of competence in their work. They recognize the boundaries of their particular competencies and the limitations of their expertise. They provide only those services and use only those techniques for which they are qualified by education, training, or experience" (APA, 1992, p. 3). A similar statement is included in the American Counseling Association's *Code of Ethics and Standards of Practice* (ACA, 1995): "Counselors practice only within the boundaries of their competence, based on their education, training, supervised experience, state and national professional credentials, and appropriate professional experience" (p. 14).

But the various test standards do not address what kinds of education, training, and supervised experience are necessary for competent test use. These standards have been left to other groups, as will be discussed in the next section.

STANDARDS RELATED TO TEST USER QUALIFICATIONS AND TRAINING

While test standards devote considerable space to the technical characteristics of tests and to test use, little is said about the qualifications of the test users. The only mention of this topic in the 1985 *Standards* appears in the section on general principles of test use. This states: "Responsibility for test use should be assumed by or delegated only to those individuals who have the training and experiences necessary to handle this responsibility in a professional and technically adequate manner. Any special qualifications for test administration or interpretation noted in the manual should be met" (p. 42).

Faced with the limited attention to test user qualifications in the Joint Standards, states and occupational groups have created their own standards for the training, certification, and licensing of testing professionals. In addition, assessment standards for teachers and school administrators have been prepared. Test publishers have long set standards about the qualifications of test purchasers. Researchers have assessed test user qualifications. Each of these is discussed below.

There are at least two ways to design standards about test user qualifications. One is to direct the standards toward how tests are used in practice. For example, a standard reflecting the belief that a test score should be interpreted only as precisely as the test's standard error of measurement allows might state, "The practitioner considers the test's standard error of measurement in interpreting test scores." The other way is to direct the standards toward the levels of understanding needed to enable responsible practice. Using the same example, the parallel standard might be: "The practitioner understands the nature of the standard error of measurement as a measure expressing the imprecision inherent in a test score." A test user who meets this standard is equipped to engage in one aspect of responsible test use. But being equipped does not guarantee that the practitioner will act responsibly in practice. When standards for test users are directed toward what is actually done, the practitioner's actions depend on two elements: (1) the ability to engage in the behavior and (2) the motivation to do so. We assume the behavior can be taught, but a practitioner's motivation can vary from situation to situation.

Training, Certification, and Licensing Standards

Counseling, psychology, and many other professions in which tests and assessment play a major role have standards for trai. ng, certification, and licensing. Some of these standards specify the kinds of courses that must be taken. Other standards use competency statements to describe the knowledge and skills necessary in the profession. Still other standards are set forth in guidelines for the content of certification or licensing examinations and the score level required to enter into professional practice. Anastasi (1990) has pointed out that "the prevention of test misuse calls for the expansion and improvement of training facilities for test users" (p. 23). In this section, we frequently use the field of school counseling as an example of the kinds of standards required of testing professionals.

Counselor education programs are accredited by the Council for Accreditation of Counseling and Related Educational Programs (CACREP, 1994). This group requires all counseling students to have training in eight core-curriculum areas. Two of these areas, Appraisal, and Research and Program Evaluation, are relevant for testing and assessment.

In Appraisal, the program must involve "studies that provide an understanding of individual and group approaches to assessment and evaluation." These studies might include

theoretical and historical bases for assessment techniques; validity including evidence for establishing content, construct, and empirical validity; reliability including methods of establishing stability, internal and equivalence reliability; appraisal methods including environment assessment, performance assessment, individual and group test and inventory methods, behavioral observations, and computer-managed and computer-assisted methods; psychometric statistics including types of assessment scores, measures of central tendency, indices of variability, standard errors, and correlations; age, gender, ethnicity, language, disability, and culture factors related to the assessment and evaluation of individuals and groups; strategies for selection, administering, interpreting, and using assessment and evaluation instruments and techniques in counseling; and ethical considerations in appraisal.

Studies in the Research and Program Evaluation area must provide "an understanding of types of research methods, basic statistics, and ethical and legal considerations in research." These studies might involve "basic types of research methods to include qualitative and quantitative research designs; basic parametric and nonparametric statistics; principles, practices, and applications of needs assessment and program evaluation; uses of computers for data management and analysis; and ethical and legal considerations in research."

In 1993 the Teacher Programs area of the Educational Testing Service (ETS) conducted a state-by-state survey of licensing requirements in various teaching specialty areas, including guidance counselor.[1] A number of assessment-related areas were identified. Twenty-nine states require school counselors to have taken courses in measurement, evaluation, and assessment. Nineteen states require courses in assessment and interpretation of learner aptitude, interests, and achievement. Eleven states require courses in student appraisal and evaluation techniques. Two states require courses in psychological testing and measurement. Two states require courses in testing and evaluation. One state requires a course in academic and human assessment, while another requires a course in the analysis of verbal and nonverbal behavior. In addition to assessment courses, many states require that counselors have training in research and evaluation. Often, these courses provide training in statistical concepts that are important in interpreting assessments as well as in carrying out research. Thirty-six states require counselors to have taken courses in program evaluation. Thirty states require courses in research and the interpretation of professional literature.

Standards based on courses taken ensure that the testing professional has been exposed to the knowledge necessary for appropriate test use. But this exposure may not result in competent job performance. Several groups are now trying to develop standards that describe test user competencies.

The National Association of State Directors of Teacher Education and Certification has standards (NASDTEC, 1991) for the approval of programs for school counselors (as well as school psychologists and other education professionals). There are 13 standards that emphasize the competencies expected of school counselors. Three of these are assessment related.

The program shall require demonstrated competence in assessing and interpreting learning aptitudes, interests, and achievement.

The program shall require demonstrated competence in career counseling, including career development theory, assessment and decision-making.

The program shall require demonstrated competence in consulting with parents, students, and professional personnel relative to the assessment of students' academic, social, cognitive, and physical functioning, and the subsequent planning, development, and implementation of the student's program.

A committee composed of representatives of the American School Counselor Association and the Association for Assessment in Counseling is in the process of drafting a statement on the standards for school counselor competence in assessment and evaluation. This statement is intended to be consistent with the CACREP and NASDTEC standards discussed above. It differs in emphasizing the skills of the individual school counselor rather than the nature of counselor education and training. It is intended that this statement will be of use to counselor and assessment educators as a guide to the development of school counselor preparation programs, workshops, inservice training, and other continuing education opportunities. It is also intended that this statement will be of use to school counselors in evaluating their own professional development and continuing education needs and to counselor certification agencies and school districts in evaluating the performance of and clarifying expectations for school counselors and counselor applicants.

Assessment Competence Standards for School Personnel

One of the major uses of tests occurs in the schools. Some of this testing is done by or under the supervision of testing professionals such as school counselors and school psychologists. At other times, testing is done by teachers or is carried out under the oversight of school administrators.

Both administrators and teachers are, typically, less well prepared to carry out and use assessments than are testing professionals (see, e.g., Impara & Plake, 1995). Two recent projects have identified desirable assessment competencies for teachers and for school administrators.

In 1990, a committee with representatives from the American Association of Colleges for Teacher Education (AACTE), the American Federation of Teachers (AFT), the NCME, and the National Education Association (NEA) completed development of a statement of *Standards for Teacher Competence in Educational Assessment of Students*. This statement, which was approved by AFT, NCME, and NEA (1990), describes five areas in which teacher competence in assessment is needed and sets forth seven standards for teacher competence that underlie these activities (Schafer, 1991a).

The American Association of School Administrators (AASA), National Association of Elementary School Principals (NAESP), National Association of Secondary School Principals (NASSP), and NCME have developed a draft statement of similar standards for school administrators (AASA, NAESP, NASSP, & NCME, 1994). This draft was guided by a survey in which nearly 1,700 administrators described how frequently they engage in 24 assessment-related tasks and evaluated their needs for knowledge, skills, and abilities in 13 areas in order to carry out these tasks. Ten standards resulted.

In 1995 the National Council on Measurement in Education approved a code of professional responsibilities to guide its members (NCME, 1995). This document can be used by teachers, school administrators, school counselors, school psychologists, and other educational assessment professionals.

Test Publishers' Standards

In 1954, the American Psychological Association introduced a three-tiered system for categorizing tests in terms of the qualifications that test users must have to employ the tests properly. The intent was to create a safeguard that would help protect the public against test misuse.

As described in the 1954 *Technical Recommendations for Psychological Tests and Diagnostic Techniques*, Level A tests are those that "can be adequately administered, scored, and interpreted with the aid of the manual" (e.g., achievement tests). Level B tests "require some technical knowledge of test construction and use, and of supporting psychological and educational subjects such as statistics, individual differences, and psychology of adjustment, personnel psychology, and guidance" (e.g., aptitude tests, adjustment inventories with normal populations). Level C tests "require substantial understanding of testing and supporting psychological subjects, together with supervised experience in the use of these devices" (e.g., projective tests, individual mental tests). In practice, Level A tests have been distributed with few, if any, restrictions, while Level B tests typically required evidence of a master's degree and Level C a doctoral degree.

These test levels have not been included in the more recent Joint Standards. Test publishers are considering if this classification system should be replaced. They have suggested a purchaser classification system that would recognize "that tests may be employed for different purposes and that it is these different purposes which should determine whether or not an individual is qualified to purchase a given test" (Simner, 1993). It has been suggested that publishers terminate the practice of providing waivers to purchasers based on occupation, professional membership, or level of graduate training.

Brown (1995) has called for development of a new system to establish and enforce test user qualifications.

Interdisciplinary Standards

Recognizing that professional credentials and occupational titles may not be adequate to screen test purchasers, a working group of the Joint Committee on Testing Practices used job analysis methods to analyze critical incidents of test misuse and assess test user qualifications (Moreland, Eyde, Robertson, Primoff, & Most, 1995). Eighty-six test user competencies were identified. These can be summarized in two comprehensive elements: (1) knowledge of the test and its limitations and (2) accepting responsibility for competent use of the test. Twelve competencies that are minimum requirements for all test users were also identified. A factor analysis identified seven areas of potential misuse of specific tests.

TRENDS AND EMERGING ISSUES

The trends discussed in this chapter, with growing emphasis on ensuring appropriate test use and on the concerns of test takers, are likely to continue. Changes in the nature of tests themselves, especially the growth of performance assessment, a revised conceptualization of validity, more concern about equity issues in testing, and the use of computer-based tests and interpretations, present problems to be addressed by new and revised test standards.

The 1985 *Standards for Educational and Psychological Testing* were undergoing revision as this chapter was being written. This revision is likely to include standards for performance assessments (Camara & Brown, 1995; Linn, 1994; Messick, 1995a), including issues of validity (Guion, 1995; Messick, 1994, 1995a), generalizability (Brennan & Johnson, 1995), equating and comparability of scores (Green, 1995), standard setting (Jaeger, 1995), and bias and fairness (Bond, 1995).

How will the revised *Standards* treat validity (Camara & Brown, 1995)? Will validity evidence continue to be categorized as construct/content/criterion related (Messick, 1995b; Moss, 1995)? For a number of years, measurement specialists (Cronbach, 1991; Schafer, 1991b) and test users (Ellis & Blustein, 1991a, 1991b) have questioned if all validity evidence might not be conceptualized as construct validity evidence. Messick (1995b) offers a unified concept of validity by providing a comprehensive theory of construct validity that addresses score meaning and the social consequences of test score use. In Messick's writing (1995b, p. 749) he concludes that "validity and values are one imperative, not two, and test validation implicates both the science and the ethics of assessment, which is why validity has force as a social value."

Some professional organizations fear that if they do not adequately regulate their own members, they may be faced with legislation that restricts test use. There is also a growing consumer protection emphasis. Finally, the changes in the nature of tests themselves, especially the growth in performance assessment and in the use of computer-based tests and interpretations, present new problems. All of these will undoubtedly be addressed by new and revised test standards.

Although test standards are intended primarily as guidelines for test developers and test users, and as a criterion against which tests and test practices can be evaluated, they also are used by the courts when there are cases involving malpractice, improper treatment, discrimination, and adverse impact in employment selection (Novick, 1984). As Faggen (1990) has pointed out, there are tensions and conflicts when the results of certification and licensing examinations are challenged. Existing standards do not always address these legal issues.

The revised *Standards* will likely include new material on test fairness and equity issues. One concern is fairness when tests are administered by computer and when computerized adaptive testing is used. It is important to ensure that the test results reflect the construct being measured, not the subject's familiarity with computers. It is also important to address the comparability of scores from paper-and-pencil, computer-administered, and computerized adaptive tests, especially when they are used interchangeably in an assessment situation. There are also concerns about fairness in other examinations where some or all of the items are selected by the examinee and when the assessment is based on a portfolio.

The passage of the Americans with Disabilities Act (ADA) in 1990 created a challenging situation for the testing profession. Tests are being modified when they are administered to individuals with documented disabilities. But there remains a need to provide valid assessments, ensuring that scores on a modified test can be equated to the original test and will have the same meaning. A related issue is whether or not the modified test scores should be ''flagged'' to alert those interpreting the results to the fact that the test was not given under standardized conditions. Some of the measurement issues raised by the ADA requirements are addressed by Fisher (1994), Geisinger (1994), and Phillips (1994).

The assessment of language minorities and of individuals from different racial/ethnic groups remains a challenge for the profession. These have been addressed differently in the various test standards. A useful compilation of various standards relating to multicultural assessment is Prediger (1993). A detailed discussion of issues related to multicultural assessment may be found in Suzuki, Meller and Ponterotto (1996).

There is a growing concern, both among testing professionals and the public, regarding test user qualifications. If professional organizations do not adequately regulate their own members, they may be faced with legislation that restricts test use (Brown, 1995). Test standards certainly have important implications for the measurement curriculum (Frisbie & Friedman, 1987) and continuing education of testing professionals (Elmore, Ekstrom, & Diamond, 1993). All agree that testing professionals should be properly prepared. Just what this preparation should be is difficult to describe since it depends on the test being used and the purpose for the assessment. Increasingly, testing professionals are acknowledging that a degree or an occupational title, by itself, is an inadequate indicator of test user qualifications. Most testing professionals would agree that test users must have received training that will enable them to administer, score, and interpret a test in a manner appropriate for the intended use and one that meets the guidelines set forth in the test manual. How best to ensure that this occurs is one of the major challenges facing the testing profession.

NOTE

1. The authors wish to thank Catherine Havrilesky and Lori Ingwerson of the ETS Teacher Programs area for providing information about and access to the survey.

REFERENCES

American Association for Counseling and Development/Association for Measurement and Evaluation in Counseling and Development. (1989). *Responsibilities of users of standardized tests*. Alexandria, VA: Author.

American Association of School Administrators, National Association of Elementary School Principals, National Association of Secondary School Principals, & National Council on Measurement in Education. (1994). Competency standards in student assessment for educational administrators. *Educational Measurement: Issues and Practice, 13* (1), 44–47.

American Council on Education, Credit by Examination Program. (1995). *Guidelines for computerized-adaptive test development and use in education*. Washington, DC: Author.

American Counseling Association. (1995). *Code of ethics and standards of practice*. Alexandria, VA: Author.

American Federation of Teachers, National Council on Measurement in Education, & National Education Association. (1990). *Standards for teacher competence in educational assessment of students*. Washington, DC: Author.

American Personnel and Guidance Association/Association for Measurement and Evaluation in Guidance. (1978). *Responsibilities of users of standardized tests*. Falls Church, VA: Author.

American Psychological Association. (1954). *Technical recommendations for psychological tests and diagnostic techniques*. Washington, DC: Author.

American Psychological Association. (1986). *Guidelines for computer-based tests and interpretations*. Washington, DC: Author.

American Psychological Association. (1992). *Ethical principles of psychologists and code of conduct*. Washington, DC: Author.

American School Counselor Association. (1992). *Ethical standards for school counselors*. Alexandria, VA: Author.

Anastasi, A. (1988). *Psychological testing* (6th ed.). New York: Macmillan.

Anastasi, A. (1990). What is test misuse? Perspectives of a measurement expert. In *The uses of standardized tests in America*. Proceedings of the 1989 ETS Invitational Conference. Princeton, NJ: Educational Testing Service.

Aschbacher, P. R., & Herman, J. L. (1991). *Guidelines for effective score reporting* (CSE Technical Report 326). Los Angeles, CA: National Center for Research on Evaluation, Standards, and Student Testing.

Bond, L. (1995). Unintended consequences of performance assessment: Issues of bias and fairness. *Educational Measurement: Issues and Practice, 14* (4), 21–24.

Brennan, R. L., & Johnson, E. G. (1995). Generalizability of performance assessments. *Educational Measurement: Issues and Practice, 14* (4), 9–12.

Brown, D. C. (1995). Test user qualifications. *The Score, 18* (2), 8–9.

Camara, W. J., & Brown, D. C. (1995). Educational and employment testing: Changing concepts in measurement and policy. *Educational Measurement: Issues and Practice, 14* (1), 5–11.

Code of fair testing practices in education. (1988). Washington, DC: Joint Committee on Testing Practices.

Council for Accreditation of Counseling and Related Educational Programs. (1994). *CACREP accreditation standards and procedures manual*. Alexandria, VA: Author.

Council on Licensure, Enforcement, and Regulation. (1996). *The Americans with Disabilities Act: Information and recommendations for credentialing examinations.* Lexington, KY: Author.

Cronbach, L. J. (1991). A moderate view: Response to Ellis and Blustein. *Journal of Counseling and Development, 69* (6), 556–557.

Ellis, M. V., & Blustein, D. L. (1991a). Developing and using educational and psychological tests and measures: The unificationist perspective. *Journal of Counseling and Development, 69* (6), 550–555.

Ellis, M. V., & Blustein, D. L. (1991b). The unificationist view: A context for validity. *Journal of Counseling and Development, 69* (6), 561–563.

Elmore, P. B., Ekstrom, R. B., & Diamond, E. E. (1993). Counselors' test use practices: Indicators of the adequacy of measurement training. *Measurement and Evaluation in Counseling and Development, 26* (2), 116–124.

Eyde, L. D., Moreland, K. L., Robertson, G. J., Primoff, E. S., & Most, R. B. (1988). Test user qualifications: A data-based approach to promoting good test use. *Issues in scientific psychology.* Report of the Test User Qualifications Working Group of the Joint Committee on Testing Practices. Washington, DC: American Psychological Association.

Eyde, L. D., Nester, M. A., Heaton, S. M., & Nelson, A. V. (1994). *Guide for administering written employment examinations to persons with disabilities.* Washington, DC: U.S. Office of Personnel Management.

Faggen, J. (1990). The profession's evolving standards. *Educational Measurement: Issues and Practice, 9* (4), 3–4.

Fisher, R. J. (1994). The Americans with Disabilities Act: Implications for measurement. *Educational Measurement: Issues and Practice, 13* (3), 17–26, 37.

Fremer, J., Diamond, E. E., & Camara, W. J. (1989). Developing a code of fair testing practices in education. *American Psychologist, 44* (7), 1062–1067.

Frisbie, D. A., & Friedman, S. J. (1987). Test standards: Some implications for the measurement curriculum. *Educational Measurement: Issues and Practice, 6* (3), 17–23.

Geisinger, K. F. (1994). Psychometric issues in testing students with disabilities. *Applied Measurement in Education, 7* (2), 121–140.

Green, B. F. (1995). Comparability of scores from performance assessments. *Educational Measurement: Issues and Practice, 14* (4), 13–15, 24.

Guion, R. M. (1995). Commentary on values and standards in performance assessment. *Educational Measurement: Issues and Practice, 14* (4), 25–27.

Haney, W. (1981). Validity, vaudeville, and values: A short history of social concerns over standardized testing. *American Psychologist, 36* (10), 1021–1034.

Haney, W., & Madaus, G. (1991). The evolution of ethical and technical standards for testing. In R. K. Hambleton & J. N. Zaal (Eds.), *Advances in educational and psychological testing* (pp. 395–425). Boston: Kluwer Academic Publishers.

Impara, J. C., & Plake, B. S. (1995). Comparing counselors', school administrators', and teachers' knowledge in student assessment. *Measurement and Evaluation in Counseling and Development, 28* (2), 78–87.

Jaeger, R. M. (1995). Setting standards for complex performances: An iterative, judgmental policy-capturing strategy. *Educational Measurement: Issues and Practice, 14* (4), 16–20.

Linn, R. L. (1994). Performance assessment: Policy promises and technical measurement standards. *Educational Researcher, 23* (9), 4–14.

Loesch, L. C. (1983). Standards in measurement and evaluation. Professional preparation guidelines: An AMEG imperative. *Measurement and Evaluation in Counseling and Development, 16,* 161–165.

Lord, F. M. (1977). Practical applications of item characteristic curve theory. *Journal of Educational Measurement, 14,* 117–138.

Mahaffey, C. (1992). *Accommodating employment testing to the needs of individuals with disabilities.* Glendale, CA: Psychological Services, Inc.

Messick, S. (1994). The interplay of evidence and consequences in the validation of performance assessments. *Educational Researcher, 23* (2), 13–23.

Messick, S. (1995a). Standards of validity and the validity of standards in performance assessment. *Educational Measurement: Issues and Practice, 14* (4), 5–8.

Messick, S. (1995b). Validity of psychological assessment: Validity of inferences from a person's responses and performances as scientific inquiry into score meaning. *American Psychologist, 50* (9), 741–749.

Moreland, K. L., Eyde, L. D., Robertson, G. J., Primoff, E. S., & Most, R. B. (1995). Assessment of test user qualifications. *American Psychologist, 50* (1), 14–23.

Moss, P. A. (1995). Themes and variations in validity theory. *Educational Measurement: Issues and Practice, 14* (2), 5–13.

National Association of School Psychologists. (1992). *Professional conduct manual.* Silver Spring, MD: National Association of School Psychologists.

National Association of State Directors of Teacher Education and Certification. (1991). *Manual on certification and preparation of educational personnel in the United States.* Dubuque, IA: Kendall/Hunt Publishing Company.

National Council on Measurement in Education. (1995). *Code of professional responsibilities in educational measurement.* Washington, DC: Author.

Novick, M. R. (1981). Federal guidelines and professional standards. *American Psychologist, 36* (10), 1035–1046.

Novick, M. R. (1984). Importance of professional standards for fair and appropriate test use. In C. W. Daves (Ed.), *The uses and misuses of tests.* San Francisco: Jossey-Bass.

Phillips, S. E. (1994). High-stakes testing accommodations: Validity versus disabled rights. *Applied Measurement in Education, 7* (2), 93–120.

Prediger, D. J. (1993). *Multicultural assessment standards: A compilation for counselors.* Alexandria, VA: Association for Assessment in Counseling.

Schafer, W. D. (1991a). Essential assessment skills in professional education of teachers. *Educational Measurement: Issues and Practice, 10* (1), 3–6, 12.

Schafer, W. D. (1991b). Validity and inference: A reaction to the unificationist perspective. *Journal of Counseling and Development, 69* (6), 558–560.

Schmeiser, C. B. (1992). Ethical codes in the professions. *Educational Measurement: Issues and Practice, 11* (3), 5–11.

Simner, M. L. (1993, November). Interim report of the professional affairs committee working group on test publishing industry standards. Working Group on Test Publishing Industry Standards.

Standards for educational and psychological testing. (1985). Washington, DC: American Psychological Association.

Standards for educational and psychological tests. (1974). Washington, DC: American Psychological Association.

Standards for educational and psychological tests and manuals. (1966). Washington, DC: American Psychological Association.

Suzuki, L. A., Meller, P. J., & Ponterotto, J. G. (Eds.). (1996). *Handbook of multicultural assessment: Clinical, psychological, and educational aspirations.* San Francisco: Jossey-Bass.

U.S. Congress, Office of Technology Assessment. (1992). *Testing in American schools: Asking the right questions.* Washington, DC: U.S. Government Printing Office.

4

What Makes an Aptitude Test Valid?

Malcolm James Ree and Thomas R. Carretta

Most aptitude tests measure more than a single ability. One of the earliest test factor theorists, Charles Spearman (1904), suggested that all tests measure a common core and a specific element. The common core he called g for general cognitive ability, and the specific elements were noted as $s_1 \ldots s_n$. Although multifactor theorists like Thurstone (1938) proposed alternative models, the conceptual values of g and s have not been lost. Vernon (1969) has demonstrated that ability test factors are arranged in a pyramidal hierarchy with g at the apex. Lower-order group factors are at the next level down. These lower-order factors are highly g saturated. Below the lower-order factors are individual aptitude tests. Each aptitude test measures g and one or more specific factors. An example is provided in Figure 4.1. It shows a three-level hierarchy for the Armed Services Vocational Aptitude Battery (ASVAB; Ree & Carretta, 1994b) with g at the highest level, specific factors at the middle level, and tests at the lowest level.

RESEARCH METHODS IN STUDYING APTITUDE

There are many methodological issues that make the study of aptitude or ability more difficult, but three are particularly troublesome. Confusion over them can lead to erroneous conclusions about what the tests measure and what makes them valid. Here we offer cautions about each and recommend remedies. The concerns are rotated factors, censored samples, and unreliability of measurement. See Ree (1995) for a broader treatment of methodological issues in aptitude and ability testing including sample size, capitalization on chance, and failure to use marker variables.

Figure 4.1
Hierarchical Structure of an Aptitude Battery

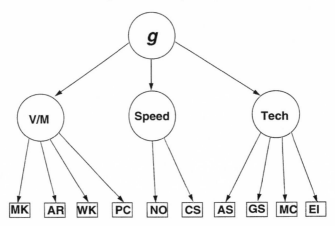

Notes: The factors were: g = General Cognitive Ability, V/M = Verbal/Math, Speed = Processing Speed, and Tech = Technical Knowledge. The tests were: MK = Math Knowledge, AR
= Arithmetic Reasoning, WK = Word Knowledge, PC = Paragraph Comprehension, NO =
Numerical Operations, CS = Coding Speed, AS = Auto & Shop Information, GS = General Science, MC = Mechanical Comprehension, and EI = Electronics Information.

Rotated Factors

The first concern stems from the use of factor analysis in aptitude research.
Factor analysis is a series of related statistical techniques used to seek latent
structure in a group of variables such as aptitude tests. The latent structure is
the set of unobservable factors that cause the observed scores (Kim & Mueller,
1978). The basic idea is that observed scores are a linear combination of unobservable underlying factors such as:

$$\text{SCORE} = \text{Factor}_1 + \text{Factor}_2 + \ldots \text{Factor}_n + \text{error}$$

The issue of concern is rotation in factor analysis. Rotation was developed to
help make factors easier to interpret. When factors are rotated, the variance
attributable to the first unrotated factor, invariably g in aptitude or ability tests
and other cognitive measures, is distributed across the other factors. The first
factor, g, therefore seems to disappear, but in reality, it becomes the dominant
source of variance in each of the now-rotated factors. These other factors each
become g and something else. It is usually the "something else" that decides
the name of the factor. The g in the factor is not acknowledged. Consider the
verbal factor found in many multiple aptitude tests. Because of rotation, it is
mostly g! We should call verbal not V but more accurately $g + v$. As a conse-

quence, the correlation among the factors in multiple aptitude tests is almost always due to g being spread across the multiple factors.

Most of the variance of multiple aptitude batteries is due to g, and very little is from the multiple specific aptitudes. Ree and Earles (1991b) have shown that the proportion of g variance in a representative multiple aptitude battery (the ASVAB) was 64 percent, and Ree and Carretta (1994b) have shown that the total proportion of reliable non-g variance was only 16 percent.

Several studies have shown that this is not unique to paper-and-pencil aptitude tests but is also found in computer-based cognitive component tests (Kranzler & Jensen, 1991; Kyllonen, 1993; Kyllonen & Christal, 1990). Although Kranzler and Jensen (1991), Kyllonen (1993), and Kyllonen and Christal (1990) used different tests, their results were similar. They demonstrated that a wide variety of computer-based elementary cognitive tasks derived from cognitive component theory measured mostly g.

The problem of the disappearing g associated with rotation can be avoided either by not rotating or by using unrotated first principal components, principal factors, or residualized hierarchical factors. Schmid and Leiman (1957) analytically demonstrated that residualization removes the effects of the higher-order factor, g in cognitive measures,[1] from the lower-order factors. Residualization and nonrotation are the only ways to get pure measures of g and s for use in comparative studies.

Censored Samples

Censored samples are the second concern in aptitude measurement. A sample is called censored when the variance of one or more variables has been reduced due to prior selection. For example, colleges do not admit all who apply, nor do employers hire all applicants. University students subjected to prior selection on the basis of test scores and academic achievement provide a common example of a censored sample. A similar situation is found in samples of job incumbents. Because of the censoring, the variance associated with the *causes* of test scores, academic achievement, or job performance would have been reduced. Censored samples have often been shown to create artifacts that lead to erroneous conclusions about aptitude or ability (Morrison & Morrison, 1995).

Correlations from censored samples are substantially downwardly biased estimators and can even change signs from their population value (Ree, Carretta, Earles, & Albert, 1994; Thorndike, 1949). The correlation of an ability test with a performance criterion when computed in a censored sample will be much lower than it should be. Thorndike (1949) provided a good illustration and discussion of the problem with an example from a large World War II military sample. A large group of applicants was admitted to aircraft pilot training without regard to aptitude test scores. Correlations with the training criterion were computed for all participants and for a subsample that would have been selected, had the standards at the end of the war been used. In the range-restricted censored sample the average decrease in validity coefficients was .29, compared to the unrestricted sample. In the unrestricted sample the most valid test had a correlation of .64 that dropped to .18 in the range-restricted sample. One test, a measure of psychomotor ability, changed sign from +.40 to −.03 from the unrestricted to the range-restricted sample! Clearly, the estimates of validity were adversely affected by range restriction. Just as clearly, wrong decisions as to which tests to implement would have been made if the range restricted correlation had been used.

Brand (1987) observed that many studies have been conducted in samples that were range restricted on g. The study participants, often college or university students, were selected, mostly on the basis of g. This reduced the variance of g and artificially reduced correlations with g. Goldberg (1991) observed that "in other words, one can always filter out or at least greatly reduce the importance of a causal variable, no matter how strong that variable, by selecting a group that selects its members on the basis of that variable" (p. 132). He noted that the more restricted the variance of a variable, the less its apparent validity.

Almost all educational and occupational samples used in studies have been selected on g. In samples from the United States Air Force, ASVAB[2] test variances frequently have been reduced from the normative 100 to 25 by prior selection. This range restriction could lead to a false conclusion that g is not strongly correlated with other variables, when, actually, the low correlation is the consequence of a statistical artifact.

Statistical corrections should be applied to reduce problems due to range restriction. If censoring has occurred on only one variable, the "univariate" corrections (Thorndike, 1949) are appropriate, but if censoring has occurred on more than one variable, the multivariate correction (Lawley, 1943; Ree, Carretta, Earles, & Albert, 1994) is suitable. These corrections provide better statistical estimates and tend to be conservative (Linn, Harnish, & Dunbar, 1981), underestimating the population parameters. The range restriction corrections should be used to provide better statistical estimates.

Unreliability of Measurement

The use of tests with poor reliability is the third problem. Unreliable tests reduce correlations (Spearman, 1904), leading to false conclusions. One solution is to lengthen unreliable tests by adding items. Alternately, removing ambiguity from the existing items can increase reliability, as can improving instructions. Failing these remedies, discard the test.

Reliability should be estimated for all tests. In some cases, internal consistency is appropriate, and in other cases, the tests should be administered in a test-retest procedure. These reliability estimates can then be used in the correction-for-attenuation formula (Spearman, 1904), and the corrected-for-attenuation correlations can be used to answer theoretical questions.

ESTIMATING *g* FOR INDIVIDUALS

To determine the causes of validity of a test, it is necessary to make estimates of the sources of variance in the test for each person. That is, it is necessary to estimate the g and $s_1 \ldots s_n$ for each individual. Using large samples (n = 9,173) and a multiple aptitude battery (Earles & Ree, 1991; Ree & Earles, 1991b), it has been shown that any set of positive weights (see Wilks, 1938) applied to the tests will yield almost identical rankings of g for the individuals. Component or factor analyses provide weighting schemes to estimate g. We estimated g as the first unrotated principal component, the first unrotated principal factor, and the highest factor from 12 hierarchical factor analyses. Correlations among g estimates ranged from .93 to over .99. Likewise, all coefficients of congruence, a measure of similarity of factor loadings, were above .99. These findings reflect the fact that all the tests, regardless of title, overt content, and form, measured g in large part.

When g is statistically removed from a test score, what remains is s, that part of the score that is due to a specific factor such as spatial or the result of experience (Cattell, 1987). The specific portions fall into two categories: specific abilities (math, perceptual, spatial, verbal, etc.) and job knowledge (aviation principles, electronics, mechanics, procedural knowledge, shop, etc.). Although these specific portions can be represented by either common factors or principal components, we prefer principal components because they include all the test variance, thus giving the s portions maximal opportunity to show validity and incremental validity. Usually, the g portions of tests or cognitive tasks measuring cognitive components account for more variance than the specific proportions. In the American military enlistment battery, g accounts for about 64 percent of the total variance (Ree & Carretta, 1994b), while in an American officer commissioning battery, g accounts for about 41 percent (Carretta & Ree, 1996). The remaining variance is either specific and distributed among the various tests or is error. Having examined what is measured by aptitude tests and how to estimate it for individuals, we then turned our attention to what causes validity. What proportion of the validity was due to g, specific abilities, and specific knowledge? Were the sources of validity the same for training and job performance?

COMPONENTS OF JOB PERFORMANCE

Job performance includes possessing the knowledge, skills, and techniques required by the job. Training success is the first component of job performance, and hands-on performance is the second. Significant aspects of most employment include training for promotions, lateral job movement, and staying current with changing responsibilities of the ''same'' job. Another job component is the performance of activities based on knowledge, skills, and techniques to achieve personal and organizational goals.

PREDICTION OF TRAINING SUCCESS

The validity of a test for predicting training success, the first component of job performance, comes predominantly from the test's measurement of g. We correlated how much each test in the ASVAB measures g, called its g-loading, with its average validity for predicting final training grades in a sample of more than 24,000 enlisted trainees in 37 diverse jobs (Jones, 1988; Ree & Earles, 1992, 1994). A broad sample of jobs such as clerk, electrical repair, mechanic, and police were included. The g-loadings of the tests were obtained from the normative sample (Ree & Wegner, 1990). The trainees constituted a range-restricted sample because they had been selected on the basis of these tests. Often, the test variances were reduced by as much as 75 percent. To reduce the effects of range restriction, the validities of the 10 tests for each training course were corrected using Lawley's multivariate theorem (Lawley, 1943; Ree et al., 1994). The Spearman rank-order (Spearman's rho) correlation between the g-loadings of the tests and their average validity was .75 (Jones, 1988). After correcting the g-loadings for unreliability, the coefficient became .98 (Ree & Earles, 1994). When computed within four broad job families (administrative, electronic, general-technical, and mechanical), the correlations were about the same (Jones, 1988). Similar results ($r = .96$) were found when this same rank-order correlation was estimated in another sample of more than 78,000 participants across 150 jobs. As the g-loading of a test increased, so did its validity. Further, the correlation of g-loading and average validity across all jobs was the same as across the job families.

Multiple aptitude test battery (ASVAB) data were used to study the incremental validity of s to g (Ree & Earles, 1989). Job training is typically the first requirement in a job. In this training, the technical and practical aspects of job performance are learned. Further, training and learning of job skills continue during all jobs, even if just to keep current with developments or to use new techniques and tools. As a consequence, job training is an important primary criterion.

Both g and s portions of the ASVAB were used to predict technical job training performance for 78,049 airmen enrolled in 89 courses. This yielded an average sample size of 876. Because the samples showed the effects of prior selection, it was necessary to correct for range restriction. Separate regressions were computed for each job with only g and compared to regressions containing g and specific abilities or specific knowledge (s). In every training course, g was the most valid predictor and the contribution of s was small or zero. The average corrected-for-range-restriction validity of g was .76. Job training performance was well and uniformly predicted by g and was incremented little or not at all by s.

The average increase by adding s to g was .02 across the 89 training courses. The second most predictive component of the test battery was provided by its measurement of specific knowledge as opposed to specific ability. For one third of the training courses, g was the only significant predictor; however, in 1 training course, s added .10 to prediction. An estimate of the expected variance of the additional predictive power of s was not made. The hypothesis that the small incremental increase in validity attributed to s was due to sampling error could not be rejected.

Next we studied if g predicted job training performance in about the same way, regardless of the kind of job or its difficulty (Ree & Earles, 1991a). This was done to determine whether g was appropriate for some job training, but specific aptitudes were more appropriate for others. In a sample of 78,041 Air Force trainees, we evaluated the suggested g versus specific ability hypothesis. Linear regression analyses were performed to determine if the relationships of g to training criteria were the same for all 82 training courses. While there was statistical evidence that the relationship of g to course performance differed, these differences were small and appeared to be of no practical effect. The relationship of g to training performance was nearly identical for each job.

To answer questions about the generalizability of g, a meta-analysis was conducted[3] of the validity coefficients for several ASVAB composites and training criteria for 88,724 trainees in 150 Air Force enlisted jobs. The meta-analysis was performed on two simple-weighted composites and job-specific linear regression composites. The first simple-weighted composite was a simple addition of the scores from the four verbal and quantitative tests, almost purely g. The second simple-weighted composite was an integer-weighted sum of all 10 tests, a more complete and diverse measure of g. An individual regression-weighted composite was estimated for each of the 150 training courses.

In this study, each correlation was individually corrected, and the Hunter and Schmidt (1990) meta-analytic model was used. Results for the two simple-weighted composites showed that mean validities were .760 and .767 and that 100 percent of the variability in correlation coefficients was due to study artifacts. This means that the validity of the composites did not differ by job. For the set of multiple regression composites, the mean validity was .768, and 73 percent of the variance in correlations was accounted for by study artifacts. However, in about 85 percent of the regression equations, negative regression weights penalized good performance on tests despite the instructions to the examinee to achieve the highest score possible. Further, when the .768 was adjusted to account for shrinkage on cross application, the average validity was reduced to .741. Clearly, there is no practical benefit to be gained from regression weighting.

Specific (non-g) portions of multiple aptitude batteries such as the ASVAB have shown little validity beyond g when they have been used to predict training success. However, special classification tests have been developed to augment the predictiveness of ASVAB for some Air Force jobs. Two additional test measures, one for the selection of computer programmers and one for the selection of intelligence operatives, were investigated to determine if they measured something other than g and to determine their validity incremental to g

(Besetsny, Earles, & Ree, 1993; Besetsny, Ree, & Earles, 1993). Training performance was the criterion. In each job, multiple regression equations containing g alone and then g and specific abilities together were tested to determine if specific abilities were incremental to g. The samples were composed of 3,547 computer programming trainees and 776 intelligence operative trainees. For the two jobs, regression analyses showed incremental validity gains for specific abilities beyond g of .00 and .02, respectively. Although intended to add unique measurement, these two tests contributed little or nothing beyond g.

For highly complex jobs such as aircraft pilot, the use of measures of g has a long history (Ree & Carretta, 1996). A study of the incremental validity of specific abilities and specific knowledge to g in prediction of work sample criteria was conducted (Olea & Ree, 1994). The Air Force Officer Qualifying Test (AFOQT; Carretta & Ree, 1996), a multiple aptitude battery measuring g and the five factors of verbal, mathematics, perceptual speed, spatial, and aircrew knowledge was used in this study. Approximately 5,500 Air Force lieutenants (all college graduates), 4,000 in pilot training and 1,500 in navigator training, were studied to determine how well g and specific abilities and knowledge predicted six pilot and six navigation criteria. The participants had tested on the AFOQT from a few months to as much as four years prior to collection of the criteria.

For the pilots, the criteria were training work samples of hands-on flying and academic grades from ground school. For the navigators, the criteria were training work samples of day and night celestial navigation and academic grades. In addition, a composite criterion was created for each job by summing the five individual criteria. Very few pilot or navigator students fail training for academic reasons. Most who fail do so because they are unable to control the aircraft (pilots) or unable to use the navigational instruments (navigators) correctly on check flights.

As with technical training performance discussed earlier, g was the best predictor of pilot and navigator composite, academic, and work sample criteria. For the composite criterion, the validity was .40 for pilots and .49 for navigators. The specific (non-g) portions provided an average increment in predictive validity of .08 for pilots and .02 for navigators. Examination of the specific portions that added validity for pilots showed that they were measures of job knowledge (aviation information and instrument comprehension) and not specific abilities (verbal, mathematics, perceptual speed, spatial). The tests used in the study did not measure specific navigation knowledge. Olea and Ree (1994) speculated that greater incremental validity would have occurred for navigators, had such tests been present, but that the amount of the increment would have been small because navigator-specific knowledge is arcane.

Recently, Ree, Carretta, and Teachout (1995) investigated the causal roles of g and prior job knowledge on sequential job knowledge acquired during training and training work sample performance for 3,428 Air Force pilots. The measures of g and prior job knowledge were from the AFOQT. The measures of job knowledge acquired during training were from 11 pilot training technical (ground school) courses. Six check flight grades were used to measure hands-on work sample performance in the primary and advanced training aircraft. General cognitive ability led to the acquisition of flying job knowledge, both prior to and during training. Further, *g* did not have a direct influence on work sample performance. Instead, it worked through job knowledge acquisition to influence hands-on flying performance during primary and advanced jet flying training. The causal role of *g* in acquisition of job knowledge and hands-on flying performance was strong.

Because some jobs require college degrees, Brodnick and Ree (1995) studied the relationship among academic performance, *g*, and socioeconomic status. The sample was 339 students in a small Catholic college in Texas. Nine observed variables including three aptitude measures from standardized college entry tests, three measures of socioeconomic status from federal financial assistance forms, and three measures of first-year academic performance grades in mandatory classes were collected for each student. Analyses showed that *g* was a good explanatory construct for academic performance. Despite common knowledge such as contained in the Coleman report, a specific latent variable for socioeconomic status added nothing to the structural models. The model with the best fit to the data included only the latent variables of *g* and academic performance.

PREDICTION OF JOB PERFORMANCE

The second component of job success, job performance, has been studied less often, particularly for the roles played by *g*, specific abilities, and specific knowledge. This is frequently because of the difficulty and expense of obtaining criterion measures.

Ree, Earles, and Teachout (1994) investigated the validity and incremental validity of *g*, specific abilities, and specific knowledge for several job performance criteria across seven jobs. On-the-job performance data were collected for 1,036 airmen with approximately two years' job experience in seven jobs. These jobs were chosen to be representative of the administrative, electrical, general-technical, and mechanical job families. All participants had taken the armed services enlistment test two to four years prior to criterion data collection. The criteria were technical interviews where the job incumbent was asked to explain in step-by-step detail how job tasks were performed, hands-on work samples of performance, and a composite of the technical interviews and work samples. Multiple criteria were used for several reasons. The technical interviews drew on a broader sample of job tasks than did the hands-on work samples. This was particularly true for job-related tasks that would have been expensive to test, presented a danger to perform, or required that machinery be temporarily removed from service. Hands-on work sample measures, on the other hand, have higher fidelity with on-the-job performance and greater face validity than the technical interviews. As for pilots and navigators, the composite criterion was considered to be the most comprehensive and, therefore, the best overall measure of job performance. As in previous studies, multiple regression equations containing measures of g and non-g or s were used to predict the criteria. Equations using g and s were compared to those using only g. As before, g was the best predictor of all the job performance measures (the range-restriction-corrected average correlation was .44). The mean increase in validity after adding s was .00 for the interviews, .03 for the work sample measures, and .02 for the composite criterion.

Similarly, McHenry, Hough, Toquam, Hanson, and Ashworth (1990) investigated the incremental validity of several variables for the prediction of job performance in a sample of about 4,000 American soldiers. The incremental validity of the variables never exceeded .03 for measures of core job performance. These incremental values were similar to those found in the technical training studies (Besetsny, Earles, & Ree, 1993; Besetsny, Ree, & Earles, 1993; Ree & Earles, 1991a, 1992) and the pilot and navigator study (Olea & Ree, 1994).

Job performance as measured by supervisory and peer ratings is also predicted by g. Carretta, Perry, and Ree (1996) demonstrated this predictiveness in a sample of 171 Air Force jet aircraft pilots. After controlling for job experience, measures of g were found to be predictive of job performance as judged by supervisors and peers. The supervisory criterion was a 31-item rating form, while the peers gave overall ratings and provided merit rankings comparing these pilots to others with whom they had flown.

The roles of g and other variables as causes of job performance have been studied. Hunter (1983, 1986) reported a path analysis relating g, job knowledge, and job performance and found that the major causal influence of cognitive ability was on the acquisition of job knowledge. In turn, job knowledge had a major impact on work sample (job) performance and supervisory ratings. Work sample performance directly influenced supervisory ratings. Figure 4.2 displays Hunter's (1986) model.

Borman, White, Pulakos, and Oppler (1991) corroborated Hunter's (1983) model in a separate sample of job incumbents but made it more parsimonious with sequential effects from ability to job knowledge to task proficiency to supervisory ratings. Borman, Hanson, Oppler, Pulakos, and White (1993) extended the causal model to supervisory job performance, showing that g influenced job knowledge and job performance as a supervisor. As found for training (Ree, Carretta, & Teachout, 1995), the causal role of g on job performance was strong.

ADDING TO THE VALIDITY OF g

Several industrial/organizational psychologists have tried to find or develop predictors to add to or replace g (see, e.g., Carretta & Ree, 1994; McHenry et al., 1990). Two of the most familiar are psychomotor tests and interviews.

Psychomotor tests and interviews are often believed to measure something

Figure 4.2
Path Model Showing the Relationship of General Cognitive Ability to Job Performance

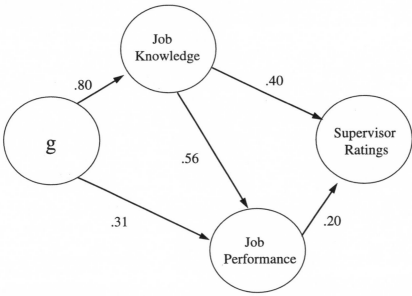

Source: Hunter (1986).

different from paper-and-pencil tests because they appear so different. The belief that outward appearance necessarily reflects what is being measured is an example of the topographical fallacy (Walters, Miller, & Ree, 1993). As the saying goes, looks can be deceiving.

In a recent study, Carretta and Ree (1994) investigated the incremental validity of psychomotor scores from a computer-based pilot selection battery, the Basic Attributes Test (BAT; Carretta, 1990),[4] above *g* for predicting completion (passing/failing) of pilot training. The AFOQT was used to estimate *g* for the 678 pilot trainees in the study. BAT psychomotor scores incremented the validity of *g* by .02 (uncorrected for range restriction). The amount of incremental validity for the BAT psychomotor scores was similar to that found in previous studies and to the increment reported by the Army (McHenry et al., 1990) for psychomotor ability. In a sample of 4,039 Army enlisted personnel, psychomotor tests added (corrected for range restriction) no more than .02 to any of their five criteria, with a mean increment of .014 across all nine jobs (McHenry et al., 1990).

Ree and Carretta (1994a) investigated the hypothesis that psychomotor tests measured *g* in addition to psychomotor ability. If this hypothesis were supported, it would help to explain why psychomotor tests have shown relatively small incremental validity to commonly acknowledged measures of *g* (e.g., tests with verbal, math, or spatial content). Some 354 Air Force enlisted trainees completed three computer-based psychomotor tracking tests that yielded eight scores. These psychomotor tests, known as Two-Hand Coordination, Complex Coordination, and Time Sharing, are computer analogues of electromechanical tests (Thorndike & Hagen, 1959) and are well known and regarded (Fleishman & Quaintance, 1984). Two verbal and two mathematics tests from the paper-and-pencil military enlistment battery were used to estimate g. The average correlation between the eight psychomotor scores and g was .21 uncorrected for range restriction and .34 after correction.

As expected, a confirmatory factor analysis demonstrated that all the paper-and-pencil scores and the psychomotor scores loaded on the first factor. A congruence analysis showed that the paper-and-pencil loadings were almost identical to the loadings found when paper-and-pencil tests were analyzed alone, with no difference larger than .04. This meant that the first factor of the cognitive scores and the psychomotor scores analyzed together was g.

Finally, a confirmatory residualized (Schmid & Leiman, 1957) hierarchical factor analysis showed that each test score (psychomotor as well as paper-and-pencil) was influenced by g. The hierarchical g factor accounted for 39 percent of the explained variance. There also was a higher-order psychomotor factor that accounted for 29 percent of the explained variance. Specific, lower-order residualized psychomotor and cognitive factors accounted for somewhat less variance: Two-Hand, 10 percent; Complex Coordination, 7 percent; Time Sharing, 7 percent; Verbal, 5 percent; and Math, 3 percent.

Rabbitt, Banerji, and Szymanski (1989) found similar results with a very complex psychomotor and reasoning test called "Space Fortress." Space Fortress requires watching a computer screen with many moving icons, learning numerous complex rules, and the manipulation of control sticks and buttons. It is not unusual to take several hours to learn Space Fortress well. Rabbitt et al. found that Space Fortress, despite its appearance, measured mostly g and that it correlated as highly with ordinary IQ tests as ordinary IQ tests correlated with each other.

The validity and incremental validity of an experimental structured interview for selecting Air Force pilot candidates were investigated by Walters, Miller, and Ree (1993). The sample was 223 U.S. Air Force pilot trainees who were administered the AFOQT, computer-based cognitive and personality tests, and the structured interview. The interview was performed by experienced Air Force pilots who had completed a brief training course in interview techniques. The interview included questions regarding educational background, self-confidence and leadership, motivation to fly, and flying job knowledge. In addition to rating pilot candidates in these four areas, interviewers rated them on probable success in pilot training, bomber-fighter flying, and tanker-transport flying. The criterion of passing-failing pilot training was the dependent measure in the validity study. The 16 AFOQT tests had an average validity of .28, the computer-based tests had an average validity of .18, and the seven interview scores had an average validity of .21. No incremental validity was found for the seven interview scores when they were added to the regression equation containing the AFOQT and computer-based test scores.

The lack of incremental validity for the interview scores beyond g occurred because the interview scores lacked unique predictive variance. Subsequent to Walters et al. (1993), linear regression analyses were done to compare full and restricted regression equations for predicting pilot training success. These analyses showed that adding the interview scores to a measure of g extracted from the AFOQT did not improve prediction. The predictive power of the interview clearly came from the measurement of g.

TRENDS IN THE MEASUREMENT OF GENERAL COGNITIVE ABILITY

Measurement approaches based on chronometric measures and neural conductive velocity are considered promising sources for new tests, because they mostly measure general cognitive ability. These approaches offer the advantage of not relying on learned material or previous experience for their content. As a result, the likelihood of observing mean test score differences that were the consequences of differential educational choices is reduced.

Examples of chronometric measures include tests based on simple reaction time, choice reaction time, and neural conductive velocity. Low, but positive, correlations with measures of intelligence (Jensen, 1980) have been found for simple reaction time tasks. These are tasks that involve the ability to give one fast response to one signal (light, picture, sound, etc.) when it appears. Moderate correlations have been found for choice reaction time tasks that require the ability to choose from among several potential alternatives and make an appropriate response such as pressing the one lighted button among eight (Jensen, 1993).

Neural conductive velocity is the speed at which an impulse is transmitted along a neuron. Measuring neural conductive velocity requires no physically invasive procedure; it can be done with simple electrodes on the skin. Typically, measurement occurs for the speed at which an impulse travels along the optic nerve. In practice, electrodes are attached to the head, and a light is flashed that the participant sees. The participant is not required to make any overt response. The instructions may be as simple as "Keep your eyes open and look at the light." Reed and Jensen (1992) have found correlations of .37 between neural conductive velocity along the optic nerve and measured intelligence.

SUMMARY AND CONCLUSION

We have reviewed several studies that examined the measurement and predictive validity of general cognitive ability (g), specific abilities, and specific knowledge. Several measurement methods were used, as were several training and job performance criteria. Results consistently showed that a variety of selection instruments including cognitive tests with varied content and method of administration, psychomotor tests, specific job knowledge tests, interviews, reaction time, and neural conductive velocity measured g. Further, the validity of these measures for predicting training and job performance comes, in part or wholly, from g. As Brand (1987) observed: "g is to psychology as carbon is to chemistry" (p. 257).

The major implication from these studies is that all research on the development of new predictors of training performance, job performance, or other occupational criteria should include measures of general cognitive ability. The uniqueness of the predictors beyond g and, when appropriate, their incremental validity beyond g should be investigated. Whenever possible, the reliability of the measures should be investigated, and samples should be corrected for the effects of range restriction. The use of corrections for unreliability and for range restriction and the use of unrotated principal components, unrotated principal factors, or residualized scores from hierarchical factor analysis is essential to avoid erroneous conclusions about what is being measured.

Additionally, the utility of g and specific predictors should be estimated in terms of cost (e.g., cost to collect measures versus training cost avoidance) where applicable or in terms of increases in expected job performance (Duke & Ree, 1996; Schmidt, 1988). The increments to g, although statistically small, could have large utility under specific large sample conditions. In any case, the utility of g as a predictor of job performance is assured. Finally, these results should not be construed to imply that g is the only construct worth investigating. Clearly, McHenry et al. (1990) showed that personality and temperament measures can predict certain job-related criteria such as "effort and leadership," "personal discipline," and "physical fitness and military bearing." However, for predicting training success, hands-on job performance, and other occupational criteria, not much more than g is needed.

NOTES

The views expressed are those of the authors and not necessarily those of the United States Air Force, Department of Defense, or the United States government.

1. Residualization is also appropriate for noncognitive measures that have a hierarchical structure.

2. The ASVAB is the enlistment qualification test battery for the U.S. military.

3. This study was conducted by Suzzane Fenske and Malcolm Ree and has been submitted for publication review.

4. The BAT contains tests in addition to the psychomotor.

REFERENCES

Besetsny, L., Earles, J. A., & Ree, M. J. (1993). Little incremental validity for a special test of abstract symbolic reasoning in an air force intelligence career field. *Educational and Psychological Measurement, 53*, 507–511.

Besetsny, L., Ree, M. J., & Earles, J. A. (1993). Special test for computer programmers? Not needed: The predictive efficiency of the Electronic Data processing test for a sample of air force recruits. *Educational and Psychological Measurement, 53,* 993–997.

Borman, W. C., Hanson, M. A., Oppler, S. H., Pulakos, E. D., & White, L. A. (1993). Role of early supervisory experience in supervisor performance. *Journal of Applied Psychology, 78,* 443–449.

Borman, W. C., White, L. A., Pulakos, E. D, & Oppler, S. H. (1991). Models of supervisory job performance ratings. *Journal of Applied Psychology, 76,* 863–872.

Brand, C. (1987). The importance of general intelligence. In S. Modgil & C. Modgil (Eds.), *Arthur Jensen: Consensus and controversy.* New York: Falmer Press.

Brodnick, R., & Ree, M. J. (1995). A structural model of academic performance, socioeconomic status, and Spearman's *g. Educational and Psychological Measurement, 55,* 583–594.

Carretta, T. R. (1990). Cross-validation of experimental USAF pilot training performance models. *Military Psychology, 2,* 257–264.

Carretta, T. R., Perry, D. C., Jr., & Ree, M. J. (1996). Prediction of situational awareness in F-15 pilots. *The International Journal of Aviation Psychology, 6,* 21–42.

Carretta, T. R., & Ree, M. J. (1994). Pilot-candidate selection method: Sources of validity. *The International Journal of Aviation Psychology, 4,* 103–117.

Carretta, T. R., & Ree, M. J. (1996). Factor structure of the Air Force Officer Qualifying Test: Analysis and comparison. *Military Psychology, 8,* 29–42.

Cattell, R. (1987). *Intelligence: Its structure, growth, and action.* The Netherlands: Elsevier Science Publishing.

Duke, A. P., & Ree, M. J. (1996). Better candidates fly fewer training hours: Another time testing pays off. *International Journal of Selection and Assessment, 4,* 115–121.

Earles, J. A., & Ree, M. J. (1991). *Air Force Officer Qualifying Test: Estimating the general ability component* (AL-TR-1991-0039). Brooks AFB, TX: Armstrong Laboratory.

Fleishman, E. A., & Quaintance, M. K. (1984). *Taxonomies of human performance: The description of human tasks.* Orlando FL: Academic Press.

Goldberg, S. (1991). *When wish replaces thought.* Buffalo, NY: Prometheus.

Hunter, J. E. (1983). A causal analysis of cognitive ability, job knowledge, job performance, and supervisor ratings. In F. Landy, S. Zedeck, & J. Cleveland (Eds.), *Performance measurement and theory* (pp. 257–266). Hillsdale, NJ: Erlbaum.

Hunter, J. (1986). Cognitive ability, cognitive aptitudes, job knowledge, and job performance. *Journal of Vocational Behavior, 29,* 340–362.

Hunter, J. E., & Schmidt, F. L. (1990). *Methods of meta-analysis.* Newbury Park, CA: Sage.

Jensen, A. R. (1980). *Bias in mental testing.* New York: Free Press.

Jensen, A. R. (1993). Why is reaction time correlated with psychometric *g? Current Directions in Psychological Science, 2,* 53–56.

Jones, G. E. (1988). *Investigation of the efficacy of general ability versus specific abilities as predictors of occupational success.* Unpublished master's thesis, St. Mary's University of Texas.

Kim, J., & Mueller, C. W. (1978). *Introduction to factor analysis.* A Sage University Paper No. 13. Newbury Park, CA: Sage.

Kranzler, J. H., & Jensen, A. R. (1991). The nature of psychometric *g*: Unitary process or a number of independent processes? *Intelligence, 15,* 397–422.

Kyllonen, P. C. (1993). Aptitude testing inspired by information processing: A test of the four-sources model. *Journal of General Psychology, 120,* 375–405.

Kyllonen, P. C., & Christal, R. E. (1990). Reasoning ability is (little more than) working memory capacity?! *Intelligence, 14,* 389–433.

Lawley, D. N. (1943). A note on Karl Pearson's selection formulae. *Proceedings of the Royal Society of Edinburgh. Section A, 62,* Part I, 28–30.

Linn, R. L., Harnish, D. L., & Dunbar, S. (1981). Corrections for range restriction: An empirical investigation of conditions resulting in conservative corrections. *Journal of Applied Psychology, 66,* 655–663.

McHenry, J. J., Hough, L. M., Toquam, J. L., Hanson, M. A., & Ashworth, S. (1990). Project A validity results: The relationship between predictor and criterion domains. *Personnel Psychology, 43,* 335–354.

Morrison, T., & Morrison, M. (1995). A meta-analytic assessment of the predictive validity of the quantitative and verbal components of the Graduate Record Examination with graduate grade point average representing the criterion of graduate success. *Educational and Psychological Measurement, 55,* 309–316.

Olea, M. M., & Ree, M. J. (1994). Predicting pilot and navigator criteria: Not much more than *g. Journal of Applied Psychology, 79,* 845–851.

Rabbitt, P., Banerji, N., & Szymanski, A. (1989). Space fortress as an IQ test? Predictions of learning and of practiced performance in a complex interactive video-game. *Acta Psychologica, 71,* 243–257.

Ree, M. J. (1995). Nine rules for doing ability research wrong. *The Industrial-Organizational Psychologist, 32,* 64–68.

Ree, M. J., & Carretta, T. R. (1994a). The correlation of general cognitive ability and psychomotor tracking tests. *International Journal of Selection and Assessment, 2,* 209–216.

Ree, M. J., & Carretta, T. R. (1994b). Factor analysis of ASVAB: Confirming a Vernon-like structure. *Educational and Psychological Measurement, 54,* 457–461.

Ree, M. J., & Carretta, T. R. (1996). Central role of *g* in military pilot selection. *The International Journal of Aviation Psychology, 6,* 111–123.

Ree, M. J., Carretta, T. R., Earles, J. A., & Albert, W. (1994). Sign changes when correcting for range restriction: A note on Pearson's and Lawley's selection formulas. *Journal of Applied Psychology, 79,* 298–301.

Ree, M. J., Carretta, T. R., & Teachout, M. S. (1995). The role of ability and prior job knowledge in complex training performance. *Journal of Applied Psychology, 80,* 721–730.

Ree, M. J., & Earles, J. A. (1989). *The differential validity of a differential aptitude test* (AFHRL-TR-89–59). Brooks AFB TX: Armstrong Laboratory, Manpower and Personnel Research Division.

Ree, M. J., & Earles, J. A. (1991a). Predicting training success: Not much more than *g. Personal Psychology, 44,* 321–332.

Ree, M. J., & Earles, J. A. (1991b). The stability of convergent estimates of *g. Intelligence, 15,* 271–278.

Ree, M. J., & Earles, J. A. (1992). Intelligence is the best predictor of job performance. *Current Directions in Psychological Science, 1,* 86–89.

Ree, M. J., & Earles, J. A. (1994). The ubiquitous predictiveness of *g*. In C. Walker, M. Rumsey, & J. Harris (Eds.), *Personnel selection and classification*. Hillsdale, NJ: Erlbaum.

Ree, M. J., Earles, J. A., & Teachout, M. (1994). Predicting job performance: Not much more than *g*. *Journal of Applied Psychology, 79*, 518–524.

Ree, M. J., & Wegner, T. G. (1990). Correcting differences in answer sheets for the 1980 Armed Services Vocational Aptitude Battery reference population. *Military Psychology, 2*, 157–169.

Reed, T. E., & Jensen, A. R. (1992). Conduction velocity in a brain nerve pathway of normal adults correlates with intelligence level. *Intelligence, 16*, 259–272.

Schmid, J., & Leiman, J. M. (1957). The development of hierarchical factor solutions. *Psychometrika, 22*, 53–61.

Schmidt, F. L. (1988). Validity generalization and the future of criterion-related validity. In H. Wainer & H. I. Braun (Eds.), *Test validity*. Hillsdale, NJ: Erlbaum.

Spearman, C. (1904). "General Intelligence," objectively determined and measured. *American Journal of Psychology, 15*, 201–293.

Thorndike, R. L. (1949). *Personnel selection*. New York: Wiley.

Thorndike, R. L., & Hagen, E. (1959). *Ten thousand careers*. New York: Wiley.

Thurstone, L. L. (1938). *Primary mental abilities*. Chicago: University of Chicago Press.

Vernon, P. E. (1969). *Intelligence and cultural environment*. London: Methuen.

Walters, L. C., Miller, M., & Ree, M. J. (1993). Structured interviews for pilot selection: No incremental validity. *The International Journal of Aviation Psychology, 3*, 25–38.

Wilks, S. S. (1938). Weighting systems for linear functions of correlated variables when there is no dependent variable. *Psychometrika, 3*, 23–40.

5

The History of Intelligence Testing in Context: The Impact of Personal, Religious, and Scientific Beliefs on the Development of Theories and Tests of Human Abilities

David F. Lohman

There are two senses in which a man may be said to know or not know a subject. I know the subject of arithmetic, for instance; that is, I am not good at it, but I know what it is. . . . There [is another way of knowing that can be seen in a] man, like Dr. Karl Pearson, who undoubtedly knows a vast amount about his subject; who undoubtedly lives in great forests of facts concerning kinship and inheritance. But it is not, by any means, the same thing to have searched the forests and to have recognised the frontiers. Indeed, the two things generally belong to two very different types of mind. . . . The students of heredity, especially, understand all of their subject except their subject. They were, I suppose, bred and born in that brier-patch, and have really explored it without coming to the end of it. That is, they have studied everything but the question of what they are studying.

—G. K. Chesterton (1922, pp. 65–66)

[I am] impressed by the discovery that more than once [in the history of intelligence testing] nonspecialists, like Walter Lippmann . . . seem to have had a better grasp of the real issues involved, in spite of misunderstandings of technical details, than the scientists themselves. War may be too important to be left to the generals.

—F. Samelson (1979, p. 141)

Science, as Gould (1981) reminds both his critics and his minions, is a gutsy human enterprise. Facts do not lie about, unfettered by experience, waiting for a dispassionate scientist to assemble them into a coherent theory. Scientists care about the theories they advocate, for reasons good and bad. And the "facts" they attempt to organize into patterns are themselves theory-laden parsings of experience. The succession of conceptual filters through which experience must pass on its way to becoming factual knowledge is shaped by personal, professional, and societal beliefs. Sometimes the distortions introduced by these filters are obvious, but often not—especially when beliefs are widely held within a culture. The purpose of this chapter, therefore, is to suggest how personal, professional, and societal beliefs have influenced thinking about intelligence.

Beliefs surely do not tell the whole story; the accumulated theory and research on human intelligence cannot be reduced to a subjective collection of opinions. Nevertheless, the tale of the construct "intelligence" and of the tests devised to measure it cannot be understood without some consideration of events beyond the journals. The explanations offered here are not hard and fast conclusions but merely suggestions for psychologists to entertain and historians to correct. I then give a thumbnail sketch of two of the major and enduring controversies in research on intelligence—whether intelligence is unitary or multiple and whether it is innate or acquired—and show how the more general issues discussed in the first part of the chapter influenced those debates.

THE IMPACT OF PERSONAL BELIEFS

Affect as Corrupter?

Sometime around 1890, a dissatisfied British army officer named Charles Spearman began reading books in psychology. One of the first texts he read was written by John Stuart Mill. The basic claim of Mill and other associationists was that experience was the foundation of all knowledge. Spearman (1930, in Fancher 1985, p. 84) later recalled that "my initial reaction to all this view was intensely negative. . . . My conviction was accompanied by an emotional heat which cannot . . . be explained on purely intellectual grounds."

Spearman's reaction is not uncommon, although his report is. Scientists routinely harbor the belief that somehow their views should be justified on a purely rational basis. Affect is considered a corrupter of cognition; theorists should strive to rise above such distractors.

Damasio (1994) takes a different view. His investigations of patients with damage to the ventromedial sector of the prefrontal cortex show the positive contributions of affect to rational cognition, particularly the ability to solve ill-structured problems.

Reason may not be as pure as most of us think it is or wish it were. . . . More directly, emotions and feelings may not be intruders in the bastion of reason at all; they may be enmeshed in its networks, for worse *and* for better. . . . In fact, the absence of emotion and feeling is no less damaging, no less capable of compromising the rationality that makes us distinctively human and allows us to decide in consonance with a sense of personal future, social convention and moral principle. (pp. ii–xii)

This is not a claim that rational processes are not important. Feelings do not solve a problem.

At their best, feelings point us in the proper direction, take us to the appropriate place in a decision-making space, where we may put the instruments of logic to good use. We are faced by uncertainty when we have to make a moral judgment, decide on the course of a personal relationship, choose some means to prevent our being penniless in old age, or plan for the life that lies ahead. (p. xiii)

A good theory invariably reaches beyond the information given; through it the theorist attempts to impose a new order on what frequently is an ill-structured problem. At the very least, then, the creation (and, for later readers, acceptance) of a theory is influenced by affect. In the extreme, the solution may merely provide rational justification for an emotional reaction to an event. More commonly, affective reactions and the beliefs they entail color the way we interpret ambiguous data.

Snyderman and Rothman (1987) provide a good example. They were annoyed by what they rightly perceived to be inaccurate accounts in the media of professional opinion on the nature of human intelligence and the value of intelligence testing. They set out, then, to survey systematically professional opinion on the matter. There was indeed a good deal of consensus among the 661 respondents to their questionnaire about the nature of intelligence. There was also evidence that these beliefs were significantly associated with political perspective: Conservatism correlated positively ($r = .31$) with a composite variable for perceived usefulness of intelligence tests and negatively ($r = -.38$) with perceived bias in such tests. These correlations were stronger than those for any other demographic or background variable they examined (including sex, age, scholarly productivity, and ethnic background). However, in their discussion, the authors chose to emphasize that these correlations with composite variables account for a small percentage of the variance in the raw data (an odd statistical twist for anyone who would defend a general factor among total scores on mental tests!). "It seems clear that despite the highly political climate surrounding testing, political ideology does not have a large influence on expert opinion" (p. 144). True. The influence is not large, but it is not dismissibly small either.

The Role of Personal Experience

Fancher (1985) claims that the story of intelligence testing comes into focus only when one begins to understand the impact of personal experience and belief on the theories publicly advocated. He begins with the disparate early childhood experiences of John Stuart Mill, who was educated by his father and shielded from knowledge of his precocity, and Francis Galton, who early in life learned that his achievements were unusual and who in his public education constantly compared himself to others. Mill later championed the environmentalist perspective and argued that one should resort to biological explanations of individual and group differences only after all reasonable environmental explanations had been explored and refuted. Galton, on the other hand, saw individual differences as largely genetic in origin and eugenics as the path to improvement.

Binet (like Spearman) came to psychology after he had finished his university work. His reaction to Mill was quite the opposite of Spearman's. [In fact, Binet later would call Mill his only master in psychology (Wolf, 1973).] For others, beliefs are most clearly evident in their earliest publications and papers. Although exceptions are noteworthy, the rule is that the earliest pronouncement about the relative importance of nature or nurture in intelligence differs little, if at all, from the one made at the end of a career. For example, in his first published article, "Experimental Tests of General Intelligence," Burt (1909) concluded that because the 13 upper-class boys in his study outperformed the 30 lower-class boys on tests he thought unaffected by practice, intelligence must be inherited "to a degree which few psychologists have hitherto legitimately ventured to maintain." By 1911, Burt had defined intelligence as "allround innate mental efficiency" (quoted in Hernshaw, 1979, p. 49), a view to which he adhered throughout his career. "It was for [Burt] almost an article of faith, which he was prepared to defend against all opposition, rather than a tentative hypothesis to be refuted, if possible, by empirical tests" (Hernshaw, 1979, p. 49).

Terman (1906) showed his hand in his dissertation "Genius and Stupidity: A Study of Some of the Intellectual Processes of Seven 'Bright' and Seven 'Stupid' Boys." Near the end of the dissertation, he speculated: "While offering little positive data on the subject, the study has strengthened my impression of the relatively greater importance of *endowment* over *training*, as a determinant of an individual's intellectual rank among his fellows" (p. 372, italics in original). Once again, experience seemed not to alter these early beliefs, as later clashes with Lippmann and the Iowa group showed.

Exceptions are noteworthy. Brigham publicly recanted his early, hereditarian interpretation of ethnic differences in intelligence, although more because the data would not support the conclusions than because the conclusions had changed (Cronbach, 1975). J. M. Hunt recounts an experience that is perhaps more familiar. His book *Intelligence and Experience* (1961) summarizes research on the effects of experience on the development of intelligence. (At the time, it also served to introduce the work of Piaget to many U.S. psychologists.) In trying to explain why belief in a fixed intelligence was so prevalent, Hunt appealed to Festinger's (1957) theory of cognitive dissonance:

In his own professional life history, the writer finds in himself some evidence of [cognitive dissonance]. So long as he was professionally identified with the testing function, it was highly comforting to believe that the characteristics tested were fixed in individuals. Evidence hinting that these characteristics were not fixed produced intense dissonance, for it threatened his belief in fixity and the adequacy of his professional function as well. Such a factor may help to explain the sometimes excessive violence of the polemics concerning the constancy of the IQ and the effects of training that were common in the years just [prior] to World War II. (pp. 14–15)

Surely cognitive dissonance may help explain why it is difficult to change beliefs. But it does not explain the "violence of the polemics." That seems better to reflect the fact that beliefs are often grounded in affect rather than merely tinged with it.

POLITICAL AND SOCIAL CLIMATE

Psychologists (including this one!) are not historians. The tales we tell each other about the origins and development of mental testing are often remarkable for their failure to consider the influence of larger political and social influences on testing. With increasing regularity, we acknowledge the impact of the broader culture on cognition and cognitive development. For example, Bronfrenbrenner (1979) argues that abilities develop through a child's interactions not only with her immediate social environment but also with the attitudes and ideologies of the broader culture in which she lives. Cultural relativism, long relegated to the extreme left wing of psychometrics, is now afforded a respected place at the table (e.g., Laboratory of Comparative Human Cognition, 1982) and a central role in at least one major theory of intelligence (e.g., Sternberg, 1985). Yet the stories we tell about the development of theories within the discipline are often remarkably devoid of such influences. In the preface of their account of intelligence testing in Britain, Evans (a psychologist) and Waites (a historian) note:

Most histories of psychology have been written by professional psychologists with a strong commitment to the body of belief accepted as achieved knowledge within their profession. . . . Such histories are not necessarily uncritical, but the critical point of view is very restricted. Past error appears merely as a series of hurdles successfully overcome on the road to current theory. (1981, p. vii)

Modern conceptions of intelligence were birthed in the second half of the nineteenth century. It is therefore impossible to understand either the theories that describe the construct or the tests developed to measure it without some understanding of the political and social ideology of the time. However, identifying the starting point is much like stepping into a stream at a particular point—perhaps where it rounds a bend—and declaring, "We will take this as the beginning." Such fictions clearly mislead, but one must begin somewhere. Herbert Spencer provides such a convenient starting point.

Social Darwinism

Spencer advocated a theory of evolution before Darwin (1859) published his *Origin of Species*. Spencer's argument, based as it was on philosophical, anthropological, and geological speculation, was largely ignored; Darwin's biologically based argument was not. Spencer soon allied himself with Darwin's theory and sought to apply the theory to the full extent of human knowledge and endeavor. The effort resulted in the 10 volumes of his *Synthetic Philosophy* (which included *The Principles of Psychology*).

Spencer saw evolution as the key to all science. Evolution, he said, proceeds from incoherent homogeneity, as is found in the lowly protozoa, to coherent heterogeneity, as is found in mankind and the higher animals.[1] More important, this heterogeneity was unidimensional. In this, both Spencer and Darwin followed the lead of Locke and Leibniz in viewing all life as falling along a continuous, unbroken scale. Leibniz said it most succintly: *Natura non facit saltum* (Nature does not make jumps). For Spencer, the tic marks on this scale marked increases in intelligence: "Gradually differentiated from the lower order of changes constituting bodily life, this higher order of changes constituting mental life assumes a decidedly serial arrangement in proportion as intelligence advances" (1897, p. 406).

The idea of a serial order—not only between species but within humankind—was brought about by an unfettered competition among individuals. "Survival of the fittest" was his phrase before it was Darwin's. If species evolved by becoming more intelligent, then to help humankind become more intelligent was to further the work of evolution. Yet Spencer held firmly to a Lamarckian view of the heritability of acquired characteristics. His theory was thus less pessimistic about the value of education than later evolutionary theories that dismissed Lamarck. On the other hand, the serial order he proposed was not the tabula rasa of Locke (1690/1959) and an earlier generation of intellectuals who, in their struggle against a hereditary monarchy and aristocracy, had emphasized the plasticity of human nature.

Doctrines of human nature as plastic and of innate human equality [popular during the revolutionary period 1780–1848] gave way to a more structured view of the mind and to concepts of innate human inequality with which to rationalize the economic and political inequalities of bourgeois society. (Evans & Waites, 1981, p. 33)

Galton was the chief exponent of this view. Like other liberals of his day, Galton advocated a meritocracy in which income and position within the social hierarchy would be based on innate ability rather than on the social status of one's parents. In his *Hereditary Genius* (1869), he argued that mental characteristics were inherited in the same manner as physical characteristics. What he lacked, though, was a way to measure innate ability so that individuals could be properly placed in the hierarchy. Tests could not fulfill this function unless they truly measured innate ability and on a single dimension. Those convinced of the need for the eugenics movement were thus more willing than they otherwise might have been to believe assertions that the new intelligence tests (which, parenthetically, confirmed *their* natural superiority) measured innate general intelligence.

Nevertheless, the American and European agendas differed. Whereas European intellectuals (particularly in England) continued to struggle against inherited privilege (see Wooldridge, 1994), Americans in- and outside of academia were more concerned with the social upheavals threatened by immigration and the explosive growth of mass education. The first led to ready acceptance for eugenic proposals, and the second for more efficient ways to conduct the business of education. Both of these agendas conflicted with the principle of equality etched in Jefferson's Declaration of Independence and thus set the stage for later debate about whether tests that showed differences between ethnic and social classes were, ipso facto, biased. Even more important, Americans then and now seemed less uniformly committed to the notion of a single rank order as their British cousins. Thus, E. L. Thorndike found no conflict in, on the one hand, advocating a genetic basis for human intelligence while, on the other hand, arguing for the existence of several intellectual abilities rather than a single, general factor.

Educational Reforms

Intelligence *testing* became a part of the American educational system not because it more fairly advanced a meritocratic agenda but because it helped solve practical problems in an educational system overrun with pupils. Schooling was expanding exponentially. From 1890 to 1918 the population of the United States increased 68%. High school attendance during this period increased 711%. On average, more than one new high school was built every day during this period (Tyack, 1974, p. 183). However, school curricula still defined a Procrustean bed in which "the wits of the slow student were unduly stretched and . . . of the quick pupils amputated" (p. 202). Many started, but few finished. Ayres (1909) showed that the number of students in each grade dropped precipitously between first and eighth grade. "The general tendency of American cities is to carry all of their children through the fifth grade, to take one half of them to the eighth grade, and one in ten through high school" (p. 4). And of those who remained in school, many in the early grades were "laggards" who had been held back. The culprit was thought to be the failure of the system to adapt itself to the intellectual abilities of its students. A variety of methods for classifying students or adapting the pace of instruction had been used in American schools for many years (Chapman, 1988). But the intelligence test was heralded as a more scientific and efficient method of performing the task. And what could be fairer than an educational system that was adapted to the natural ability levels of its students? Test publishers thus found a ready market for their products. Terman estimated that probably a million children were given a group intelligence test in 1919–1920, and 2 million the next.

Thus, as White (1977) observes, American psychology was not simply an intellectual and scientific enterprise but rather "something that was given life and form by American social concerns of the 1900's . . . particularly . . . interests in creating professional, scientific bases for children's education and socialization" (p. 29). Tests then as now provided a means for sorting and classifying people that was ostensibly objective and fair. They helped administrators in a school system newly infatuated with a corporate model of centralization, bureaucratization, and efficiency perform and defend the sorting functions they were asked to perform. Even Walter Lippmann, who is now remembered by psychologists chiefly for his debates with Terman about intelligence testing, applauded the goal:

The intelligence test promises to be more successful in grading the children. This means that the tendency of the tests in the average is to give a fairly correct sample of the child's capacity to do school work. In a wholesale system of education, such as we have in our public schools, the intelligence test is likely to become a useful device for fitting the child into the school. This is, of course, better than not fitting the child into the school, and under a more correct system of grading, such as the intelligence test promises to furnish, it should become possible even where education is conducted in large classrooms to specialize the teaching, because the classes will be composed of pupils whose capacity for school work is fairly homogeneous. (Lippmann, 1922, in Block & Dworkin, 1976, p. 18)

Nativism

The practical use of tests, however, has always followed a path largely independent of theoretical debates about the nature of intelligence. In America (as in England), Social Darwinism was the dominant view. In fact, "Spencer's writings were so dominant in discussions of society and politics that they virtually sank into the unconscious of American political deliberation, ceased to be an argument, became obvious, and became common sense" (White, 1977, pp. 36–37).

Why? The specter that most haunted American and European intellectuals during this period was the prospect of the degeneration of human kind and subsequent collapse of society. "Indeed, 'degeneration' was arguably the most potent concept in the medical and biological sciences of the period" (Wooldridge, 1994, p. 20). In Britain, politicians and military leaders blamed defeat in the Boer War on the physical unfitness of the masses. In Italy, Lambroso warned about the return of the primitive, especially "natural criminals" (cf. more recent discussions of a permanent "underclass" in the United States, as in Herrnstein & Murray, 1994). In Germany, fear of racial degeneration and the quest for racial purity found their way into medicine, the social sciences, and political thought. In France, the medical/psychiatric concept of *dégénerescence* pervaded political debates about national decline.

From Jaurès to Maurras, political discourse was obsessed by the question of national defeat and the ensuing chaos; . . . alcoholism, habitual crime, and depravity were cast through the image of a social organism whose capacity for regeneration was in question. National defeat, degeneration and social pathology appeared to be caught up in an endless reciprocal exchange. (Pick, 1989, p. 98)

A declining birthrate in France and stagnant birth rates in Germany and in Great Britain seemed to confirm fears that degeneration had set in. Fears of losing military hegemony were seen as an inevitable consequence for a nation that could not raise armies larger than its rivals, especially from a population of "stunted, anemic, demoralized slum dwellers" (Wooldridge, p. 22).

The proximal causes of degeneration were (1) the higher birth rate among the lower classes and "races," especially those confined to the growing urban ghettos, and (2) the movement of "races" outside of their natural ecologies. Thus, an African "placed outside of his 'proper' place in nature—too stimulating an intellectual or social environment, or in a climate unsuited to his 'tropical' nature could undergo a further 'degeneration,' causing the appearance of atavistic or evolutionarily even more primitive behaviors and physical structures" (Stephan, 1985, p. 98).

In America, emancipation of the slaves gave new urgency to the question of the boundaries between whites and blacks. Blacks who attempted to move away from the warmer southern states or to advance beyond their natural condition of servitude would degenerate and eventually die out. The statistician and economist Hoffman argued that blacks were "a race on the road to extinction," and thus whites—who thrived in the political and geographical climate of America—need have no fears of a newly freed black race (see Stephan, 1985).

Racial mixing also resulted in degeneration. If nature separated humans into ranks, then mixing them was not only unnatural, but an invitation to atavism. "Unnatural unions" produced a hybrid that was inferior to either parent. In America, and later in Germany, the doctrine of *rassenhygiene* (race hygiene) became the watchword for a group that looked back to a braver, purer, tectonic past as much as it looked forward to a eugenically improved race.

Thus, the specter of a complete collapse of society haunted many American and European intellectuals during this period. Evidence of the social, moral, and physical decay of humanity seemed irrefutable. And in the United States, many feared that the massive immigration of Europe's poor and degenerate was nothing short of complete folly. The new immigrants were, on the East Coast, poorer and more Catholic than before. More important, they did not as readily assimilate into the existing order but instead insisted on keeping their own language and customs. Catholics set up their own schools and achieved political control in some cities of the Northeast, thereby reviving Protestant fears of papal influence. Nativist political organizations fought against these trends.

Previously vague and romantic notions of Anglo-Saxon peoplehood were combined with general ethnocentrism, rudimentary wisps of genetics, selected tidbits of evolutionary theory, and naive assumptions from an early and crude imported anthropology (later, other social sciences at a similar stage of scientific development added their contributions) to produce the doctrine that the English, Germans, and others of the "old immigration" constituted a superior race of . . . "Nordics" or "Aryans." (Gordon, 1964, p. 97)

These beliefs were given wide currency in a book, *The Passing of the Great Race*, by the amateur zoologist Madison Grant. The obvious implication of such views was to exclude the inferior races, an end finally achieved in the restrictive immigration laws of the 1920s, but only after nativist sentiments were augmented by a postwar isolationism.

But what to do about those already admitted? Ellwood Cubberly, Terman's dean at Stanford,[2] echoed the feeling of many:

These southern and eastern Europeans are of a very different type from the north Europeans who preceded them. Illiterate, docile, lacking in self-reliance and initiative, and not possessing the Anglo-Teutonic conceptions of law, order, and government, their coming has served to dilute tremendously our national stock, and to corrupt our civic life. The great bulk of these people have settled in the cities of the North Atlantic and North Central states, and the problems of proper housing and living, moral and sanitary conditions, honest and decent government, and proper education have everywhere been made more difficult by their presence. Everywhere these people tend to settle in groups and settlements, and to set up here their national manners, customs, and observances. Our task is to break up these groups or settlements, to assimilate and amalgamate these people as part of our American race, and to implant in their children, so far as can be done, the Anglo-Saxon conception of righteousness, law and order, and popular government, and to awaken in them a reverence for our democratic institutions and for those things in our national life which we as a people hold to be of abiding worth. (Cubberly, 1909), pp. 15–16)

Eugenic Proposals

These, then, were some of the main social and political beliefs that helped form an atmosphere conducive to the development and ready acceptance of intelligence tests. The new tests fulfilled a need to sort individuals and ethnic groups on the basis of innate ability.

People approached the social changes of the turn of the century with their minds formed by Spencer and the advocates of Social Darwinism. Before Binet, or Thorndike, or Cattell, or even Galton, people had made up their minds about the centrality of intelligence as the epitome of human merit. When the tests came along, they were [viewed as] manifestations of an entity whose scientific and social sanctity was given. (White, 1977, p. 37)

The argument was simple: If the survival of a democracy depends on the ability of its citizens to make intelligent decisions, and if intelligence is innate, and individuals and groups differ in intellectual competence, then it was the moral duty of those who would improve (or at least not openly contribute to the degeneration of) humankind to restrict immigration of such peoples into the country and to stem their proliferation within society. Alarmist (and later, sober) reports of the dysgenic effects of the higher birthrate among the poor and the less intelligent led to calls for sterilization of the retarded and restrictions on immigration (see, e.g., Cattell, 1940). As late as 1940 in his massive *Human Nature and the Social Order*, E. L. Thorndike was writing that although

much in the legislation concerning sterilization is doubtless misguided, . . . on the whole its operations seem more beneficent than those of an equal amount of time and skill spent in ''social education.'' Indeed the first lesson in social education for an habitual criminal or a moral degenerate might well be to teach him to submit voluntarily to an operation that would leave his sex life unaltered but eliminate his genes from the world. The same would hold for dull or vicious epileptics and for certain sorts of dull and vicious sex perverts. (p. 455)

Although psychologists certainly contributed to the discussion of eugenic proposals, they were not the only or even the most important voices. For example, contrary to popular opinion, neither psychologists nor their army testing data exerted much influence on the restrictive Immigration Law of 1924.

[The Immigration Law of 1924] was the culmination of efforts begun in the 1890s and supported by a far-flung coalition of forces from the Immigration Restriction League all the way to the American Federation of Labor. Much of the power of this movement was based on economic issues. . . . It was predominantly the biological argument of the eugenicists and racists under the leadership of Madison Grant and C. B. Davenport that produced the scientific . . . legitimation [for this legislation]. (Samelson, 1979, pp. 135–136)

Eugenics was part of a larger zeitgeist that had at its core a belief in the improvement of humankind through the application of the methods of science to people and their institutions. Interventions ranged from the child study movement and the enactment of child labor laws, to the application of corporate methods to education, to time in motion studies of industrial production, to the enactment of eugenic proposals into sterilization laws.

The Religious Context

Finally, the ground had been prepared for the seed of intelligence testing by an even larger and earlier cultural movement: the Reformation. Salvation, Luther said, was not to be achieved through good works but through grace. Those thus saved were the new chosen people, an analogy taken quite literally in Calvinist Holland (Schama, 1987). If some were elected for salvation, then others were predestined for damnation—at least in Calvinist and Puritanical writings.[3] It is now acknowledged that these beliefs influenced an astonishing array of other— often distant—aspects of the social, political, and economic activity of these peoples and the cultures they influenced. For example, Weber (1904/1958) argued that, paradoxically, the belief in predestination fueled the economic enterprise of ascetic Protestant sects (such as the Puritans). Schama (1987) claims that the sense of self-legitimation as a "chosen" people that pervaded Dutch culture during the seventeenth and eighteenth centuries also "helps account for the nationalist intransigence of . . . the Boer *trekkers* of the South African Veldt, the godly settlers of the early American frontier, even the agrarian pioneers of Zionist Palestine" (p. 35). If so, then in America, nativism and manifest destiny were not far behind. More important, believing that some individuals and peoples were predestined for salvation or damnation is not incompatible with the belief not only that some are chosen intellectually but that such gifts might properly be used as an arbiter of individual merit and worth. "We are comfortable with the idea that some things are better than others" (p. 534), proclaim Herrnstein and Murray (1994). But they are also comfortable with the fact that some people are better than others, that the best measure of better is IQ, and that a meritocracy based on intelligence is "what America is all about" (p. 512). Perhaps it is, and perhaps that is why the study of individual differences in general and of intelligence in particular has been more popular a topic in countries where Calvinism or Puritanism once flourished than in countries where such beliefs never attained a significant following.[4]

PHILOSOPHY OF SCIENCE

The construct of intelligence as innate ability was firmly rooted in the zeitgeist of the period during which the first tests were developed. But scientists also had beliefs about the scientific enterprise. Indeed, beliefs about how knowledge is acquired and how conflicts among competing explanations are resolved form core assumptions of methods of inquiry of a discipline at a particular point in time. Collectively, these methods define (or assume) a particular philosophy of science. The question of how competing claims are arbitered is a somewhat narrower issue of epistemological values and will be discussed as such.

Positivism versus Realism

Logical positivism was the dominant philosophy of science during the late nineteenth century when the foundations of modern psychology were laid (Koch, 1959). Positivism is often distinguished from an older view of science, realism. Proponents of realism hold that the methods of science allow direct access to reality. Scientific explanations, in this view, describe the world as it really is.

Positivism is a more moderate position. According to this view, scientists form models or theories of the world based on observed regularities. Although constructs and the laws that relate them usefully explain these regularities, they are not necessarily real. However, as Slife and Williams (1995) note, it is difficult for positivists not to take the next conceptual step and begin to believe that the constructs formed to explain regularities in the world (e.g., gravity or intelligence) are in some sense real. From Spearman to the present, those who report factor analyses of correlations among tests have routinely slipped from careful statements about factors representing convenient "patterns of covariation" or "functional unities" to entities that exist in some concrete fashion in the brains of those who responded to the tests.

Like the earlier realists, positivists put great emphasis on observation. It is hard to read Wolf's (1973) biography of Binet or Joncich's (1968) biography of E. L. Thorndike (appropriately titled *The Sane Positivist*) without feeling some of the enthusiasm both felt for observation and experimentation. Application of the methods of science to human behavior promised to ameliorate many social ills. There was no worry about the extent to which theory contaminated or shaped their observations, since, in their worldview, facts existed independent of and prior to theory. Nor was there a concern whether the methods of science, rather than providing an avenue for the discovery of truth, might actually presume a certain set of beliefs about the world.

The logical positivism of the turn of the century has been replaced by a less comforting set of philosophies. One of the more important contributions was made by Popper (1963) when he pointed out the logical asymmetry of proof and disproof. A thousand confirming instances does not prove the statement "All swans are white"; but one instance of a black swan disconfirms the statement. The implication is that theories cannot be proven correct, only disproven. But Popper's science was still evolutionary; progress came in a thousand small attempted refutations. Kuhn (1970), on the other hand, argued that progress in science was more often discontinuous. A new paradigm would revolutionize thinking in a domain. Finally, an even more extreme view is taken by social constructivists (scientific "constructs" are simply shared understandings within a particular community in a particular culture at a particular point in time) and their postmodernist allies (there is no way to secure knowledge of a universal and objective reality; rather, knowledge is contextual and constructed through social and linguistic convention).

Social scientists trained in the first half of this century seemed often to believe their task was to put forth a good theory and then defend it against all attacks. (Thus, Carroll's quip that, near the end of his career, Guilford seemed to suffer from "hardening of the categories.") Those trained after Popper and Kuhn are more likely to see their task differently. For example, Anderson (1983), in the preface to a book describing a theory of cognition, announced his intention to "break" the theory. The increasingly widespread acceptance of the notion of intelligence as a cultural construct is grounded in an even more constructivist philosophy.

Epistemological Issues

Epistemology is that branch of philosophy that concerns the nature, origins, and limits of knowledge. A central epistemological issue for scientists is how to choose among competing explanations or theories: Should it be parsimony? utility? meaningfulness? perceived truth value? Test users have generally opted for utility. In America, psychological meaningfulness prevailed over parsimony in the theoretical debate at least until the 1960s. Then parsimony reasserted its challenge. This epistemological struggle underpins the first and most enduring debate about intelligence: Is it one or many things?

INTELLIGENCE: UNITARY OR MULTIPLE?

Early Statements

Probably the most persistent controversy about human intelligence is whether it is one or many. The ambiguity is clearly foreshadowed in Binet's writings. On some occasions he spoke as if it were a single dimension and at other times as if it were many things. Spearman, who early championed the unitary view, was not amused by this eclecticism: "It would seem as if, in thus inconstantly flitting hither and thither, Binet can nowhere find theoretical perch satisfactory for a moment even to himself" (Spearman, 1923, p. 10).

The unitary intelligence view was most clearly advanced by Spearman (1904) in a classic paper, " 'General Intelligence' Objectively Determined and Measured," that he published in the *American Journal of Psychology*. The opposite view was staked out by E. L. Thorndike (see Thorndike, Lay, & Dean, 1909) and Kelley (1928) in the United States and by Thomson (1916) in the United Kingdom. Both Thomson and Thorndike had challenged Spearman's methods and conclusions, although Spearman always replied with equal vigor. The multiple-ability view gained a new respectability with the introduction of Thurstone's (1935) methods of factor extraction and rotation. Thurstone, using psychological meaningfulness as a criterion, showed how arbitrary factor axes extracted by his centroid method could be rotated to define a small set of correlated "primary" ability factors, thereby dispensing with Spearman's (1904) general factor (g). There followed an explosion of factorial studies by Thurstone (1938, 1944, 1949), his students (Botzum, 1951; Carroll, 1941; Pemberton, 1952), and others, notably Guilford and his coworkers in the Army–Air Force (AAF) Aviation Psychology program (Guilford & Lacey, 1947), decomposing primary abilities into still narrower factors or identifying other factors not previously known.

Wolfe (1940) attempted an early summary of this sprawling literature. French

(1951) followed with an even more comprehensive review in which he noted how difficult it was to determine whether factors with different labels were indeed different or whether some with the same labels represented different ability dimensions. He proposed that investigators include common reference or marker tests in their studies, a procedure already followed by Thurstone in his studies and by the AAF workers in theirs. Tests selected as markers showed high loadings on one rotated factor. Typically, these were homogeneous, speeded tests. Thus, Thurstone's criterion of simple structure and the use of marker tests led to a gradual shift in the type of tests included in factorial investigations and thereby to the fractionalization of abilities that resulted.

By the mid-1950s the continued proliferation of factors was making it difficult to summarize existing work or to know where to look for new ability dimensions. Guilford (1956), reviving an earlier suggestion of Thorndike, Bregman, Cobb, and Woodyard (1926), posited a three-facet scheme for classifying existing factors and directing the search for new ones. Although many accepted Guilford's (1956) Structure of Intellect (SI) model, a few were openly skeptical. Spearman's (1927) claim that the ability space could be spanned by g and four group factors was not much more parsimonious than Thurstone's (1938) claim that seven factors would do the job if psychological meaningfulness were given priority. In fact, Thurstone explicitly invoked parsimony when he argued that the number of common factors should be relatively small even though the number of ability tests was large, even unbounded (see Guttman, 1958). However, with the prospect of Guilford's 120 independent abilities, hierarchical theories and multiple-ability theories were not equally parsimonious. McNemar (1964) in a critical review dubbed the SI model ''scatterbrained'' and advocated a return to g via the hierarchical model of Vernon (1950) and other British theorists. Indeed, Humphreys (1962) had earlier shown how a facet model such as Guilford's could be made conformable with a hierarchical model by averaging over rows and columns to define higher-order abilities, a solution Guilford ignored at the time but accepted 20 years later (Guilford, 1985).

Resurgence of g

Thus, the construct of general intelligence was at first embraced by many American psychologists—at least by those who were administering tests—then cast aside as Thurstone's methods of multiple factor analysis won favor, then rediscovered again in the guise of a hierarchical model of abilities, and most recently, challenged once again by those who would extend the domain of intelligence in old and new ways. General and special abilities have thus alternately dominated the field, one ascending while the other declined, one in favor while the other challenged. The loyal opposition has always been close at hand.

Explanations for Differences in Theory

Reasons for the recurring rise and fall of different theories of intelligence are many. Those who arrived at different conclusions often started with more or less variegated samples of subjects and tests, used different methods of factor analysis, adhered to different social and political philosophies, or held different personal theories about the nature of human abilities. For example, Spearman often used age-heterogeneous samples of children, whereas Thurstone preferred age-homogeneous groups of young adults. Guilford preferred even more *g*-restricted samples. For example, in their study of figural-spatial abilities, Hoffman, Guilford, Hoepfner, and Doherty (1968) used architecture students at the University of Chicago! Although differences in subject samples are sometimes noted, methodologists are quick to ascribe the differences between the American multiple-ability view and the British *g*-centered view to different methods of factor analysis and, by implication, different epistemological criteria: American factorists emphasized psychological meaningfulness and thus preferred systems of parallel abilities, whereas British factorists emphasized parsimony and thus preferred hierarchical theories. However, since these different factorial solutions are mathematically equivalent, other influences seem likely. One of these is tradition: Spearman's shadow extends even to the present in British psychometrics. Similarly, Thorndike (at Columbia) and later Thurstone (at Chicago) each influenced a generation of graduate students. Another is social stratification: The American social system has never been as staunchly ordered from high to low as the English system. This more democratic view allows that a child might excel (or fail) in one cognitive dimension while not excelling (or failing) in others. The English view conforms better with the belief in a natural aristocracy of ability, which, from Spencer onward, was seen more as a unidimensional than as a multidimensional affair.

Limitations of Hierarchy

On this view, then, as long as there is controversy over method, or differences in the social, political, and personal philosophies of individuals, there will be controversy about the nature of human abilities. The expectation that one theory will triumph is seen as a holdover from turn-of-the-century logical positivism. When rival views persist, it may also signal that each has merit but important limitations as well (see E. Hunt, 1986). A hierarchical model that posited both broad and narrow abilities thus seemed to preserve the best of both worlds, while uniting them in a common framework. In reality, however, the hierarchical model has enhanced the status of g and diminished the status of narrower ability factors. This may or may not be a good thing. Certainly there is less tendency to attribute effects to special ability constructs that could more parsimoniously be attributed to general ability. However, parsimony is only one of several criteria that may be used to arbiter such decisions. Psychological meaningfulness is perhaps equally important but has fared less well in more recent epistemological struggles with parsimony than it did in Thurstone's and later Guilford's day. Indeed, one could argue that psychological clarity declines as factor breadth increases. In other words, the broadest individual difference dimension—although practically the most useful—is also psychologically the most obscure.

Debate over the meaning of factors such as verbal fluency or spatial ability has never even approximated that which routinely attends discussion of g.

It is ironic that many latter-day advocates of Vernon's (1950) hierarchical model seem unaware that he never claimed psychological validity for the model or for the factors it specified.

I do not think it is correct to say that I regard, or have ever regarded, hierarchy as a psychological model. It is . . . simply . . . a convenient way for classifying test perform-ances. . . . *Qua* psychological model, I think it is open to a lot of difficulty because successive group factors do not have any obvious psychological meaning. Thus, my verbal-educational and spatial-mechanical factors do not represent mental abilities; they are the residual common variance left when one has taken out . . . the g factor. Similarly, the minor factors are residuals of residuals. (Vernon, 1973, p. 294)

Interestingly, he claims that "the same sort of difficulty would arise if we started from oblique primary factors and calculated . . . higher-order factors from correlations between the primaries" (p. 294). However, "Burt's hierarchy is different in that . . . it does owe a good deal to neurological and psychological theory. . . . But then his model is not a straight representation of the correlations of a battery of tests" (p. 294). Thus, the theoretical parsimony and practical utility of Vernon's hierarchical model were purchased at the price of psycho-logical meaningfulness.

But there were also practical reasons why the theories of Thurstone and Guil-ford fell into disfavor. Much to the dismay of defenders and publishers of mul-tiple aptitude test batteries, it was discovered that predictions of course grades from one or more special ability scores were usually no better than prediction from g (McNemar, 1964). Even more discouraging was the finding that tests of general abilities were also more likely to interact with instructional manipula-tions (Cronbach & Snow, 1977). In personnel psychology, Schmidt and Hunter (1977) also touted the virtues of general ability and argued that the importance of special abilities for the prediction of job performance had been grossly over-stated by a common failure to attend to sampling variability of small-sample correlations. Utility has ever been a strong value for Americans; theories that do not work are generally discarded, no matter how appealing they might be.

There are, of course, dissenters. Horn (1985) argues that "what is called intelligence is a mixture of quite different things—different attributes having different genetical and environmental determinants and different developmental courses over the life span" (p. 268). He argues that, like facial beauty, intelli-gence is composed of distinctive components. Evidence for heritability of the whole does not confer ontological status. In a similar vein, Cronbach (1977) argues that intelligence, like "efficacy," is a word that describes the system. One cannot locate the efficiency of a factory in one of its many departments. It is not a thing but rather one of many indices that describe the functioning of the whole. Neither Horn nor Cronbach argues that the statistical dimension commonly called g lacks utility. Rather, they claim that practical utility does not imbue psychological meaningfulness. These and other critics claim that Thorndike, Thomson, and their followers were more nearly right than were Spearman and his followers. Some would even expand the domain of intelligence tasks not only to include social intelligence, which Thorndike (1920) and Guilford (1956, 1985) recognized, but also to include musical and bodily kinesthetic abilities as well (Gardner, 1983). Thus, the ongoing battle between advocates of g and of multiple abilities is probably the major theme in the story of intelligence.

INTELLIGENCE: INNATE OR ACQUIRED?

The second major, recurring controversy in discussion of human intelligence concerns whether it is best understood as innate capacity or as acquired competence. With rare exceptions—and those exceptions often seem more rhetorical than convictional (e.g., Kamin, 1974)—the issue here is one of emphasis. All acknowledge both factors. Various other debates hang on the coattails of this argument—some appropriately so, some not. Among individual difference theorists, those (such as Burt, 1958; or Terman, 1922) who see intelligence as innate are more likely to emphasize the influence of heredity, whereas those who see intelligence as acquired (such as Davis, 1949) emphasize the environment. Among experimental psychologists, those who see it as innate are more likely to explain individual differences in cognition on the basis of the capacity of basic cognitive structures, such as working memory (e.g., Just & Carpenter, 1992) or the speed or efficiency of cognition in general (e.g., Jensen, 1982) or particular cognitive processes (e.g., E. Hunt, 1986). Those who see abilities as acquired competencies tend to emphasize the importance of knowledge in cognition (Glaser, 1984), to study the development of abilities rather than the dimensions of individual differences at a particular point in development (Kail & Pellegrino, 1985), and to view intelligence as a product of formal schooling, not simply as a predictor of success in that medium (Snow & Yalow, 1982).

There are other correlates of positions on the innate-acquired debate. Those who emphasize the acquired aspects are more likely to believe that social and cultural factors loom large not only in the definition of behaviors valued as ''intelligent'' within a culture (Sternberg, 1985) but also their development and expression (Laboratory of Comparative Human Cognition, 1982). On the other hand, those who emphasize innate aspects are more likely to look for physiological correlates and explanations of behavioral differences (Matarazzo, 1992). Eysenck gives clear expression to this position. Following Hebb (1949), Eysenck (1988) distinguished among biological intelligence, psychometric intelligence, and social intelligence. Biological intelligence ''refers to the structure of the human brain, its physiology, biochemistry, and genetics which are responsible for the possibility of intelligent action'' (p. 3). Eysenck considers biological intelligence to be the purest, most fundamental intelligence because it is ''least adulterated by social factors.'' He claims it can be measured by the electroen-cephalogram (EEG), evoked potentials, galvanic skin responses, and perhaps reaction times. Eysenck defines psychometric intelligence as that intelligence that is measured by psychometric tests. In addition to the core of biological intelligence, psychometric intelligence is determined by cultural factors, edu-cation, family upbringing, and socioeconomic status. However, since only a fraction of the variance in psychometric intelligence (i.e., IQ) can be attributed to genetic factors (Eysenck estimates 70 percent), IQ should not be confused with biological intelligence. Finally, social intelligence reflects the ability to solve problems an individual encounters in life. But since so many noncognitive factors are reflected in such performances, Eysenck (1988) argues that ''social intelligence is far too inclusive a concept to have any kind of scientific mean-ing'' (p. 45). Thus, for Eysenck, intelligence is a concept that is best studied at the physiological (or even neurological) level, only indirectly represented in intelligence tests, and obscured almost entirely in performances in the real world. Those who emphasize the social, contextual, and cultural aspects of intelligence would, of course, reject such a view.

Those who espouse an innate view are also more likely to see ability factors (whether general or narrower) as at least grounded in (if not the direct reflection of) structures and processes in the brain rather than as merely statistical abstrac-tion (Thomson, 1916) or as emergent properties of behavior. Thus, the innate view is more closely allied with a Realist philosophy of science. Critics who view factors as constructs call this ''reification''—the fallacy of believing ''whatever received a name must be an entity or being, having an independent existence of its own'' (Mill, in Gould, 1981, p. 151).

Finally, theorists who take positions on the innate-acquired controversy tend to emphasize different aspects of the data or to use different types of scores. Hilgard (1988) claims that a major difference between hereditarians and envi-ronmentals lies in which aspect of the data is captured in their analyses: ''Those who favor heredity tend to rely chiefly on *correlational* data, whereas those who favor environment rely chiefly on *changes in mean IQ*'' (p. 23). Similarly, those who emphasize the growth of abilities tend to prefer raw or developmental scores (such as mental age), whereas those who emphasize constancy prefer status scores (such as IQ or other measures of rank within group). Critics of status scores—from Lippmann (1922, in Block & Dworkin, 1975) to the present (Kail & Pellegrino, 1985; Lohman, 1993)—have noted the fallacy of inferring fixity in ability from the constancy in status scores.

[The IQ within-grade constancy of average IQ] may be useful in school administration, but it can turn out to be very misleading for an unwary theorist. If instead of saying that Johnny gained thirty pounds one year, twenty-five the next and twenty the third, you said that measured by the average gain for children of his age, Johnny . . . weighed as much [then] as he does today. And if you dodged that mistake, you might nevertheless come to think that since Johnny classified year after year in the same position, Johnny's diet had no influence on his weight. (Lippmann, 1922, in Block & Dworkin, 1975, p. 27)

Relationship to One versus Many Controversy

There is surprisingly little relationship between a theorist's stance on the one versus many controversy and his or her stance on the innate-acquired debate. One might expect that those who argued for a general factor might be more inclined to the hereditarian position than those who emphasized the environmental position. However, both Thorndike (see, e.g., Thorndike, Bregman, Cobb, & Woodyard, 1926) and Thurstone (1938), who championed the multiple factor interpretation, sided with the hereditarian position. For example, although Thurstone allowed that some ability factors might be defined in terms of experience and schooling, on the whole

[I]nheritance plays an important part in determining mental performance. It is my own conviction that the arguments of the environmentalists are too much based on sentimentalism. They are often even fanatic on this subject. If the facts support the genetic interpretation, then the accusation of being undemocratic must not be hurled at the biologists. If anyone is undemocratic on this issue, it must be Mother Nature. To the question whether the mental abilities can be trained, the affirmative answer seems to be the only one that makes sense. On the other hand, if two boys who differ markedly in visualizing ability, for example, are given the same amount of training with this type of thinking, I am afraid that they will differ even more at the end of the training than they did at the start. (1946, p. 111)

Similarly, in his chapter-length history of intelligence testing, Carroll (1982) notes:

In the early years of factor analysis investigations, there has not been time to assemble evidence on whether the underlying factors were of genetic or of environmental origin, or of some combination of these origins. The common opinion, however (possibly influenced by the intellectual climate of the time), seems to have been that the "factors" identified in factor-analytic investigations were largely genetic in origin. (p. 71)

Nevertheless, the educational and social implications of a multiple-ability view were invariably less conservative than the single-ability view. In fact, "meritocratic, single-rank-order selection is only a shade less conservative than the aristocratic selection it replaced, since to a significant degree it also perpetuates advantage of birth" (Cronbach & Snow, 1977, p. 8). Both Thurstone's (1938) seven primary mental abilities and Gardner's (1983) seven intelligences allowed social planners and educators to envision developing the talents of a much larger segment of society, even though abilities (or "intelligences") were seen as grounded in physiology.

CONCLUSIONS

It is something of a truism that those who advocated the use of intelligence tests were themselves their beneficiaries. Some benefited financially, but all received a new justification for their own (and their children's) superiority or chosenness. The intellectually "gifted" are the new chosen people, and the argument about heredity versus environment is a modern version of our earlier theological debate about whether salvation came through predestination or good works.

But to identify the existence and effects of such factors—either broad, simplifying beliefs in a society or narrower, self-serving beliefs in individuals—is *not* to claim that debate and discord is prior belief writ large. Evidence matters. Some are persuaded by it to change their minds. And sometimes data force conclusions that conflict with at least some beliefs:

If the world were as I would like it to be, what I think I have learned about intelligence would not be true. I think that individual differences in intelligence, as assessed by standardized tests, relate to what individuals learn in schools and to their social mobility. And I think that scores on such tests are related, albeit weakly related, to race and social class background. In addition, I think we do not know how to substantially modify or eliminate individual differences in intelligence or the relationship between individual differences in intelligence and what is learned in schools. As long as this is true, individual differences in intelligence will relate to various important social outcomes. In my utopia, children would be equally capable of learning and everyone would be well educated. Differences in status associated with different occupations would be minimized or eliminated. Individual differences, in whatever would be analogous to intelligence in such a world, would be of little relevance. That world is not the world in which we live. (Brody, 1992, pp. ix–x)

If the Snyderman and Rothman (1987) survey is to be believed, then Brody's view is nearer to the modal view of experts in the domain than is the view of luminaries such as Sternberg (1985) or Gardner (1983), on the one hand, or Jensen (1982) and Eysenck (1988), on the other hand. The essential claim of this chapter, though, is that all such beliefs—great and small—are influenced not only by the data but also by personal proclivity and professional experiences; by beliefs about science and how it is conducted; and by larger social, political, and religious themes that form the fabric of the culture.

NOTES

1. William James, the once-believer-turned-critic of Spencer, parodied this view to his classes as: "Evolution is a change from a no-howish untalkaboutable all-alikeness to a somehowish and in general talkaboutable not-all-alikeness by continuous stick-togetherations and somethingelseifications" (cited in Hofstadter, 1992, p. 129).

2. The trail does not stop here. Cubberley's boss—Stanford's President David Starr Jordan—was a well-known biologist and leader in the eugenics movement.

3. It is useful to distinguish between the simple predestination of Paul (some are predestined for salvation) and the double predestination of Augustine, Luther, and Calvin

(some are predestined for salvation, others for damnation). The latter view is more congenial with eugenic proposals to eliminate the unfit.

4. The medieval church certainly recognized differences among people in social status, but its view differed from the post-Darwinian view in two major respects: First, from Aristotle through Aquinas it was believed that humans differed qualitatively from other animals by virtue of their reason, intellect, or immortal souls. The classic definition of man as a rational animal saw the possession of a rational faculty as the key difference not only between man and other animals but also among men. For Aquinas and his followers, then,

human dignity arises from the fact that man is not only the creature, but the child of God; alone in the created world he possesses a rational nature which renders him capable of a supersensible good—a vision of God in his true essence. Every human being, therefore, has the moral right always to be treated in a manner which accords with this exalted prerogative. (Burtt, 1939, pp. 131–132)

As one defender of this orthodoxy put it, "Once we step down from that tall and splintered peak of pure insanity we step on to a tableland where one man is not so widely different from another. Outside the exception, what we find is the average" (Chesterton, 1922, p. 38). Second, differences among men in learning or wealth or social status—while important in this world—had no bearing on their status in the next.

REFERENCES

Anderson, J. R. (1983). *The architecture of cognition*. Cambridge, MA: Harvard University Press.

Ayres, L. P. (1909). *Laggards in our schools: A study of retardation and elimination in city school systems*. New York: Charities Publication Committee.

Botzum, W. A. (1951). A factorial study of reasoning and closure factors. *Psychometrika, 16*, 361–386.

Brody, N. (1992). *Intelligence* (2nd ed.). San Diego: Academic Press.

Bronfrenbrenner, U. (1979). *The ecology of human development*. Cambridge, MA: Harvard University Press.

Burt, C. (1909). Experimental tests of general intelligence. *British Journal of Psychology, 3*, 94–177.

Burt, C. (1958). The inheritance of mental ability. *American Psychologist, 13*, 1–15.

Burtt, E. A. (1939). *Types of religious philosophy*. New York: Harper & Brothers.

Carroll, J. B. (1941). A factor analysis of verbal abilities. *Psychometrika, 6*, 279–307.

Carroll, J. B. (1982). The measurement of intelligence. In R. J. Sternberg (Ed.), *Handbook of human intelligence* (pp. 29–120). New York: Cambridge University Press.

Cattell, R. B. (1940). Effects of human fertility trends upon the distribution of intelligence and culture. In G. M. Whipple (Ed.), *The thirty-ninth yearbook of the National Society for the Study of Education. Intelligence: Its nature and nurture* (pp. 221–234). Bloomington, IL: Public School Publishing Company.

Chapman, P. D. (1988). *Schools as sorters: Lewis M. Terman, applied psychology, and the intelligence testing movement, 1890–1930*. New York: New York University.

Chesterton, G. K. (1922). *Eugenics and other evils*. New York: Cassell and Company, Ltd.

Cronbach, L. J. (1975). Five decades of public controversy over mental testing. *American Psychologist, 30*, 1–14.

Cronbach, L. J. (1977). *Educational psychology* (3rd ed.). New York: Harcourt, Brace, Jovanovich.

Cronbach, L. J., & Snow, R. E. (1977). *Aptitudes and instructional methods: A handbook for research on interactions.* New York: John Wiley & Sons.

Cubberly, E. P. (1909). *Changing conceptions of education.* Boston: Houghton Mifflin.

Damasio, A. R. (1994). *Descartes' error: Emotion, reason, and the human brain.* New York: Putnam.

Darwin, C. (1859). *The origin of species by means of natural selection, or, the preservation of favored races in the struggle for life.* London: J. Murray.

Davis, A. (1949). Poor people have brains too. *Phi Delta Kappan, 30*, 294–295.

Evans, B., & Waites, B. (1981). *IQ and mental testing: An unnatural science and its social history.* Atlantic Highlands, NJ: Humanities Press.

Eysenck, H. (1988). The concept of "intelligence": Useful or useless? *Intelligence, 12*, 1–16.

Fancher, R. E. (1985). *The intelligence men: Makers of the IQ controversy.* New York: W. W. Norton.

Festinger, L. (1957). *A theory of cognitive dissonance.* Evanston, IL: Roco, Peterson.

French, J. W. (1951). The description of aptitude and achievement tests in terms of rotated factors. *Psychometric Monographs*, No. 5.

Gardner, H. (1983). *Frames of mind: The theory of multiple intelligences.* New York: Basic Books.

Glaser, R. (1984). Education and thinking: The role of knowledge. *American Psychologist, 39*, 93–104.

Gordon, M. M. (1964). *Assimilation in American life: The role of race, religion, and national origins.* New York: Oxford University Press.

Gould, S. J. (1981). *The mismeasure of man.* New York: W. W. Norton.

Guilford, J. P. (1956). The structure of intellect. *Psychological Bulletin, 53*, 267–293.

Guilford, J. P. (1985). The structure-of-intellect model. In B. B. Wolman (Ed.), *Handbook of intelligence* (pp. 225–266). New York: Wiley.

Guilford, J. P., & Lacey, J. I. (Eds.). (1947). *Printed classification tests* (Army Air Force Aviation Psychology Research Report No. 5). Washington, DC: Government Printing Office.

Guttman, L. (1958). What lies ahead for factor analysis? *Educational and Psychological Measurement, 18*, 497–515.

Hebb, D. O. (1949). *The organization of behavior.* New York: Wileg.

Hernshaw, L. S. (1979). *Cyril Burt, psychologist.* Ithaca, NY: Cornell University Press.

Herrnstein, R. J., & Murray, C. (1994). *The bell curve: Intelligence and class structure in American life.* New York: Free Press.

Hilgard, E. R. (1988). The early years of intelligence measurement. In R. Linn (Ed.), *Intelligence: Measurement, theory, and public policy* (pp. 7–25). Urbana: University of Illinois Press.

Hoffman, K. I., Guilford, J. P., Hoepfner, R., & Doherty, W. J. (1968). *A factor analysis of the figure-cognition and figural-evaluation abilities* (Representative No. 40). Los Angeles: Psychological Laboratory, University of Southern California.

Hofstadter, R. (1992). *Social Darwinism in American thought.* Boston, MA: Beacon Press.

Horn, J. L. (1985). Remodeling old models of intelligence. In B. B. Wolman (Ed.), *Handbook of intelligence* (pp. 267–300). New York: Wiley.

Humphreys, L. G. (1962). The organization of human abilities. *American Psychologist, 17*, 475–483.

Hunt, E. (1986). The heffalump of intelligence. In R. J. Sternberg & D. K. Detterman (Eds.), *What is intelligence? Contemporary viewpoints on its nature and definition* (pp. 101–108). Norwood, NJ: Ablex.

Hunt, J. M. (1961). *Intelligence and experience.* New York: Ronald Press Company.

Jensen, A. (1982). Reaction time and psychometric *g*. In H. J. Eysenck (Ed.), *A model for intelligence* (pp. 93–132). New York: Springer.

Joncich, G. M. (1968). *The sane positivist: A biography of Edward L. Thorndike.* Middletown, CT: Wesleyan University Press.

Just, M. A., & Carpenter, P. A. (1992). A capacity theory of comprehension: Individual differences in working memory. *Psychological Review, 99*, 122–149.

Kail, R., & Pellegrino, J. W. (1985). *Human intelligence: Perspectives and prospects.* New York: W. H. Freeman.

Kamin, L. J. (1974). *The science and politics of IQ.* Potomac, MD: Erlbaum.

Kelley, T. L. (1928). *Crossroads in the mind of man.* Stanford, CA: Stanford University Press.

Koch, S. (1959). *Psychology: A study of science.* New York: McGraw-Hill.

Kuhn, T. S. (1970). *The structure of scientific revolutions.* Chicago: Universi of Chicago Press.

Laboratory of Comparative Human Cognition. (1982). Culture and intelligence. In R. J. Sternberg (Ed.), *Handbook of human intelligence* (pp. 642–719). New York: Cambridge University Press.

Lippmann, W. (1976). The abuse of the tests. In N. J. Block & G. Dworkin (Eds.), *The IQ controversy: Critical readings* (pp. 18–20). New York: Pantheon Books.

Locke, J. (1690/1959). *Essay concerning human understanding.* New York: Dover.

Lohman, D. F. (1993). Teaching and testing to develop fluid abilities. *Educational Researcher, 22*, 12–23.

Matarazzo, J. D. (1992). Psychological testing and assessment in the 21st century. *American Psychologist, 47*, 1007–1018.

McNemar, Q. (1964). Lost: Our intelligence? Why? *American Psychologist, 19*, 871–882.

Pemberton, C. (1952). The closure factors related to other cognitive processes. *Psychometrika, 17*, 267–288.

Pick, D. (1989). *Faces of degeneration: A European disorder. c. 1848–c. 1918.* Cambridge, UK: Cambridge University Press.

Popper, K. R. (1963). *Conjectures and refutations: The growth of scientific knowledge.* New York: Harper and Row.

Samelson, F. (1979). Putting psychology on the map: Ideology and intelligence testing. In A. R. Buss (Ed.), *Psychology in social context.* New York: Halsted Press.

Schama, S. (1987). *The embarrassment of riches: An interpretation of Dutch culture in The Golden Age.* London: William Collins Sons and Co. Ltd.

Schmidt, F. L., & Hunter, J. E. (1977). Development of a general solution to the problem of validity generalization. *Journal of Applied Psychology, 62*, 529–540.

Slife, B. D., & Williams, R. N. (1995). *What's behind the research? Discovering hidden assumptions in the behavioral sciences.* Thousand Oaks, CA: Sage Publications.

Snow, R. E., & Yalow, E. (1982). Education and intelligence. In R. J. Sternberg (Ed.),

Handbook of human intelligence (pp. 493–585). Cambridge, England: Cambridge University Press.

Snyderman, M., & Rothman, S. (1987). *The IQ controversy, the media, and public policy.* New Brunswick, NJ: Transaction Publishers.

Spearman, C. (1904). ''General intelligence'' objectively determined and measured. *American Journal of Psychology, 15,* 201–293.

Spearman, C. E. (1923). *The nature of intelligence and the principles of cognition.* London: Macmillan.

Spearman, C. E. (1927). *The abilities of man.* London: Macmillan.

Spencer, H. (1897). *The principles of psychology.* New York: Appleton and Company.

Stephan, N. (1985). Biology and degeneration: Races and proper places. In J. E. Chamberlin & S. L. Gilman (Eds.), *Degeneration: The dark side of progress* (pp. 97–120). New York: Columbia.

Sternberg, R. J. (1985). *Beyond IQ: A triarchic theory of human intelligence.* Cambridge, England: Cambridge University Press.

Terman, L. M. (1906). Genius and stupidity: A study of some of the intellectual processes of seven ''bright'' and seven ''stupid'' boys. *Pedagogical Seminary, 13,* 307–373.

Terman, L. M. (1922). Were we born that way? *World's Work, 5,* 655–660.

Thomson, G. H. (1916). A hierarchy without a general factor. *British Journal of Psychology, 8,* 271–281.

Thorndike, E. L. (1920). Intelligence and its uses. *Harper's Magazine, 140,* 227–235.

Thorndike, E. L. (1940). *Human nature and the social order.* New York: Macmillan.

Thorndike, E. L., Bregman, E. O., Cobb, M. V., & Woodyard, E. (1926). *The measurement of intelligence.* New York: Columbia University, Teachers College.

Thorndike, E. L., Lay, W., & Dean, P. R. (1909). The relation of accuracy in sensory discrimination to general intelligence. *American Journal of Psychology, 20,* 364–369.

Thurstone, L. L. (1935). *The vectors of the mind.* Chicago: University of Chicago Press.

Thurstone, L. L. (1938). Primary mental abilities. *Psychometric Monographs,* No. 1.

Thurstone, L. L. (1944). A factorial study of perception. *Psychometric Monographs,* No. 4.

Thurstone, L. L. (1946). Theories of intelligence. *Scientific Monthly,* February, 101–112.

Thurstone, L. L. (1949). *Mechanical aptitude: III. Analysis of group tests* (Psychometric Laboratory Report No. 55). Chicago: University of Chicago Press.

Tyack, D. B. (1974). *The one best system: A history of American urban education.* Cambridge, MA: Harvard University Press.

Vernon, P. E. (1950). *The structure of human abilities.* London: Methuen.

Vernon, P. E. (1973). Multivariate approaches to the study of cognitive styles. In J. R. Royce (Ed.), *Multivariate analysis and psychological theory* (pp. 125–148). New York: Academic Press.

Weber, M. (1958). *The Protestant ethic and the spirit of capitalism* (T. Parsons, Trans.). New York: Scribner. (Original work published 1904.)

White, S. H. (1977). Social implications of IQ. In P. L. Houts (Ed.), *The myth of measurability* (pp. 23–44). New York, NY: Hart Publishing Company.

Wolf, T. (1973). *Alfred Binet.* Chicago: University of Chicago Press.

Wolfe, D. (1940). Factor analysis to 1940. *Psychometric Monographs,* No. 3.

Wooldridge, A. (1994). *Measuring the mind: Education and Psychology in England. c. 1860–c.1990.* Cambridge, UK: Cambridge University Press.

6

Ability Profiles

Jan-Eric Gustafsson and Richard E. Snow

INTRODUCTION

In the previous chapter on the history of intelligence testing, Lohman contrasted theorists who emphasized a general ability construct (G) with those who favored one or another list of multiple, more specialized abilities. As he noted, one way of resolving this dispute is to construct hierarchical models of ability organization, with G at the top and various differentiations of more specialized abilities beneath it. Then, ability constructs can be chosen from different levels of referent generality to serve further theory, research, and practice as needed (see also Coan, 1964; Cronbach, 1990). The criterion is thus the usefulness, not the truthfulness, of the different levels. However, hierarchical models of ability organization not only provide identification of ability constructs at different levels but also allow for explicit contrasts among constructs within and between levels. These contrasts are often expressed as ability profiles.

The present chapter examines the nature, uses, misuses, strengths, and limitations of special ability constructs and, particularly, profiles of such constructs. We begin with a brief definition of the problem, for both research and practice. We then present a conceptual framework and some of the basic psychometrics of profiles. Next we review some examples of profile use, noting several problems that need to be addressed and misuses that need to be avoided. Finally, we examine some extant research on profiles and suggest some potentially profitable lines for further work.

PROBLEM DEFINITION FOR RESEARCH AND PRACTICE

If G is defined as the general ability construct that accounts for the positive correlations commonly found across all cognitive tests, then special ability constructs can be defined to account for positive correlations within subsets of cognitive tests that exceed the level of correlation expected, based on G alone. In the language of factor analysis, the general factor loads all of the tests in a battery administration and approximates G if the sampling of tests and persons is sufficiently representative. One or more additional group factors then will account for clusters of test correlations that remain to be explained after G has been defined. These group factors identify special abilities. A vast literature demonstrates that some number of special abilities in addition to G must be posited to account for the extant correlational evidence (Carroll, 1993). The further research question has long been: Which special abilities are important to distinguish, and can they be organized into a coherent taxonomy?

In practical terms also, it has long seemed evident that different special abilities govern success in particular performance situations. Thus, in practice, the question has been: How can we measure and use profiles of these multiple special abilities to local advantage? Usually, to form an ability profile, two or more separate ability scores have been computed on a common scale and graphed side by side to allow comparison. The array might or might not include G along with the special abilities. Standard scores, factor scores, and various other common derivations have been used. Sometimes difference scores are designed to represent the contrast quantitatively. Ability profiles are used in research and practice whenever it is thought that an analysis of relative strengths and weaknesses will be important in understanding performance. For example, although a G measure may be sufficient for some individual selection or program evaluation purposes, classifying students or employees into alternative treatments or jobs may benefit from matching profiles to special features of instruction or job requirements. As another example, most guidance and counseling purposes are better served by client profiles across a variety of abilities than by the unidimensional summary provided by G testing. Actually, most major intelligence tests are designed as multitest batteries precisely because it is thought that profiles can be used to identify different kinds of mental functions and malfunctions. Thus, a variety of research and practical purposes are served by profile comparisons.

However, there have been major disputes about the relative power and value of G measures versus profile measures for many testing purposes. Evidence has been accumulating on both sides of the issue (see, e.g., Carroll, 1993; Cronbach, 1990; Jensen, 1992; Ree & Earles, 1992; Schmidt & Ones, 1992; Sternberg, Wagner, Williams, & Horvath, 1995). It appears that a significant part of the problem involves the proper definition and measurement of ability profiles.

CONCEPTUAL FRAMEWORK

Unless more than one ability can be reliably and meaningfully measured, of course, it is not possible to describe patterns of performance in terms of profiles. As noted above, the question of which ability dimensions can and should be measured is thus the first question to be faced. To address this question, we need to elaborate briefly on Lohman's history. We can then turn to the measurement problem.

Theories of Multiple Abilities

Research on individual differences in cognitive performance has resulted in a proliferation of models, but all agree that multiple dimensions are necessary (see, e.g., Carroll, 1993; Gustafsson & Undheim, 1996). Thus, all models suggest the importance of studying profiles of performance. However, the models differ greatly in the number of dimensions they identify and how they organize them.

Spearman (1904) presented the first formalized and empirically based model of the structure of cognitive abilities. In his view, performance on any intellectual task is affected by two factors: one general factor common to all tasks (g) and one factor that is specific to each task (s). Spearman (1927) proposed methods for estimating scores on g and s factors to be used in profile descriptions. However, his model was shown to be too simple to fit the data and was rejected in favor of models with multiple dimensions of ability.

Thurstone (1938), in contrast, postulated a limited set of specialized intellectual abilities, each of which is important for performance in a limited domain of tasks (e.g., spatial, perceptual, numerical, verbal, memory, fluency, and inductive reasoning). Thurstone's (1931) view came from his newly developed method of factor analysis, which yielded descriptions in terms of multiple uncorrelated dimensions of ability. Whereas Spearman had posited one broad ability and many narrow abilities, Thurstone's so-called Primary Mental Abilities (PMAs) were all of the same degree of generality. Although he aimed to identify independent abilities that would be useful in profiles, further research showed that the PMAs were not uncorrelated. Thurstone (1947) then developed multiple factor methods to allow correlations among the factors in his model. Further research also identified a large number of new abilities, so the list of PMAs was soon considerably extended (see, e.g., French, 1951). In a recently published review and reanalysis of much of this century's evidence on human cognitive abilities, Carroll (1993) identified at least 60 factors of the PMA type.

Guilford (1967) mounted the major attempt to create a taxonomy for this growing list of PMAs. He classified each test and factor into a three-dimensional system, with "content," "operation," and "product" as facets. When the elements of the three facets are combined in all possible ways, 120 possible ability factors are obtained. Even more would be added by distinguishing audio and visual media for test content. Guilford (1972; see also Guilford & Hoepfner, 1971) showed that almost all the PMAs could be classified this way and also that new tests could be developed to measure abilities predicted from the model. In the original formulation, all factors were assumed to be orthogonal. In the last steps of development, however, correlations were allowed among the primary factors. But Guilford (1981) expected that any broader ability constructs that might be based on these correlations would still follow the lines of his taxonomic system. Thus, although it was Guilford's intention to organize the growing number of individual difference factors and reach an integrated understanding of them, he actually contributed substantially to the further proliferation of narrow factors.

The large number of abilities, along with the correlations among abilities, dampened the original optimism about creating ability profiles to be used for diagnosis, counseling, and prediction. Much further work in recent decades has sought to address the problems that arise from the need to account theoretically and practically for multiple correlated abilities.

Hierarchical Models of Ability Structure

When abilities are intercorrelated, the possibilities of observing profiles that mix low and high scores are restricted. However, correlations between abilities may also indicate the presence of broad overarching dimensions under which several narrow abilities are subsumed. Then, the profiles of observed scores can be reorganized to reflect both broad and narrow abilities at different levels. Models that include both broad and narrow abilities are referred to as *hierarchical* models. Although available in various forms in earlier British work (e.g., Vernon, 1950), this type of model has gained increasing attention over recent decades as a means of organizing the many obtained PMAs into fewer, broader constructs. Because hierarchical models are of particular interest in the analysis of ability profiles, the most important hierarchical models are described below in some detail.

Through factorization of tests and factors at the PMA level, Cattell and Horn (e.g., Cattell, 1963; Horn, 1968; Horn & Cattell, 1966) identified several broad overarching abilities. The two dimensions of most central importance in the Cattell-Horn formulation are Fluid Intelligence (G_f) and Crystallized Intelligence (G_c); their model is often referred to as G_f-G_c theory. The G_c dimension represents broad verbal and academic ability thought to reflect individual differences associated with influences of acculturation and schooling. The G_f dimension represents broad abstract analytic reasoning ability and is thought to reflect more the effects of genetic, neurological, and early experience influences.

In the early formulation of G_f-G_c theory, Horn and Cattell (1966) identified some additional broad abilities: General Visualization (G_v), General Speediness (G_s), and General Fluency (G_r). In later work, still other broad abilities have been added (e.g., General Auditory Ability, G_a). The model has also been given significant theoretical elaborations. Horn (1986, 1989) offered an information-processing interpretation of the hierarchy with levels of sensory reception, associational processing, perceptual organization, and relation eduction. Cattell (1971, 1987) developed the hierarchical model with concepts quite different from those used by Horn. His so-called Triadic Theory includes abilities of three different kinds. "General capacities" (e.g., G_f, G_s, and G_r) represent limits to brain action as a whole. Another class of abilities is referred to as "provincial powers." These correspond to sensory area factors, such as visualization, auditory structuring ability, and motor and kinesthetic abilities. The third class of abilities is referred to as "agencies" involved in performing in different areas of cultural content. The agencies largely correspond to PMAs.

Recently, Carroll (1993) also formulated a hierarchical model with factors at three levels of generality, based on the results of his reanalysis of almost 500 correlation matrices collected throughout the history of research on human cognitive abilities. The three-stratum division corresponds to a classification of abilities in narrow, broad, and general categories. The PMAs belong to the category of narrow abilities. Carroll also identified 10 broad abilities. These are essentially the same factors identified in the Cattell-Horn model, namely, Fluid Intelligence (G_f), Crystallized Intelligence (G_c), Broad Visual Perception (G_v), Broad Retrieval Ability (G_r), and Broad Auditory Perception (G_a). In addition, Carroll identified a broad memory factor (General Memory and Learning, G_y) as well as factors reflecting Broad Cognitive Speediness (G_s) and Reaction Time (G_t). Carroll's model also explicitly includes a general factor (G) at the third level, whereas the Cattell-Horn model is unclear on this point; Cattell (1971) has posited an antecedent, historical G_f as a kind of G at the fourth level, but Horn (1989) seems to reject a final unitary G level.

As noted previously, British research represents a separate tradition of hierarchical models that include a general factor; these may be regarded as elaborations of Spearman's Two-Factor Theory. British researchers have relied on the so-called hierarchical group factor technique, which starts by extracting a general factor and then extracts group factors that become successively more narrow. The most influential summary of the results achieved with this approach was presented by Vernon (1950). At the top of his hierarchical model is Spearman's g factor. The model also includes two major group factors: the verbal-numerical-educational (*v:ed*) factor and the practical-mechanical-spatial-physical (*k:m*) factor. These major group factors are subdivided into several minor group factors. The *v:ed* factor subdivides into different scholastic factors such as verbal and number abilities. The *k:m* factor is then subdivided into minor group factors such as perceptual, spatial, and mechanical abilities. It would appear that the Carroll or Cattell-Horn G_c and the *v:ed* factors are virtually identical and that the G_v and *k:m* factors largely overlap. However, there is no explicit general factor in the Cattell-Horn G_f-G_c model, and the Vernon model does not recognize any major group factor clearly corresponding to G_f.

But comparisons between the American and British hierarchical models using confirmatory factor analysis (e.g., Gustafsson, 1984, 1988; Undheim, 1981, Undheim & Gustafsson, 1987) have shown that the correlation between G_f and a higher-order g factor is so close to unity that these factors must be considered identical. Thus, in the Vernon model the g factor accounts for all the systematic variance in the tests, leaving no variance remaining to define a subordinate G_f factor.

The differences in the patterns of result of the American and British hierarchical factorists thus seem due to the way in which the analyses have been performed. The G_f-G_c model is constructed with the narrow factors as building blocks for the broader factors; the analysis is conducted from bottom up, using what Gustafsson and Balke (1993) labeled a *higher-order* modeling approach. In the British tradition, the analysis starts at the top and goes down, using a *nested-factor* modeling approach. Because in both cases the analysis stopped with a two-level model, different interpretations resulted. If, however, the bottom-up approach is extended to include a level above the second-order factors, a general factor appears as well. And if the top-down approach is extended down below the level of major group factors, it yields a large number of narrow factors corresponding to the primary abilities. In both cases the result is a hierarchy with factors at three levels similar to that reported by Carroll (1993). It also may be noted that there are different ways of conceptualizing the relations between factors at different levels of hierarchy. Researchers who rely on the higher-order approach tend to regard the narrow factors as indivisible. However, in the nested-factor approach, factors at lower levels in the hierarchy are freed from the variance due to the broader factors. The hierarchical model is thus formulated with orthogonal factors, some of which are broad and some of which are narrow, and observed performance is seen as influenced by both broad and narrow factors. It is, however, also possible to transform the higher-order model into one with hierarchical orthogonal dimensions, using procedures devised by Schmid and Leiman (1957). This transformation was used by Carroll (1993) in his reanalyses. Thus, in the end, the different models seem to fit into a common scheme; they appear essentially to be transforms of one another.

A Hypothetical Example

The different types of models can be described in more concrete terms using a small hypothetical example presented by Muthén (1994). Figure 6.1 shows a model with three correlated factors (I, V, and S) that account for performance on six cognitive tests (I1, I2, V1, V2, S1, and S2). According to the given data the correlations among the abilities are quite substantial: .82 for I and V, .93 for I and S, and .76 for V and S. These correlations are somewhat higher than what is typically found in real data, but the exaggeration helps the patterns to appear more clearly.

The high correlations between the three abilities may be accounted for by a

Figure 6.1
A Model with Three Correlated Abilities

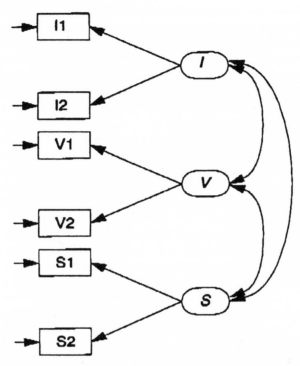

Source: Muthén (1994).

second-order factor (G), as shown in Figure 6.2. In this higher-order model, parameter values have been chosen in such a way that G accounts for all the variance in I. There is, thus, no residual left in the I factor. However, for both V and S, there is a residual (V' and S', respectively) that represents the variance not accounted for by G in the first-order factors.

However, the hierarchy may also be constructed as a nested-factor model, shown in Figure 6.3. Here the ability factors are all directly related to the tests. Because the G factor accounts for variance in the tests to which V and S are related, these narrow factors are residual factors in this model, too. In this model, there is also no I' (or I) factor because the G factor leaves no systematic variance unaccounted for in I1 and I2.

The three models all account for the same data, but they have quite different interpretations. Thus, in the model with correlated factors, it is assumed that the three dimensions represent different ability constructs, which although correlated are conceptually distinct. This model also implies that the tests each measure only one ability, so they adhere to the principle of simple structure formulated by Thurstone (1947). However, from the other two models, it follows that test

Figure 6.2
A Higher-Order Model with Three Primary Abilities and One Second-Order Ability

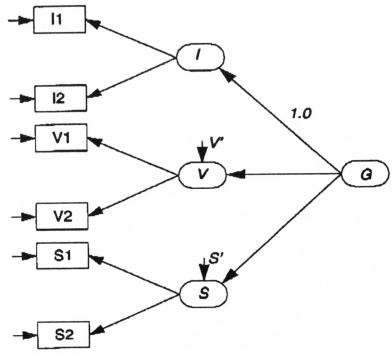

Source: Muthén (1994).

performance is accounted for by at least two factors and that the tests are thus indicators of more than one ability. In the hierarchical models, the principle of simple structure breaks down, because the correlations among the factors are also brought into the model. The complexity of the tests is most clearly seen in the nested-factor model in Figure 6.3, but it is also implicit in the higher-order model in Figure 6.2 because this model implies that the residual factors V' and S' also account for variance in the tests.

When Thurstone introduced the PMAs, high expectations were raised that profiles of abilities would be useful for purposes of diagnosis, counseling, and prediction. Such ability profiles remain of value, within certain limits (see Cronbach, 1990), in counseling and in some diagnostic situations. However, differential aptitude batteries have not been found to have much differential predictive power for achievement in different subject matter areas or performance in different jobs (see, e.g., Humphreys, 1981; McNemar, 1964). Even though profiles of abilities of the PMA type, on the surface at least, should be easy to match with different tasks and types of treatments, empirical research has not shown strong support (Cronbach & Snow, 1977; Gustafsson, 1976).

Figure 6.3
A Nested-Factor Model with One Broad and Two Narrow Factors

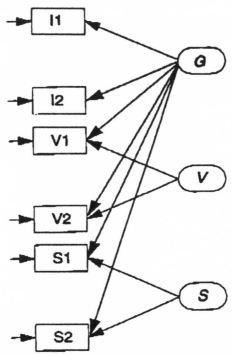

Source: Muthén (1994).

Gustafsson and Balke (1993) have suggested that this results because broad and narrow abilities have not been properly separated in studies of differential prediction; a hierarchical model with both broad and narrow abilities should be more parsimonious and theoretically clear than a model with correlated narrow abilities. But there are also methodological reasons why profiles based on correlated narrow abilities may yield misleading results. This can be demonstrated in relation to the hypothetical example already introduced.

Muthén (1994) compared the three models shown in Figures 6.1–6.3, along with others, in a hypothetical prediction problem. It was assumed that a dependent variable (Y) is predicted from the three latent variables of Figure 6.3, with standardized regression coefficients set to .65, .23, and .13 for G, V', and S', respectively. The covariance matrix thus generated was then analyzed under the assumption that the model shown in Figure 6.1 fit the data. This analysis resulted in standardized regression slopes of .00, .40, and .35 for I, V, and S. This absurd result suggests, quite wrongly, that the single most important predictor according to the true model has in this analysis no influence whatsoever on Y! The model with three correlated factors also fails to reveal the true differential predictive strength of V and S. However, when the hierarchical model that generated the data are used to predict Y, the correct estimates are, of course, obtained.

The lesson is that the correlated factors approach cannot properly estimate the relative importance of predictors when broad factors influence two or more of the predictors because the partial regression coefficients express the importance of a predictor with all the other independent variables held constant. To the extent that there are sources of variance that overlap two or more of the independent variables, this common variance will be partialed out. Thus, the importance of variables measuring broad factors will be underestimated, and the importance of variables measuring both broad and narrow factors will be over-estimated (Muthén, 1994). This is why the I factor appears to have no influence on the dependent variable when the prediction is made from correlated factors, and why the relative importance of V and S is distorted. Findings similar to those reported here with simulated data were also found by Gustafsson (1989, pp. 220–221) with actual empirical data.

Recommendations for Ability Construct Selection

Given the above, it is clear that, whenever possible, ability constructs should be chosen as orthogonal factors from a hierarchical model obtained either from a nested-factor model or from a higher-order-factor model transformed using the Schmid-Leiman technique. For interpretation purposes, careful attention should be paid to the hierarchical level of each construct chosen.

Of course, the selection of special ability constructs for a score profile obviously should also be adapted to the research or practical problem at hand. And the most important decisions to be made in this selection concern the breadth of reference constructs needed and the amount of detail appropriate for the particular purpose. For some problems in educational counseling the full spectrum of broad abilities is likely to be useful, whereas differentiation of abilities beneath this level is usually not necessary. When classifying persons for different occupations, however, differentiations at a finer level of detail may be needed. Any focus of assessment may be as finely differentiated as needed through the addition of more measures at the lowest level of the hierarchical model, even including test-specific components that may be of particular interest (see Spearman, 1927).

For many research purposes, it is useful to include reference measures for constructs at all three levels of the hierarchy: G, to distinguish general from special individual differences variance in interpreting results; the group factors closest to the phenomenal domain of interest; and the particular ability distinctions closest to the actual performances to be studied. We especially recommend the constructs distinguished in the Carroll (1993) hierarchical model for general reference purposes in research in differential, educational, industrial, and counseling psychology, with the proviso that G and G_f be treated as identical (Gustafsson, 1984). The Carroll model offers the broadest survey and the most systematic and consistent analysis of this century's evidence on ability tests available. For any given purpose, of course, useful distinctions can also be drawn from the Cattell (1987) and Horn (1989) hierarchical models, from the Guilford (1967) taxonomy, or from the extant catalogue of psychomotor and physical abilities (Fleishman & Quaintance, 1984). But the Carroll model ought to be the prime base for profile selection.

Recently, Gardner (1983, 1993) has suggested an alternative classification of abilities, developed without reference to the mass of evidence from psychometric research. His review of literature from developmental psychology, neuropsychology, and cross-cultural research led Gardner to posit seven intelligences: linguistic intelligence, including the skills involved in reading, writing, listening, and talking; logical-mathematical intelligence, which enters, for example, mathematical and scientific thinking and a wide range of everyday situations requiring analysis and judgment; spatial intelligence, involving the accurate perception of the visual world, as well as transformations and modifications of the initial perceptions; musical intelligence, which is involved in music production and appreciation; bodily-kinesthetic intelligence, which enters into activities such as dancing, athletics, acting, and surgery; interpersonal intelligence, which represents abilities to discern other persons' moods, temperaments, motivations, and intentions; and finally, intrapersonal intelligence, which involves the ability to understand oneself and to behave in ways that are appropriate to one's needs, goals, and abilities. Gardner emphasizes the need for assessing student profiles across these categories and for providing a spectrum of opportunities for their development in educational settings. Assessments would be formed from the processes and products of student work, and portfolios of these would represent student strengths and weaknesses.

For the most part, Gardner's categories correspond to abilities identified in psychometric research: linguistic intelligence is part of G_c; logical-mathematical intelligence combines parts of G_f and G_c; spatial intelligence equals G_v; musical intelligence includes G_a; bodily-kinesthetic intelligence corresponds to the domain of physical and psychomotor abilities; and interpersonal and intrapersonal intelligence corresponds to the old domain of social intelligence (see Ford, 1986, Thorndike, 1920). Gardner's viewpoint helps to consider the diversity of talent developments and outcomes important in education, and some of his work in these categories may suggest interesting further ability measures to study. However, assessment development and evaluation does not yet justify the use of profiles based on his scheme. Furthermore, Gardner's model excludes the other group factors commonly seen in psychometric research and postulates that his seven intelligences are uncorrelated, biological modules. Because it ignores contrary evidence, particularly the correlational evidence for G and hierarchical organization, the model has been broadly criticized (see, e.g., Anderson, 1992; Brody, 1992; Messick, 1992; Snow, 1985).

PSYCHOMETRICS OF ABILITY PROFILES

Given a provisional list of ability constructs such as those identified above, there remains a series of critical questions concerning the reliable and meaningful measurement of profile differences. Due to practical limits, in most cases, it will only rarely be possible to administer a battery sufficient to compute a hierarchical model with a full range of general, broad, and narrow ability factors. Many practical compromises impose problems in smaller studies. Even in large studies, it is often difficult to obtain satisfactory reliability estimates for profiles. Problems associated with unreliability of scores are more severe when profiles are in focus than when single abilities are measured, as are the problems of securing appropriate norms. Another source of problems relates to the above discussion about the structure of abilities; in smaller studies it is often not clear how measures should best be organized into profiles. These and related psychometric problems have hindered progress in the understanding and use of ability profiles.

An Example

To set discussion in a concrete context, consider the example of one test battery specifically designed to measure profiles of ability. The General Aptitude Test Battery (GATB) was developed by the United States Employment Service for use in counseling and in matching job applicants with jobs. The GATB yields nine scores, each on a scale with a mean of 120 and a standard deviation of 20 (see, e.g., Cronbach, 1990, pp. 394–395):

V—Verbal (Vocabulary)

N—Numerical (Computation, Arithmetic Reasoning)

S—Spatial (Three-Dimensional Space)

P—Form Perception (Tool Matching, Form Matching)

Q—Clerical Perception (Name Comparison)

K—Motor Coordination (Mark Making)

F—Finger Dexterity (Assemble, Disassemble)

M—Manual Dexterity (Place, Turn)

G—General (Vocabulary, Three-Dimensional Space, and Arithmetic)

As originally designed, the profile of scores for an individual applicant for a job was to be compared to a set of multiple cutoff scores, each set of cutoff scores being different for each occupation. For example, to be recommended as an egg candler the job seeker had to achieve a score of 80 on P, 85 on K, and 100 on M; the other six scores would not enter into this particular recommendation (see Cronbach, 1990, p. 395).

There are several problems with this procedure. First, it is based on single scores, most of which have low reliability. Because the standard error of measurement is large, each score comparison entering into the multiple cutoff rule involves a risk of being in error. This risk becomes larger the lower the reliability of each score, and it increases also as a function of the number of scores used in the decision rule. A second problem is that the cutoff criteria are often more or less arbitrary, because it is not possible to establish multiple cutoff scores with empirical methods for a large number of occupations, many of which also have requirements that change over time. As emphasized by Cronbach (1990, pp. 399–400), the choice of reference groups for establishing norms against which individual profiles are evaluated also is of fundamental importance in the job placement decision. Still another problem is that typically a job applicant is not evaluated against the requirements of only a single job or category of jobs. For example, in counseling, a person's GATB profile is often matched to an "optimal" education or occupation. Such recommendations are based on the pattern, that is, the difference among scores over all nine scales. However, differences between scores are even more unreliable than are single scores. The reliability of a difference score is a function of the correlation between the variables and the reliability of each (e.g., Cronbach, Gleser, Nanda, & Rajaratnam, 1972; Stanley, 1971). For example, if two scores correlate .60 and each has a reliability of .70, the reliability of their difference score is only .25. Because GATB scores tend to be unreliable and also highly intercorrelated, the many difference scores that may be computed from them tend to be quite unreliable. It is therefore difficult to decide whether particular profiles arise from errors of measurement or reflect true differences.

To minimize these problems, scores should be made as reliable and as uncorrelated as possible. Toward this end, it is now recommended that the 12 tests of the GATB be combined into three scores instead of nine: a manual-dexterity (MFK) composite; a spatial-perceptual (SPQ) composite; and a general-cognitive (GVN) composite. These three composites show higher reliability and lower intercorrelation, relative to individual scores. Cronbach (1990, p. 390) argued, however, that scale combination may have gone too far. In the composites, no distinction is made between V and N, or between S and Q, even though these contrasts match differential job requirements. Also, the Three-Dimensional Space test is included in both the G score and the S score; this creates artificial overlap between the general-cognitive and the spatial-perceptual composites.

Thus, difficult psychometric problems are involved in constructing and interpreting ability profiles. Some of these problems are solved or reduced if the newly developed approaches to hierarchical structure of cognitive abilities described above are adopted. The hierarchical approach allows multiple, correlated, and typically quite unreliable measures to be combined into a limited number of orthogonal composites, at least some of which have good reliability. It also allows both broad and narrow abilities into the profile, so that the relative importance of different levels of abilities can be determined empirically in each instance. When hierarchical models are estimated with structural equation modeling techniques the abilities are estimated as error-free latent variables. Problems related to errors of measurement are avoided altogether. However, this approach is far from generally applicable. When decisions must be made about individuals, it is necessary to obtain scores for individuals, either through estimation of factor scores or through creation of composite scores. Also, translation of the hierarchical structure into a particular profile design must be adapted to the problem at hand. These two problems are discussed below.

Factor Scores and Composite Scores

Several methods can be used to estimate factor scores (see, e.g., Harman, 1967), and a selection of these is available in common statistical packages. Because factor scores are estimated as weighted composites of the individuals' test scores, they tend to be more reliable than any single test score. It must be remembered, however, that these estimates are themselves afflicted by errors of measurement (Horn, 1969). Because lower-order factors in the hierarchical model are estimated as difference scores, these estimates tend to be less reliable than estimates of the apex factor.

For practical or theoretical reasons, computation of factor scores may sometimes not be an available option. However, composites formed as weighted or unweighted sums or differences of test scores may be a useful approximation. Cronbach and Snow (1977) demonstrated applications of one such approach, which comes close conceptually to the hierarchical factor models. A general ability score is constructed as a sum of the test scores available, along with one or more contrast scores, formed as differences between particular test scores. For example, if verbal (V) and spatial (S) abilities have been measured, a general score may be formed as V + S, and a contrast score as V − S. These scores will be more or less orthogonal and may be combined in regression equations to study the relative importance of general ability versus the verbal-spatial profile. Cronbach and Snow (1977) recommended this strategy particularly for forming orthogonal aptitude predictors in aptitude-treatment interaction research, but it is appropriate in many other kinds of uses. Contrast scores of this sort still run the risk of low reliability, so formulas for estimating reliability of composites and difference scores should be applied (see, e.g., Stanley, 1971, pp. 401–402). Each score dimension would also have its associated standard error of measurement. For individual interpretation, then, confidence bands could also be established to help judge what size difference between any two ability factor or composite scores should be considered significant. Each dimension would also be represented with reference to a clearly defined norm sample. For practical purposes, there may need to be separate norms for different comparison samples of interest. Beyond the reliability and norm reference concerns, however, there is also the assumption of interval scale measurement, which may not hold for the difference score even when it holds for each constituent; for example, a unit difference between verbal and spatial ability at the high end of both scales may be quite different psychologically from a unit difference at the low end, though the two differences are equal quantitatively. Distributional anomalies can also occur, as when the range of the verbal-spatial difference is large only for persons scoring in the midrange of G.

Another good example of such approximation procedures comes from work with the Wechsler intelligence scales, probably the most widely used ability tests in practice. The Weschler tests were designed from the start to provide a verbal versus performance IQ contrast, and profiles across the constituent scale scores within each, as well as a general or total IQ. The hope was that profile differences could be helpful in diagnosing different kinds of disabilities and thus suggesting differential treatments. Over the years, substantial clinical experience has grown to support some uses of profiles if appropriate guidelines are followed. But controversy surrounds profile interpretation because the empirical evidence for its validity remains mixed and weak and because the G factor seems to take up much of the variance, leaving little for systematic subscore differences. Now, the newly revised Wechsler Intelligence Scale for Children–Third Edition (WISC–III) provides factor score indexes for four distinct factors, in addition to the traditional verbal-performance contrast and the individual scale scores. Thus, it is now possible to include the factors in the profile design; they distinguish verbal comprehension and freedom from distraction within verbal IQ and perceptual organization and speed of processing within performance IQ. Kaufman (1994) has also provided guidelines for deciding when it is appropriate to interpret the verbal-performance IQ contrast, using confidence bands for the contrast itself, differences between the two verbal factors and between the two performance factors, and a measure of range or scatter among the scale scores within each IQ category. For further discussion of individual Wechsler profile interpretation using this approach, and the history of research and controversy about it, see Kaufman (1979, 1994) but also McDermott, Fantuzzo, and Glutting (1990) and McDermott, Glutting, Watkins, and Baggaley (1992).

Continuing research offers the possibility of further improvement in Wechsler profile design. The Wechsler factors described above, even though empirically distinguishable, are still highly correlated; they mix general and special ability variance. Our alternative approach would fit a nested-factor model to allow a general factor and orthogonal second-order factors. One such analysis of WISC–III obtained G and three residual factors, representing verbal-crystallized ability, visual perception, and speed (Gustafsson, 1992; Gustafsson & Undheim, 1996). Profiles based on this model would allow sharper distinctions among the subordinate abilities, and between them and G, and thus potentially more sensitive description of intra- as well as interindividual differences for diagnostic purposes.

Profile Contrast Scores

Traditionally, ability test scores are normative, also described as norm-referenced or nomothetic. That is, it is assumed that each ability exists in some amount for all persons; the score then describes each person's standing relative to other members of the norming reference population for that test and ability. Factor scores or composite scores such as those discussed above are similarly norm-referenced in the sense that they are weighted combinations of normative test scores to represent the latent ability continuum in the reference population. Profiles of such scores thus represent the person's relative standing across the set of abilities in the norm population. To contrast any two such normative scores across persons, difference scores are often constructed, as noted previously. But it is also possible to build other kinds of profile contrast scores. So-called ipsative scores and idiothetic scores offer potentially useful alternatives to normative, nomothetic scores. There are also categorical and ordinal as well as interval scale versions of each. We note the strengths and weaknesses of each kind of score briefly in the following paragraphs.

Ipsative scores have sometimes been used as alternatives to normative difference scores. They are designed to contrast different abilities (or other attributes) within persons, that is, across each person's ability profile. Kaufman's (1994) measure of range or scatter across an individual's scale scores on the WISC–III is an example of ipsative scoring. Another, quite old example is Thorndike's (1912) rank ordering of achievement in different academic subject matters, for each person, to correlate with a similar rank ordering of interest in each subject matter. Ipsative scores actually combine within-person and between-person viewpoints, at least in most uses; they show the strength of each ability relative to other abilities for that person, but also relative to the population of persons used in norming the measures. Except in the controversies surrounding individual profile interpretation of Wechsler scores, as previously noted, ipsative scoring has not been subjected to much systematic research in ability measurement. The forced-choice format for questionnaires is a frequently seen example of ipsative measurement in research on personality and stylistic characteristics.

Another new proposal for personality measurement is called idiothetic scaling (see Lamiell, 1981, 1987; Rorer, 1990). To our knowledge, it has not been studied in relation to ability measurement or profile design, though it may have some uses in this connection. In this approach, an attribute is scored relative to an absolute standard ranging from zero to some maximum (whether or not either end point is actually definable or obtainable), rather than relative to a population of persons or other attributes. One might imagine, for example, persons judging their own abilities or those of others on personal standards or on objectively anchored standards, with or without contrasts among abilities, but without resort to comparisons among persons. Lohman and Rocklin (1995) have pointed out that in most uses idiothetic scores are interpreted with reference to the collection of items used in the measure. This is essentially the same kind of score interpretation reached in achievement and ability tests that are criterion referenced or domain referenced. Scores indicate the degree to which the person has mastered the defined domain.

Of course, quantitative profile analysis can also lead to categorization into types. Type constructs are implicitly profile contrasts. They are useful today in some areas of personality research and in interest assessment (see, e.g., Holland, 1985). But they seem to be used in ability research mainly as labels to imply broader personality differences associated with ability contrasts such as verbal versus spatial or verbal versus mathematical. The notion of aptitude complexes similarly implies profile differences combining ability and personality constructs. For example, some research suggests that individual differences in general ability, anxiety, and achievement via independence versus conformance combine to identify groups of persons who benefit from contrasting instructional treatments (Snow, 1977, 1987). The possibility of such complex constructs is one of several questions being pursued in further research on ability profiles.

PROBLEMS AND PROSPECTS: SOME RESEARCH EXAMPLES

In this final section, we examine some examples of empirical work that uses ability profiles. These example studies show that profiles can be useful in research and practice but that serious misrepresentations can arise when the psychometric and substantive problems of profile contrasts are not addressed.

Group Differences in Ability Profiles

One area in which profile contrasts have played an important role is research on group differences. The gender difference in verbal versus spatial ability provides a leading example, but there also have been studies of ability profile differences among racial, ethnic, and socioeconomic groups.

In one early line of work, Waber (1976) sought to compare male and female adolescents who differed in age and physical maturation as well as strength in verbal versus spatial ability. She used Wechsler Digit Symbol, Stroop Color Naming, and PMA Word Fluency tests as a combination score to represent verbal ability, and Wechsler Block Design, Embedded Figures, and PMA Spatial subtests combined to represent spatial ability. A difference score for verbal minus spatial ability was then computed for each person; it correlated $-.14$ with a total IQ score, and so seemed mostly free of G variance. Figure 6.4 shows the result. Clearly, maturation and not age or sex related to the verbal versus spatial difference; early maturers appear stronger in verbal ability, whereas late maturers appear stronger in spatial ability. Early maturation may allow early development of facility in verbal symbolic processing, which in turn may interfere with continuing development of the more primitive, visual spatial processing facility. Late maturation may allow more early development of spatial ability as well as delayed development of verbal ability. The oft-noted verbal versus spatial difference between males and females thus perhaps arises primarily from the fact that females mature earlier than males on average; maturation, not gender, may be the important underlying mediator of the ability profile difference.

Figure 6.4
Mean Values of Difference Scores for Each Grouping of Sex, Maturation, and Age Level

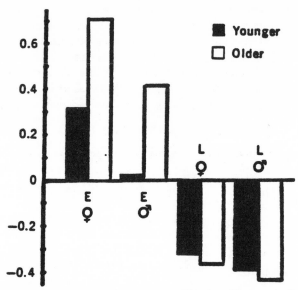

Source: Reprinted with permission from Waber, D. P. (1976) Sex differences in Cognition: A function of maturation rate? *Science, 192*, 572–573. Copyright 1976 American Association for the Advancement of Science.
Note: Positive values indicate that the verbal score is greater than the spatial score, and negative values indicate that the spatial score is greater than the verbal score.

Lohman (1994) elaborated the verbal versus spatial profile contrast for males and females by arraying ability tests along a continuum according to the size of the average gender differences each displayed. This is shown in Figure 6.5. The data came from a battery of ability tests administered to a large sample of high school students (see Marshalek, Lohman, & Snow, 1983). The continuum sharpens considerably our focus on the tests and constructs that do and do not distinguish males and females. The average female advantage appears in perceptual speed, spelling, sequencing, and verbal fluency, not primarily in verbal comprehension. The average male advantage appears in Gestalt closure identification, visualization, visual ideational fluency, and field independence. Lohman also brought in other evidence that fast phonological coding versus vivid visual imagery is a key to the contrast. And he added research by Riding (1983; Riding & Dyer, 1980) suggesting that an ipsative score contrasting imagery versus semantic coding relates strongly to personality; children showing more imagistic processing are more likely to be introverted, whereas children preferring semantic processing are likely to be extroverted. It is also known that extroversion and introversion develop at different rates and relate to ability and achievement

Figure 6.5
A Continuum of Sex Differences in Abilities

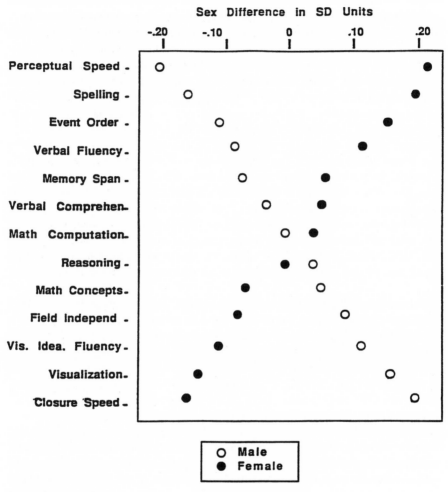

Source: Lohman (1994).

differently across ages and gender groups. Maturation differences may also mediate some of these relationships. Thus, it is a misleading and simplistic over-
generalization to characterize the profile difference merely as gender-linked
verbal versus spatial ability. The more complex profile difference would appear
to provide entry into a deeper psychology that has practical as well as theoretical
significance. But the complex interrelations of cognitive and personality development and maturation need much further analysis.

In a study with a somewhat different approach, Rosén (1995) also investigated gender differences in profiles of cognitive abilities. She fitted a hierarchical model to a battery of 32 tests administered to a large sample of 12- and 13-year-old males and females and identified 13 factors of different degrees of generality. Among the factors obtained were a general factor (G), interpretable as G_f, and the broad factors of G_c and G_v. Several narrow spatial, verbal, and numerical achievement factors were also identified. Rosén then went on to study gender differences in means and variances of the latent variables of the hierarchical model and found, among other things, average differences in favor of females with respect to G and G_c, and differences favoring males on G_v and numerical achievement. There also were differences favoring males on some of the narrow spatial and verbal factors.

Rosén also investigated gender differences in the traditional, univariate manner, studying one test at a time. Interestingly, the univariate and the multivariate analyses yielded quite different results, there being many fewer gender differences in the univariate analyses. Thus, univariate analysis failed to bring out the differences in favor of males in spatial and numerical abilities and the difference with respect to G in favor of females. One reason for the differences in pattern of results is that the multivariate representation of profile differences reorganizes the many observed variables into a more limited number of latent variables, which allows for a more powerful analysis. But another reason is that the univariate approach fails to disentangle the multiple sources of influence on each test score. For example, according to the hierarchical model, performance on a spatial test is influenced by G and G_v, as well as by a narrow spatial factor. If there are gender differences in opposite directions on these latent variables (i.e., females higher on G, males higher on G_v), these will cancel, leaving no observable gender differences in test performance.

Other work has examined racial, ethnic, and socioeconomic differences in ability profiles. Studies conducted by Lesser and his colleagues (see Lesser, Fifer, & Clark, 1965; Stodolsky & Lesser, 1967) reported ability profile differences for first-grade children in four racial-ethnic groups in New York and Boston. Figure 6.6 shows the average profiles for Jewish, Chinese, African-American, and Puerto Rican children on verbal, reasoning, numerical, and spatial ability (using tests similar to Thurstone's PMA tests of the same name). Social class differences were also investigated, but the profile differences seemed to be associated only with race-ethnicity; social class related only to the average level of each ability, not to the profile variations.

However, Feldman (1973; Feldman & Johnson, 1971; see also Lesser, 1973) criticized the methods used in this work on various grounds. The main concern, for our present purposes, was that the group profiles might not validly reflect the actual profiles of the individuals in each group. It is well known that aggregating individual profiles (or learning curves; see Estes, 1956) can result in group profiles that represent no one in the group. Feldman therefore reanalyzed the Lesser data using a measure of individual profile similarity that ignored racial-ethnic or social group membership and then a scaling and clustering pro-

Figure 6.6
Average Profiles of Normalized Mental Abilities Scores for Four Ethnic Groups

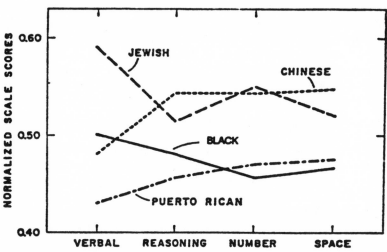

Source: Adapted from Feldman (1973).

cedure to identify groups of persons with empirically similar profiles. Some 26 profile groups could be distinguished in this way; using further rules, these could be reduced to 10 profile families. But neither profile groups nor families could be mapped easily into the matrix of four racial-ethnic groups by two social class–level groups with which Lesser and his colleagues had started. Thus, individual ability profiles and average group profiles can be quite different; one often cannot predict one from the other. It is evident that individual differences in profiles should be examined first. Generalizations about groups can then be conditioned by knowledge of individual distributions. This admonition applies to the previous work on gender as well as it does in the present connection.

Multidimensionality of Educational Achievement

Educational achievement is often represented by a single score, but there is much to be gained by looking at profiles of outcomes instead. Several studies illustrate this point.

Early work by Härnqvist (1968), among others, demonstrated the effect of education on the development of intelligence. In a replication and extension of Härnqvist's study, Balke-Aurell (1982) went on to investigate effects of type of education and occupation on profiles of verbal and spatial abilities. Data came from a Swedish longitudinal study of about 10,000 students who were followed from age 13 to age 18. In the first wave of data collection in grade 6, three cognitive tests (verbal, spatial, and inductive) were administered. At age 18, as part of military enlistment, practically every male in the sample performed a test battery with four tests (verbal, spatial, inductive, and technical). Every year, course choice and, when relevant, occupation were also recorded. Courses and occupations were then classified into verbal and spatial/technical categories. In the analysis, changes in verbal and spatial abilities were investigated as a function of types of education and occupation, controlling for abilities at age 13. This analysis showed an effect of type of education on the profile of abilities, such that students with spatial/technical courses increased their spatial ability, whereas students with verbally oriented courses increased their verbal ability.

Muthén, Khoo, and Goff (1994) reanalyzed some of the 1992 National Assessment of Educational Progress (NAEP) data for mathematics in grades 8 and 12. First, they used a latent variable modeling approach to investigate whether one general mathematics achievement factor sufficed to account for performance differences. The model was specified as an incomplete data model (see, e.g., Muthén, Kaplan, & Hollis, 1987), which for each grade comprised 26 groups of cases that had been given different combinations of 49 "testlets" in a matrix sampling design. This approach made it possible to study the dimensionality of a large set of mathematics items, which differed in response format and content. A one-factor model did not fit the data; to achieve an acceptable level of fit the model had to be extended with several special achievement factors, representing performance in Measurement, Data Analysis and Statistics, Geometry, and Algebra. These factors were taken to be orthogonal to one another and to the general mathematics factor.

Having established multidimensionality, Muthén et al. (1994) went on to formulate a structural equation model relating the outcome dimensions to background variables, such as gender, ethnicity, and courses taken. The latent outcome variables were found to be differently related to the background variables, and the authors suggested that such differential patterns may reflect differences in curricular emphasis, differences in opportunity to learn, and the effects of differential course choice. For example, it was found that Asian-American students showed much higher performance than Euro-American students on algebra but that there was only a small difference between the groups with respect to the general factor.

In a study with similar purposes, mathematics and science achievement tests at grades 8 and 10 in the National Educational Longitudinal Study of 1988 (NELS:88) were subjected to item-level factor analyses as well as cognitive process analyses (for details, see Hamilton, Nussbaum, Kupermintz, Kerkhoven, & Snow, 1995; Kupermintz, Ennis, Hamilton, Talbert, & Snow, 1995). Separate achievement factors could be established to represent Math Knowledge (MK), Math Reasoning (MR), Quantitative Science (QS), Spatial Mechanical Reasoning (SM), and Basic Science Knowledge and Reasoning (BKR). Regression analyses then demonstrated that achievement factors related to different patterns of prior achievement predictors and also other educational and personal characteristics. For example, course-taking patterns and instructional variables predicted MK more strongly than they did MR, and different courses predicted the different science factors. Moreover, gender and ethnic differences showed quite different patterns across the achievement factors. Males averaged higher than females on MR, QS, and especially on SM; no difference occurred on BKR, and on MK, females averaged slightly higher than males. Asian-American students averaged higher than Euro-Americans on MK, not on MR. African-American students averaged lower than Euro-Americans particularly on MR and SM; much smaller differences occurred on BKR, MK, and QS. The results clearly suggested that profile differences could be constructed to represent multidimensional achievement with significant value for further research and evaluation purposes.

Still another study demonstrates the multidimensionality of educational achievement in a different way. Gustafsson and Balke (1993) investigated relations between a battery of tests of cognitive abilities administered in the sixth grade and school achievement in the ninth grade. The test battery, which was administered to 866 students, comprised 16 ability tests. To these tests a latent variable model with orthogonal factors was fitted. The model included a general factor, interpretable as G_f, along with the broad factors G_c and G_v. There were also about half a dozen narrow factors, representing, among others, narrow spatial abilities. School achievement was measured with course grades in 17 different subject matter areas. The course grades were used as dependent variables in a series of regression analyses, and a latent variable model was also fitted to the grades. This model included a general achievement factor, along with domain-specific achievement factors in science, social science, language, and spatial-practical performance. When course grades were regressed onto ability factors, it was found that G_f and G_c were related to all outcomes, and G_v contributed some variance to achievement in Technology, Handicraft, and Drawing. However, even though G_f and G_c showed significant relation to all outcomes, the relative importance of these abilities varied for different outcomes. For English, for example, G_f and G_c contributed about equally, but for Mathematics, G_f was much more important than G_c. The differentiation was brought out even more clearly when the latent variables in the model for course grades were used as dependent variables. In this analysis, G_f and G_c were both related to the general achievement factor, but only G_f related to the narrow science achievement factor. For high achievement on the narrow spatial-practical factor, only G_v and a narrow visualization ability were of any importance.

These results all show that it is worthwhile to consider multiple outcomes, and they also demonstrate that more than one general cognitive ability factor is needed in the prediction of school achievement; at a minimum, it seems that differentiation between the broad abilities G_f, G_c, and G_v is important. This study also provides indications that it may be necessary to bring more narrow abilities into such analyses in the future.

Predictions of Job Performance

As already noted, many studies seem to indicate that little is gained by considering special abilities over and above G in predicting job performance. But there is reason to believe that the methodological problems also identified above may have contributed to this negative conclusion about the value of ability profiles. Consider this last example.

Muthén and Gustafsson (1996; also Gustafsson & Muthén, 1996) compared a hierarchical latent variable approach with a regression approach for assessing the predictive validity of the Armed Services Vocational Aptitude Battery (AS-VAB). The study was a reanalysis of some of the data from Project A's Concurrent Validity study (Campbell & Zook, 1991), in which the ASVAB was augmented with tests measuring spatial ability, psychomotor skills, perceptual speed, and reasoning. Hands-on performance scores were also collected for nine military jobs. A model with six factors was fitted to a subset of the variables in the test battery. One of these was a general factor, which clearly could be interpreted as G_f. Other factors were G_c, and Perceptual Speed (PS), Mathematical Achievement (Math), and a broad spatial factor with an emphasis on mechanical tests (G_v/Mech).

When the criterion performance scores were regressed onto the six orthogonal latent variables, it was generally found that two or three latent variables showed significant relation to outcome. For all jobs, G_f was a significant predictor. G_v/Mech was a significant predictor for all jobs except for Administrative. For many jobs, the contributions of G_f and G_v/Mech were about the same size (e.g., Infantryman, Cannon Crewman, Tank Crewman). For Vehicle Mechanic, the G_v/Mech contribution was considerably larger than the G_f contribution, and for some jobs, G_f contributed substantially more than G_v/Mech (e.g., Radio Operator, Medical, and Military Police). For most of the jobs, G_c was not a significant predictor, but it did contribute some variance for Radio Operator, Motor Transport, and Medical jobs. The narrow abilities typically did not contribute any variance, but PS did predict for Vehicle Mechanic.

Regression analyses also were conducted in which composite scores derived from the ASVAB were used as independent variables. These included, for example, the overall Air Force Qualification Test (AFQT) score and a Technical score, or Verbal (V), Quantitative (Q), or Technical (T) scores. The pattern of contributions of abilities to the criterion performance tests was in these analyses quite different from that obtained in the analyses of latent variables. For example, for Cannon Crewman, where the latent variable analysis showed G_f and G_v/Mech to be equally strong predictors, only the Technical composite had a significant contribution when entered along with the AFQT. When V, Q, and T were used as three correlated independent variables, none of the partial regression coefficients reached significance. These results thus agree with the implications of our analysis of artificial data demonstrated in Figures 6.1 through 6.3; namely, an orthogonal model of latent broad and narrow ability factors will often show the value of ability profile distinctions, where models based on correlated predictors will fail to do so. It appears that ability profiles have at least sometimes been dismissed as useless based on faulty methodology.

SUMMARY

Ability profiles have a checkered history. As theories of multiple abilities grew through this century, high hopes for the usefulness of profiles grew with them. Some evidence has indeed shown the value of ability profiles in research and in various practical uses. But much evidence has also called their use into question. Profiles have often appeared to add little beyond a global G measure, especially in prediction studies. It is clear, however, that profiles involve complicated psychometrics that, if not properly addressed, can subvert intended uses. Moreover, important weaknesses in some of the standard methods used in evaluating profiles may have often misrepresented their strengths and weaknesses.

When properly constructed, validated, and interpreted, ability profiles can be useful. They should be valuable in academic and career counseling. They can aid in diagnosing malfunctions in cognitive performance and in isolating particular learning disabilities. And they can be useful in research on differences in multiple dimensions, among groups as well as individuals, in both aptitude and achievement. Although the evidence in support of profile use for selection and classification in education, training, and employment situations is currently scattered, specialized, and quite weak overall, further research with improved methodology seems justified. Given the hierarchical model of ability organization, new research using the methods suggested here should tell us where and when a global construct of G is sufficient and how different profiles of more specialized broad and narrow ability factors come into important play in particular situations.

REFERENCES

Anderson, M. (1992). *Intelligence and development. A cognitive theory.* Oxford: Blackwell.

Balke-Aurell, G. (1982). *Changes in ability as related to educational and occupational experience.* Göteborg: Acta Universitatis Gothoburgensis.

Brody, N. (1992). *Intelligence* (2nd ed.). San Diego: Academic Press.

Campbell, J. P., & Zook, L. M. (1991). *Improving the selection, classification, and utilization of army enlisted personnel: Final report on Project A* (Research Report 1597) Alexandria, VA: U.S. Army Research Institute for the Behavioral and Social Sciences.

Carroll, J. B. (1993). *Human cognitive abilities. A survey of factor-analytic studies.* Cambridge: Cambridge University Press.

Cattell, R. B. (1963). Theory of fluid and crystallized intelligence: A critical experiment. *Journal of Educational Psychology, 54,* 1–22.

Cattell, R. B. (1971). *Abilities: Their structure, growth, and action.* Boston: Houghton Mifflin.

Cattell, R. B. (1987). *Intelligence: Its structure, growth and action.* New York: North-Holland.

Coan, R. W. (1964). Facts, factors and artifacts: The quest for psychological meaning. *Psychological Review, 71,* 123–140.

Cronbach, L. J. (1990). *Essentials of psychological testing* (5th ed.). New York: Harper and Row.

Cronbach, L. J., Gleser, G. C., Nanda, H., & Rajaratnam, N. (1972). *The dependability of behavioral measurements: Theory of generalizability for scores and profiles.* New York: Wiley.

Cronbach, L. J., & Snow, R. E. (1977). *Aptitudes and instructional methods.* New York: Irvington.

Estes, W. K. (1956). The problem of inference from curves based on group data. *Psychological Bulletin, 53,* 134–140.

Feldman, D. H. (1973). Problems in the analysis of patterns of abilities. *Child Development, 44,* 12–18.

Feldman, D. H., & Johnson, L. E. (1971, April). *A reanalysis of Lesser's patterns of mental abilities data.* Paper presented at the annual meeting of the Society for Research in Child Development, Minneapolis.

Fleishman, E. A., & Quaintance, M. K. (1984). *Taxonomies of human performance: The description of human tasks.* Orlando, FL: Academic Press.

Ford, M. E. (1986). A living systems conceptualization of social intelligence: Outcomes, processes, and developmental change. In R. J. Sternberg (Ed.), *Advances in the psychology of human intelligence* (Vol. 3, pp. 119–171). Hillsdale, NJ: Lawrence Erlbaum Associates.

French, J. W. (1951). The description of aptitude and achievement tests in terms of rotated factors. *Psychometric Monographs,* No. 5.

Gardner, H. (1983). *Frames of mind: The theory of multiple intelligences.* New York: Basic Books.

Gardner, H. (1993). *Multiple intelligences: The theory in practice.* New York: Basic Books.

Guilford, J. P. (1967). *The nature of human intelligence.* New York: McGraw-Hill.

Guilford, J. P. (1972). Thurstone's primary mental abilities and structure-of-intellect abilities. *Psychological Bulletin, 77,* 129–143.

Guilford, J. P. (1981). Higher-order structure-of-intellect abilities. *Multivariate Behavioral Research, 16,* 411–435.

Guilford, J. P., & Hoepfner, R. (1971). *The analysis of intelligence.* New York: McGraw-Hill.

Gustafsson, J. E. (1976). *Verbal and figural aptitudes in relation to instructional methods. Studies in aptitude-treatment interactions.* Göteborg: Acta Universitatis Gothoburgensis.

Gustafsson, J. E. (1984). A unifying model for the structure of intellectual abilities. *Intelligence, 8,* 179–203.

Gustafsson, J. E. (1988). Hierarchical models of individual differences in cognitive abilities. In R. J. Sternberg (Ed.), *Advances in the psychology of human intelligence* (Vol. 4, pp. 35–71). Hillsdale, NJ: Lawrence Erlbaum Associates.

Gustafsson, J. E. (1989). Broad and narrow abilities in research on learning and instruction. In R. Kanfer, P. L. Ackerman, & R. Cudeck (Eds.), *Abilities, motivation, and methodology. The Minnesota symposium on learning and individual differences* (pp. 203–237). Hillsdale, NJ: Erlbaum.

Gustafsson, J. E. (1992). The relevance of factor analysis for the study of group differences. *Multivariate Experimental Research, 27*(2), 239–247.

Gustafsson, J. -E., & Balke, G. (1993). General and specific abilities as predictors of school achievement. *Multivariate Behavioral Research, 28*(4), 407–434.

Gustafsson, J. -E., & Muthén, B. (1996). *The nature of the general factor in hierarchical models of the structure of cognitive abilities: Alternative models tested on data from regular and experimental military enlistment tests.* Unpublished manuscript, School of Education, UCLA.

Gustafsson, J. -E., & Undheim, J. O. (1996). Individual differences in cognitive functions. In D. C. Berliner & R. C. Calfee (Eds.), *The handbook of educational psychology* (pp. 186–242). New York: Macmillan.

Hamilton, L. S., Nussbaum, E. M., Kupermintz, H., Kerkhoven, J. I. M., & Snow, R. E. (1995). Enhancing the validity and usefulness of large-scale educational assessments: II. NELS:88 science achievement. *American Educational Research Journal, 31*, 555–581.

Harman, H. (1967). *Modern factor analysis,* Chicago: University of Chicago Press.

Härnqvist, K. (1968). Relative changes in intelligence from 13 to 18. II. Results. *Scandinavian Journal of Psychology, 9*, 65–82.

Holland, J. L. (1985). *Making vocational choices: A theory of vocational personalities and work environments.* Englewood Cliffs, NJ: Prentice-Hall.

Horn, J. L. (1968). Organization of abilities and the development of intelligence. *Psychological Review, 72*, 242–259.

Horn, J. L. (1969). On the internal consistency reliability of factors. *Multivariate Behavioral Research, 4*, 115–125.

Horn, J. L. (1986). Intellectual ability concepts. In R. J. Sternberg (Ed.), *Advances in the psychology of human intelligence* (Vol. 3, pp. 35–77). Hillsdale, NJ: Lawrence Erlbaum Associates.

Horn, J. L. (1989). Models of intelligence. In R. L. Linn (Ed.), *Intelligence. Measurement, theory and public policy* (pp. 29–73). Urbana: University of Illinois Press.

Horn, J. L., & Cattell, R. B. (1966). Refinement and test of the theory of fluid and crystallized intelligence. *Journal of Educational Psychology, 57*, 253–270.

Humphreys, L. G. (1981). The primary mental ability. In M. P. Friedman, J. P. Das, & N. O'Connor (Eds.), *Intelligence and learning* (pp. 87–102). New York: Plenum.

Jensen, A. R. (1992). Commentary: Vehicles of G. *Psychological Science, 3* (5), 275–278.

Kaufman, A. S. (1979). *Intelligent testing with the WISC–R.* New York: Wiley.

Kaufman, A. S. (1994). *Intelligent testing with the WISC–III.* New York: Wiley.

Kupermintz, H., Ennis, M. N., Hamilton, L. S., Talbert, J. E., & Snow, R. E. (1995). Enhancing the validity and usefulness of large-scale educational assessments: I. NELS:88 mathematics achievement. *American Educational Research Journal, 31*, 525–554.

Lamiell, J. T. (1981). Toward an idiothetic psychology of personality. *American Psychologist, 36*, 276–289.

Lamiell, J. T. (1987). *The psychology of personality: An epistomological inquiry.* New York: Columbia University Press.

Lesser, G. S. (1973). Problems in the analysis of patterns of abilities: A reply. *Child Development, 44,* 19–20.

Lesser, G. S., Fifer, G., & Clark, D. H. (1965). Mental abilities of children from different social-class and cultural groups. *Monographs of the Society for Research in Child Development, 30* (4).

Lohman, D. F. (1994). Spatially gifted, verbally inconvenienced. In N. Colangelo, S. G. Assouline, & D. L. Ambroson (Eds.), *Talent development: Vol. II.* Proceedings from the 1993 Henry B. and Jocelyn Wallace National Research Symposium on Talent Development (pp. 251–264). Dayton, OH: Ohio University Press.

Lohman, D. F., & Rocklin, T. (1995). Current and recurring issues in the assessment of intelligence and personality. In D. H. Saklofske & M. Zeidner (Eds.), *International handbook of personality and intelligence* (pp. 447–474). New York: Plenum.

Marshalek, B., Lohman, D. F., & Snow, R. E. (1983). The complexity continuum in the radex and hierarchical models of intelligence. *Intelligence, 7,* 107–128.

McDermott, P. A., Fantuzzo, J. W., & Glutting J. J. (1990). Just say no to subtest analysis: A critique on Wechsler theory and practice. *Journal of Psycho-educational Assessment, 8,* 290–302.

McDermott, P. A., Glutting, J. J., Watkins, M. W., & Baggaley, A. R. (1992). Illusions of meaning in the ipsative assessment of children's ability. *Journal of Special Education, 25,* 504–526.

McNemar, Q. (1964). Lost: Our intelligence? Why? *American Psychologist, 19,* 871–882.

Messick, S. (1992) Multiple intelligences or multilevel intelligence? Selective emphasis on distinctive properties of hierarchy: On Gardner's *Frames of mind* and Sternberg's *Beyond IQ* in the context of theory and research on the structure of human abilities. *Psychological Inquiry, 3,* 365–384.

Muthén, B. (1994). *A note on predictive validity from a latent variable perspective.* Unpublished manuscript, School of Education, UCLA.

Muthén, B., & Gustafsson, J. -E. (1996). *ASVAB-based job performance prediction and selection. Latent variab; modeling versus regression analysis.* Unpublished manuscript, School of Education, UCLA.

Muthén, B. O., Kaplan, D., & Hollis, M. (1987). On structural equation modeling with data that are not missing completely at random. *Psychometrika, 52,* 431–462.

Muthén, B. O., Khoo, S. T., & Nelson Goff, G. (1994). *Multidimensional description of subgroup differences in mathematics achievement data from the 1992 National Assessment of Educational Progress.* Paper presented at the annual meeting of the American Educational Research Association.

Ree, M. J., & Earles, H. A. (1992). Intelligence is the best predictor of job performance. *Current Directions in Psychological Science, 1,* 86–89.

Riding, R. J. (1983). Extraversion, field independence, and performance on cognitive tasks in twelve-year-old children. *Research in Education, 29,* 1–9.

Riding, R. J., & Dyer, V. A. (1980). The relationship between extraversion and verbal-imagery learning. *Personality and Individual Differences, 1,* 273–279.

Rorer, L. G. (1990). Personality assessment: A conceptual survey. In L. A. Pervin (Ed.), *Handbook of personality: Theory and research* (pp. 693–718). New York: Guilford Press.

Rosén, M. (1995). Gender differences in structure, means and variances of hierarchically ordered ability dimensions. *Learning and Instruction, 5*(1), 37–62.

Schmid, J., & Leiman, J. M. (1957). The development of hierarchical factor solutions. *Psychometrika, 22,* 53–61.

Schmidt, F. L., & Ones, D. S. (1992). Personnel selection. *Annual Review of Psychology, 43,* 627–670.

Snow, R. E. (1977). Research on aptitudes: A progress report. In L. S. Shulman (Ed.), *Review of research in education* (Vol. 4, pp. 50–105). Itasca, IL: Peacock.

Snow, R. E. (1985, November). Review of Gardner, H. (1983). *Frames of mind: The theory of multiple intelligences. American Journal of Education,* pp. 101–112.

Snow, R. E. (1987). Aptitude complexes. In R. E. Snow and M. J. Farr (Eds.), *Aptitude, learning, and instruction: Vol. 3. Conative and affective process analyses* (pp. 11–34). Hillsdale, NJ: Lawrence Erlbaum Associates.

Spearman, C. (1904). ''General intelligence,'' objectively determined and measured. *American Journal of Psychology, 15,* 201–293.

Spearman, C. (1927). *The abilities of man.* London: Macmillan.

Stanley, J. C. (1971). Reliability. In R. L. Thorndike (Ed.), *Educational measurement* (pp. 356–442). Washington, DC: American Council on Education.

Sternberg, R. J., Wagner, R. K., Williams, W. M., & Horvath, J. A. (1995). Testing common sense. *American Psychologist, 50,* 912–927.

Stodolsky, S. S., & Lesser, G. S. (1967). Learning patterns in the disadvantaged. *Harvard Educational Review, 37* (4), 546–593.

Thorndike, E. L. (1912). The permanence of interests and their relation to abilities. *Popular Science Monthly, 81,* 449–456.

Thorndike, E. L. (1920). Intelligence and its uses. *Harper's Magazine, 140,* 227–235.

Thurstone, L. L. (1931). Multiple factor analysis. *Psychological Review, 38,* 406–427.

Thurstone, L. L. (1938). Primary mental abilities. *Psychometric Monographs,* No. 1.

Thurstone, L. L. (1947). *Multiple factor analysis.* Chicago: University of Chicago Press.

Undheim, J. O. (1981). On intelligence II: A neo-Spearman model to replace Cattell's theory of fluid and crystallized intelligence. *Scandinavian Journal of Psychology, 22,* 181–187.

Undheim, J. O., & Gustafsson, J. -E. (1987). The hierarchical organization of cognitive abilities: Restoring general intelligence through the use of linear structural relations (LISREL). *Multivariate Behavioral Research, 22,* 149–171.

Vernon, P. E. (1950). *The structure of human abilities.* London: Methuen.

Waber, D. P. (1976). Sex differences in cognition: A function of maturation rate? *Science, 192,* 572–573.

7

Intelligence Revised: The Planning, Attention, Simultaneous, Successive (PASS) Cognitive Processing Theory

Jack A. Naglieri and J. P. Das

THE PASS THEORY

The concept of human intelligence is one of the most important contributions made by psychologists since its beginnings more than a century ago (Anastasi, 1988). In that time psychologists have developed a considerable base of knowledge about human intellectual functioning in theoretical and applied areas. Theoretical work related to intelligence was conducted by individuals such as: Anokhin (1969), Bernstein (1967), Carroll (1993), Cattell (1963, 1971), Das (1972), Eysenck (1939), Gardner (1983), Gazzaniga (1970), Guilford (1967), Hernandez-Peon (1966), Horn (1985), Hunt (1990), Jensen (1982), Leontiev (1978), Lindsley (1960), Luria (1966), Magoun (1963), Miller, Galanter, and Pribram (1960), Neisser (1967), Piaget (1950), Pribram (1971), Spearman (1927), Sternberg (1977), Thurstone (1938), and Vygotsky (1978). Some of the theories of intelligence differ substantially from each other—for example, the view that intelligence is best described as a single general factor (e.g., Jensen) or is multifaceted (e.g., Guilford), which has been a long-standing conflict among many theorists. Another important distinction is that some based their view on extensive statistical methods to uncover mental structures (e.g., Horn, Jensen), while others rely on the author's interpretation of psychological observations and experimental findings (e.g., Gardner, Piaget), and still others use neuropsychological, information-processing, or cognitive psychological research as the basis for their theories (e.g., Luria, Lindsley, Pribram).

In contrast to theoretical research on intelligence were the efforts of those who published *tests* to meet the needs of applied psychologists. IQ tests were essentially developed in a parallel manner to theoretical positions and typically with little influence from theoretical views. For example, even though the Stanford-Binet scale is based on the view of general ability, Thorndike, Hagen, and Sattler clearly state that "there is no evidence that Binet and his successors were influenced by Spearman's theorizing, or that Spearman had Binet's test-making activities specifically in mind as he developed his formulation of g and the multitudinous s specifics" (1986, p. 1). Moreover, according to Vernon (1979), there is no reason to believe that the Binet-Simon scale consisted of more than a "haphazard collection of mental tasks" (p. 4).

The actual tests that have been used to measure intelligence have remained essentially the same despite the accumulation of considerable psychological knowledge about human intelligence. The isolation of theoretical and applied psychology relating to intelligence is apparent in Brody's (1992) statement: "I do not believe that our intellectual progress has had a major impact on the development of tests of intelligence" (p. 355). Nevertheless, the Wechsler scales remain the most often used measure of intelligence in educational and clinical settings. It should be remembered, however, that the Wechsler and Binet tests (often referred to as "tradition tests" [Naglieri, 1996a]) were most recently developed in 1916 by Binet and in 1939 by Wechsler. Notwithstanding the fact that these tests have been revised several times during this century, they remain essentially the same as when they were initially introduced. Even though they could be seen as dated technology, these tests have dominated practice by psychologists for more than 50 years and have often been used as the criterion measures of intelligence in psychology.

Rationale for the PASS Theory

The PASS theory was developed to integrate contemporary knowledge from both theoretical and applied areas in psychology. To do so, we have provided a theory of intelligence that has its focus on cognitive processes and a battery of tests to measure these processes (Das•Naglieri Cognitive Assessment System [CAS]; Naglieri & Das, 1996). We seek to improve intelligence at both a theoretical and applied level by providing a theory and approach to its measurement. We have replaced the term intelligence with cognitive functions, and focus on processes rather than on abilities and have summarized some of our assumptions below:

1. Traditional intelligence tests have defined intelligence and dominated intelligence testing in psychology and education because of their good standardization and psychometric properties, but they have not changed substantially since their introduction in 1916 (Binet) and 1939 (Wechsler).

2. Psychology's research on cognitive functioning has advanced considerably during the 1900s, especially since the 1960s.

3. In spite of elaborate methods, such as profile analysis, to interpret traditional IQ tests,

these methods offer limited ways to understand the diverse forms of individual intellectual variations that are found, therefore offering a limited understanding of academic failures, as well as successes, and intervention options.

4. Traditional intelligence tests have limitations when used for differential diagnosis, especially, for example, with those who have learning disabilities, attention deficits, and traumatic brain injury because they are based on a general view of ability that offers little theoretical or practical specificity.

5. We agree with Crocker and Algina (1986) that "psychological measurement, even though it is based on observable responses, would have little meaning or usefulness unless it could be interpreted in light of the underlying theoretical construct" (p. 7). The PASS theory provides a framework for the essential elements of human cognitive functioning that interact with and influence the base of knowledge and provide an important dimension of human performance.

Given these considerations, the following aims of the PASS theory are provided:

1. A theory of intelligence should be based on the view that intelligence is best described within the context of cognitive processes, and the term *cognitive processing* should be used to replace *intelligence*.

2. A theory of cognitive processing should inform the user about those processes that are related to academic and job successes and difficulties, have relevance to differential diagnosis, and provide guidance to the development of effective programming for intervention.

3. A view of cognitive functioning should be firmly based on a contemporary theory that has been proposed, tested, and shown to have validity on several dimensions.

4. A test of cognitive processing should follow closely from the theory of cognition on which it is based.

5. A multidimensional theory of cognitive functioning and a means to measure the constructs could provide the advantage of both a theoretically specified group of cognitive functions and an alternative to traditional intelligence tests.

6. A test of cognitive processing should evaluate an individual using tests that are as free from acquired knowledge as possible, accepting that no such test can be completely free from knowledge base.

PASS Theory of Cognitive Processing

The PASS theory is the result of the merging of both theoretical and applied psychology most recently summarized by Das, Naglieri, and Kirby (1994). Das and his colleagues (Das, Kirby, & Jarman, 1979) initiated the link between Luria (1966, 1970, 1973, 1976, 1980, 1982), the "most frequently cited Soviet scholar in American, British, and Canadian psychology periodicals" (Solso & Hoffman, 1991, p. 251), and the field of intelligence when they suggested that intelligence could be seen from the cognitive perspective we now call PASS.

The theoretical work described by Luria has its roots in experimental psychological research and writings published during the middle part of this century. Luria's recognition of those whose ideas he incorporated into a cohesive view of the working brain is apparent in his writings (especially Luria, 1966, 1973). When he described research on the "reticular formation, the *first* functional unit of the brain . . . —an apparatus maintaining cortical tone and waking state and regulating these states in accordance with the actual demands confronting the organism" (Luria, 1973, p. 47), he credited the discovery to works of French, Hernandez-Peon, and Livingston (1955), Hernandez-Peon (1969), Lindsley (1960, 1961), Magoun (1958, 1963), Moruzzi and Magoun (1949), Pribram (1960, 1966b, 1967), and Segundo, Naquet, and Buser (1955). The workings of the *second* functional unit, which includes the "two basic forms of activity of the cerebral cortex, by which different aspects of the outside world may be reflected" (Luria, 1966, p. 74), were originally described by Sechenov (1878) and later by Arana (1961), Goldstein (1927), Sokolov (1960), and Ajuriaguerra and Hecaen (1960) (cited in Luria, 1966). Finally, Luria (1973) credits knowledge about the *third* functional unit, which provides for the regulation of human conscious activity, to Anokhin (1978), Bernstein (1935, 1957, 1966), Jacobsen (1935), Miller, Galanter, and Pribram (1960), and Pavlov (1949). Additionally, Luria recognized the contributions of Vygotsky (1978), Leontiev (1959), and Zaporozhets (1960) that "higher mental processes are formed and take place on the basis of speech activity," especially within the context of social interaction (Luria, 1973, p. 93). These and other researchers and scholars provided the theoretical base for the theory we call PASS.

The initial work on the PASS theory began with the examination by Das (1972) of the differences between persons with and without mental retardation using tasks that were interpreted as measuring simultaneous and successive processes. This study and others that shortly followed—for example, a cross-cultural investigation of these two processes (Das, 1973)—led to the suggestion that simultaneous and successive synthesis could be included as an information-processing model for cognitive abilities (Das, Kirby, & Jarman, 1979). In their book *Simultaneous and Successive Cognitive Processes*, Das, Kirby, and Jarman (1979) described the information-integration model and tasks used to operationalize these processes along with a discussion of the need to further develop measures of attention and planning (see p. 54). At that point, evidence was provided that it was reasonable to use Luria's description of the three functional units to reconceptualize intelligence even though only simultaneous and successive tasks were developed. The use of planning, simultaneous, and successive experimental tasks was first reported by Ashman and Das (1980), who showed the distinctiveness of the tests used to measure these processes. Attention and planning tasks were developed and tested several years later and reported in the literature by Naglieri and Das (1988), Naglieri, Braden, and Gottling (1993), and Naglieri, Welch, and Braden (1994). The development and refinement of experimental tests to measure the various PASS processes and to evaluate their practical utility and validity are provided in more than 100 published papers and several books. There include, for example, works by Ashman (1978, 1982), Cummins and Das (1977, 1978, 1980), Das (1972, 1980, 1983, 1984), Das and Cummins (1979, 1982), Jarman (1978, 1980a, 1980b), Kirby (1982, 1984), Kirby and Das (1977, 1978, 1990), Kirby and Williams (1991), Leong (1980, 1984), Naglieri (1989a, 1989b, 1992, 1996b), and Naglieri and Das (1987, 1988, 1990). The relationships among these lines of research are provided in Figure 7.1.

The combination of theoretical and applied efforts that underlie the PASS theory have sufficient breadth and depth to give us ample evidence to support the view expressed by Das more than 20 years ago that Luria's description of the three functional units of the brain offers a viable conceptualization of human cognitive functioning. We therefore suggest that intelligence be reconceptualized as cognitive processes and defined as follows: Human intelligence is based upon the four essential activities of Planning, Attention, Simultaneous, and Successive cognitive processes that employ and alter an individual's base of knowledge. Planning processes are responsible for the generation and control of activity, the control of attentional and simultaneous/successive processes, and the utilization of knowledge; attention is responsible for focused cognitive activity; and simultaneous/successive processes are two forms of operating on information. These dimensions form the PASS theory we have proposed that views intelligence from the perspective of cognitive processes:

Human cognitive functioning includes three components:

attentional processes that provide focused cognitive activity;

information processes of two t nes (simultaneous and successive process); and

planning processes that provide the control of attention, utilization of information processes and knowledge, and intentionality and self-regulation to achieve a desired goal.

PASS Processes Defined

Planning. Planning is a mental process by which the individual determines, selects, and uses efficient solutions to problems. This includes intentionality, the development of plans of action, the evaluation of the effectiveness of these plans, regulation of the plans, verification, self-correction, and impulse control. The planning process provides an individual with the means to solve a problem for which no method of solution is immediately apparent. It may apply to complex or simple tasks and may involve attentional, simultaneous, and successive process. Once the need for a plan is apparent, the individual may search his or her base of knowledge for an approach. If one is not within the knowledge base, an initial plan of action may be developed and examined to decide if it is

Figure 7.1
Selected Research Underlying the PASS Theory

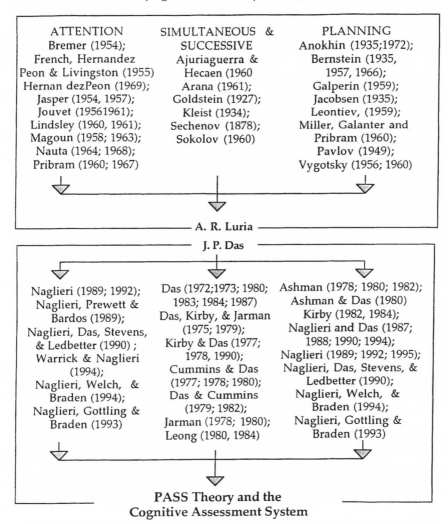

PASS Theory and the
Cognitive Assessment System

reasonable or not. If it is accepted, the plan is carried out until it produces an acceptable result or is revised or rejected in favor of a new plan. When a plan is put into action, its effectiveness may be monitored to determine if it should be continued, modified to achieve a more efficient result, or discarded and a new one generated. Planning is integral to all activities that involve intentionality and where there is a need for some method to solve a problem.

Attention. Attention is a mental process by which the individual selectively attends to a particular stimulus and inhibits attending to competing stimuli. Although both arousal and selective attention comprise this component of the PASS model, adequate arousal is assumed, and selective attention is the dimension of greatest interest. Selective attention is a "specialized form of activation" (Luria, 1973, p. 265) that presumes a filter allowing selection of relevant stimuli and ignoring of others. Attention is involved in all activities requiring the focus of cognition. For example, a child's listening to a teacher's instruction over the noise in a classroom requires attentional process. Attention becomes increasingly difficult when nontarget stimuli are more salient than the target stimuli. Similarly, attention is important when examining the differences between different numbers with the same numerals such as 16.0, 61.0, 16.6, 16.1 (see Das, Naglieri, & Kirby, 1994).

Simultaneous. Simultaneous is a mental process by which the individual integrates stimuli into groups. The essence of simultaneous processing is that the elements of the stimuli must be interrelated for successful completion, what Luria (1966) called "surveyability." Simultaneously processed information is said to be surveyable because the elements are interrelated and accessible to inspection either through examination of the stimuli during the activity (as in design copying) or through recall of the stimuli (as in reproduction of a design from memory). Simultaneous processing may take place when stimuli are perceived (as when a child copies a design such as a cube), remembered (when the design is drawn from memory), or conceptualized (when the child reasons about a design as in Raven's [1956] or Naglieri's [1985, 1996c] figural matrices). Simultaneous processing is needed in language involving logical grammatical relations—for example, in comprehension of the question, Who is the person in the following statement: "My mother's father was his only son"? Thus, simultaneous processing can be applied to tests having nonverbal (matrices, block design) or verbal (logical-grammatical, or passage comprehension) content.

Successive. Successive is a mental process by which a person integrates stimuli in their specific serial order that forms a chainlike progression. The distinguishing quality of successive processing is that each element is only related to those that precede it, and these stimuli are not interrelated. For example, successive processing is needed for skilled movements (e.g., writing) because this activity requires "a series of movements which follow each other in a strictly defined order . . . without surveyability" (Luria, 1966, p. 78). In the early stages of the formation of the skilled movement, each successive link exists as a separate unit and may be taught as a specific step in a larger behavior. Only when each aspect becomes automatic can the initial stimulus in the chain become the signal that leads to the automatic execution of the complete successive action. Linguistic tasks involving successive processing require appreciation of the linearity of stimuli with no requirement for interrelating of the parts. For example, to answer the question, The girl hit the boy; who got hurt? the ordering of the words within the sentence must be considered and appreciated.

Aspects of the PASS Processes

The PASS processes, corresponding to the three functional units described by Luria (1966), form a "functional system (the term introduced and developed by Anokhin, 1935; 1940; 1949; 1963; 1968; 1972)" (Luria, 1973, p. 27) that has interrelated interdependent components that are closely related to the base of knowledge and are influenced by the cultural experiences of the individual. Knowledge base not only is conceptualized as a storehouse of knowledge and experience acquired in the individual's society and through formal education but also provides the motivational and affective orientation for the cognitive processing in which the individual is engaged. The PASS processes form functional systems, or a "working constellation" (Luria, 1966, p. 70) of cognitive activity, that allows individuals to perform the same task with the contribution of various processes and the participation of knowledge base as shown in Figure 7.2.

Functional System. The concept of functional system (composed of functional units) is important to the PASS theory because it provides an explanation of how individuals may solve the same task through the application of different combinations of processes and knowledge utilization. As described by Luria (1973, p. 28), a specific task can be performed using variable processes to bring about a constant result. What makes a functional system distinctive is that the components are interdependent and interacting to achieve various goals and that it is defined by its goal and not by its methods (Luria, 1973) (Naglieri & Sloutsky, 1995). This was illustrated by Hunt (1974), who described how progressive matrices could be solved using a gestalt or analytic approach, and Lawson and Kirby (1981), Kirby and Das (1990), and Kirby and Lawson (1983), who found that the application of these simultaneous or successive approaches to solving matrix items can be influenced by training. Although "the way in which the task is performed may vary considerably" (Luria, 1973, p. 28), that is, using a simultaneous or successive solution, the same result was obtained (selection of the option).

Interrelated Interdependent Functional Systems. "Man's mental processes in general, and his conscious activity in particular, always take place with the participation of all three units" (Luria, 1973, p. 43). Thus, cognitive activities related to specific brain structures provide processes that allow the individual to function so that environmental demands may be addressed and these demands influence which processes may dominate. The PASS processes are interdependent, and at the same time, each process "plays its own part in the organization" of activity (Luria, 1966, p. 44). The four processes act in concert as part of a complex functional system in all tasks performed in everyday life (Luria, 1973), although not every process is equally involved in every task. Effective functioning is accomplished through the integration of planning, attention, simultaneous, and successive process (as well as the base of knowledge) as demanded

Figure 7.2
The PASS Theory

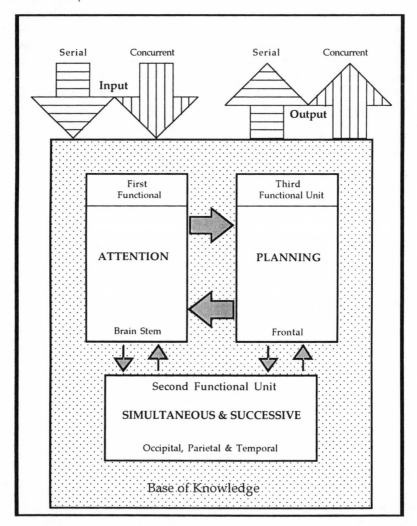

by the particular task. Although each type of process is an independent component with distinct functions, they merge in cognitive activity to form a complex functional system. Thus, planning, simultaneous, and successive processes interact to facilitate acquisition of knowledge, and at the same time, these higher functions depend on a proper state of arousal and attention to provide the opportunity for focused cognitive activity.

The interrelated nature of the PASS processes includes use of information to be processed through any of the receptors (eyes, ears, skin, muscle movements, etc.) and received in a serial (i.e., over time) or synchronous (i.e., concurrent) manner. That is, several stimuli may be presented to the individual at one time, or several stimuli may be presented one at a time (e.g., hearing two different words at the same time or two words in a series). Despite the type of presentation, the information is typically processed according to the requirements of the task and with the participation of all processes. An important implication of the interrelated nature of the PASS processes is that we view the four processes as interdependent. For example, planning, simultaneous, and successive processes require an adequate state of arousal and attention so that plans can be generated and applied and simultaneous and successive processes utilized.

Base of Knowledge. Cognitive processes rely on (and influence) the base of knowledge, which may be temporary (as in working memory) or more long term (that is, knowledge that is well learned). This includes, for example, what can be called declarative knowledge (one's base of knowledge about facts, reading, writing, etc.) and procedural knowledge (or what one knows about how to do something or how to use various processes), as well as knowing the conditions under which each is called for. The base of knowledge is the result of the interaction of the individual with the environment, and it supports tools of cognition (e.g., language, arithmetic operations, ideas, culturally based information, technologies, etc.) (Naglieri & Sloutsky, 1995). The acquisition of new knowledge and skills or the loss of old knowledge can profoundly change cognitive activity (e.g., Luria, 1973, 1976; Vygotsky, 1978; Vygotsky & Luria, 1993). For example, a child who is instructed to solve a task in a particular way (e.g., using a phonetic decoding method to read a word) has been encouraged to rely on one type of cognitive processes (successive) to solve the reading problem. Similarly, a child may be taught to remember a particular solution to a mathematic problem provided by the teacher (heavy reliance on rote learning) rather than being taught to consider and reflect upon how tasks of a certain type could be solved. The latter is a solution that facilitates planfulness through a reflective, self-reliant approach described as cognitive instruction by Scheid (1993). In both instances, the base of knowledge provided by a significant person in the child's environment can influence process utilization. Knowledge base influences all aspects of learning and other cognitive processes. Because all cognitive processing must occur within the reality as constructed by children and adults, their affect, motivation, and personality predispositions are part of this reality as much as their cognitive tools. For example, in mathematics learning, educators and practicing psychologists cannot ignore that math anxiety could prevent children from performing optimally in math problems.

RELEVANCE OF PASS TO INTERVENTION

There are many dimensions of the PASS theory that we have already discussed regarding its operationalization, profiles for exceptional children, implications for improved diagnostic validity, and related validity issues (see Das,

Naglieri, & Kirby, 1994). In the remainder of this chapter, we will focus on one dimension, utilization of the information PASS provides toward instructional and remedial decisions. We provide this summary assuming that the learning successes and difficulties children experience may be caused by many factors, including, but not limited to, quality of instruction; psychological status of the child; the home environment; family attitudes toward learning; characteristics of the class, school, and teacher; and the focus of this chapter, the PASS characteristics of the child. Our intent is that the PASS theory should provide a way to examine the cognitive characteristics of the child to help determine if these processes influence academic performance. When the critical variable is PASS, then there are some methods one could select that can be appropriate.

Our presentation of the relationship between PASS and intervention or instruction presented in this chapter is intended to be a summary of some of the research reported to date and a discussion of the trajectory these findings suggest. It is not our goal to give fixed or determined plans of action but rather to provide a beginning point for the application of PASS scores for the evaluation of the fitness of instruction and the design of remediation for children on the basis of their specific cognitive needs. We, therefore, provide several approaches that have been suggested and/or used by researchers interested in building a bridge between cognitive processing and instruction. We provide these summaries with the understanding that details are omitted and encourage interested readers to examine the original sources for additional information.

PASS Remedial Program for Improving Reading

Cognitive process–based training has gained acceptance as a branch of applied cognitive psychology, using both the rules and tools from the cognitive psychology of instruction (Lochhead & Clements, 1979) as well as dynamic assessment and intervention (Haywood & Tzuriel, 1992). The PASS Remedial Program (PREP; Das, Carlson, Davidson, & Longe, 1997) is theoretically oriented on the PASS theory and a process-based training approach described in some detail by Das, Naglieri, and Kirby (1994) and in a recent research paper (Das, Mishra, & Pool, 1995). PREP is designed to address those processes that are related to a child's difficulty in acquiring reading, especially successive and simultaneous processes. More specifically, PREP is designed to improve reading decoding skills based on the concept that a phonological coding deficit and an underlying successive processing are directly related to word reading difficulties. This approach recognizes the burgeoning literature on the bases of decoding deficits and phonological awareness and, through a series of procedures, reduces the deficits; consequently, word reading improves (Das, Mishra, & Pool, 1995).

Background of PREP

There are three developments that formed the impetus for PREP. First, early work in the area of memory (Atkinson & Shiffrin, 1968) led to an attempt to improve rehearsal as a control process (Belmont & Butterfield, 1971), but it was soon observed that rehearsal training did not lead to transfer of learning (Resnick, 1981). Programs for developing general learning skills that began in the late 1980s (e.g., Glaser & Bassok, 1989) provided a rationale for the efficacy of a program like PREP. Essentially, these programs were based on two general assumptions about a learner's characteristics: (1) Change in the learner is self-directed; that is, the learner tries to search for causes and explanations, thus extending the boundaries of his or her knowledge; and (2) learning is a process of internalization that has a social origin, as Vygotsky observed where the learner makes the skills his or her own.

Second, cognitive stimulation early in life could be effective (Haywood & Tapp, 1966), and cognitive training has improved the intellectual performance of culturally disadvantaged children (Feuerstein, 1979). In addition, Bradley and Bryant (1983) found that preschoolers who were poor in their perception of rhyming words eventually show reading difficulty, and hence, an early training in rhyming detection could lead to improved reading.

Lastly, PREP has been much influenced by Vygotsky, especially his concepts of internalization and sociocultural mediation (Das & Conway, 1992). Children have to make external instruction and knowledge their own, assisted by inner speech, to learn by the collaborative process of mediation. Its essence is contained in Vygotsky's statement: "What children can do with assistance of others might be in some sense more indicative of their mental development than what they can do alone" (Vygotsky, 1978, p. 85). PREP has been constructed to facilitate spontaneous acquisition of processing strategies, in contrast to deductive rule-learning, so that children learn through experience as they internalize the principles through an inductive process.

Description of PREP

The ultimate purpose of the PREP remediation program is to improve word decoding difficulties via two methods. First, global process training provides children with the opportunity to internalize strategies in their own way, thus maximizing generalization and facilitating transfer. Second, the program provides "bridges," that is, training in strategies that have been shown to be relevant for the academic skills of reading and spelling. These two parts of PREP encourage the application of the strategies to academic tasks through verbal mediation and internalization processes.

There are eight tasks included in the PREP program. They are designed to provide remediation of successive (six tasks) and simultaneous (two tasks) processing deficiencies but will also have small effects on other related processes, such as planning and attention. Thus, the PREP program was constructed to induce successive and simultaneous processing while promoting planning and attention. The goals for the tasks are:

1. To provide a structure for the child, which by design uses the targeted process.

2. To provide a scaffolding network through a series of prompts that provides the child with only the amount of assistance that is necessary to successfully complete the tasks, ensuring maximal success for the child.

3. To provide a monitoring system by which we are able to assess when the material is at too difficult a level for the child, as well as when the child is able to progress successfully to a more difficult level. The tasks contain such procedures as rehearsal, categorization, monitoring of performance, prediction, revision of prediction, and sound blending. The children develop their skill to use these procedures through experience with the tasks.

4. To encourage the children to become aware of the use of underlying cognitive processes through discussion of what they are doing during and following the tasks. Growth in the use of the processes and awareness of appropriate opportunities for use occur over the course of remediation. This inductive approach (in contrast to a direct instructional method) is taken to facilitate transfer.

Summary of Studies using PASS Remedial Program (PREP)

Early forms of PREP were initially developed in 1976 and have been found to be effective in improving reading (Crawford & Das, 1992; Brailsford, Spencer, Snart, & Das, 1989; Kaufman & Kaufman, 1978; Krywaniuk & Das, 1976). These early studies are described in Das, Naglieri, and Kirby (1994). A more recent version of PREP (Das, Carlson, Davidson, & Longe, 1997) is also described by Das, Naglieri, and Kirby (1994) and utilized in two recent investigations, one by Carlson and Das (1992), a second by Das, Mishra, and Pool (1995), and a third by Boden and Kirby (1995). What follows is a summary of recent investigations of PREP.

Carlson and Das (1992). The PREP program was used by Carlson and Das (1992) for improving reading in underachieving children in Chapter 1 programs in Hemet, California. In their study, pairs of children were instructed in two 50-minute sessions per week for three months. Both the PREP (n = 22) and control (n = 15) group samples continued to participate in the regular Chapter 1 program. Word Attack and Letter-Word Identification subtests of the Woodcock Reading Mastery Test (Woodcock, 1987) were administered at the start and finish of the study. The results showed that not only was there improvement in pre- to postperformance following training in the PREP group, but there were significant interaction effects. That is, the PREP children who received remediation gained substantially (almost one year in word decoding), as shown in Figure 7.3. While comparing the treated and nontreated students, it is important to remember that the gains achieved for the group exposed to PREP were compared to untreated students in the control group who were receiving remedial education in their resource room. Overall, these data provide support for the utility of the PREP program in improving word reading.

Figure 7.3
Pre- and Postintervention Reading Scores for Experimental and Control Groups—Word Decoding

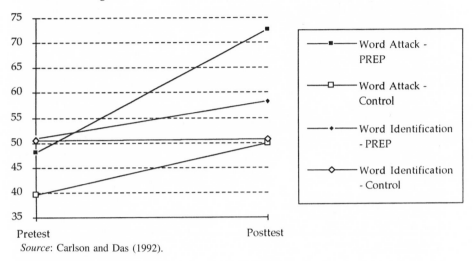

Pretest   Posttest
Source: Carlson and Das (1992).

Das, Mishra, and Pool (1995). Das, Mishra, and Pool (1995) applied the PREP program to a group of students with reading disability in grade 4 in Edmonton, Canada. The study involved 51 students aged 8 to 11 years from four public schools. The students in the treatment group (n = 31) was exposed to PREP, whereas the control group (n = 20) was not. The experimental group was given PREP approximately two times per week for a total of 15 sessions in groups of 4 students. The PREP group was compared to a no-intervention group for pre- and posttests on reading decoding as assessed by the Woodcock Reading Mastery Test—Revised (Woodcock, 1987). The results, shown in Figure 7.4, illustrate the improvements made by the subjects exposed to PREP over those seen for the control group. There were, in fact, significant differences found, supporting the utility of the PREP program. These results, like that found in the Carlson and Das (1992) study, which also provides evidence for the efficacy of the PREP program, combine to support this cognitive approach. For more details and other results, see Das, Mishra, and Pool (1995).

Boden and Kirby (1995). Boden and Kirby (1995) examined the effectiveness of PREP for a younger sample of children. They randomly assigned a total of 16 male and female students from two elementary schools to either a control or experimental groups. Poor readers were identified from the overall sample based on their average grade equivalent scores on the Gates-MacGinitie Comprehension and Vocabulary tests. Two teachers gave the PREP program (adapted for the grade 5/6 level and for groups of 4) so that half received the program from one instructor and half from the other instructor. Each group received remediation for approximately three hours a week for seven weeks for an average of

Figure 7.4
Pre- and Postintervention Reading Scores for Experimental and Control Groups
with Reading Disability

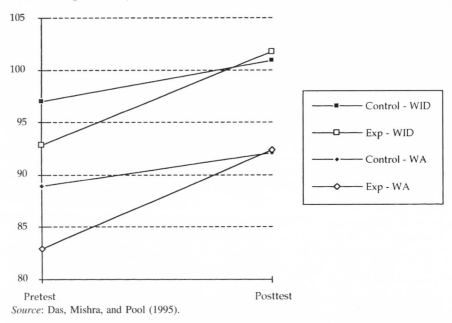

Source: Das, Mishra, and Pool (1995).

about 14 hours of remediation per student. The results showed significant differences between the control and PREP groups on word identification and word
attack after treatment. In relation to previous years' reading scores, the PREP
group performed significantly better than the control group. This study provided
preliminary evidence that the PREP instruction in phonological decoding and
successive processing was effective for poor readers. See Boden and Kirby
(1995) for more details.

PREP Conclusions

The PREP program is composed of tasks having specific cognitive demands
with a system of prompts that have been specifically designed to provide the
structure the student needs to encourage the utilization of specific cognitive
processes. The three investigations described here conducted by Carlson and
Das (1992), Das et al. (1995), and Boden and Kirby (1995) showed that significant positive results in word attack and word decoding were achieved after
the instructional program's completion. Taken as a whole, these results suggest
that the PREP program can be effective with elementary school–aged students
with reading decoding problems. These results also suggest that children with
poor reading, related to successive processing problems, but who have average

to superior scores in simultaneous processing are good candidates for this remedial program. Because reading words requires both processes to some extent (decoding requires successive, whereas blending the decoded sounds requires simultaneous processing), a poor simultaneous and average successive process can still result in poor reading. Therefore, PREP contains training tasks for both processes. Depending on the cognitive profile of the poor reader, a greater emphasis on mainly successive or mainly simultaneous training then becomes a logical strategy for remediation. In contrast to reading decoding, reading comprehension involves a greater demand on simultaneous processing. Therefore, when comprehension is weak but word decoding is not, all of the simultaneous training tasks along with some successive tasks are given. We recommend the use of both types of tasks in training for reading with different degrees of emphasis.

Facilitation of Planning for Nonacademic and Academic Tasks

There has been a series of studies that have investigated the relationship between planning and instruction. The first two involved nonacademic tasks (e.g., solution of nonverbal matrices), whereas the third and fourth involved academic content taken directly from the curriculum. In these studies, students who had poor scores on measures of planning improved more than those who had high scores in planning when given the same instruction designed to facilitate planfulness. The interventions that facilitate control and regulation of cognitive activity should have beneficial effects, especially for those who are poor in planning as defined by the PASS theory. Because it was anticipated that students would differentially benefit from the intervention, matching the instruction to the specific cognitive weakness of the child is the goal. These studies illustrated how the encouragement of strategy use (via verbalization) can be effective because the procedure encouraged planning processes for those children who otherwise did not adequately utilize it.

The instruction utilized in the four studies all centered on the position that a student's use of planning processes should be facilitated rather than directly instructed. This concept hinges on the idea of what is often referred to as discovery learning—that the student discovers the value of strategies that are appropriate for them. But they not only do this without being specifically told to; they sometimes cannot articulate the strategies they use. This use of inductive inference that we are able to do because of experience is also used in PREP discussed above. In the studies that are given in summary form below, the students verbalize to themselves how they did the task and what they can do next. This self-talk facilitates the utilization of planning processes and is especially important for those who are low in planning. The studies presented below provide a description of the brief intervention and report its effectiveness in facilitating planfulness.

Figure 7.5
**Comparison of Progressive Matrices Scores under Control and Experimental
Conditions for Children with Good or Poor Planning Scores**

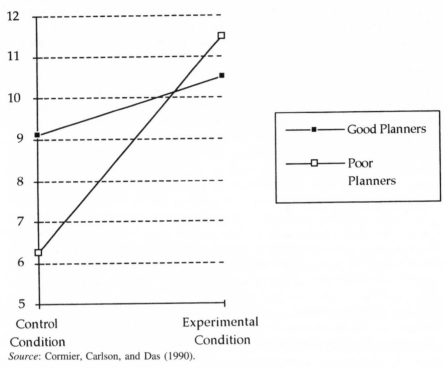

Source: Cormier, Carlson, and Das (1990).

Cormier, Carlson, and Das (1990). The first in a series of investigations to
find that students differentially benefited from a verbalization technique intended
to facilitate planfulness was published by Cormier, Carlson, and Das (1990).
They used the PASS theory as a measure of individual differences to understand
why differential improvement might be found. Their sample of 118 students was
organized into four groups—good and poor in planning with control and experimental testing conditions. The students in the experimental condition were
instructed to solve progressive matrices while verbalizing the problem, then
justify why their choice was correct, and finally explain why each of the other
options was not correct. The role of the experimenter was to facilitate the child's
verbalizations through the use of prompts such as "Now tell me what you see"
or "How would you describe it?" They found that, following this instruction,
which encouraged careful analysis of the problem, self-monitoring, and self-
correction, subjects who performed poorly on measures of planning earned significantly higher scores than those with good scores on planning measures (see

Figure 7.5). The verbalization technique facilitated a planful and organized examination of the component parts of the task and analysis of the relevant information (good planning) for those that needed to do this the most (those with low planning scores). This study suggested a differential benefit of instruction based on the PASS characteristics of the child. See Cormier, Carlson, and Das (1990) for more details.

Naglieri and Gottling (1995). The differential effects of instruction designed to facilitate planfulness using academic content (mathematics) taken directly from the class curriculum was recently reported by Naglieri and Gottling (1995). They extended the research by Cormier et al. (1990) by using a method designed to facilitate planning and in individual tutoring sessions. The results of their study showed that the intervention helped those with low scores in planning considerably more than those with high planning scores on multiplication problems. This study was the first to examine the usefulness of training planning processes as part of mathematics instruction for learning disabled students with low versus average scores on planning. Because their results suggested that students benefited differentially from the instruction based upon their cognitive processing scores, matching the instruction to the cognitive weakness (or strength) of the child was again suggested (see Naglieri and Gottling [1995] for more details). This study was expanded and replicated by Naglieri and Gottling (1996).

Naglieri and Gottling (1997). The most recent study in this series involved a classroom curriculum–based math instruction presented by the student's regular teachers. Naglieri and Gottling (1997) studied a sample of 12 elementary school students who attended an independent school that specializes in the treatment of students with significant learning problems who had made minimal educational progress in public special education programs. Two teachers who provided instruction to the learning disabled students on a regular basis participated in this study. The method of administrating the instruction was established in an initial one-hour collaborative session where initial guidelines for prompting were first established. During the time the experiment was under way, the authors consulted with the teachers weekly to assist in the execution of the intervention, monitor the progress of the students, consider ways of facilitating classroom discussions, and so on.

Students completed mathematics work sheets in a sequence of 7 baseline and 21 intervention sessions over about a two-month period. In the intervention phase, there was a 10-minute period for completing a math page; a 10-minute period was used for facilitating planning and a second 10-minute period for math. All students were exposed to 21 sessions that involved the three 10-minute segments of math/discussion/math in half-hour instructional periods. During the group discussion periods, self-reflection and discussion were facilitated with the goal that the children would gain a recognition of the need to be planful and utilize an efficient strategy when completing the math problems. To achieve this general goal the children were encouraged to (1) determine how they completed the work sheets; (2) verbalize and discuss their ideas; (3) explain which methods work well and which work poorly; (4) and be self-reflective. In order to facilitate self-reflection, probes were given by the teachers. For example, they said things like: "Let's talk about how you did the work sheet. How did you do the problems? Can anyone tell me anything about these problems? What could you have done to get more correct? Why did you do it that way? What will you do next time?" The students responded with comments such as: "I'll do all the easy ones first. I have to keep the columns straight. I do them row by row. I do the ones with 1's, 0's, and 10's in them because they're easy. If it's a big problem (all big numbers on the top) you don't have to borrow, so do it first." During this time, however, the teacher did not make statements such as "That is correct" or "Remember to use that same strategy"; no feedback on the number correct was provided; and at no time was mathematics instruction provided by the teachers.

The number correct per page was calculated for each student's 28 math work sheets, and contrast groups were identified on the basis of their planning scores. The results show that the low and high groups differentially benefited from the instruction even though both groups had similar initial baseline scores in math computation (see Figure 7.6). Students who were low in planning improved 80 percent overall and consistently across the three intervention segments, whereas the students with high planning scores improved 42 percent overall and inconsistently. The maximal effect for the students with low planning scores (113 percent) was achieved as the result of very consistent improvement across the three segments. The students with high planning scores improved somewhat; however, their improvement was about 50 percent less than that seen for students with low planning scores. These data, in conjunction with the previous three studies, provide support for the concept that children with low planning scores benefit more than those with high planning scores when given an instruction designed to facilitate planfulness. See Naglieri and Gottling (1996) for more details.

Section Conclusion. The group of studies taken as a whole provide a framework for practitioners to design instruction that facilitates planfulness. This method can be given by teachers to their class as a group and is expected to have differential effects based upon the cognitive characteristics of the individual students. It is anticipated that students with low planning scores will improve more than those with high scores in planning because this instruction meets their need to be more planful. In the last two studies, increased planning led to increased performance in math, which was anticipated because planning has been shown to be important for mathematics computation (Garofalo, 1986). Similar improvements in academic areas that involve planning (e.g., written composition

Figure 7.6
**Mean Number of Math Problems Correct during Baseline and Intervention
Sessions for Students with Low and High Average Planning Scores**

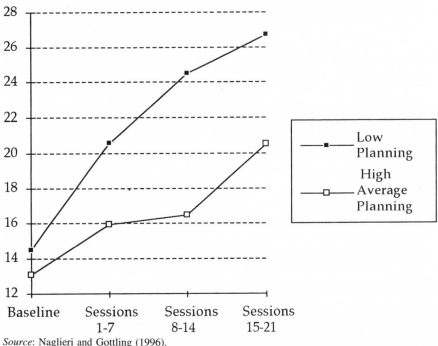

Baseline   Sessions   Sessions   Sessions
                 1-7   8-14   15-21

Source: Naglieri and Gottling (1996).

and other tasks that require the child to make many decisions about what and
how to do things) can be expected if this technique is similarly applied. Thus,
teaching control and regulation of cognitive activity (planning) can be expected
to have beneficial effects for many students but was especially helpful for those
poor in planning as defined by the PASS theory, and matching the instruction
to the cognitive weakness in planning is implied.

Teaching of Planning at the Classroom Level

In their book *Using Cognitive Methods in the Classroom*, Ashman and Conway (1993b) present a cognitive strategy training method called Process-Based
Instruction (PBI). This method was developed to ensure that processes are
learned through the integration of PBI plans within regular classroom activities.
PBI was designed to help classroom teachers provide a strategy for learning and

problem solving and a general framework for instruction that can be readily integrated into a teacher's usual classroom practices (Ashman & Conway, 1993a). The approach places emphasis on the process and use of planning that is accomplished through the systematic introduction and reinforcement of plan use. PBI "involves teaching students to be metacognitive about their learning and problem solving behavior by using plans as the vehicles" (Ashman & Conway, 1993a, p. 75). The task of the teacher is to develop the student's knowledge of how to generate, use, and adapt specific as well as general plans as circumstances demand, assist understanding of problem-solving methods appropriate to the particular developmental level, and encourage students to anticipate when planning strategies may be effective or not. According to Ashman and Conway (1993a), PBI plans are sequences of actions and metacognitions that are used to complete a task successfully. These plans may be written, pictorial, oral, or any combination of these forms but involve four essential components: (1) a cue for the child to look for information that initiates a planning sequence; (2) actions; (3) monitoring of progress; and (4) verification that the task goal is achieved.

Ashman and Conway (1993a). The effectiveness of PBI was recently examined in a study conducted by Ashman and Conway (1993a). Academic achievement scores were obtained from 147 students in grades 4 though 7 who attended regular primary classes in which PBI had been used and from students in comparable classes in which the program was not used. The students (58 experimental and 89 control) attended eight schools located in the metropolitan area of Brisbane, Australia. The PBI instructional program included four phases: first, "Introduction," where plans and planning are initially discussed; second, "Establishment," where plans are selected, modified, and applied to similar curriculum tasks; third, "Consolidation," where plans are identified, chosen, developed, and applied across curricular areas; and last, "Incorporation," where plans are modified and adapted in various domains and applied to learning in general. These phases were applied over a six-month interval.

Measures of achievement were obtained for the PBI and control groups on a pre/post treatment basis. The Class Achievement Test in Mathematics (Australian Council for Educational Research, 1976, 1986) was used to evaluate arithmetic skill areas of measurement, money, space, and time, and the Test of Reading Comprehension (Mossenson, Hill, & Masters, 1987) was given to evaluate the comprehension of 14 reading passages. The results of this study (shown in Figures 7.7 and 7.8) for math and reading comprehension demonstrated that those students who participated in the PBI program made statistically significant performance gains when compared to the control group. These results supported the utilization of a planning-based instructional format.

Figure 7.7
Pre- and Posttest Math Scores for Students in PBI and Control Groups

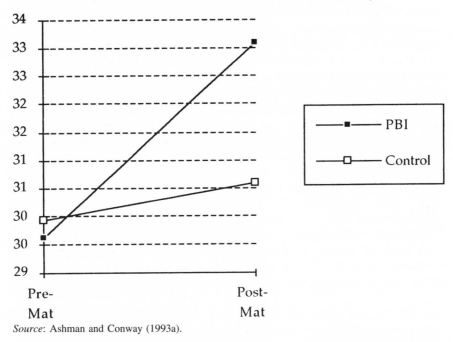

Source: Ashman and Conway (1993a).

Section Conclusions. The PBI method provides a means to encourage planning in children within the regular classroom activities in a way that is unobtrusive and relatively easily applied. The results of the study described above provide some reason to be optimistic about the positive effects of PBI on whole classroom teaching and learning. Taken in relation to the approaches used by Cormier et al. (1990) and Naglieri and Gottling (1995, 1996), this group of studies further encourages the application of methods that attempt to facilitate the use of planning processes in the classroom. Whereas the PBI group was not organized according to high or low planning processing scores, and examination of differential benefits of this planning-based instructional method was not reported, the results of Ashman and Conway's study still has implications for application of PASS. We suggest that PBI may be a viable method, especially for those who have poor planning processing scores, when the teacher wishes to instruct the class as a whole, rather than provide specific instruction to specific students. Targeted instruction to smaller groups of individuals with low scores in planning may be accomplished using PBI.

Figure 7.8
Pre- and Posttest Reading Scores for Students in PBI and Control Groups

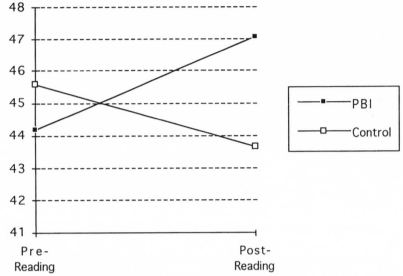

Source: Ashman and Conway (1993a).

CHAPTER CONCLUSIONS

In this chapter, we have provided a description of the PASS theory and a picture of the current status of our understanding of the relationships between PASS and several methods of instruction and intervention. As developments in this field emerge, these findings will come into greater focus, and more details of the methods and applications will emerge. We anticipate that because the PASS theory provides a view of intelligence that has greater breadth of measurement than traditional IQ tests, scores obtained from the Cognitive Assessment System (Naglieri & Das, 1997) may be relevant for instructional and intervention design.

REFERENCES

Anastasi, A. (1988). *Psychological testing* (6th ed.). New York: Macmillan.

Anokhin, P. K. (1969). Cybernetics and the integrative activity of the brain. In M. Cole & I. Maltzman (Eds.), *A handbook of contemporary Soviet psychology*. New York: Basic Books.

Ashman, A. F. (1978). *The relationship between planning and simultaneous and successive synthesis*. Unpublished doctoral dissertation, University of Alberta.

Ashman, A. F. (1982). Cognitive processes and perceived language performance of retarded persons. *Journal of Mental Deficiency Research, 26*, 131–141.

Ashman, A. F., & Conway, R. N. F. (1993a). Teaching students to use process-based learning and problem solving strategies in mainstream classes. *Learning and Instruction, 3*, 73–92.

Ashman, A. F., & Conway, R. N. F. (1993b). *Using cognitive methods in the classroom.* London: Routledge.

Ashman, A. F., & Das, J. P. (1980). Relation between planning and simultaneous-successive processing. *Perceptual and Motor Skills, 51*, 371–382.

Atkinson, R., & Shiffrin, R. (1968). Human memory: A proposed system and its control processes. In K. W. Spence & J. T. Spence (Eds.), *The psychology of learning and motivation: Advances in theory and research* (Vol. 2, pp. 89–125). New York: Academic Press.

Australian Council for Educational Research. (1976). *Class achievement test in mathematics.* Hawthorn, Vic.: Author.

Australian Council for Educational Research. (1986). *Class achievement test in mathematics—Year 6/7 teacher's manual* (2nd ed.). Hawthorn, Vic.: Author.

Belmont, J., & Butterfield, E. (1971). What the development of short-term memory is. *Human Development, 14*, 236–248.

Bernstein, N. A. (1967). *The coordination and regulation of movements.* Oxford: Pergamon Press.

Boden, C., & Kirby, J. R. (1995). Successive processing, phonological coding, and the remediation of reading. *Journal of Cognitive Education, 4*, 19–32.

Bradley, L., & Bryant, P. (1983). Categorizing sounds and learning to read: A casual connection. *Nature, 301*, 419–421.

Brailsford, A., Snart, F., & Das, J. P. (1984). Strategy training and reading comprehension. *Journal of Learning Disabilities, 17*, 287–290.

Broadbent, D. E. (1958). *Perception and communication.* Oxford: Pergamon.

Brody, N. (1992). *Intelligence* (2nd ed.). San Diego: Academic Press.

Carlson, J., & Das, J. P. (1992). *The cognitive assessment and reading remediation of Chapter 1 students.* Riverside: California Educational Research Cooperative of the University of California, Riverside.

Carroll, J. B. (1993). *Human cognitive abilities: A survey of factor-analytic studies.* Cambridge: Cambridge University Press.

Cattell, R. B. (1963). Theory for fluid and crystallized intelligence: A critical experiment. *Journal of Educational Psychology, 54*, 1–22.

Cattell, R. B. (1971). *Abilities: Their structure, growth and action.* Boston: Houghton Mifflin.

Cormier, P., Carlson, J. S., & Das, J. P. (1990). Planning ability and cognitive performance: The compensatory effects of a dynamic assessment approach. *Learning and Individual Differences, 2*, 437–449.

Crawford, S. A. S., & Das, J. P. (1992). Teaching for transfer. A program for remediation in reading. In J. Carlson (Ed.), *Advances in cognitive and educational practice* (Vol. 1B, pp. 73–103). Greenwich, CT: JAI Press.

Crocker, L., & Algina, J. (1986). *Introduction to classical and modern test theory.* New York: Holt, Rinehart and Winston.

Cummins, J. P., & Das, J. P. (1977). Cognitive processing and reading difficulties: A framework for research. *Alberta Journal of Educational Research, 23*, 246–256.

Cummins, J. P., & Das, J. P. (1978). Simultaneous and successive syntheses and linguistic processes. *International Journal of Psychology, 13*, 129–138.

Cummins, J. P., & Das, J. P. (1980). Cognitive processing, academic achievement, and WISC–R performance in EMR children. *Journal of Consulting and Clinical Psychology, 48*, 777–779.

Das, J. P. (1972). Patterns of cognitive ability in nonretarded and retarded children. *American Journal of Mental Deficiency, 77*, 6–12.

Das, J. P. (1973). Structure of cognitive abilities: Evidence for simultaneous and successive processing. *Journal of Educational Psychology, 65*, 103–108.

Das, J. P. (1980). Planning: Theoretical considerations and empirical evidence. *Psychological Research, 41*, 141–151.

Das, J. P. (1983). Process training and remediation of reading disability: Examples of some Soviet tasks. *Mental Retardation and Learning Disability Bulletin, 11*, 32–41.

Das, J. P. (1984). Cognitive deficits in mental retardation: A process approach. In P. H. Brooks, R. Sperber, & C. McCauley (Eds.), *Learning and cognition in the mentally retarded* (pp. 115–128). Hillsdale, NJ: Erlbaum.

Das, J. P., Carlson, J., Davidson, M. B., & Longe, K. (1997). *PREP: PASS remedial program.* Toronto: Hogrefe Publishing Company.

Das, J. P., & Conway, R. N. F. (1992). Reflections on remediation and transfer: A Vygotskian perspective. In H. C. Haywood & D. Tzuriel (Eds.), *Interactive assessment* (pp. 94–118). New York: Springer-Verlag.

Das, J. P., & Cummins, J. (1979). Academic performance and cognitive processes in EMR children. *American Journal of Mental Deficiency, 83*, 197–199.

Das, J. P., & Cummins, J. (1982). Language processing and reading disability. *Advances in Learning and Behavioral Disabilities, 1*, 3–24.

Das, J. P., Kirby, J. R., & Jarman, R. F. (1979). *Simultaneous and successive cognitive processes.* New York: Academic Press.

Das, J. P., Mishra, R. K., & Pool, J. (1995). An experiment on cognitive remediation of word-reading difficulty. *Journal of Learning Disabilities, 28*, 66–79.

Das, J. P., Naglieri, J. A., & Kirby, J. R. (1994). *Assessment of cognitive processes.* Needham Heights, MA: Allyn & Bacon.

Eysenck, H. J. (1939). Primary mental abilities. *British Journal of Educational Psychology, 37*, 81–98.

Feuerstein, R. (1979). *The dynamic assessment of retarded performers: The learning potential assessment device, theory, instruments, and techniques.* Baltimore: University Park Press.

Gardner, H. (1983). *Frames of mind: The theory of multiple intelligences.* New York: Basic Books.

Garofalo, J. F. (1986). Simultaneous synthesis, behavior regulation and arithmetic performance. *Journal of Psychoeducational Assessment, 4*, 229–238.

Gazzaniga, M. S. (1970). *The bisected brain.* New York: Appleton-Century-Crofts.

Glaser, R., & Bassok, M. (1989). Learning theory and the study of instruction. *Annual Review of Psychology, 40*, 631–666.

Guilford, J. P. (1967). *The nature of human intelligence.* New York: McGraw-Hill.

Haywood, H. C., & Tapp, J. T. (1966). Experience and the development of adaptive behavior. In N. R. Ellis (Ed.), *International review of research in mental retardation* (Vol. 1, pp. 109–151). New York: Academic Press.

Haywood, J., & Tzuriel, D. (1992). *Interactive assessment.* New York: Springer-Verlag.

Hernandez-Peon, R. (1966). Neurophysiology of attention. In P. J. Vinken and G. W. Bruyn (Eds.), *Handbook of clinical neurology* (Vol 3). Amsterdam: North Holland Publishing Company.

Horn, J. L. (1985). Remodeling old models of intelligence. In B. B. Wolman (Ed.), *Handbook of intelligence* (pp. 267–300). New York: Wiley.

Hunt, E. B. (1974). Quote the Raven? Nevermore! In L. Gregg (Ed.), *Knowledge and cognition*. Potomac, MD: Erlbaum.

Hunt, E. B. (1990). A modern arsenal for mental assessment. *Educational Psychologist, 25*, 223–242.

Hunt, E., & Lansman, M. (1986). Unified model of attention and problem solving. *Psychological Review, 93*, 446–461.

Jarman, R. F. (1978). Patterns of cognitive ability in retarded children: A reexamination. *American Journal of Mental Deficiency, 82*, 344–348.

Jarman, R. F. (1980a). Cognitive processes and syntactic structure: Analyses of paradigmatic and syntagmatic associations. *Psychological Research, 41*, 153–169.

Jarman, R. F. (1980b). Modality-specific information processing and intellectual ability. *Intelligence, 4*, 201–217.

Jensen, A. R. (1982). Reaction time and psychometric *g*. In H. J. Eysenck (Ed.), *A model for intelligence*. Berlin: Springer-Verlag.

Kaufman, D., & Kaufman, P. (1992). Strategy training and remedial techniques. *Journal of Learning Disabilities, 16*, 72–78.

Kirby, J. R. (1982). Cognitive processes, school achievement, and comprehension of ambiguous sentences. *Journal of Psycholinguistic Research, 11*, 485–499.

Kirby, J. R. (1984). *Cognitive strategies and educational performance*. New York: Academic Press.

Kirby, J. R., & Das, J. P. (1977). Reading achievement, IQ, and simultaneous-successive processing. *Journal of Educational Psychology, 69*, 564–570.

Kirby, J. R., & Das, J. P. (1978). Information processing and human abilities. *Journal of Educational Psychology, 70*, 58–66.

Kirby, J. R., & Das, J. P (1990). A cognitive approach to intelligence: Attention, coding and planning. *Canadian Psychology, 31*, 320–331.

Kirby, J. R., & Lawson, M. J. (1983). Effects of strategy training on progressive matrices performance. *Contemporary Educational Psychology, 8*, 127–139.

Kirby, J. R., & Williams, N. H. (1991). *Learning problems: A cognitive approach*. Toronto: Kagan and Woo.

Krywaniuk, L. W., & Das, J. P. (1976). Cognitive strategies in native children: Analysis and intervention. *Alberta Journal of Educational Research, 22*, 271–280.

Lawson, M. J., & Kirby, J. R. (1981). Training in information processing algorithms. *British Journal of Educational Psychology, 51*, 321–335.

Leong, C. K. (1980). Cognitive patterns of ''retarded'' and below-average readers. *Contemporary Educational Psychology, 5*, 101–117.

Leong, C. K. (1984). Cognitive processing, language awareness, and reading in grade 2 and grade 4 children. *Contemporary Educational Psychology, 9*, 369–383.

Leontiev, A. N. (1978). *Activity, consciousness, and personality*. Englewood Cliffs, NJ: Prentice-Hall.

Lindsley, D. B. (1960). Attention, consciousness, sleep and wakefulness. In J. Field (Ed.), *Handbook of physiology*. Springfield, IL: Thomas.

Lochhead, J., & Clements, J. (Eds.). (1979). *Cognitive process instruction: Research on teaching thinking skills*. Philadelphia: Franklin Institute Press.

Luria, A. R. (1966). *Human brain and psychological processes*. New York: Harper & Row.

Luria, A. R. (1970). The functional organization of the brain. *Scientific American, 222*, 66–78.

Luria, A. R. (1973). *The working brain: An introduction to neuropsychology*. New York: Basic Books.

Luria, A. R. (1976). *Cognitive development: Its cultural and social foundations*. Cambridge, MA: Harvard University Press.

Luria, A. R. (1980). *Higher cortical functions in man* (2nd ed., rev. and exp.). New York: Basic Books.

Luria, A. R. (1982). *Language and cognition*. New York: Wiley.

Magoun, H. W. (1963). *The waking brain* (2nd ed.). Springfield: Thomas.

Miller, G., Galanter, E., & Pribram, K. (1960). *Plans and the structure of behavior*. New York: Henry Holt and Company.

Mossenson, L., Hill, P., & Masters, G. (1987). *Test of reading comprehension manual*. Melbourne, Vic.: Australian Council for Educational Research.

Naglieri, J. A. (1985). *Matrix Analogies Test—Expanded Form*. San Antonio: Psychological Corp.

Naglieri, J. A. (1989a). A cognitive processing theory for the measurement of intelligence. *Educational Psychologist, 24*, 185–206.

Naglieri, J. A. (1989b). Planning, attention, simultaneous, and successive cognitive processes: A summary of recent studies with exceptional samples. *Mental Retardation and Learning Disability Bulletin, 17*, 3–22.

Naglieri, J. A. (1992). Two roads diverged in the wood: Choosing "g" or PASS cognitive processes. In J. Carlson (Ed.), *Cognition and educational practice: An international perspective* (pp. 111–126). Greenwich, CT: JAI Press.

Naglieri, J. A. (1996a). Cognitive assessment. In T. Fagan & P. Warden (Eds.), *Encyclopedia of school psychology* (pp. 70–72). Westport, CT: Greenwood Publishing Group.

Naglieri, J. A. (1996b). Planning, attention, simultaneous, and successive (PASS) and the cognitive assessment system: A theory based measure of intelligence. In D. P Flanagan, J. L. Genshaft, & P. L. Harrison (Eds.), *Beyond traditional intellectual assessment: Contemporary and emerging theories, tests, and issues* (pp. 247–267). New York: Guilford.

Naglieri, J. A. (1996c). *Naglieri Nonverbal Ability Test*. San Antonio: Psychological Corp.

Naglieri, J. A., Braden, J., & Gottling, S. (1993). Confirmatory factor analysis of the planning, attention, simultaneous, successive (PASS) cognitive processing model for a kindergarten sample. *Journal of Psychoeducational Assessment, 11*, 259–269.

Naglieri, J. A., & Das, J. P. (1987). Construct and criterion related validity of planning, simultaneous, and successive cognitive processing tasks. *Journal of Psychoeducational Assessment, 5*, 353–363.

Naglieri, J. A., & Das, J. P. (1988). Planning-Arousal-Simultaneous-Successive (PASS): A model for assessment. *Journal of School Psychology, 26*, 35–48.

Naglieri, J. A., & Das, J. P. (1990). Planning, attention, simultaneous, and successive (PASS) cognitive processes as a model for intelligence. *Journal of Psychoeducational Assessment, 8,* 303–337.

Naglieri, J. A., & Das, J. P. (1997). *Das•Naglieri Cognitive Assessment System.* Chicago, IL: Riverside Publishing Company.

Naglieri, J. A., & Gottling, S. H. (1995). A cognitive education approach to math instruction for the learning disabled: An individual study. *Psychological Reports,* 1343–1354.

Naglieri, J. A., & Gottling, S. H. (1997). Mathematics instruction and PASS cognitive processes: An intervention study. *Journal of Learning Disabilities,* in press.

Naglieri, J. A., & Sloutsky, V. N. (1995). Re-inventing intelligence: The PASS theory of cognitive functioning. *General Psychologist, 31,* 11–17.

Naglieri, J. A., Welch, J. A., & Braden, J. (1994). Factor structure of planning, attention, simultaneous, successive (PASS) cognitive processing tasks and the Wechsler PIQ for a hearing impaired sample. *Journal of School Psychology, 32,* 371–384.

Neisser, U. (1967). *Cognitive psychology.* New York: Appleton-Century-Crofts.

Piaget, J. (1950). *The psychology of intelligence.* London: Routledge.

Pribram, K. H. (1971). *Languages of the brain: Experimental paradoxes and principles in neuropsychology.* Englewood Cliffs, NJ: Prentice-Hall.

Raven, J. C. (1956). *Coloured progressive matrices: Sets A, Ab, B.* London: H. K. Lewis.

Resnick. L. (1981). Instructional psychology. *Annual Review of Psychology, 32,* 659–704.

Scheid, K. (1993). *Helping students become strategic learners.* Cambridge, MA: Brookline.

Solso, R. L., & Hoffman, C. A. (1991). Influence of Soviet scholars. *American Psychologist, 46,* 251–253.

Spearman, C. (1927). *The nature of intelligence and the principles of cognition.* London: Macmillan.

Spencer, F., Snart, F., & Das, J. P. (1989). A process-based approach to the remediation of spelling in students with reading disabilities. *Alberta Journal of Educational Research, 35,* 269–282.

Sternberg, R. J. (1977). *Intelligence, information processing, and analogical reasoning: The componential analysis of human abilities.* Hillsdale, NJ: Erlbaum.

Thorndike, R. L., Hagen, E. P., & Sattler, J. M. (1986). *Stanford-Binet Intelligence Scale* (4th ed.). Chicago: Riverside Publishing Company.

Thurstone, L. L. (1938). *Primary mental abilities.* Chicago: University of Chicago Press.

Vernon, P. E. (1979). *Intelligence: Heredity and environment.* San Francisco: Freeman.

Vygotsky, L. S. (1978). *Mind in society: The development of higher psychological processes.* Cambridge: Harvard University Press.

Vygotsky, L. S., & Luria, A. R. (1993). *Studies on the history of behavior: Ape, primitive, and child.* Hillsdale: Lawrence Erlbaum.

Woodcock, R. W. (1987). *Woodcock reading mastery tests—Revised.* Circle Pines, MN: American Guidance Service.

8

Dynamic Testing

A goal as important as any in education or psychology is to derive measures of intelligence, ability, and aptitude that are sensitive or accurate measures of the abilities and processes of interest. Clearly, accurate assessment of intellectual abilities is fundamental to all attempts to validate theories of intelligence and development. Moreover, such sensitive measurement is essential to determinations of academic growth or technical competence.

WHAT IS DYNAMIC TESTING?

Researchers and diagnosticians have demonstrated considerable recent interest in the theory and methods of dynamic assessment. *Dynamic testing* refers to those efforts at involving an examinee in an assessment situation that, in some way, allows the learner to participate more actively in testing and thus is more similar to the manner in which information acquisition actually occurs (hence, the term *dynamic*) than is the case under standard psychometric measurement. The major assumption underlying the various efforts, not always well articulated, is that dynamic assessment of intellectual abilities provides more reliable, valid, and diagnostically and prescriptively useful estimates of the tested abilities, or competence, than would be the case if the same tests were administered under traditional psychometric methods.

Beyond this point, the consensus diminishes. The interest in dynamic testing, coupled with theoretical divergence in the emerging literature, makes it necessary to clarify certain issues. In this chapter, I articulate what I believe to be a set of important issues or questions that stem from ambiguities in the dynamic testing literature. In addition, I provide examples of the manner in which dynamic testing approaches bear on the following questions or issues.

Here, our task is to ask, What, at the level of cognitive-processing phenomena, is dynamic testing supposed to accomplish? Concern is with competencies that either are not isolated by traditional assessment or are measured more veridically under dynamic assessment. Concern also is with processes that can be fostered or enhanced through dynamic testing. The area of dynamic assessment has been fueled by the theoretical and psychodiagnostic considerations discussed in this chapter.

Dynamic Testing and Intelligence Theory

With respect to intelligence theory, dynamic testing paradigms are motivated by changing conceptions of the nature of intelligence and from resulting beliefs regarding how best to measure the abilities derived from these new views of intelligence. Validity issues provide important sources of impetus for the use of dynamic procedures.

At a more aggregative level of analysis, we can see that test performance improves under dynamic procedures to a greater extent for some individuals than for other individuals. Dillon and Carlson (1978) found a no effect–effect–no effect pattern for children ages 5–6/7–8/9–10. The youngest group of examinees showed no facilitative effect under testing-the-limits procedures because of apparent structural limitations. Similarly, the oldest group showed no differences in test performance as a function of dynamic procedures; their competence was manifested spontaneously on this task without the need for external inducement. The transitional group benefited from dynamic assessment procedures because they possessed the competence to perform well on the items but did not manifest this competence spontaneously. In Carlson and Wiedl's (1992) terminology, these latter examinees demonstrated ''suboptimal application of actual intelligence'' under standard procedures, due to the nature of the standard testing condition. The mediation through verbalization and elaborated feedback served to reduce the competence-performance discrepancy; subjects were able to demonstrate a level of performance that was closer to their actual competence.

Another very important reason for using dynamic testing procedures is that they enable researchers to identify and isolate cognitive processes that would be difficult or impossible to understand without such techniques. Identification of ability differences in cognitive processes is important on both theoretical and practical grounds. From a theoretical perspective, dynamic testing allows intelligence researchers to gain information regarding the nature of mediation, dual coding, and solution monitoring and regarding the roles of these processes in intelligent performance.

It is important to note two points about both optimizing procedures and learning potential. The extent to which individuals profit from either testing-the-limits procedures or learning potential assessment depends on task factors such as the nature and difficulty of test items and on individual difference dimensions. In the latter regard, subjects differ in the extent to which they spontaneously use multiple representations, elaborate, monitor, and employ other procedures invoked through dynamic assessment. And subjects differ in their responsiveness to intervention—that is, the extent to which they can learn to perform these procedures through dynamic assessment. Note also that developmental factors play a role in responsiveness to intervention.

An individual's responsiveness to intervention appears to vary independently of performance level. Consequently, inclusion of this phenomenon in the conceptualization of intelligence may define intelligence more accurately and increase validity, regardless of whether the criterion taps life experience factors or academic success.

Differing Conceptions of Intelligence and Resulting Principles of Assessment

Carlson and Wiedl (1992) articulate the manner in which different conceptions of intelligence spawn different principles of dynamic assessment. They discuss three types of cognitive capacity. An important point to note is that differences between Intelligence C and Intelligence B, the so-called competence-performance distinction, is at the core of one of the central goals of dynamic testing: to render an individual's test performance as close an approximation of actual competence as possible.

Intelligence A. This type of cognitive capacity refers to the general potential to profit from environmental stimulation, and it is believed to be neurobiological in nature. Researchers in this camp concern themselves with learning potential, rehabilitation potential, and learning ability. The assessment programs in this category focus on assessment of training gains.

Intelligence B. Intelligence B is considered to be an individual's actual intelligence and is composed of the structural, motivational, attentional, and metacognitive aspects of thinking and problem solving.

Intelligence C. Intelligence C refers to performance on mental ability measures. Note that Intelligence B is inferred from Intelligence C.

Psychometric Motivation for Dynamic Testing

With respect to the psychometric motivation for using dynamic assessment procedures, widespread consensus exists that traditional testing approaches fail to provide accurate measures of intelligent academic, training, or job performance. Moreover, such assessments fail to deal adequately with issues of adverse impact (see Dillon, 1989a). A consistent body of literature exists to demonstrate that validity is improved when the cognitive tests or tasks of interest are administered dynamically rather than statically (see Campione & Brown, 1987, 1990; Carlson & Dillon, 1977; Carlson & Wiedl, 1980, 1992; Dillon, 1981, 1986a, 1986b; Dillon & Carlson, 1978, Lidz, 1992, for experiments using a range of tasks, ability, and subject groups).

A few examples of previous train-within-test validity studies will be given. In the first study, Jerry Carlson and I (Dillon & Carlson, 1978) reported increased performance for Caucasian, Hispanic, and black children when analogical reasoning items were presented under train-within-test procedures of subject verbalization and elaborated feedback rather than standard procedures. A similar finding emerged for profoundly deaf children in the same age range (Carlson & Dillon, 1977). Dynamic assessment improves validity on a wide range of tasks in addition to tests of reasoning and general thinking skills. In an example from the reading literature, Swanson (1992) demonstrates that dynamic testing procedures enhance the prediction of reading performance.

DYNAMIC TESTING PARADIGMS

Two classes of dynamic testing paradigms have received greatest attention. The approaches, as well as a mixed approach, are considered below.

Intelligence as Elaborated Thinking (the Genotype-Environment Interaction)

In comparing the definitions of *intelligence as elaborated thinking* and *intelligence as the ability to profit from experience*, the terms *activation* versus *training* are particularly useful. Intelligence researchers who equate intelligence with an examinee's current level of functioning see their goal as the activation of underlying competence. Researchers in this camp (see Dillon, 1989a, and Jitendra & Kameenui, 1993, for reviews of this work) seek to test the limits of performance, and they believe that the most veridical assessment of intelligence derives from activating the competence that underlies an individual's current performance. The competence is believed to be structural in nature. The environment serves as a catalyst, with the goal of activating underlying cognitive competence, not altering cognitive abilities. More specifically, by asking examinees to "think aloud" during item solution, or by providing examiner-generated elaborated feedback following solution of each item, dynamic procedures are believed to enhance the extent to which individuals build internal connections between test elements, generate multiple representations for test items, engage in dual coding of stimulus materials, and employ self-monitoring of solution tactics. Such train-within-test paradigms allow researchers and educators to measure intelligence or ability by activating underlying competence. The accepted consensus of proponents is that such procedures activate the competence that an individual currently possesses and that they do not train or change actual competence.

Intelligence as the Ability to Profit from Experience

Researchers in this group measure learning potential rather than current level of functioning. In this dynamic way of measuring aptitude, the individual's competence is trained or changed. Thus, the examinee's current level of intelligent performance is not believed to be the best measure of intelligence; rather, intelligence is seen as the ability to profit from experience.

Three dynamic assessment paradigms are included in this category of models: (1) test-train-test; (2) learning potential mediational assessment; and (3) the continuum of assessment model, with mediated and graduated prompting (although developmental factors play a role in responsiveness to intervention under this latter approach). The test-train-test approach to measuring learning potential was conceptualized by Budoff (1974) for use with educably mentally handicapped children. The cornerstone of the approach is the belief that, by incorporating training into assessment, faulty performance resulting from test-relevant experiential deficits will be reduced. The result of this intervention is said to be more competent intellectual performance—a performance that is closer to the individual's actual intellectual competence than is found under standard testing conditions. The approach involves pretest, training, and posttest phases. Training uses standardized procedures to help examinees understand task expectations, facilitate positive rapport, and provide training in solution monitoring. Budoff (1987) reports performance gains using this approach. Curriculum efforts have focused on utilizing individuals' strengths in designing instruction.

Feuerstein's (Feuerstein, Rand, & Hoffman, 1979) mediational approach to learning potential assessment is based on the premises that (1) mediated learning is the essence of cognitive acquisition and (2) a lack of mediated learning experiences, not limitations in cognitive structures, often impedes cognitive performance. Consequently, proponents believe that task performance under standard testing conditions is not an accurate measure of an individual's learning potential. Instead, accurate measurement of an examinee's strengths and limitations in basic learning abilities is said to result from coupling learning potential assessment with intervention designed to provide mediated learning experiences.

Feuerstein's Learning Potential Assessment Device (Feuerstein, Rand, Hoffman, & Miller, 1980) permits the examiner to infer the effect that the test-teach-retest procedures have on an individual's ability to show cognitive change. Performance improvements following instruction are believed to be indicators of learning potential. The approach is designed to isolate the sources of deficient cognitive functioning in intellectual skills and also to measure the consequences of intervention. Providing clinical intervention, the facilitator's role is to serve as the mediational interface between the examinee and external influences, helping the individual gain facility at making inferences and processing information. The examiner uses task analysis procedures to isolate the source of a given performance failure. Common sources of difficulty include lack of familiarity with task content, difficulties with particular presentation modalities, and deficiencies in information-processing componential operations or other cognitive functions. Intervention then provides mediation that is targeted at specific deficiencies.

The Continuum of Assessment model (e.g., Burns, Haywood, Delclos, & Siewart, 1987; Vye, Burns, Delclos, & Bransford, 1987) combines mediation assessment with graduated prompting assessment. This model is especially experiential and assumes that adequate learning of skills such as planning and monitoring requires mediated experiences. Such experiences can be brought about through graduated prompting. Mediation is necessary to bring performance up to the level of competence for examinees who fail to receive full activation from the graduated prompting component of the program. Brief scripted interventions are used during guided prompting (Burns, 1985; Tzuriel & Klein, 1987; Vye et al., 1987). The program focuses on enhancing familiarization with task materials, teaching the rules for successful performance, and practice with elaborated feedback. In this part of the testing program, prompts are contingent upon the examinee's performance. In contrast, during the graduated prompting portion of the program, predetermined prompts are given as needed. Tasks include measures of higher cognitive abilities and academic skills.

Note that both theory and individual differences might motivate use of this paradigm. With respect to theory, some intelligence researchers believe that learning ability is one component in a multifaceted model of intelligence (see Sternberg's [1985] discussion of knowledge acquisition components and components of novelty). With respect to the role of individual differences in testing, individuals clearly differ in task-relevant experiences, apart from the ability differences the diagnostician seeks to measure—for example, experiential differences in the use of computers during test taking. So training approaches may be used because the researcher believes that one facet of intelligence is the ability to profit from experience or because the individuals being tested lack important task-relevant experiences, the lack of which would contaminate assessment of the competencies under investigation. Feuerstein, for example, would assert that an individual's current level of functioning may not be a good predictor of future academic success to the extent that the individual, relatively speaking, has not had adequate "mediate learning experiences." As an example of the latter concern, an individual may desire admission to a particular program of study. For this individual, content and/or process dimensions of the predictor task may be unfamiliar, due to sociocultural or other experiential differences that affect current test performance but that need not be relevant to performance in the program to which the individual seeks admission.

The work of Budoff and his colleagues (Budoff, Meskin, & Harrison, 1971) and Feuerstein and his colleagues provides several examples of other types of experiential shortcomings that may prevent an individual's actual competence from being revealed under standard testing procedures. Feuerstein's Learning Potential Assessment Device (LPAD; Feuerstein et al., 1980) and the accompanying mediated learning program (Feuerstein, Rand, & Hoffman, 1979) measures and trains directly the types of processes that can be isolated through dynamic techniques.

Mixed Paradigms

One type of mixed approach is found at the interface of Intelligence A and Intelligence B. The work is exemplified by the Graduated Prompting approach. In this developmental approach, a gradual transfer of control of learning from adult examiner to child examinee characterizes developmental attainments (Vygotsky, 1962, 1978). This transfer of control is the theoretical underpinning of the Vygotsky model and is operationalized in the Graduated Prompting Assessment procedure. Central to this model is the notion of the Zone of Proximal Development. This zone is the distance from the examinee's initial unassisted cognitive performance to the level that the examinee can attain when given assistance. Preassessment is followed by sequential sets of prompting activities. The activities are designed to quantify the amount of assistance needed to reach post levels. Proponents of this approach use the Zone of Proximal Development to quantify the individual's readiness to learn. Children with broad zones are believed to profit markedly from intervention. In contrast, individuals with narrow zones are not expected to improve significantly beyond their initial levels of unassisted performance. The test-train-test approach to graduated prompting used by Campione and Brown (Brown & French, 1979; Campione, Brown, & Ferrerra, 1982) demonstrates the usefulness of this approach for determining readiness to learn. According to Vygotsky, when a child moves from the necessity for external control of a given intellectual activity to internalization of the processes responsible for attainment in that activity, learning and consequent activation of higher cognitive processes have occurred. Instruction creates changes in the Zone of Proximal Development, and susceptibility to instruction varies as a function of the individual's level of functioning for particular cognitive attainments.

Note in this framework that intelligence is a developmentally linked, dynamic structural capacity rather than a constant structural capacity. So this approach links Intelligence A and Intelligence B because the extent of the individual's ability to profit from experience varies from one point in development to another. So the Zones of Proximal Development differ throughout each individual's development.

In a second type of mixed approach, current intellectual functioning is altered through training and then validated against criterion measures that tap current functioning. Larson, Alderton, and Kaupp's (1991) work is an example of a mixed approach. Larson and his colleagues combine analytic/reflective strategy training, rule combination training, and modeling in a pretraining package. The training package is a nice example of the test-train-test dynamic approach. In this work, dynamic testing constitutes a training program that is designed to change intellectual competence, but it is validated against a g-type battery designed to measure current intelligence. Interpretation of findings from such mixed approaches may be problematic because investigators alter intellectual competence through explicit training and validate this performance against concurrent IQ test–type performance, administered statically. Table 8.1 provides a summary of the dynamic assessment models.

VALIDITY OF DYNAMIC ASSESSMENT TECHNIQUES

In this section, I consider first the choice of dynamic assessment approaches and the distinction between dynamically measured performance versus practice. Subsequently, I consider criterion development issues.

Which Paradigm Should I Use?

The choice of dynamic procedures, then, depends on two factors. First, choice of approach is relevant to the researcher's views regarding the nature of intelligence (e.g., whether processes such as mediation, monitoring, dual coding, or learning are important components of intelligence) and its measurement (i.e., whether current competence or learning potential is of primary importance). Second, individual differences provide an important source of concern. Factors such as sociocultural differences in relevant experiences or differences in relevant motivation may impact the choice of dynamic assessment paradigm.

Optimal Performance versus Practice

Practice alone does not account for the greater performance demonstrated by learners on complex tasks administered dynamically versus statically. Missiuna and Samuels (1989) found that practice alone did not improve analogical reasoning for preschool special needs children. Keane and Kretschmer (1987) reported that deaf students demonstrated enhanced performance under conditions of mediation, with no practice effects identified. In related work, Reinharth (1989) and Thomas (1986) found that mediation resulted in higher scores on the Preschool Learning Assessment Device (Lidz, 1991) than did practice. The results of this work indicate that some type of elaboration of problem-solving processes is responsible for greater or improved learner performance.

Choices of Assessment Tasks

As Bransford, Delclos, Vye, Burns, and Hasselbring (1987) note, it is important to distinguish the general concept of dynamic assessment from the use of a particular set of tasks and procedures such as the LPAD. Bransford et al.'s concern distinguishes the use of dynamic assessment for measuring learning potential and current competence from the use of dynamic assessment for diagnosis of current academic shortcomings—measuring intelligence versus pre-

Table 8.1
Models of Dynamic Assessment

Model	Testing the Limits	Test-Train-Test	Learning Potential Assessment	Graduated Prompting	Continuum of Assessment
Type of Intelligence	Intelligence B	Intelligence A	Intelligence A	Intelligence A & B Interface	Intelligence A
View of Intelligence	Activation of Competence	Trainability	Mediated Learning Experiences Facilitate Changes in Learning and Development; Ability to Learn	Depends on Readiness to Learn; Large Gains in Independent Functioning with Guided Experience	Learning Results from Direct Experience
Purpose of Dynamic Assessment	Activate and Measure Full Intellectual Competence	Identify Examinees Who Can Profit From Optimal Instruction	Measure Responsiveness to Intervention	Measure Learning and Transfer Ability and Efficiency	Assess Effects of Learning as a Function of Different Instructional Components
Tasks	Reasoning, Planning and Visual Search Tasks	Nonverbal IQ-type Tasks	Visual-Motor, Higher Cognitive Tasks with Memory Components	Inductive Reasoning, Math and Reading, and Trouble-Shooting in Technical Environments	Perceptual Tasks, Math and Reading

Assessment Component of the Model	Standardized Procedures Involving Examinee Verbalization and Elaborated Feedback during Testing	Pre- and Post-assessments with Separate Intervention; Responsiveness Measured by Residualized Gain Scores	Pre- and Post-assessments with Separate Intervention	Preassessment; Then Quantifies Amount of Assistance Needed to Reach Post-Levels and Transfer	Initial Administration of Static Measure, Graduated Prompting Assessment, and if Necessary, Mediation
Intervention Component of the Model	No Interference Before or After Testing	Helping Examinees Understand Task Expectations, Building Rapport, Solution Monitoring, Facilitating Organization and Dual Coding	Problem Solving, Selecting, Focusing and Feedback	Sequential Sets of Teaching or Prompting Activities, From Most General to Most Specific	Nonstandardized Mediation and Standardized Graduated Prompting

Source: The material in this table provides a synthesis of work reported in Carlson and Wiedl (1992) and Jitendra and Kameenui (1993). Copyright 1993 by Remedial and Special Education. Adapted with permission.

scribing remediation. One might advocate dynamic assessment using a general test like the LPAD or using train-within-test procedures with IQ test–type tasks such as the Advanced Progressive Matrices (APM) (Raven, 1962), if one's purpose is to predict overall potential to succeed in school, training, or on the job. On the other hand, if one's purpose is to identify learners' domain-specific limitations and provide specific teaching prescriptions, dynamic procedures used with tests of relevant academic content knowledge could be used. Both types of dynamic assessment provide important sources of information about learners. Campione and Brown (1987, 1990) demonstrate this interface in the diagnosis and remediation of reading comprehension. Bransford et al. (1987) used dynamic assessment of math problems to identify learning difficulties, thereby suggesting specific teaching strategies. Further, they report that use of these teaching strategies has positive effects on learning among math-delayed children. Results from this type of research point to the need to include domain-specific tasks when seeking domain-specific recommendations for remediating content knowledge deficiencies.

The work of Feuerstein and others reminds us of the benefit of using dynamic procedures to identify strengths and limitations in general processes such as mediation. Elucidation of both domain-specific knowledge and general cognitive processes is important for predicting general potential to succeed. Moreover, it is important to interface content with these types of general processes in developing thought-based curricula. Such an interface enables students to learn and use "higher-order" thinking techniques to develop lower-order skills.

Criterion Development

Two studies, one using a train-within-test approach and one using a test-train-test approach, address the important issue of the criterion in validity studies of dynamic assessment. Using the testing-the-limits (train-within-test) method, Carlson and Wiedl (1980) demonstrated that while static IQ measurement may be a good predictor of traditional school achievement, dynamically IQ task performance was the best predictor of criterion performance under an adapted teaching condition. The dynamic teaching procedure emphasized verbalization, scanning, and self-correction. Using the learning potential (test-train-test) method, Babad and Bashi (1975) demonstrated that when the criterion is a process-oriented curriculum-based test, learning potential is a better predictor than IQ, regardless of ability.

MECHANISMS OF DYNAMIC ASSESSMENT

Having established that dynamic assessment techniques can, at times, provide more valid estimates of current intellectual competence and learning potential than traditional testing procedures, it is important to consider how these paradigms accomplish the two goals. Just what do investigators believe is going on during dynamic testing that occurs naturally during thinking but is inhibited during typical intelligence and ability testing? That is, what are the enhanced cognitive mechanisms during dynamic assessment?

Carlson and Wiedl (1980, 1992) offer a theoretical formulation to guide dynamic testing work that seems to be quite useful in framing much of the dynamic testing research. The authors suggest that four problem-solving factors are impacted by dynamic procedures: structures, processes, components, and levels of knowledge. The authors suggest, further, that dynamic testing affects heuristic structures, analytic processes, procedural characteristics of increased planfulness, reflectivity, exactness, flexibility, and sharpening of responses, as well as operator and orientation components and the examinee's level of conceptual knowledge. Dynamic procedures also are believed to lead to decreased anxiety.

Recent data from my laboratory on the direct assessment of cognitive flexibility indicates that dynamic procedures increase flexibility. Examination of solution protocols during flexibility testing indicates that dynamic assessment increases the use of multiple problem representations, helps examinees' building of internal connections, improves solution monitoring, and facilitates self-regulation.

With respect to building internal connections, examinees are encouraged through dynamic procedures specifically to understand the relations between problem elements. At a molecular level of analysis, changes are seen under dynamic versus standard procedures in the execution of the different information-processing stages underlying task solution. In recording ongoing eye movement patterns during dynamic versus standard assessment of analogical reasoning, I demonstrated that dynamic procedures result in more efficient and more thorough encoding and rule inference than is the case for standard techniques (Dillon, 1985). Tactical differences also were found in the sequencing of information-processing components. In terms of solution monitoring, dynamic testing helps point out inconsistencies in the examinee's thinking (Carlson & Wiedl, 1992). Again using data from eye movement patterns recorded during solution of complex analogical reasoning items, I demonstrated that solution monitoring occurs *within* components under dynamic techniques, thereby eliminating the examinee's perceived need for double-checking (Dillon, 1985). Under dynamic, as opposed to traditional, procedures, greater processing resources are devoted to the important components of encoding and rule inference, and less processing is devoted to rule application and confirmation activities—differences that reflect greater information-processing efficiency. Sternberg and Rifkin's (1979) work on expert-novice differences in execution of analogical reasoning components is consistent with these data.

Metacognitive theorists have linked thinking aloud during problem solving to self-regulated aspects of learning. The term *self-regulation* reflects many analogous processes to *solution monitoring*. In two reports of testing-the-limits effects on Das planning tasks, Cormier, Carlson, and Das (1990) and Kar, Dash, Das, and Carlson (1993) identify planning and selective attention effects of examinee verbalization. Poorer planners show greatest benefit from dynamic testing, although good planners also benefit from the dynamic procedures.

DIAGNOSTIC, PRESCRIPTIVE, AND TRAINING ADVANTAGES OF DYNAMIC PROCEDURES

In the context of diagnosis and prescription, dynamic testing procedures possess certain advantages over traditional methods of testing. With respect to diagnosis of intellectual abilities, dynamic procedures have two advantages. First, these procedures allow researchers to identify cognitive processes through dynamic techniques that cannot be isolated under standard procedures, such as certain types of solution monitoring. Moreover, investigators can extract a ''real-time'' account of cognitive processing through, for example, thinking-aloud techniques. Second, dynamic techniques permit identification of strengths and limitations in the processing abilities *underlying* test performance. We must keep in mind that the very different patterns of strengths and limitations in underlying processing abilities may be manifested in the same test score. Use of test scores, therefore, may not enable researchers to get certain crucial data regarding information-processing substrates of test performance. Advances in dynamic testing also make it possible to target education and training efforts at learner strengths and limitations in specific cognitive processes. Work using the range of dynamic assessment paradigms has been very fruitful in elucidating processes underlying test performance.

Testing-the-Limits Procedures

Using testing-the-limits procedures, Kirby and Woodhouse (1994) report that subjects' verbalizations during text processing elucidate depth of processing indices. Gilman and McFadden (1994) note the important information provided by dynamic assessment, with respect to the processes that are at work when examinees with special language and learning needs function successfully in contexts that require interpersonal and academic communication. Studying kindergarten children, Spector (1992) demonstrates that a dynamic measure of phonemic awareness enhances prediction of progress in beginning reading, relative to traditional assessment. The numerous studies reported by Jerry Carlson and his colleagues as well as work completed in my laboratory that were discussed above provide other examples of the importance of train-within-test paradigms for diagnosis and prescription.

Test-Train-Test Paradigms

A large number of studies using training-type paradigms point to the psychodiagnostic utility of dynamic assessment procedures. The work of Borland and Wright (1994) and Bolig and Day (1993) underscores the important role of dynamic assessment procedures in elucidating abilities among gifted individuals and understanding the relationship between ability and economic status. The authors present validation data in support of dynamic assessment for kindergarten children who are potentially intellectually gifted *and* economically disadvantaged. In acknowledging the importance of this work, we must bear in mind the belief shared by researchers embracing the genotype-environment interaction that intelligence can be understood as the ability to profit from experience. Central to this perspective is the notion that experiential deficiencies often mask accurate assessment of intellectual competence. Thus, we recognize the importance of work that permits us to study directly, and at an early age, the interface between economic disadvantage and intellectual giftedness. Numerous reports of the important role of dynamic assessment training approaches for other types of exceptional learners are offered in the literature. Gerber, Semmel, and Semmel (1994) demonstrate the usefulness of computer-based dynamic assessment of mathematical operations for providing instructional prescriptions for students with learning disabilities.

Jitendara, Kameenui, and Carnine (1994) employed dynamic assessment procedures in a test-train-test context with third-grade students who were performing mathematical operations. Data indicate that dynamic assessment facilitates use of strategies for understanding connections between mathematical concepts, and use of such strategies facilitates performance on a range of mathematical operations.

Using a test-train-test approach (Budoff, Meskin, & Harrison, 1971) and a graduated prompting approach (Campione & Brown, 1987, 1990), researchers report impressive bodies of literature on the usefulness of intervention approaches for diagnosing and improving general cognitive abilities and processes. As an example of this latter work, a study on four- and five-year-olds indicates that dynamic assessment scores are better predictors of residualized gain than static IQ (Campione & Brown, 1990).

Molina and Perez (1993) demonstrate the importance of learning potential assessment for diagnosing planning as well as simultaneous and successive processing deficits among children with Down's syndrome. Simmons (1992) reports that familiarization with task materials and rule and strategy instruction with feedback are dynamic assessment procedures that enhance performance and near transfer for four- and five-year-old children on solving a stencil design–type task. In related work, Burns, Delclos, Vye, and Sloan (1992) describe use of a continuum of assessment approach to demonstrate the role of mediation in strategy execution for three- to five-year-old handicapped and regular classroom children.

Lidz (1992) describes the usefulness of a preschool form of the learning potential assessment paradigm for diagnostic investigation of children aged three to five years. Processes assessed in this ambitious work include attention, stimulus detection, encoding, decoding, declarative knowledge, intersensory interactions, discrimination, flexibility, comparison, pattern detection, memory, planning, abstract thinking, impulse control, self-awareness, transfer, motivation, and interaction with adults.

Gutierrez-Clellen and Quinn (1993) successfully use dynamic assessment with training of culture-specific narrative contextualization rules to assess language abilities of culturally and linguistically diverse children. With respect to preschool language assessment, Pena, Quinn, and Inglesias (1992) demonstrate that dynamic language assessment effectively differentiates language-disabled from nondisabled preschoolers.

Another use of dynamic assessment and training is in complex technical environments. LaJoie and Lesgold (1992) use a graduated prompting-type intervention paradigm to assess and improve proficiency at solving avionics troubleshooting tasks. Using a related approach to assess academic abilities, Carney and Cioffi (1990, 1992) demonstrate the usefulness of a response to instruction technique in elucidating learning potential for word recognition and comprehension processes. Appropriate remedial intervention then is tied to examinees' performance.

Budoff (1987) uses a test-train-test approach to assess learning potential among experientially disadvantaged learners. According to Budoff, the procedures distinguish learners who are ill-prepared from learners who are incapable of success. An important point noted in Budoff's research concerns the robustness of learning potential predictions. Budoff found that children who perform competently following dynamic assessment also function better in other learning and social situations. For example, Budoff, Meskin, and Harrison (1971) demonstrate that end-of-term performance of special education students of high learning potential is equivalent to their peers in the regular classroom, in elementary science. Working in a mainstreaming context, Budoff and Gottlieb (1976) note that students of high learning potential demonstrate higher achievement than students who do not benefit as much from dynamic assessment, regardless of their class placement (i.e., initial tested intelligence). Students with high learning potential also believe that their peers view them as competent to a greater extent than low learning potential students. The above work demonstrates again that dynamic procedures identify differences in performance among individuals who previously were thought be grouped homogeneously.

An additional advantage of dynamic testing bears on the effects of dynamic assessment on teachers' opinions about students' competence or learning potential. Two experiments (Delclos, Burns, & Vye, 1993; Vye, Burns, Delclos, & Bransford, 1987) provide data to demonstrate that teachers who view videotapes of handicapped students participating in a dynamic assessment session report more positive expectations of the performance of examinees than without such exposure. Like the work of Feuerstein and Budoff, the impact of this research is to shift attribution for learning failure from the learner to the instructional techniques.

The robustness of dynamic assessment is underscored further by noting that its importance extends beyond cognitive abilities and academic subject areas per se to the domain of psychotherapy. Dynamic analysis of the psychotherapy process enables researchers to understand interaction plans at a process level (Richter, Schiepek, Kohler, & Schutz, 1995).

By providing information regarding an individual's strengths and limitations in cognitive processes underlying task performance, recommendations for selection, classification, and training can be made at a useful level. Diagnosis of individual differences in information-processing abilities can form the basis for selection, classification, and training efforts. Remediation can be tailored to an individual's particular limitations rather than providing the same training for all students. Increased efficiency and effectiveness should result. Finally, adverse impact is reduced when dynamic procedures are used (Dillon & Carlson, 1978; Lidz, 1987, 1992).

Transfer

Generalization of dynamic testing effects is another important issue in evaluating the utility of particular dynamic assessment paradigms. In a testing-the-limits context, the durable effect of verbalization and elaborated feedback on cognitive processes executed during inductive reasoning has been demonstrated (e.g., Dillon, 1978).

The Graduated Prompting Assessment work is promising in terms of demonstrating durable and generalizable effects. The processes in Feuerstein's Learning Potential Assessment program, if trained effectively, should prove durable and generalizable. Research in this area is needed.

WHEN IS DYNAMIC TESTING PARTICULARLY IMPORTANT?

The answer to this question pertains to purpose as well as individual difference factors. Each factor is considered below.

Purposes of Testing

With respect to the purposes of testing, an ample body of literature, discussed earlier, points to the increased criterion-related validity that results when learners are tested under dynamic as opposed to standard testing procedures. Often, important decisions are being made regarding an examinee's access to services or opportunities—example, voluntary admission to or exclusion from particular education or training opportunities. On these occasions, it is essential to have the most sensitive measures possible regarding the individual's current level of functioning and his or her ability to profit from the opportunities for which the individual is being considered. Examples range from provision of remedial training to securing a coveted slot in a prestigious medical school. Given the demonstrated importance of dynamic testing procedures for increasing the sensitivity of psychoeducational measurement, these testing techniques should be considered viable diagnostic options under such circumstances.

Learner Characteristics

Use of dynamic testing procedures is motivated also by individual difference concerns. Experiential, motivational, sociocultural, and remedial attributes all play roles in deriving an accurate measure of intelligence or ability. In earlier research using the train-within-test approach, Carlson & Dillon (1977) demonstrated that analogical reasoning among profoundly deaf children was greater under testing-the-limits procedures than under standard procedures, with this group of examinees performing at a level that was comparable to their hearing peers under dynamic assessment. In addition, ethnic group differences in analogical reasoning performance have been eliminated under dynamic procedures (Dillon & Carlson, 1978).

The work of Gutierrez-Clellen and Quinn (1993) extends consideration of the relationship between sociocultural factors and task performance to the measurement of narrative contextualization processes. The authors provide data to support the premise that such processes are culture specific and must be considered in assessment. Data are provided to advocate the use of dynamic training of the context-specific narrative rules that are valued in American schools before learning potential can be assessed veridically.

Feuerstein's work, of course, is similar in underlying motivation. Feuerstein's subjects have included experientially disadvantaged adolescents, for whom the use of training prior to testing to reduce task-relevant experiential deficiencies is believed to be justified if comparisons are to be made across sociocultural groups. Examinees report, during debriefing, greater enjoyment of the testing sessions during testing-the-limits procedures (Dillon, 1996) and greater academic self-efficacy following learning potential procedures, compared to standard methods of assessment.

Coupling Dynamic Testing Procedures with Individual Difference Dimensions

In discussing the issue of when dynamic testing is particularly important, I noted that particular experiential, sociocultural, and other individual difference dimensions render traditional assessments particularly limited in their power to predict educational or occupational success for certain learners. An interesting question is whether mechanisms of dynamic assessment are related to learners' cognitive processing preferences. At an applied level, researchers may consider the usefulness of matching or accommodating *particular* dynamic testing procedures to specific individual differences.

As an example of this type of work, I tested college undergraduates on one set of complex figural analogies under thinking-aloud procedures and a second set of items under elaborated feedback. A preference measure was computed for each subject, based on item set scores. Eighty-five percent of the subjects demonstrated a clear preference for internally imposed mediation or externally induced mediation. One half of the subjects then were matched to their preferred condition for administration of a third set of items, while the remaining subjects were mismatched to condition. Performance and validity were greater when subjects were matched to their preferred type of mediation (Dillon, 1980).

A second type of experiment concerned the effects of matching versus mismatching subjects to their preferred item presentation modality (Campbell & Dillon, 1992). One set of syllogisms was presented under auditory procedures, while a second set of items was administered visually. Subjects either were matched or mismatched to their preferred condition for a third set of syllogisms. Performance is found to be greater under matched conditions than when preferred presentation modality and testing condition are mismatched.

A third type of experiment coupled planning ability with dynamic procedures, revealing a similar benefit when planning ability and type of dynamic technique are matched (Kar, Dash, Das, & Carlson, 1993). Data from these experiments demonstrate that mechanisms of dynamic assessment are related to individual differences in cognitive processes and presentation modality.

Coupling Dynamic Testing with Other Procedures

Dynamic testing may be coupled with other procedures to yield even greater information than is available by either approach alone. As an example of this work, information-processing techniques may be used to record ongoing data from tests that are being administered dynamically. Such an approach permits identification of the effects of dynamic testing directly on information-processing components. As noted earlier, work in my laboratory (Dillon, 1985) permitted identification of the role of testing-the-limits procedures on problem representation, processing efficiency, and solution monitoring.

LINKING DYNAMIC TESTING WITH PROBLEM-SOLVING TRAINING

Feuerstein (e.g., Feuerstein, Rand, & Hoffman, 1979) maintains that basic cognitive processes, rather than traditional academic abilities, should be the objects of direct instruction. His position has support among cognitive components researchers (e.g., Sternberg, 1985). A common view among these researchers is that fundamental representational and solution processes should be trained *directly* rather than simply training traditional academic subjects and assuming that problem representation, encoding, inference, rule application, response selection, and monitoring will be improved. Dynamic assessment procedures provide one means of facilitating this training by making possible identification of strengths and limitations at the process level.

SUMMARY

A great deal can be said regarding the usefulness of dynamic testing. With respect to the study of intelligence, dynamic procedures permit identification of cognitive processes that may be difficult or impossible to measure directly through other means. Processes elucidated by means of dynamic testing include attention, stimulus detection, encoding, decoding, memory, flexibility, building internal connections, metacognitive processes such as solution monitoring, transfer, personality factors such as decreased anxiety, basic academic skills, and complex technical skills including troubleshooting. Such procedures go hand in hand with advances in intelligence theory.

Dynamic testing is believed to work by affecting cognitive structures and processes. Testing and/or intervention is targeted at these specific phenomena.

From an applied psychodiagnostic perspective, a strong body of literature exists to demonstrate that performance is increased dramatically when dynamic as opposed to standard testing methods are used. Validity is increased as well, with effects being most dramatic when criteria involve process dimensions. The beneficial effects of dynamic assessment are seen also in durable and generalizable effects on cognitive processes. Dynamic procedures may provide essential experiential training for individuals who are socioculturally or experientially disadvantaged, relative to their peers of comparable age and ability. The above point notwithstanding, the benefits of dynamic testing are seen across the ability spectrum and across developmental levels. Moreover, diagnosis and training effects run the gamut from basic information-processing componential and metacognitive abilities to academic subject areas and complex technical skills.

Dynamic testing procedures also inform selection and classification efforts. Assessment of either general competence to succeed or learning potential is possible. Coupling train-within-test or test-train-test techniques with tests of general reasoning or items such as those found on the LPAD is useful in this regard. When specific difficulties in particular school subject matter must be remediated, dynamic procedures can be coupled with tests of math or reading, for example, to inform prescriptions for remediation.

Dynamic procedures can be coupled with other techniques to enhance diagnostic power and to make possible the identification of abilities and processes that cannot be elucidated by either technique alone. Dynamic procedures can reveal, for example, the manner in which, how efficiently, and when in the sequence of problem solution the processes fostered through dynamic testing are occurring.

Finally, in examining research relating individual differences to dynamic assessment procedures, we see that experientially different individuals perform at a comparable level to their nondisadvantaged peers when testing procedures encourage (or provide practice in) forming multiple representations for problems, building internal connections, solution monitoring, and self-regulation.

It is interesting to note just how far the area of dynamic testing has come in the past two decades, since the first published reports of the success of dynamic procedures in enhancing reasoning test performance and criterion-related validity (e.g., Carlson & Wiedl, 1980, 1992; Dillon, 1979; Dillon & Carlson, 1978). Researchers now have eager audiences for their dynamic testing work.

REFERENCES

Babad, E., & Bashi, J. (1975). *Final report: An educational test of learning potential measurement.* Cambridge, MA: Research Institute for Educational Problems.

Bolig, E. E., & Day, D. (1993). Dynamic assessment and giftedness. *Roeper Review, 16,* 110–113.

Borland, J. H., & Wright, L. (1994). Identifying young, potentially gifted, economically disadvantaged students. *Gifted Child Quarterly, 38,* 164–171.

Bransford, J. D., Delclos, V. R., Vye, N. J., Burns, M. S., & Hasselbring, T. S. (1987). State of the art and future directions. In C. S. Lidz (Ed.), *Dynamic assessment: An interactional approach to evaluating learning potential* (pp. 479–496). New York: Guilford Press.

Brown, A. L., & French, L. A. (1979). The zone of potential development: Implications for intelligence testing in the year 2000. *Intelligence, 3,* 255–273.

Budoff, M. (1974). *Learning potential and educability among the educable mentally retarded* (Final Report Project No. 312312). Cambridge, MA: Research Institute for Educational Problems, Cambridge Mental Health Association.

Budoff, M. (1987). The validity of learning potential assessment. In C. S. Lidz (Ed.), *Dynamic assessment: An interactional approach to evaluating learning potential* (pp. 52–81). New York: Guilford Press.

Budoff, M., & Gottlieb, J. (1976). Special class EMR children mainstreamed: A study of an aptitude (learning potential) × treatment interaction. *American Journal of Mental Deficiency, 81,* 1–11.

Budoff, M., Meskin, J., & Harrison, R. H. (1971). An educational test of the learning potential hypothesis. *American Journal of Mental Deficiency, 76,* 159–169.

Burns, M. S. (1985). *Comparison of "graduated prompt" and "mediational" dynamic assessment and static assessment with young children.* Nashville, TN: J. F. Kennedy Center for Research on Education and Human Development, Vanderbilt University.

Burns, M. S., Delclos, V. R., Vye, N. J., & Sloan, K. (1992). Changes in cognitive strategies in dynamic assessment. *International Journal of Dynamic Assessment and Instruction, 2,* 45–54.

Burns, M. S., Haywood, H. C., Delclos, V. R., & Siewart, L. (1987). Young children's problem-solving strategies: An observational study. *Journal of Applied Developmental Psychology, 8,* 113–121.

Campbell, C., & Dillon, R. F. (1992, March). *Matching students to preferred reasoning conditions.* Paper presented at the Annual Phi Delta Kappa Research and Projects Field Day, Carbondale, IL.

Campione, J. K., & Brown, A. (1987). Linking dynamic assessment with school achievement. In C. Lidz (Ed.), *Dynamic assessment: An interactional approach to evaluating learning potential.* New York: Guilford.

Campione, J. C., & Brown, A. (1990). Guided learning and transfer: Implications for approaches to assessment. In N. Frederiksen, R. Glaser, A. Lesgold, & M. G. Shafto (Eds.), *Diagnostic monitoring of skill and knowledge acquisition*. Hillsdale, NJ: Erlbaum.

Campione, J. C., Brown, A. L., & Ferrerra, R. A. (1982). Mental retardation and intelligence. In R. J. Sternberg (Ed.), *Handbook of human intelligence* (pp. 392–490). Cambridge, England: Cambridge University Press.

Carlson, J. S., & Dillon, R. F. (1977, January; 1979). *The use of activation variables in the assessment of competence*. Paper presented at the Seventh Annual International Interdisciplinary Conference of Piagetian Theory and the Helping Professions, Los Angeles. Also *Journal of Educational Measurement, 16*, 19–26.

Carlson, J. S., & Wiedl, K. H. (1980). Applications of a dynamic testing approach in intellectual assessment: Empirical results and empirical formulations. *Zeitschrift für Differentielle und Diagnostische Psychologie, 1*, 303–318.

Carlson, J. S., & Wiedl, K. H. (1992). Principles of dynamic assessment: The application of a specific model. *Learning and Individual Differences, 4* (Special Issue), 153–166.

Carney, J. J., & Cioffi, G. (1990). Extending traditional diagnosis: The dynamic assessment of reading abilities. *Reading Psychology, 11* (Special Issue: Comprehension), 177–192.

Carney, J. J., & Cioffi, G. (1992). The dynamic assessment of reading abilities. *International Journal of Disability, Development, and Education, 39*, 107–114.

Cormier, P., Carlson, J. S., & Das, J. P. (1990). Planning ability and cognitive performance: The compensatory effects of a dynamic assessment approach. *Learning and Individual Differences, 2*, 437–449.

Delclos, V. R., Burns, M. S., & Vye, N. J. (1993). A comparison of teachers' responses to dynamic and traditional assessment reports. *Journal of Psychoeducational Assessment, 11*, 46–55.

Dillon, R. F. (1978). *The durable effects of dynamic assessment procedures*. Unpublished manuscript.

Dillon, R. F. (1979). Testing for competence: Refinement of a paradigm and its application to the hearing impaired. *Educational and Psychological Measurement, 39*, 363–371.

Dillon, R. F. (1980). Matching students to their preferred testing conditions: Improving the validity of cognitive assessment. *Educational and Psychological Measurement, 40*, 999–1004.

Dillon, R. F. (1981). Analogical reasoning under different methods of test administration. *Applied Psychological Measurement, 5*, 341–347.

Dillon, R. F. (1985). Eye movement analysis of information processing under different testing conditions. *Contemporary Educational Psychology, 10*, 387–395.

Dillon, R. F. (1986a, October). Development of a new system of measurement. In *Proceedings of the 1986 meeting of the Military Testing Association*. Mystic, CT: Military Testing Association.

Dillon, R. F. (1986b). Information processing and testing. *Educational Psychologist, 20*, 163–174.

Dillon, R. F. (1989a). Information processing and intelligent performance. In R. J. Sternberg (Ed.), *Advances in the psychology of human intelligence* (Vol. 5). Hillsdale, NJ: Erlbaum.

Dillon, R. F. (1989b). New approaches to aptitude testing. In R. F. Dillon & J. W. Pellegrino (Eds.), *Testing: Theoretical and applied perspectives*. New York: Praeger.

Dillon, R. F. (1992). Components and metacomponents of intelligence among navy and air force personnel. In *Proceedings of the 34th Annual Conference of the Military Testing Association*. San Diego: MTA.

Dillon, R. F. (1996). *Cognitive flexibility as a mechanism of dynamic assessment*. Unpublished manuscript.

Dillon, R. F., & Carlson, J. S. (1978). Testing for competence in three ethnic groups. *Educational and Psychological Measurement, 39*, 437–443.

Elliott, T. (1993). Assisted assessment: If it is "dynamic" why is it so rarely employed? *Educational and Child Psychology, 10*, 48–58.

Feuerstein, R. Y., Rand, Y., & Hoffman, M. B. (1979). *Dynamic assessment of retarded performers*. Baltimore: University Park Press.

Feuerstein, R., Rand, Y., Hoffman, M., & Miller, R. (1980). *Instrumental enrichment: An intervention program for cognitive modifiability*. Baltimore: University Park Press.

Gerber, M. M., Semmel, D. S., & Semmel, M. I. (1994). Computer-based dynamic assessment of multidigit multiplication. *Exceptional Children, 61*, 114–125.

Gilman, R., & McFadden, T. U. (1994). Redefining assessment as a holistic discovery process. *Journal of Childhood Communication Disorders, 16*, 36–40.

Gutierrez-Clellen, V. F., & Quinn, R. (1993). Assessing narratives of children from diverse cultural/linguistic groups. *Language, Speech, and Hearing Services in Schools, 24*, 2–9.

Jitendra, A. K., Kameenui, E. J. (1993). Dynamic assessment as a compensatory assessment approach: A description and analysis. *Remedial and Special Education, 14*, 6–18.

Jitendra, A. K., Kameenui, E. J., & Carnine, D. W. (1994). An exploratory evaluation of dynamic assessment and the role of basals on comprehension of mathematical operations. *Education and Treatment of Children, 17*, 139–162.

Kar, B. C., Dash, V. N., Das, J. P., & Carlson, J. (1993). Two experiments on the dynamic assessment of planning. *Learning and Individual Differences, 51*, 13–29.

Keane, K. J., & Kretschmer, R. E. (1987). Effect of mediated learning intervention on cognitive task performance with a deaf population. *Journal of Educational Psychology, 79*, 49–53.

Kirby, J. R., & Woodhouse, R. A. (1994). Measuring and predicting depth of processing in learning. *Alberta Journal of Educational Research, 40* (Special Issue: Cognition and assessment), 147–161.

LaJoie, S. P., & Lesgold, A. M. (1992). Dynamic assessment of proficiency for solving procedural knowledge tasks. *Educational Psychologist, 27*, 365–384.

Larson, G. E., Alderton, D. L., & Kaupp, M. A. (1991). Dynamic administration of a general intelligence test. *Learning and Individual Differences, 3*, 123–134.

Lidz, C. S. (1987). Historical perspectives. In C. S. Lidz (Ed.), *Dynamic assessment: An interactional approach to evaluating learning potential* (pp. 3–34). New York: Guilford.

Lidz, C. S. (1991). *Practitioner's guide to dynamic assessment*. New York: Guilford.

Lidz, C. S. (1992). The extent of incorporation of dynamic assessment into cognitive assessment courses: A national survey of school psychology trainers. *Journal of Special Education, 26* (Special Issue: Interactive assessment), 325–331.

Missiuna, C., & Samuels, M. T. (1989). Dynamic assessment of preschool children with special needs: Comparison of mediation and instruction. *Remediation and Special Education, 10*, 53–62.

Molina, S., & Perez, A. A. (1993). Cognitive processes in the child with Down syndrome. *Developmental Disabilities Bulletin, 21*, 21–35.

Pena, E., Quinn, R., & Inglesias, A. (1992). The application of dynamic methods to language assessment: A nonbiased procedure. *Journal of Special Education, 26* (Special Issue: Interactive assessment), 269–280.

Raven, J. C. (1962). *Advanced progressive matrices, Set II*. San Diego, CA: Psychological Corporation.

Reinharth, B. M. (1989). *Cognitive modifiability in cognitively delayed children*. Unpublished doctoral dissertation, Yeshiva University.

Richter, K., Schiepek, G., Kohler, M., & Schutz, A. (1995). Towards sequential plan analysis (SPA): A method for the dynamical analysis interactional plans within the client-therapist relationship. *Psychotherapie Psychomatik Medizinische Psychologie, 45*, 24–36.

Simmons, S. (1992). Instructional components of mediation in dynamic assessment: Performance and behavior effects. *International Journal of Dynamic Assessment and Instruction, 2*, 7–20.

Spector, J. E. (1992). Predicting progress in beginning reading: Dynamic assessment of phonemic awareness. *Journal of Educational Psychology, 84*, 353–363.

Sternberg, R. J. (1985). *Beyond IQ: A triarchic theory of human intelligence*. New York: Cambridge University Press.

Sternberg, R. J., & Powell, J. S. (1983). The development of intelligence. In J. H. Flavell & E. M. Markman (Eds.), *Handbook of child psychology* (Vol. 3, pp. 341–419). New York: Wiley.

Sternberg, R. J., & Rifkin, B. (1979). The development of analogical reasoning processes. *Journal of Experimental Child Psychology, 27*, 195–232.

Swanson, H. L. (1992). Generality and modifiability of working memory among skilled and less skilled readers. *Journal of Educational Psychology, 84*, 473–488.

Thomas, C. M. (1986). *The effects of mediation on the performance of disadvantaged preschool children on two cognitive tasks*. Unpublished doctoral dissertation, Bryn Mawr College, Bryn Mawr, PA.

Tzuriel, D. (1989). Dynamic assessment of learning potential in cognitive education programs. *The Thinking Teacher, 5*, 1–4.

Tzuriel, D., & Klein, P. S. (1987). Assessing the young child. Children's analogical thinking modifiability. In C. S. Lidz (Ed.), *Dynamic assessment: An interactional approach to evaluating learning potential* (pp. 268–287). New York: Guilford.

Vye, N. J., Burns, S., Delclos, V. R., & Bransford, J. D. (1987). A comprehensive approach to assessing intellectually handicapped children. In C. S. Lidz (Ed.), *Dynamic assessment: An interactional approach to evaluating learning potential* (pp. 327–359). New York: Guilford.

Vygotsky, L. S. (1962). *Thought and language* (E. Hanfmann & G. Vakar, Trans.). Cambridge, MA: MIT Press. (Original work published 1934)

Vygotsky, L. S. (1978). *Mind in society: The development of higher psychological process* (M. Cole, V. John-Steiner, & E. Souerman, Eds. & Trans.). Cambridge, MA: Harvard University Press.

9

Army Alpha to CAT-ASVAB: Four-Score Years of Military Personnel Selection and Classification Testing

Brian K. Waters

BACKGROUND

The United States military presents a massive personnel management challenge. Since the buildup for World War I, it has had to select, train, assign, lead, and manage millions of young men and women, most of whom have never held prior full-time employment. The challenge of selecting and assigning eligible recruits fairly, efficiently, and accurately has been met by military cognitive testing experts, primarily by the service research laboratories and their contractors.

The instruments and procedures that the U.S. military has developed over the past seven decades have become models for cognitive ability testing for education, job selection and promotion, and ability measurement throughout the world. This chapter provides a brief history of personnel selection and classification testing in the military over those seven decades, primarily focused on the enlisted force but touching on officer selection and assignment in the final sections.

Military Personnel Selection Testing

The demand for new enlisted recruits by the Army, Navy, Marine Corps, and Air Force is great, running from about a quarter of a million young men and women annually during peacetime to several million during mobilizations. The pool from which the military draws its recruits is young (generally ranging in age from 18 to the early 20s). Most often they arrive without advanced education (i.e., college education) or much previous employment history. Further, the military needs recruits who must often withstand physical demands well beyond comparable civilian jobs and who may be required to risk their lives to accomplish their missions. Thus, military testing is not limited only to cognitive assessment but also encompasses evaluating the physical, medical, emotional, and attitudinal characteristics of its potential recruits. The scope of the requirements for military testing is unmatched in any other psychological measurement application. The lives of millions of American youth and our national security rest in part upon an effective selection testing system in the U.S. military.

Military Personnel Classification Testing

Classification, in this context, is the system for assigning selected applicants into jobs. Military enlisted personnel must be selected to fill hundreds of different jobs, from cooks to riflemen to computer specialists. The aim of testing is not only to provide an estimate of general aptitude but also to provide a method for assigning recruits to particular jobs in which they show potential. Although the technical requirements for military jobs have increased greatly since World War I, the basic functions of selecting and assigning new recruits in the military have remained constant. This chapter now turns to military testing's roots: World War I, when an entirely new group-administered way of measuring people's abilities was born.

WORLD WAR I[1]

Alfred Binet's work on the measurement of human intelligence in the early 1900s provided the impetus for large-scale ability testing in the military during World War I. During 1917–1919, Robert M. Yerkes, the "father" of military psychology, applied Binet's individual intelligence measurement work to military testing. In considering the early months of 1917, Yerkes wrote:

The war demanded of us the speedy mobilization of our military machine and in addition the organization and training of an immense supplementary armed force. . . . Never before in the history of civilization was brain, as contrasted with brawn, so important; never before, the proper placement and utilization of brain power so essential to success. (Yerkes, 1919)

Army Alpha and Beta

Yerkes recommended that the Army use group testing to select and classify recruits on the basis of their intellectual ability, as well as to eliminate the unfit and identify the exceptionally superior. He proposed to develop three types of tests: the written Army Alpha for groups of literate recruits, the pictorial Beta for groups of illiterates and men who had failed the Alpha, and individual examinations—some version of the Binet scales—for those who failed the Army Beta.

The Army Alpha included eight types of test items: Directions or Commands, Arithmetical Problems, Common Sense, Synonym-Antonym, Disarranged Sentences, Number Series Completion, Analogies, and General Information (Martin, 1994). The Beta pictorial test included block counting, number similarities, mazes, drawing completion, and figure similarities. Many of the constructs measured by Army Alpha are present today in both military and civilian multiple aptitude test batteries.

Because of the scope of military selection for World War I, group-administered testing was essential to process the millions of potential recruits efficiently. An enduring effect of the World War I testing was the impetus it gave to mental testing itself. The Army tests were the first written tests of mental ability to be accepted generally by the testing professional community. As they were group administered, they provided a feasible method for ranking large numbers of persons for many different purposes, such as educational selection and placement, job selection and assignment, and professional licensing and certification. Most impressive was the use of tests for both employment and educational purposes. The Army's testing program was the first by any large organization, public or private, to assess its members' capabilities and to assign them accordingly (Van Riper, 1958, p. 252, cited in Zeidner & Drucker, 1988, p. 19). The basic work by Army test developers prior to and during World War I provided the foundation for the modern psychological testing industry.

WORLD WAR II

After the end of World War I, industry and government personnel managers deluged military test developers with requests for help in establishing testing programs based upon World War I military testing procedures. Industrial psychologists recognized the value of better personnel selection as a means for coping with absenteeism, turnover, and industrial inefficiency problems. The boom faded, however, when users found that testing was not the all-purpose single panacea for industrial personnel problems that many had hoped.

By the late 1930s, however, the forthcoming war began to place extraordinary demands on the personnel systems of both military and civilian agencies and rekindled interest in large-scale testing. During the summer of 1940, the Army established the Personnel Research Section (PRS) under Walter V. Bingham (this agency was the predecessor to today's Army Research Institute; Zeidner & Drucker, 1988) to develop a new general classification test and an examination for non-English-speaking men and illiterates. Tests of specific aptitudes required for clusters of jobs were also needed.

AGCT/Special Mental Tests[2]

The first major product of the PRS was the Army General Classification Test (AGCT)—Forms 1a and 1b—in October 1940 and Forms 1c and 1d in October 1941. Two Spanish-language versions were published in April 1941. The tests contained 140 to 150 multiple choice items covering vocabulary, arithmetic, and block counting items. The AGCT largely replaced the tests of World War I (Eitelberg, Laurence, Waters, with Perelman, 1984, pp. 14–15). By 1946, numerous forms of the AGCT had been fielded. AGCT Forms 3a and 3b included four tests: Reading and Vocabulary, Arithmetic Reasoning, Arithmetic Computation, and Pattern Analysis. During the 1940–1949 period, the Army Classification Battery (ACB) gradually replaced the AGCT (Uhlaner & Bolanovich, 1952). Over 9 million men, both enlisted and officer candidates, took the AGCT or ACB during the war.

As in World War I, there was a need during World War II for special mental tests. Three such additional tests were developed by PRS for classification purposes; for example, the Mechanical Aptitude Test (MAP) contained mechanical information, mechanical comprehension, and surface development items. MAP scores were used for assigning men to military occupational specialties (MOSs) as, for example, clerks, aircraft warning operators, and airplane mechanics. The Clerical Aptitude Test, used for selection into clerical and administrative jobs, included name checking, coding, catalog numbers, verbal reasoning, number checking, and vocabulary items. The Army Trade Screening Tests and Experience Checklists were developed in clerical, mechanical, and other technical fields to verify skill status for specific MOSs.

PRS scientists considered almost every type of selection device that could be standardized and empirically evaluated. Cognitive, psychometric, personality, biographical inventories, sensory, and psychomotor tests were assessed for various selection and classification purposes. Interviews, essays, ratings, performance-based measures, and assessment center techniques were also tried as selection tools. All were accompanied by vigorous attempts to obtain reliable and relevant criterion measures. The information was the best available testing data on ability testing for training and employment. It provided the standard of quality for future industrial psychological research. However, the ready acceptance of psychological tests in the military during World War II could be attributed to the pioneering work done during World War I and the broad acceptance of tests during the 1920s in industry and in academia.

The transition from broad classification measurement categories (qualified/not qualified) to differential ability testing was gradual. The AGCT-3a was the first manifestation of a full battery of selection and classification tests. By the fall of 1947, 10 tests (later to make up the Army Classification Battery) had been in use for classification (Zeidner & Drucker, 1988).

After the war, the services each developed their own selection tests. The Navy used the Basic Test Battery (BTB); the newly independent Air Force developed its Airman Classification Battery, and the Army used the ACB. Each of these test batteries was developed and validated with the services' missions and jobs in mind (Zeidner & Drucker, 1988).

THE ARMED FORCES QUALIFICATION TEST[3]

In 1948, the services convened a working group to develop a single, uniform aptitude test that could be used for enlisted selection and classification by each of the services.

Four basic requirements of the test were specified:

- Represent a "global" measure of ability.
- Contain vocabulary, arithmetic reasoning, and spatial relations items.
- Minimize the importance of speed so that slow performers would not be penalized.
- Minimize the difficulty of verbal instruction relating to test items (Eitelberg et al., 1984, pp. 15–16).

The service research laboratory test developers introduced the Armed Forces Qualification Test (AFQT) in July 1950. The AFQT was modeled after the AGCT and statistically linked to the World War II mobilization population, both enlisted members and officers, who were on active duty as of December 31, 1944. Thus, scores on the AFQT meant the same as scores on the earlier battery of selection tests used by the separate service branches.

The AFQT was designed to be used only as an initial screening device, not both as selection and classification measures as the earlier AGCT had been. Each service continued to use its own classification tests for assigning recruits to specific jobs. Although the tests making up the AFQT score have changed somewhat over the ensuing 40-plus years, the AFQT remains today the primary selection measure for Army, Navy, Marine Corps, Air Force, and Coast Guard enlisted recruits. Readers interested in the early development of the AFQT should refer to Uhlaner and Bolanovich (1952).

THE ARMED SERVICES VOCATIONAL APTITUDE BATTERY

In September 1968, the Air Force began using the Armed Services Vocational Aptitude Battery (ASVAB)-Form 1 for testing students under the Department of Defense (DoD) High School Testing Program (HSTP). ASVAB-1 included the then-current AFQT selection tests (Word Knowledge, Arithmetic Reasoning, Tool Knowledge, and Space Perception) and also classification tests (Mechanical Comprehension, Shop Information, Automotive Information, Electronics Information, and Coding Speed). Scores from the non-AFQT tests were combined into "composite" test scores that predicted performance in Air Force jobs and clusters of jobs.

In 1974, the decision was made that all of the services would use a single, common test battery for both selection and classification. The ASVAB, developed by the Air Force, was being used in the DoD-HSTP, as well as by the Marine Corps and Air Force for operational selection and classification testing. A revised version of the ASVAB (Forms 5, 6, and 7) became the DoD-wide aptitude test battery on January 1, 1976 (Eitelberg et al., 1984). The AFQT composite score included the Word Knowledge, Arithmetic Reasoning, and Space Perception tests, while nine other tests (Mathematics Knowledge, Numerical Operations, Attention to Detail, General Science, General Information, Mechanical Comprehension, Shop Information, Automotive Information, and Electronics Information) made up the classification components of the ASVAB.

Oops! The Miscalibration of the ASVAB

Great time pressures were thrust upon service laboratory test development specialists in 1975 and 1976 to get the ASVAB operational as soon as possible (Maier, 1993; Maier & Truss, 1983; Sims & Truss, 1980). The result of hurrying the implementation was a catastrophic error: a miscalibration of the new test battery; that is, percentile scores were grossly overestimated for many examinees. Errors in AFQT score, for example, led to the enlistment of thousands of recruits between January 1, 1976, and October 1, 1980, who would have been ineligible for military service according to then-existing enlistment standards.

Figure 9.1 displays the dramatic effect of the miscalibration on the actual levels of new recruit general ability scores (note that each year's data point shown in Figure 9.1 represents over one quarter of a million new recruits). The impact of the 1976–1980 scaling error was substantial (the percent scoring above the 50th percentile on the AFQT did not return to the pre-1976 level until the mid-1980s). After four years of scientific study and policy analyses (see ASVAB Working Group, 1980; Department of Defense [DoD], 1980a, 1980b; Jaeger, Linn, & Novick, 1980), DoD replaced the faulty test scales with a revised version of the ASVAB (ASVAB Forms 8, 9, and 10).

With the implementation of the new battery, the quality of the enlisted recruits immediately began to improve, and the belabored military test developers were able to put the ASVAB miscalibration brouhaha behind them. In the meantime, however, the services, particularly the Army, had admitted several hundred thousand potentially ineligible enlisted troops (PIs) to their ranks. A detailed analysis of the PIs may be found in Laurence and Ramsberger (1991).

ASVAB (1980–1997)

In conjunction with the recalibration of the ASVAB, DoD arranged for the development of a nationally representative normative base for the battery by

Figure 9.1
Percent Scoring AFQT 50 or Higher, 1952–1994

**Percent Scoring AFQT 50 or Higher:
1952-1994**

— NPS Accessions %
> AFQT 50

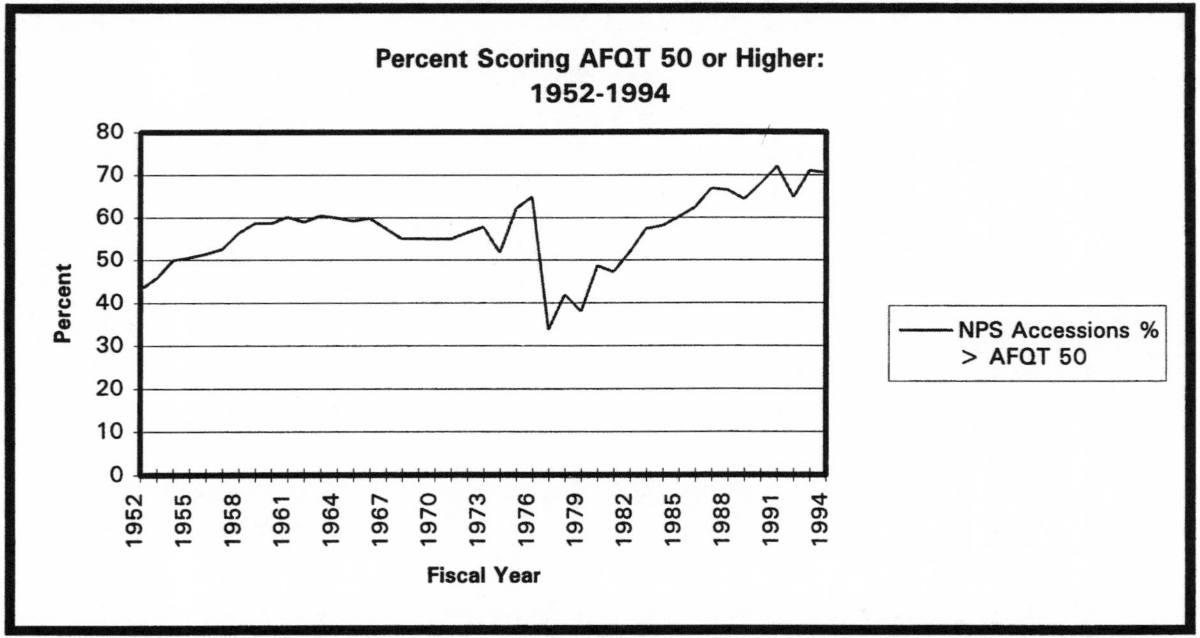

Source: Department of Defense (1994, table D-8).

administering ASVAB-Form 8A to respondents in the Department of Labor's 1979 National Longitudinal Survey of Youth Labor Force Behavior (NLSY79) data collection. Nearly 12,000 American youth from 16 through 23 years old took the entire ASVAB as part of their participation in the 1980 Profile of American Youth (PAY80) study. A new comparison population of test scores was developed to replace the 1944 reference population, which had served as the score reference base for military entrance test scores for nearly four decades (see Department of Defense, 1982). The PAY80 study provided the score scale for ASVAB for the next 16 years. Since 1980, new versions of the battery are developed every three or four years to keep the test content current and prevent compromise of the battery.

The content of the current version of the battery (ASVAB Forms 20, 21, and 22) is shown in Table 9.1. Scores are currently referenced to the PAY80 norms. As with earlier versions, the individual services develop their own composites for classification purposes. A concise description of current military selection and classification uses of ASVAB can be found in Sands and Waters (1997).

1998 AND BEYOND: CAT-ASVAB

Beginning in the 1960s, DoD became interested in supporting research to computerize its testing. A new technology, Computerized Adaptive Testing (CAT), was being developed in academic testing research that showed considerable promise for improving the efficiency and accuracy of aptitude testing. The U.S. military provided the majority of the financial support for the development of CAT for over two decades. CAT came into operational fruition in 1996 due to that support.

Computerized Adaptive Testing (CAT)[4]

As the name implies, a computerized adaptive test is computer administered. The test dynamically adapts itself to each examinee's ability *during* the course of test administration. In a conventionally administered, paper-and-pencil test, every examinee takes the same items, typically in the same order, regardless of the item's appropriateness for his or her ability level. Administering easy items to a high-ability examinee is wasteful, as correct responses provide relatively little information about that examinee's ability. In addition, the person may become bored with a less challenging test and respond carelessly, introducing additional measurement error. Administering hard items to a low-ability examinee is similarly wasteful, as incorrect answers do not provide much information. Moreover, when low-ability examinees find most items too difficult for them, they may become frustrated and respond randomly, degrading the accuracy of the ability estimate. In contrast, a CAT instrument has the ability to "tailor" the test to each examinee as information is being collected and evaluated during the test's administration. Thus, CAT offers an adaptive process for selecting and administering a test item, scoring an examinee's response, updating his or her ability estimate, and choosing the next item for administration, which continues until the examinee's ability is accurately estimated (see McBride, 1996, for discussion). Using CAT rather than paper-and-pencil testing results in time savings of approximately 50 percent, as the process quickly hones in on those test items that best assess each examinee's ability.

CAT-ASVAB

As occurred in the PAY80 study, DoD will join with the Department of Labor's 1997 National Longitudinal Study of Youth to renorm the ASVAB. This new normative base, a nationally representative sample of 12- through 23-year-olds, will be gathered on personal computers at contract testing centers, using a CAT version of ASVAB. Data will also be collected on a new space perception test (Assembling Objects) and a DoD-developed interest inventory, the Interest Finder (IF). As with PAY80, PAY97 will establish the score scales for ASVAB and for IF as well. The testing will require over one hour less time on the average than the 1980 data collection. The PAY97 norming will put DoD at the leading edge of state-of-the-art aptitude testing. It will represent the largest application of CAT technology in history.

OFFICER SELECTION AND CLASSIFICATION TESTING[5]

Traditionally, the military services have publically released less data and policy statements about the selection and classification testing of their officers than about their enlisted forces. Unlike the enlisted selection, there is no single aptitude test used across services to identify the best-qualified officer candidates. Even within each service, there are various commissioning paths (e.g., Service Academy, Reserve Officer Training Corps [ROTC], Officer Candidate School [OCS], or direct commissioning), whose selection procedures vary widely. Each path has its own selection methods, measures, and standards.

Numerical requirements for officer accessions are only about one seventh of the number of recruits needed annually. Today, new officer candidates to all of the services are required to be college graduates. This effectively places the onus on the educational community to provide the screening (cognitive as well as behavioral) function that the ASVAB provides for the enlisted force. Certainly, selection testing plays an important part in who goes to college (e.g., the Scholastic Assessment Test [SAT] or American College Test [ACT] college admission tests), however, the services demand much more than just academic ability of their officer corps. Graduating from college requires technical knowledge (e.g., engineering or scientific skills), plus demonstration of less specifically definable characteristics such as perseverance, maturity, leadership and management skills, and logical thinking.

This section provides a brief overview of how officer selection has evolved

Table 9.1
ASVAB Tests: Description, Number of Questions, and Testing Time

ASVAB Test Title and Abbreviation	Description	Number of Questions	Testing Time (Minutes)
General Science (GS)	Measures knowledge of physical and biological sciences	25	11
Arithmetic Reasoning (AR)	Measures ability to solve arithmetic word problems	30	36
Word Knowledge (WK)	Measures ability to select the correct meaning of words presented in context and to identify best synonym for a given word	35	11
Paragraph Comprehension (PC)	Measures ability to obtain information from written passages	15	13
Mathematics Knowledge (MK)	Measures knowledge of high school mathematics principles	25	24
Numerical Operations (NO)	Measures ability to perform arithmetic computations in speeded context	50	3

Coding Speed (CS)	Measures ability to use a key in assigning code numbers to words in a speeded context	84	7
Auto and Shop Information (AS)	Measures knowledge of automobiles, tools and shop terminology and practices	25	11
Mechanical Comprehension (MC)	Measures knowledge of mechanical and physical principles and ability to visualize how illustrated objects work	25	19
Electronics Information (EI)	Measures knowledge of electricity and electronics	20	9
Total All Tests		334	144[a]

Source: Sands and Waters (1997, p. 6).

[a]Administrative time is 36 minutes, for a total testing and administrative time of three hours.

over the past seven decades. The enlisted selection was covered in greater detail not only because little has been documented in the literature on officer selection policies but also because the processes are so complex across and within the individual services. Readers interested in an excellent in-depth discussion of the subject should refer to "Becoming Brass: Issues in the Testing, Recruiting, and Selection of American Military Officers" by Eitelberg et al. (1992).

World War I Officer Selection

By January 31, 1919, Yerkes and the PRS had presided over test adminis-tration to 42,000 officer-candidates, using the Army Alpha and other tests and evaluative techniques (Zeidner & Drucker, 1988). Many underclass officer-candidates enrolled in service academy or ROTC college programs at that time were assigned directly from the campus to the battlefield to fill the bur-geoning requirements for officers in Europe. This World War I policy likely served as a precedent for the current college education requirement for all of-ficers.

World War II Officer Selection

As in World War I, a critical need for officers grew as U.S. entry into World War II approached. After World War I, the majority of officers re-turned to civilian life as the military made its transition to peacetime status. Many officers retained inactive reserve status with their service. Some of those experienced officers were still on board as the buildup for World War II evolved, and they were recalled to active duty. But, clearly, other sources of officer-candidates were needed. The Officer Candidate Test was developed and implemented to predict OCS performance. The candidates' "ability to deal with people" was rated through interviews and other measurement de-vices such as projective tests (e.g., the Rorschach, the Thematic Apperception Test, and the Philo-Phobe). Test scores were evaluated and used as tools to predict candidates' leadership ability. New tests were developed—some for special populations—such as the Women's Classification Test, which was used to predict Women's Army Corps (WAC) OCS grades. A Combat Adapt-ability Rating Scale was developed, and used in conjunction with an inter-view, performance situations, and stress situations, but it failed to correlate with leadership ratings adequately.

The U.S. Office of Strategic Services (OSS) developed its renowned multiple assessment techniques during World War II for the selection of officer-candidates (OSS Assessment Staff, 1948). The referenced book is the classic documentation of the OSS program, authored by the Army staff and consultants who developed it. The OSS techniques are the forerunner of modern assessment center selection procedures. It is highly recommended for readers interested in assessment centers and their historical development.

The Role of Testing in Current Officer Selection

Across all of the services, aptitude test scores are only one part of their officer selection processes. The so-called whole person is assessed, including leadership potential, technical skills, character, recommendations, school grades, and interview performance. Selections are made by boards of senior officers and personnel specialists. Potential costs of making an errant selection can be enormous, currently up to a quarter of a million dollars at the academies, not taking into account the operational costs and consequences of having a ''bad'' officer enter the system. The complex, expensive, and unique systems used by each of the services to identify their officers appropriately reflect the importance of reliable and valid decisions in deciding who becomes their brass (Eitelberg et al., 1992).

Current Military Officer Selection Policies

At the end of fiscal year 1993, there were 239,293 officers on active duty and 149,430 in the reserves. During that year, 15,351 new officers entered active duty, and there were 18,561 new reservists (DoD, 1994). Table 9.2 shows officer selection tests and academic criteria used by the services in 1987–1988 (Eitelberg et al., 1992). Each of the unique service tests depicted in Table 9.2 are described briefly.

Army Officer Selection Battery (OSB). Originally developed in 1972, the OSB Forms 1 and 2 measure cognitive abilities, interest in combat leadership, technical-managerial leadership, and career potential. It is currently the selection test for Army OCS. OSB Forms 3 and 4 were developed in 1986 for ROTC nonscholarship students, based upon job analysis of the administration: They measure communication, interpersonal manner, technical knowledge, and combat performance.

Navy Officer Aptitude Rating (OAR), Aviation Qualification Test (AQT) and Flight Aptitude Rating (FAR). Navy aviation candidate selection testing began in the 1920s, covering physical measures, intelligence, motivation, and character. In 1942, the Flight Aptitude Rating (FAR) was developed from a combination of the Bennet Mechanical Comprehension Test (MCT) and the Purdue Biographical Inventory (BI). A year later, the Aviation Classification Test (ACT) was administered along with the FAR for Navy officer selection. In 1971, the Navy created the Aviation Selection Test Battery (ASTB), which included the AQT (a replacement for the ACT), the MCT, the BI, and a new test—the AQT and MCT, was developed for use in selection of nonaviation candidates. The FAR and the AQT are still in use for Naval and Marine aviation candidates, and the OAR is used for the Navy OCS program. The ASTB (also referred to as the Officer Candidate Tests) is currently in operational use by the Navy. It has recently been revised. The ASTB is designed to measure ''academic, mechanical, and spatial aptitudes, . . . basic knowledge of aerospace, mature judgment, risk-taking willingness and other person attributes'' (Eitelberg et al., 1992, pp. 113–114).

Table 9.2
Aptitude Tests and Academic Criteria Used to Screen Officer Candidates,
by Program and Service, 1987–1988

Program	Army	Navy	Marine Corps	Air Force
Service Academy	SAT/ACT HS Rank	SAT/ACT HS Rank	---[a]	SAT/ACT HS Rank
ROTC Scholarship	SAT/ACT HS Rank College GPA	SAT/ACT HS Rank HS GPA	---[a]	SAT/ACT HS Rank College GPA AFOQT
ROTC Non-Scholarship	OSB 3 & 4	Varies by Unit	---[a]	AFOQT SAT/ACT College GPA
OCS/OTS and Other	OSB 1 & 2 GT	OAR	SAT/ACT EL	AFOQT College GPA
Aviation OCS	N/A	AQT-FAR	SAT/ACT EL AQT-FAR	N/A

[a] Same as Navy. Up to 16% of Naval Academy and naval ROTC graduates may be commissioned as Marine Corps officers.

Abbreviations

SAT	Scholastic Assessment Test	ASVAB	Armed Services Vocational Aptitude Battery
ACT	American College Test	GT	General Technical Composite of ASVAB
HS	High School	OAR	Officer Aptitude Rating
GPA	Grade Point Average	AQT-FAR	Aviation Qualification Test-Flight Aptitude Rating
AFOQT	Air Force Officer Qualifying Test	OTS	Officer Training School
OSB	Officer Selection Battery	EL	Electronic Composite from ASVAB
OCS	Officer Candidate School	N/A	Not Applicable
ROTC	Reserve Officer Training Corps		

Source: Eitelberg et al. (1992, p. 111).

Air Force Officer Qualifying Test. The Air Force Officer Qualifying Test (AFOQT) was developed in 1951 and has been revised numerous times over the past four decades. It currently contains over 300 items clustered into 16 tests that together require about four hours to complete. Five composite scores are generated: Pilot, Navigator-Technical, Academic Aptitude, Verbal, and Quantitative, which are used for both selection and classification to Air Force officer specialties.

ASVAB Composites Used in Officer Selection. The Army uses the General-Technical (GT) composite (scores from the Arithmetic Reasoning, Word Knowledge, and Paragraph Comprehension tests) from the ASVAB as a selection measure for OCS for Army enlisted personnel applying for officer training. Similarly, the Marine Corps uses the Electronics Repair (EL) ASVAB composite score (General Science, Arithmetic Reasoning, Mathematics Knowledge, and Electronics Information tests) in selecting between OCS applicants. Since all enlisted personnel have ASVAB scores in their records, evaluation of initial OCS applicants is both efficient and inexpensive for the Army and Marine Corps.

EPILOGUE

Testing and measurement are big business in DoD. This brief overview of military selection and classification testing only skims the surface. For example, personnel testing in the military is used for psychological testing in clinical and medical applications, in all aspects of training, in specialized content areas such as foreign language proficiency, unit performance and individual proficiency measurement, promotion testing, and in determination of qualifications for awards and decorations, but these are only a handful of their applications in the military.

In many ways, military testing is a mirror of the more general subject of testing in the civilian world. DoD, however, has paved the way for much of the research and development of testing technology throughout this century. Because relatively small improvements in the technology yield such big payoffs and affect so large a scale, military testing will continue to be at the leading edge of research and development in the testing profession into and throughout the twenty-first century.

NOTES

Many Human Resources Research Organization and Department of Defense colleagues reviewed and critiqued drafts of this chapter. The author appreciates their efforts. However, the author remains responsible for the final version.

1. This section draws heavily from Zeidner and Drucker (1988, pp. 7–19).

2. Drawn primarily from Zeidner and Drucker (1988).

3. Much of the information in this section came from Zeidner and Drucker (1988), Eitelberg et al. (1984), and Maier (1993).

4. Drawn heavily from Sands and Waters (1997).

5. Drawn heavily from Eitelberg, Laurence, and Brown (1992).

REFERENCES

ASVAB Working Group. (1980). *History of the Armed Services Vocational Aptitude Battery (ASVAB) 1974–1980.* A report to the Principal Deputy Assistant Secretary of Defense (Manpower, Reserve Affairs, and Logistics). Washington, DC: Office of the Assistant Secretary of Defense (Manpower, Reserve Affairs, and Logistics).

Department of Defense. (1969). *Project 100,000: Characteristics and performance of "new standards" men.* Washington, DC: Office of the Assistant Secretary of Defense (Manpower, Reserve Affairs, and Logistics).

Department of Defense. (1980a). *Aptitude testing of recruits*. A report to the House Committee on Armed Services. Washington, DC: Office of the Assistant Secretary of Defense (Manpower, Reserve Affairs, and Logistics).

Department of Defense. (1980b). *Implementation of new Armed Services Vocational Aptitude Battery and actions to improve the enlistment standards process*. A report to the House and Senate Committees on Armed Services. Washington, DC: Office of the Assistant Secretary of Defense (Manpower, Reserve Affairs, and Logistics).

Department of Defense. (1982). *Profile of American youth: 1980 nationwide administration of the Armed Services Vocational Aptitude Battery*. Washington, DC: Office of the Assistant Secretary of Defense (Manpower, Reserve Affairs, and Logistics).

Department of Defense. (1994). *Population representation in the military services: Fiscal year 1993*. Washington, DC: Office of the Assistant Secretary of Defense (Force Management Policy).

Eitelberg, M. J., Laurence, J. H., & Brown, D.C. (1992). Becoming brass: Issues in the testing, recruiting, and selection of American military officers. In B. R. Gifford & L. C. Wing, (Eds.), *Test policy in defense: Lessons from the military for education, training, and employment*. Boston: Kluwer Academic Publishers.

Eitelberg, M. J., Laurence, J. H., Waters B. K., with Perelman, L. S. (1984). *Screening for service: Aptitude and education criteria for military entry*. Washington, DC: Office of the Assistant Secretary of Defense (Manpower, Installations, and Logistics).

Jaeger, R. M., Linn, R. L., & Novick, M. R. (1980). A review and analysis of score calibration for the Armed Services Vocational Aptitude Battery. In Department of Defense, *Aptitude testing of recruits, Appendix B*. Washington, DC: Office of the Assistant Secretary of Defense (Manpower, Installations, and Logistics).

Laurence, J. H., & Ramsberger, P. F. (1991). *Low-aptitude men in the military: Who profits, who pays?* New York: Praeger.

Maier, M. H. (1993). *Military aptitude testing: The past fifty years* (DMDC TR 93–007). Monterey, CA: Personnel Testing Division, Defense Manpower Data Center.

Maier, M. H., & Truss, A. R. (1983). *Original scaling of ASVAB Forms 5/6/7: What went wrong.* (CRC 457). Alexandria, VA: Center for Naval Analyses.

Martin, C. J. (1994). *Army Alpha to Navy Theta*. Paper presented at the 36th Annual Conference of the International Military Testing Association, Rotterdam, The Netherlands.

McBride, J. R. (1996). Innovations in computer-based ability testing: Promise, problems, and peril. In M. D. Hakel (Ed.), *Beyond multiple choice: Evaluating alternatives to traditional testing for selection*. Hillsdale, NJ: Laurence Erlbaum Associates.

OSS Assessment Staff. (1948). *Assessment of men: Selection of personnel for the Office of Strategic Services*. New York: Rinehart and Company, Inc.

Sands, W. A., & Waters, B. K. (1997). "Introduction to ASVAB and CAT." In W. A. Sands, B. K. Waters, & J. R. McBride (Eds.), *CATBOOK—Computerized adaptive testing: From inquiry to operation*. Washington, D.C.: American Psychological Association.

Sims, W. H., & Truss, A. R. (1980). *A reexamination of the normalization of the Armed Services Vocational Aptitude Battery (ASVAB) Forms 6, 7, 6E and 7E* (CNA Study 1152). Alexandria, VA: Center for Naval Analyses.

Staff, Personnel Research Section (The Adjutant General's Office). (1945). The Army General Classification Test. *Psychological Bulletin, 42*, 760–768.

Uhlaner, J. E., & Bolanovich, D. J. (1952). *Development of Armed Forces Qualification Test and predecessor Army screening tests, 1946–1950* (PRS Report 976). Washington, DC: Office of the Personnel Research Section, Department of the Army.

Van Riper, P. (1958). *History of the United States Civil Service*. Evanston, IL: Row, Peterson & Company.

Waters, B. K., Laurence, J. H., & Camara, W. J. (1987). *Personnel enlistment and classification procedures in the U.S. military*. Washington, DC: National Academy Press.

Yerkes, R. M. (1919). Report of the Psychology Committee of the National Research Council. *Psychological Review, 26*, 317–328.

Zeidner, J., & Drucker, A. J. (1988). *Behavioral science in the Army: A corporate history of the Army Research Institute*. Alexandria, VA: United States Army Research Institute for the Behavioral and Social Sciences.

10

The Use of Computerized Adaptive Testing in the Military

Kathleen E. Moreno, Daniel O. Segall, and
Rebecca D. Hetter

The United States Armed Services use the Armed Services Vocational Aptitude Battery (ASVAB) to assess military applicants. This battery consists of 10 subtests and is typically administered by conventional, paper-and-pencil (P&P) methods. It is administered to approximately 600,000 applicants annually by the United States Military Entrance Processing Command as part of their production testing program.

Currently, there is a major effort under way to implement a Computerized Adaptive Testing version of the ASVAB (CAT-ASVAB). CAT-ASVAB uses item response theory to tailor a test to the ability level of an individual examinee. Items are selected from large, precalibrated item pools, matching the difficulty of the next test item to the current ability level of the examinee. After each item response, the examinee's ability estimate is updated. Adaptive testing makes it possible to administer short tests that provide precise measurement across all ability levels. Computer administration makes it possible to use this procedure, plus provides such benefits as standardization of test administration procedures, item security, and increased accuracy of scoring and recording of data.

The CAT-ASVAB research effort can be broken down into two phases. The purpose of the first phase was to develop, evaluate, and implement a CAT system in a small number of operational sites. Lessons learned from this first phase are being used in the second phase of the project: development and implementation of CAT-ASVAB on a nationwide scale.

The first phase of the project has been completed. Item pools and test administration procedures were developed and evaluated, hardware was selected and procured, software development was completed, and the CAT-ASVAB system was implemented at six operational sites. This chapter describes the psychometric development and evaluation of this system. It also briefly describes system implementation.

PROJECT BACKGROUND

During the past decade, military research laboratories have conducted extensive research in the area of Computerized Adaptive Testing. As early as 1977, the Navy Personnel Research and Development Center (NPRDC), in conjunction with the University of Minnesota, was administering computerized adaptive tests designed to be similar in content to several of the subtests in the P&P-ASVAB. Tests were administered to military recruits for research purposes only.

Results of these early studies were very encouraging. Comparisons of reliability estimates obtained from CAT to those obtained from P&P tests showed that CAT could achieve the same level of reliability as P&P with about half the number of items as P&P (McBride & Martin, 1983). A factor analytic study showed that CAT subtests appeared to be measuring the same abilities as corresponding P&P-ASVAB subtests (Moreno, Wetzel, McBride, & Weiss, 1984). The same study also showed that the CAT subtests correlated as highly with corresponding P&P-ASVAB subtests as another form of the P&P-ASVAB.

The early studies showed that the potential of CAT for personnel selection is promising. Based on these findings, an experimental CAT system, to include all ASVAB content areas, was designed and developed (Quan, Park, Sandahl, & Wolfe, 1984). The hardware used for the experimental system consisted of Apple /// computers connected to a Corvus hard disk drive. The computer keyboard was modified so that only those keys needed to take the test were exposed. The power subtests were administered using stratified maximum information combined with a randomization procedure for item selection (Wetzel & McBride, 1985). Owen's Bayesian sequential scoring (Owen, 1975) was used to estimate ability. The speeded subtests were administered in a conventional fashion, and number-correct scoring was used.

The experimental CAT system was used to conduct a joint-service validity study (Moreno, Segall, & Kieckhaefer, 1985). Over all four services, 7,515 military recruits were tested on CAT-ASVAB and those P&P-ASVAB subtests that were used in computing a recruit's school selection composite score. Training school performance data were also collected for each recruit. CAT-ASVAB and P&P-ASVAB were compared in terms of how well each predicted performance in about six training schools per service. Results showed that even though the number of items per subtest in CAT-ASVAB was substantially less than in P&P-ASVAB, CAT-ASVAB predicted school performance as well. Also, these data showed that CAT-ASVAB has a similar factor structure to that of the P&P-ASVAB.

While the empirical studies mentioned above are only a few of the research studies conducted as part of this project, they have served as key elements in evaluating the potential of CAT-ASVAB. Other studies, both simulation and empirical, have been conducted primarily to develop, evaluate, and/or refine the psychometric procedures to be employed in CAT-ASVAB. Some of these studies will be described in the next section.

CAT-ASVAB PSYCHOMETRIC DEVELOPMENT

CAT-ASVAB contains nine power subtests: General Science, Arithmetic Reasoning, Word Knowledge, Paragraph Comprehension, Automotive Information, Shop Information, Mathematics Knowledge, Mechanical Comprehension, and Electronics Information; it also has two speeded subtests: Numerical Operations and Coding Speed. These subtests correspond to those in the P&P-ASVAB, with the exception that the P&P-ASVAB Automotive and Shop Information subtest has been broken into two subtests due to concerns about dimensionality. This section describes item pool development for each of these content areas and test administration procedures that will be used in CAT-ASVAB. Please note that the description applies to the first two forms developed for CAT-ASVAB. Procedures for form development and test administration may vary in the future.

Item Pool Development

The item pool used in an adaptive test has a major influence on the precision of the test. In developing the pools for CAT-ASVAB, certain steps were taken to ensure that the final pools would provide accurate measurement of ability. Procedures for CAT-ASVAB item pool development can be roughly divided into five steps: (1) item writing and calibration, (2) item screening, (3) assessment of dimensionality, (4) creation of alternate forms, and (5) elimination of unused items.

Items for the nine power subtests were developed and calibrated by an Air Force Human Resources Laboratory contractor (Prestwood, Vale, Massey, & Welsh, 1985). Over 200 items in each content area were calibrated using P&P data collected from military applicants at Military Entrance Processing Stations nationwide. This data collection effort resulted in approximately 2,500 responses per item. Item parameters were estimated using a joint maximum likelihood procedure based on the three-parameter logistic model. The ASCAL computer program was used to provide these estimates (Vale & Gailluca, 1985).

After item calibration, all items were screened by a panel of NPRDC researchers. Item reviews were based on: (1) recommendations provided by service representatives and by an NPRDC contractor (Kershaw & Wainer, 1985) addressing sensitivity and quality concerns, (2) empirical checking of item keys using point biserial correlations for each alternative, and (3) suitability for display on the computer screen. Those items found to be unacceptable were dropped from the pools.

Item response theory, on which the adaptive testing methods are based, requires that a test be unidimensional. However, empirical results show that the model is suitable when the items have one dominant dimension (Green, Bock, Humphreys, Linn, Reckase, 1982). Data collected for item calibration were used to assess the dimensionality of the power subtest item pools. Item responses were analyzed using the TESTFACT computer program (Wilson, Wood, & Gibbons, 1984). This program employs "full information" item factor analysis based on item response theory (Bock & Aitkin, 1981). Results showed that the majority of the content areas appeared to be multidimensional, showing more than one factor. However, the reason for the item clustering appeared to be unrelated to specific item content and confounded by item difficulty. The exception was General Science, which appeared to have three factors: physical science, life science, and chemistry.

In CAT-ASVAB, all power subtests, except General Science, are treated as unidimensional. General Science has been divided into the three content areas listed above, with content balancing being used during test administration. This will ensure that the same numbers of items from each General Science content area will be administered to each examinee.

The next step in item pool development was to divide the item pool for each content area into alternate forms. Two forms are needed for retesting of examinees and for security purposes. The goal of the alternate form assignment was to minimize the weighted sum-of-squared differences between the two test information functions. These squared differences were weighted by an N (0, 1) density. For General Science, alternate forms were created for the life, physical, and chemistry content areas. Figure 10.1 shows a graph of the alternate forms for Math Knowledge.

The final step in item pool development was to eliminate items that would not be used in test administration because of low item information. This step was necessary because of limited memory in the test administration computers. Simulations were conducted, using the adaptive testing procedures described in the section below on test administration. Simulated test sessions were generated for 500 examinees at each of 31 different ability levels, equally spaced along the -3, $+3$ interval. Items that were not selected for administration in the simulations were dropped from the pools.

Test Administration Procedures

This section describes the item selection and scoring procedures used in CAT-ASVAB. It also describes the stopping rule used to end a subtest and the use of "seeded" items in CAT-ASVAB.

Power Subtests. Items are selected using maximum information. To save computation time, an information "look-up" table is used. To create the tables, all items within a content area were rank ordered by item information at each of 37 theta levels, ranging from -2.25 to $+2.25$. Typically, using this type of item

Figure 10.1
Test Information Functions for Math Knowledge

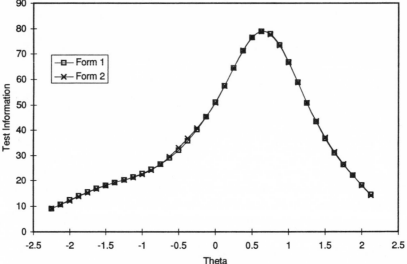

selection procedure, the most informative item at the level closest to an examinee's current ability estimate is administered. However, this procedure results in some items being overused. Consequently, CAT-ASVAB item selection incorporates an algorithm for exposure control (Sympson & Hetter, 1985). This algorithm reduces the exposure rate of certain highly informative items, while increasing the exposure rate for other items. The result is an upper ceiling on the exposure of a test item. For those subtests used for applicant selection (Word Knowledge, Paragraph Comprehension, Math Knowledge, and Arithmetic Reasoning), the most frequently used items are administered to approximately one sixth of the examinees. For those subtests used for classification to job, the most frequently used items are administered to approximately one third of the examinees.

While item selection for General Science uses the procedure described above, it is slightly different from the other power subtests in that there are three information tables. Items are selected and administered in the following sequence:

P L P L P L P L P L P L P L C,

where P = physical, L = life, and C = chemistry.

Owen's approximation to the posterior mean (Owen, 1975) is used to update the ability estimate during subtest administration. For each subtest, the prior distribution has a mean of 0.0 and a standard deviation of 1.0. Owen's is not used as the final theta estimate since it is affected by the order of item admin-

Table 10.1
CAT-ASVAB Item Pools

Content Area	Number of Items Used		Time Limits (mins.)	Test Length[1]	
	Form 1	Form 2		CAT	P&P
General Science	72	67	8	16	25
Arithmetic Reasoning	94	94	39	16	30
Word Knowledge	95	99	8	16	35
Paragraph Comprehension	50	52	22	11	15
Numerical Operations			3	50	50
Coding Speed			7	84	84
Auto Information	53	53	6	11	20
Shop Information	51	49	5	11	20
Math Knowledge	84	85	18	16	25
Mechanical Comprehension	64	64	20	16	25
Electrical Information	61	61	8	16	25

[1]Test length includes one seeded item per content area.

istration. Use of Owen's estimator could result in different ability estimates for examinees that give identical responses to the same set of items. This situation could arise when the same set of items are administered in two different orders. Consequently, at the end of a subtest, the Bayesian posterior mode, which is order independent, is computed, then transformed to the number-right metric using the test characteristic function (Lord, 1980). The Bayesian posterior mode was chosen over other scoring methods as the final theta estimate because it is well established in the research literature and computation time is fairly rapid.

Each subtest is terminated after a fixed number of items. Table 10.1 shows the test length for each of the power subtests. Fixed-length testing is used in CAT-ASVAB because (1) empirical research has shown that this type of stopping rule results in adequate reliabilities and validities, (2) administering the same number of items to all examinees avoids public relations problems associated with variable-length testing, (3) fixed-length testing is administratively easier to handle, and (4) further research is needed to evaluate the relative precision of variable-length testing and the operational implications of using this method. However, terminating the test after some criterion is met, such as standard error of measurement, may be an option for the future.

For each power subtest, a nonoperational item is interspersed among the operational items. These items are referred to as seeded items. The purpose of administering seeded items is to collect data needed to check the calibration or to calibrate an item under operational conditions.

Speeded Subtests. The items in the speeded subtests were generated by the Air Force Human Resources Laboratory and conform to the P&P-ASVAB taxonomy. The speeded subtests are administered in a conventional fashion, with examinees answering the same items in the same sequence. In Numerical Operations, items are displayed one at a time on the screen. The subtest terminates when a time limit of three minutes is reached or when the examinee has answered all 50 items. In Coding Speed, 7 items are displayed on a screen. This is similar to the format used in P&P-ASVAB and the same as the format used in the joint-service validity study. The subtest terminates when a time limit of seven minutes is reached or when the examinee has answered all 84 items. The score on a speeded subtest is a rate score: proportion of attempted items that are correct divided by the geometric mean of the screen time (Wolfe, 1985). The rate score is adjusted for guessing.

SYSTEM DEVELOPMENT

The hardware used in this first operational version of CAT-ASVAB is the Hewlett Packard Integral. The keyboard has been modified so that only those keys needed during the test are accessible. At the time of hardware selection (1985), the Hewlett Packard Integral came closer than other microcomputers to meeting the functional specifications for CAT-ASVAB. The primary system requirements were (1) portability, (2) on-line data storage, (3) high-resolution graphics, and (4) networking capabilities (Tiggle & Rafacz, 1985).

In the typical network setup, individual examinee testing stations are networked with a test administrator's station. Prior to testing, the test administrator downloads software and the item pools to random access memory in the individual stations. During the test, the test administrator's station is used to key enter examinee personal data, monitor examinee progress, and receive data from the individual stations (Rafacz, 1986). In case of network failure or when only one or two examinees are being tested, an examinee testing station can operate in a ''stand-alone'' mode, needing no external support. This type of design provides both the efficiency of networking and the safety of independence, when needed.

When an examinee sits down at the computer, he or she first completes a familiarization sequence that is designed to teach the examinee how to use the computer keyboard. After completion of this sequence, the examinee is given some general test instructions, then begins the first subtest. At the beginning of each subtest, instructions for that subtest and a practice question are given.

During the power subtests a status line appears at the bottom of the screen, telling the examinee the current item number and the time remaining to complete the subtest. When an examinee completes one subtest, he or she goes immediately to the next subtest.

To determine if there are any human/machine interaction problems with the CAT-ASVAB system, a pretest was conducted at the San Diego Military Entrance Processing Station and the San Diego High School. Examinees took CAT-ASVAB, followed by a questionnaire, and in some cases, an interview. Examinees participating in this study had taken the P&P-ASVAB at an earlier date. A few minor problems were encountered that resulted in changing some instructional screens. Overall, examinees were very enthusiastic about the test. They felt the computer was extremely easy to use, much more so than the printed answer sheet, and that instructions were clear. Examinees especially liked the self-paced nature of the test. Test administrators felt that the test was easy to administer and monitor and that when an examinee had trouble, built-in software functions easily identified that examinee to the test administrator.

OPERATIONAL CONSIDERATIONS

During planning for operational implementation of CAT-ASVAB, certain issues arose that were, in some cases, of administrative concern but that could impact examinee performance and/or system development. As work progressed on the CAT-ASVAB system, it became increasingly clear that administrative issues, psychometric concerns, and system development were not separate issues but closely intertwined. This section will give the reader an idea of some of the problems encountered and the solutions used in this first version of CAT-ASVAB.

Time Limits

ASVAB test administrators at some testing sites are hired for a certain period of time, and in many cases, applicants are processed according to a set schedule. Consequently, time limits for CAT-ASVAB subtests are necessary. This was not a problem for the speeded subtests, since by nature they are timed. However, power subtests administered adaptively are typically not timed. Setting time limits imposed problems such as determining what the limits should be and how to score an examinee if he or she ran out of time. For CAT-ASVAB, power subtest time limits were initially set based on empirical data from the joint-service validity study. In this study, power subtests were untimed. For each subtest, the distribution of total time was obtained, and the average item time for those individuals at the 95th percentile was computed. The CAT-ASVAB subtest time limits were the number of items in a given subtest multiplied by this average item time. These time limits were later adjusted using data collected in an operational setting. The final time limits are shown in Table 10.1. This technique results in liberal time limits that are sufficient for the majority of examinees to complete the subtest (Segall, Moreno, Blokom, & Hetter, in press).

Since a very small percentage of examinees do run out of time before answering all items, scoring these incomplete tests presented a special problem in the context of adaptive testing. The bias associated with the Bayesian estimator regresses the estimated score toward the mean of the prior and is inversely related to test length. Consequently, for short test lengths, the bias is large, and an examinee could use this fact to game the test. For an examinee of below-average ability, the optimal test-taking strategy would be to answer zero items. In the absence of any data, the Bayesian score would be simply the mean of the prior (a score equivalent to the mean). If a minimum test length were imposed, then the optimum strategy for a below-average examinee would be to answer the minimum allowable number of items.

To invalidate any coachable strategy for gaming the test, a penalty is applied to incomplete tests. This procedure (Segall, 1987) provides a final score that is equivalent (in expectation) to the score obtained by guessing at random on the unfinished items. For each subtest, the size of the penalty depends on the provisional Bayesian estimate and the number of completed items. The procedure has three desirable qualities: (1) the size of the penalty is positively related to the number of unfinished items, (2) applicants with the same number of answered items and same provisional ability estimate will receive the same penalty, and (3) the procedure eliminates coachable test-taking strategies.

Help Calls

Another issue was how to determine when an examinee was having trouble understanding the instructions or operating the keyboard and what course of action to follow under these circumstances. ''Help'' calls have been built into the system; however, we wanted to avoid unnecessary calls to the test administrator. In CAT-ASVAB, liberal screen timeouts have been set so that if an examinee is taking too long on a screen, the test administrator is called. Also, if an examinee presses an invalid key (i.e., the enter key when the only valid response is A through E) three times in a row, the test administrator is called. The examinee also has the option of pressing the key labeled ''HELP'' at any point in the test.

When the help function is invoked either by the system or by the examinee, the test administrator can bring up instructional screens, if necessary, and will monitor the examinee's progress for awhile. When a help call occurs during a power subtest, after the appropriate action is taken, the subtest continues with the item that the examinee was on when help was invoked. During a speeded test the same sequence is followed; however, the response(s) to the item(s) on the interrupted screen is not scored. As mentioned earlier, these procedures worked well during the pretest of the system.

Figure 10.2
Score Information Functions for Math Knowledge

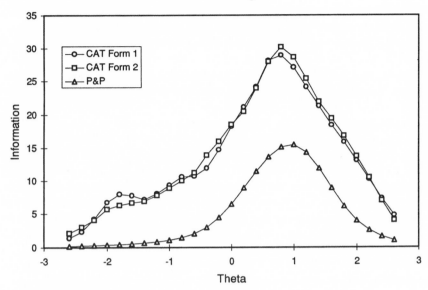

EVALUATION OF CAT-ASVAB

Simulation Studies

Once item pools and test administration procedures were finalized, simulation studies were conducted to evaluate the precision of the CAT-ASVAB power subtest item pools. Two measures of precision were examined: (1) score information (Lord, 1980) and (2) a reliability index. The two precision criteria were computed for both CAT-ASVAB and P&P-ASVAB, with P&P-ASVAB being used as a baseline (Hetter & Segall, 1986; Segall, 1987).

For most power subtests, score information for CAT-ASVAB was higher across all ability levels than that for P&P-ASVAB. Figure 10.2 shows this comparison for Math Knowledge. For two of the content areas, Arithmetic Reasoning and Word Knowledge, score information for CAT-ASVAB was lower than P&P-ASVAB at some ability levels. As a result, these two areas were supplemented with items from the experimental CAT-ASVAB pools. The supplemental Arithmetic Reasoning and Word Knowledge item parameters were transformed to the metric of the "operational" items using the Stocking and Lord (1983) procedure. After supplementing, score information functions for these two content areas met the criterion of being higher than P&P-ASVAB. Table 10.1 shows the number of items in the final pools, after supplementing.

Test-retest reliabilities were estimated for the power subtests in each CAT-ASVAB form and for Form 9A of the P&P-ASVAB. Simulated scores were generated for 1,900 simulees. The estimated CAT-ASVAB reliability indices exceeded corresponding P&P-ASVAB values for all subtests (Hetter & Segall, 1986).

Empirical Studies

Upon completion of system development, studies were conducted to empirically evaluate both the psychometric characteristics of CAT-ASVAB and the functioning of the system overall.

Cross-Correlation Check. As a final check on the precision of the CAT-ASVAB item pools, an empirical study was conducted to evaluate the alternate form reliability of CAT-ASVAB and to determine if CAT-ASVAB subtests measure the same traits as the P&P battery (Moreno & Segall, in press). In this study, examinees were randomly assigned to one of two conditions: (1) administration of two forms of CAT-ASVAB or (2) administration of two forms of P&P-ASVAB. After eliminating cases with incomplete data, the sample sizes were 744 for condition one and 726 for condition two. Correlational analyses were conducted to compare the alternate form reliabilities for the two versions of the ASVAB, CAT, and P&P. A structural analysis was conducted to determine if the two versions measured the same traits.

Results of the correlational analyses are shown in Table 10.2. Six of the 10 CAT-ASVAB subtests had significantly higher reliabilities than the corresponding P&P-ASVAB subtests. The other 4 had reliabilities equal to those of the P&P version. In addition, correlations between CAT subtests and the operational P&P-ASVAB (the test used to qualify for military service) were as high as or higher than correlations between the P&P forms given as part of this study and the operational P&P-ASVAB.

Results of the structural analysis showed that for 9 of the 10 subtests, the disattenuated correlations between CAT-ASVAB and the P&P-ASVAB power tests were not significantly different from 1.00. For one of the speeded tests, Coding Speed, the disattenuated correlation was .86, which is significantly different from 1.00, with $p = .002$. Coding Speed is a nonadaptive test, with the computer administration almost identical in format to the P&P administration. Nevertheless, these results indicate that for Coding Speed the difference in medium of administration may result in a slight difference in what the test is measuring.

Item Calibration Media. Initially, there was some concern that while the item parameters were estimated from a P&P administration, they should have been estimated using data from computer administration of the items. There may be some difference in the way an examinee responds to an item administered by computer as opposed to P&P. Several simulation studies were conducted to evaluate this concern. Segall (1986) found that even with substantial parameter misspecification, there was little loss in reliability. Using empirical data, Divgi (1986) found that scores change very little as a result of the medium of admin-

Table 10.2
Alternate Form and Cross-Medium Correlations

	Alt. Form Rel.		Correlations with Operational P&P-ASVAB			
			CAT		P&P	
Subtest	CAT	P&P	Form 1	Form 2	Form 1	Form 2
General Science	.84**	.74	.83	.82	.79	.73
Arithmetic Reasoning	.83**	.77	.81	.75	.76	.72
Word Knowledge	.83	.81	.83	.81	.81	.78
Paragraph Comprehension	.54	.48	.54	.43	.48	.38
Numerical Operations	.82	.71	.60	.60	.65	.56
Coding Speed	.77	.75	.57	.54	.65	.62
Auto & Shop Information	.89**	.78	.83	.83	.76	.74
Math Knowledge	.88**	.82	.86	.83	.83	.80
Mechanical Comprehension	.75*	.70	.69	.64	.66	.65
Electronics Information	.73**	.65	.73	.72	.66	.65

*Statistically significant ($p < .05$).
**Statistically significant ($p < .01$).

istration. In addition to these simulations, an empirical study was conducted to evaluate the effect of calibration medium on the reliability and validity of test scores (Hetter, Segall, & Bloxom, 1994).

Examinees were randomly assigned to one of three groups. Groups 1 and 2 were administered a fixed block of items by computer, and group 3 was administered the same fixed block by P&P. Data from groups 1 and 3 were used for item calibration, resulting in two sets of parameters, one set obtained from a computer administration and another obtained from a P&P administration. Data from the second group were used to conduct CAT real-data simulations, resulting in scores obtained using parameters from the two different calibration media.

Covariance structure analysis was conducted to address the equality of scores from the two different calibration media. Details of the formal model and variables involved are described in Hetter, Segall, and Bloxom (1994). Results showed that item parameters calibrated from a P&P administration can be used in CAT administration without changing the construct being measured and without lowering the reliability. A comparison of the difficulty parameters across the two media showed little or no distortion in the scale.

Equating CAT and P&P Score Scales. The final step in psychometric development for CAT-ASVAB was the equating of CAT-ASVAB scores to P&P-ASVAB scores. This step was necessary since both batteries are in operational use. At some testing sites, applicants are accessed using scores from the CAT-ASVAB, while at other sites applicants are enlisted using scores obtained on the P&P-ASVAB. In order to make comparable enlistment decisions across the adaptive and conventional versions, an equivalence relation (or equating) between CAT-ASVAB and P&P-ASVAB has been obtained (Segall, in press). The primary objective of this equating is to provide a transformation of CAT-ASVAB scores that preserves the flow rates currently associated with the P&P-ASVAB. In principle, this can be achieved by matching the P&P-ASVAB and equated CAT-ASVAB subtest and composite distributions. This equating allows cut-scores associated with the existing P&P-ASVAB scale to be applied to the transformed CAT-ASVAB scores without affecting flow rates into the military or into various occupational specialties.

The equating study was designed to address three concerns. First, the equating transformation applied to CAT-ASVAB scores should preserve flow rates associated with the existing cut-scores based on the P&P-ASVAB score scale. This concern was addressed by using an equipercentile procedure for equating the CAT-ASVAB and P&P-ASVAB. This equating procedure by definition identifies the transformation of scale that matches the cumulative distribution functions. Although this procedure was applied at the subtest level, the distributions of all selector composites were evaluated to ensure that no significant differences existed across the adaptive and conventional versions.

A second concern addressed by the study addressed the motivation of examinees used to develop the scale transformation. Specifically, it is highly desirable that the equating transformation be based on operationally motivated applicants, since the affect of motivation on CAT-ASVAB equating has not been thoroughly studied. This concern over motivation was addressed by conducting the CAT-ASVAB equating in two phases: (1) Score Equating Development (SED) phase and (2) Score Equating Verification (SEV) phase. The purpose of SED was to provide an interim equating of the CAT-ASVAB. During that study, both CAT-ASVAB and P&P-ASVAB were given nonoperationally to randomly equivalent groups. The tests were nonoperational in the sense that test performance had no impact on the applicants' eligibility for the military—all participants in the study were also administered an operational P&P-ASVAB form used for enlistment decisions. This interim equating was used in the second SEV phase to select and classify military applicants. During the second phase (SEV), applicants were administered either an operational CAT-ASVAB or an operational P&P-ASVAB. Both versions used in the SEV study impacted applicants' eligibility for military service. This new equating obtained in SEV was based on operationally motivated examinees and was later applied to applicants participating in the OT&E study.

A third concern addressed by the equating study dealt with subgroup performance on the CAT-ASVAB. Specifically, members of targeted subgroups taking CAT-ASVAB should not be placed at a disadvantage relative to their subgroup counterparts taking the P&P-ASVAB. This third concern was addressed through a series of analyses conducted on data collected as part of the score equating study. These analyses examined the performance of blacks and females for randomly equivalent groups assigned to CAT-ASVAB and P&P-ASVAB conditions. Results indicate that although it is desirable for exchangeability considerations to match distributions for subgroups as well as the entire group, this may not be possible for a variety of reasons. First, differences in precision between the CAT-ASVAB and P&P-ASVAB versions may magnify existing differences between subgroups. Second, small differences in dimensionality, such as the verbal loading of a test, may cause differential subgroup performance. Although several subgroup differences observed in CAT-ASVAB are statistically significant, their practical significance on qualification rates is small. Once CAT-ASVAB becomes fully operational, the exchangeability issue will become less important. The small differences in subgroup performance displayed by CAT-ASVAB may be a positive consequence of greater precision and lower verbal contamination. Ultimately, in large-scale administrations of CAT-ASVAB, we may observe higher classification efficiency and greater predictive validity than is currently displayed by its P&P counterpart.

IMPLEMENTATION

The empirical evaluation of CAT-ASVAB showed that, psychometrically, CAT-ASVAB could replace the P&P-ASVAB, resulting in a substantial savings in testing time. Other factors, however, needed to be considered. Prior to investing a substantial amount of funds into purchasing computer equipment, the cost effectiveness of CAT-ASVAB and the impact of implementation on operational procedures needed to be determined.

To provide data for these evaluations, in 1992, CAT-ASVAB was implemented operationally in six sites. The primary areas evaluated were (1) test administrator training and performance, (2) processing of test scores, (3) equipment needs, (4) the use of self-paced testing, (5) user acceptance, and (6) system performance.

Results showed that implementation of CAT-ASVAB is cost-effective (Wise, Curran, & McBride, in press). Overall, the system performed extremely well. Test administrators found the test easy to give and much more efficient than giving the P&P-ASVAB. Examinees and recruiters, in general, liked the shorter testing time and immediate test scores. As a result of these favorable findings, the joint services approved implementation of CAT-ASVAB nationwide, at all Military Entrance Processing Stations. Implementation started in October 1996. Prior to this implementation, the CAT-ASVAB software was converted to run on IBM-PC–compatible machines. This step was necessary in that the Hewlett Packard system is now obsolete. While certain procedures were streamlined, based on results of the limited implementation, overall the IBM-PC–based system is very similar in function to the Hewlett Packard–based system.

Nationwide implementation of CAT-ASVAB begins a new era in military testing. While many improvements in testing will be realized through the use of CAT, the delivery platform, the computer, provides even greater potential for expansion of methods of individual assessment.

REFERENCES

Bock, R. D., & Aitkin, M. (1981). Marginal maximum likelihood estimation of item parameters: An application of an EM algorithm. *Psychometrika, 46*, 443–459.

Divgi, D. R. (1986). *Sensitivity of CAT-ASVAB scores to changes in item response curves with the medium of administration* (CNA Research Memorandum 86–189). Alexandria, VA: Center for Naval Analysis.

Green, B. F., Bock, R. D., Humphreys, L. G., Linn, R. L., & Reckase, M. D. (1982). *Evaluation Plan for the Computerized Adaptive Vocational Aptitude Battery* (Technical Report 82–1). San Diego, CA: Navy Personnel Research and Development Center.

Hetter, R. D., & Segall, D. O. (1986, November). *Relative precision of paper-and-pencil and computerized adaptive tests*. Paper presented at the 28th Annual Meeting of the Military Testing Association, Mystic, CT.

Hetter, R. D., Segall, D. O., & Bloxom, B. M. (1994). A comparison of item calibration media in computerized adaptive testing. *Applied Psychological Measurement, 18*, 197–204.

Kershaw, S. W., & Wainer, H. (1985). Reviewing an item pool for its sensitivity to the concerns of women and minorities: Process and outcome. *Proceedings of the 27th Annual Conference of the Military Testing Association, I*, 288–293.

Lord, F. M. (1980). *Applications of items response theory to practical testing problems*. Hillsdale, NJ: Lawrence Erlbaum Associates.

McBride, J. R., & Martin, J. T. (1983). Reliability and validity of adaptive ability tests in a military setting. In D. J. Weiss (Ed.), *New horizons in testing* (pp. 223–236). New York: Academic Press.

Moreno, K. E., & Segall, D. O. (in press). Reliability and construct validity of CAT-ASVAB. In W. A. Sands, B. K. Waters, and J. R. McBride (Eds.), *Computerized adaptive testing: From inquiry to operation*.

Moreno, K. E., Segall, D. O., & Kieckhaefer, W. F. (1985). A validity study of the Computerized Adaptive Testing version of the Armed Services Vocational Aptitude Battery. *Proceedings of the 27th Annual Conference of the Military Testing Association, I*, 29–33.

Moreno, K. E., Wetzel, D. C., McBride, J. R., & Weiss, D. J. (1984). Relationship between corresponding Armed Services Vocational Aptitude Battery (ASVAB) and Computerized Adaptive Testing (CAT) subtests. *Applied Psychological Measurement, 8*, 155–163.

Owen, R. J. (1975). A Bayesian sequential procedure for quantal response in context of adaptive mental testing. *Journal of the American Statistical Association, 40*, 351–356.

Prestwood, J. S., Vale, C. D., Massey, R. H., & Welsh, J. R. (1985). *Armed Services Vocational Aptitude Battery: Development of an adaptive item pool* (Technical Report 85–19). San Antonio, TX: Air Force Human Resources Laboratory.

Quan, B., Park, T. A., Sandahl, G., & Wolfe, J. H. (1984). *Microcomputer network for Computerized Adaptive Testing (CAT)* (Technical Report 84–33). San Diego, CA: Navy Personnel Research and Development Center.

Rafacz, B. A. (1986, November). Development of the test administrator's station in support of ACAP. *Proceedings of the 28th Annual Conference of the Military Testing Association, I*, 606–611.

Segall, D. O. (1986). *Effects of item characteristic curve mis-specification on CAT precision.* Unpublished manuscript.

Segall, D. O. (1987). *CAT-ASVAB item pools: Analysis and recommendations.* Unpublished manuscript.

Segall, D. O. (in press). Equating the CAT-ASVAB. In W. A. Sands, B. K. Waters, and J. R. McBride (Eds.), *Computerized adaptive testing: From inquiry to operation.*

Segall, D. O., Moreno, K. E., Bloxom, B., & Hetter, R. D. (in press). Psychometric procedures for administering CAT-ASVAB. In W. A. Sands, B. K. Waters, and J. R. McBride (Eds.), *Computerized adaptive testing: From inquiry to operation.*

Stocking, M. L., & Lord, F. M. (1983). Developing a common metric in item response theory. *Applied Psychological Measurement, 7*, 201–210.

Sympson, J. B., & Hetter, R. D. (1985, October). Controlling item exposure rates in computerized adaptive tests. *Proceedings of the 27th Annual Conference of the Military Testing Association, I*, 973–980.

Tiggle, R. B., & Rafacz, B. A. (1985). Evaluation of three local CAT-ASVAB network designs. *Proceedings of the 27th Annual Conference of the Military Testing Association, I*, 23–28.

Vale, C. D., & Gailluca, K. A. (1985). *ASCAL: A microcomputer program for estimating logistic IRT item parameters* (Research Report ONR 85–4). St. Paul, MN: Assessment Systems Corp.

Wetzel, C. D., & McBride, J. R. (1985). Reducing the predictability of adaptive item sequences. *Proceedings of the 27th Annual Conference of the Military Testing Association, I*, 43–48.

Wilson, D., Wood, R., & Gibbons, R. D. (1984). *TESTFACT: Test scoring, item statistics, and item factor analysis.* Mooresville, IN: Scientific Software, Inc.

Wise, L. L., Curran, L. T., & McBride, J. R. (in press). CAT-ASVAB cost and benefit Analysis. In W. A. Sands, B. K. Waters, and J. R. McBride (Eds.), *Computerized adaptive testing: From inquiry to operation.*

Wolfe, J. H. (1985). Speeded tests: Can computers improve measurement? *Proceedings of the 27th Annual Conference of the Military Testing Association, I*, 49–54.

11

Steps toward an Improved Pilot Selection Battery

William C. Tirre

Aviation psychologists have been concerned with improving pilot selection for decades, though a recent survey (Hilton & Dolgin, 1991) suggests that only modest progress has been made since the World War II aviation psychology program (Guilford & Lacey, 1947; Melton, 1947). In this chapter, I discuss some problem areas for pilot selection batteries and then outline some steps toward an improved technology. These steps call for systematic task analysis, basic research to broaden the sampling of abilities beyond traditional psychometrics, construction of battery utilizing multiple indicators of each proposed ability, preliminary validation against meaningful criteria in laboratory, and validation against automated and conventional criteria obtained in training aircraft.

THE CURRENT SITUATION

This chapter is primarily concerned with research on selection of pilots for the military and especially the United States Air Force (USAF), though much of what is addressed here also applies to the selection of candidates for commercial ab initio pilot training programs. In the typical military situation, pilot candidates are administered printed cognitive tests and sometimes computer-administered tests as part of the selection process. In the USAF, test scores are considered along with other data including prior flying experience and interview responses by a selection board composed of senior USAF pilots. USAF candidates in the Reserve Officer Training Corps must also pass the Flight Screening Program (FSP), which consists of 22 hours of instruction on piloting a T-3 (Slingsby Firefly, a single propeller, low-wing, aerobatic-capable aircraft). Air

Force Academy students receive the same training in T-3s prior to commission, and recommendations for Undergraduate Pilot Training (UPT) are based on performance during training. Once selected, candidates report for UPT consisting of about 200 training hours, first in a subsonic jet aircraft (T-37, 89 hours), and then in either a supersonic jet aircraft (T-38, 119 hours) or a twin-engine Beechcraft 400A Jet (T-1 Jayhawk, 104 hours), depending on the student's assignment to the fighter, bomber, attack, or reconnaissance aircraft track or the tanker and transport track, respectively. This training is followed by a three- to six-month period of advanced specialized training involving the transition to operational aircraft. Assignment of pilots to the various types of aircraft is basically a classification problem. The various aircraft differ substantially in both mission and the types of processing demands made of the pilot, but as of this writing, the USAF does not attempt systematic classification other than basing prestigious fighter-attack assignments on T-37 training performance. At the end of T-37 training, students are ranked on overall training performance. Then students are allowed to select their aircraft assignment, with the highest-ranking students making their selections first, and so on, down the ranks. Upon graduation, the new pilot is assigned to an operational flying unit. At the end of three or four years the pilot may be considered for another type of aircraft, according to the needs of the USAF. Information on pilot selection and training in the other services (army, navy, marines, and coast guard) is most readily available in Wiener (1989).

Pilot training attrition is one concern of the armed forces, because each failure costs the USAF an estimated $50,000 to $80,000 (Hunter, 1989). Over a 20-year period, there was an attrition rate of 25 percent in the USAF program (Hunter, 1989), though recently the figure is more like 15 percent. Increasingly, the USAF has emphasized the concept of mission readiness as the goal for its training and selection programs. And so the appropriate emphasis in pilot selection research is on identifying candidates who will become the most proficient pilots in the least amount of time and those who will most easily make the transition to new aircraft and weapons systems.

THE STATE OF THE ART IN PILOT SELECTION RESEARCH

I will not attempt a thorough review of pilot selection research in this chapter. Narrative reviews are provided by Hilton and Dolgin (1991) and Hunter (1989), and a meta-analysis of several hundred correlations is provided by Hunter and Burke (1995b). The most comprehensive treatment of pilot selection is provided by Hunter and Burke (1995a) in their *Handbook of Pilot Selection*.

Meta-analysis Results

Pilot selection batteries have not been as successful as one would hope. Hunter and Burke (1995b) reported in their meta-analysis of 468 correlations that the predictor categories considered in the sampled studies yielded moderated validations (10 to 16 cases) and nongeneralizable validities (6 of 16 cases). Moderator variables included type of aircraft, air force versus other performing organization, nationality, and time period of study. Time period of study had the strongest effect: The mean validity (unweighted and uncorrected) was .28 (range: .21 to .35) for studies published from 1940 to 1960 and .14 (range: .09 to .22) for studies published from 1961 to 1990. The most successful categories of predictors were job samples (mean $r = .34$), gross dexterity (mean $r = .32$), mechanical (mean $r = .29$), and reaction time (mean $r = .28$). The least successful were education (mean $r = .06$), fine dexterity and personality (mean $r = .10$), age (mean $r = -.10$), and quantitative ability (mean $r = .11$). General ability was likewise a poor predictor (mean $r = .13$). The two best predictor categories, gross dexterity and job sample, both show strong moderator effects. Job sample predictors were moderated by nationality such that studies conducted in the United States showed lower mean validity and variability. Gross dexterity showed significant moderator effects of time period, performing organization, and aircraft type. Non-USAF studies showed lower mean validity and larger sampling error. The same was true for studies of rotary-winged aircraft.

It is difficult to draw any strong conclusions from this meta-analysis other than pilot selection research results are quite complicated, and level of prediction is quite low, given the importance of pilots for national defense and public safety.[1] My response to this situation is to attempt a classification of approaches to the design of pilot selection batteries, select successful examples of each category for closer examination, and determine where to go next, given the gathered intelligence.

Two Approaches to Pilot Aptitude Measurement

For the purposes of simplification, let us say that there are two approaches to the design of pilot selection batteries, which I will call the *basic attributes approach* and the *learning sample approach*. The basic attributes approach attempts to measure the cognitive, perceptual, motor, and personality correlates of successful pilot performance. An excellent example is (no surprise here) the USAF Basic Attributes Test (BAT). The BAT is a computer-based battery of basic cognitive, perceptual, and psychomotor tasks, plus personality measures designed to supplement the Air Force Officer Qualification Test (AFOQT) in predicting UPT outcomes. Carretta (1989) reported that a model that combines AFOQT and BAT variables accounted for 19 percent of the variance in UPT pass/fail. More recently, Carretta and Ree (1994) reported that the same model accounted for 12 percent of the variance in pass/fail (86 percent pass) and 15 percent in class rank (all correlations corrected for range restriction). Cognitive tests from the AFOQT contributed the most to prediction, followed by psychomotor tests. Information-processing speed tests (e.g., encoding speed, mental rotation, short-term memory search) did not contribute significantly. Note that except for the significant contribution of psychomotor tests (called gross dexterity by Hunter and Burke, 1995b), the Carretta and Ree results appear to contradict the meta-analysis results. Carretta and Ree suggest that general cognitive ability is capturing the lion's share of the variance in predicting pilot training outcomes and that reaction time/information-processing speed does not make a significant independent contribution when psychomotor and general cognitive ability are already in the equation. Hunter and Burke were talking about simple correlations and not unique contributions (increments to R-square), and so it is possible that reaction time demonstrates simple correlation but no unique contribution. The apparent disagreement over general cognitive ability may stem from differences in operational definition. Hunter and Burke may have defined general cognitive ability differently (with substantially different tests) than Carretta and Ree, but we are unable to resolve this from the information given.[2]

The learning sample approach (basically the same as the job sample category in Hunter & Burke, 1995b) attempts to sidestep the process of identifying components of the job task by presenting the candidate with a simulation of the job that the candidate must learn to perform. An example is the Canadian Automated Pilot Selection System (CAPSS; Spinner, 1991), which built on earlier USAF work by Long and Varney (1975). CAPSS presents the pilot candidates with brief instruction on how to perform a set of eight basic flight maneuvers in a flight simulator and then records flight parameters as they attempt to perform the maneuver. On the derivation sample of 225 already selected pilot candidates, Spinner found that CAPSS accounted for 58 percent of the variance in primary flight school pass/fail (proportion passing was .70). On the cross-validation sample of 172 candidates, CAPSS accounted for 22 percent of the variance in pass/fail (proportion passing was .70).[3]

PROBLEMS WITH THE BASIC ATTRIBUTES APPROACH

What are some possible reasons for lack of success with the basic attributes approach that are unique to it? I thought of four general areas of concern:

- The ability domain has not been adequately sampled.
- Abilities chosen are too narrow in bandwidth.
- Tests chosen to indicate abilities have inadequate stability.
- Tests were constructed without adequate attention to theory, making informed revision difficult.

We will cover each of these points in more detail, but first let us consider some background on what might be called the *cognitive paradigm* in abilities research.

Cognitive Paradigm in Abilities Research

Basic research on human abilities was largely dormant from the 1950s until the late 1970s when cognitive psychologists such as Hunt (1978) and Sternberg (1977) sparked fresh interest in the topic. Research focused on trying to understand the components of complex cognitive activities such as reasoning (e.g., Sternberg, 1977), verbal ability (Hunt, 1978), reading (Frederiksen, 1981), and comprehension (Gernsbacher, Varner, & Faust, 1990), to name some representative abilities. Two related methodologies emerged for the study of complex cognitive abilities. One was the componential approach typified by Sternberg (1977) in which the investigator attempted identification of basic information processes called performance components that combine to account for task performance. Performance components such as encoding, inference, and mapping relations were measured through response time to tasks designed to evoke a particular component. The second was the cognitive correlates approach typified by Hunt (1978, 1987) in which complex task performances were related to parameters extracted from elementary cognitive tasks (ECTs) such as lexical decision, short-term memory search, and name versus physical identity, to name a few. ECTs, which did not resemble subtasks of the complex criterion task, were selected to measure in isolation one component of task performance. It was generally thought that componential analysis would lead to a better understanding of scores on intelligence tests, and so the emphasis was on particular classes of tasks such as analogies, series, and classification items that are used to measure intelligence. Cognitive correlates analysis was more often applied to potentially more complex tasks such as reading.

Pilot selection battery development has been closer in form and content to cognitive correlates analysis than to componential analysis. Typically, however, tests in pilot selection batteries have varied in complexity from elementary cognitive tasks such as the Sternberg memory search paradigm to complex mathematical reasoning items.

The Ability Domain Has Not Been Adequately Sampled

Pilot selection batteries employing the basic attributes approach have largely relied on psychometric theories of ability that emerged in the 1942–1971 time period, with 1942 marking the founding of the Aviation Psychology Program and 1971 marking the publication of Guilford's *Analysis of Intelligence* (Guilford & Hoepfner, 1971), which summarized the Structure of Intellect (SOI) abilities research program. Guilford's SOI theory, in fact, was developed to impose some order on the empirical findings of the World War II research program. Few operational pilot selection batteries have taken advantage of theory and measurement technologies that have emerged since the late 1970s. Componential analysis, for example, might be used to identify the major components of cockpit skills. Measurement of these cockpit skill components might, in turn, be related to tests of cognitive, perceptual, and motor abilities that have been studied in cognitive laboratories. The cognitive paradigm in abilities research has identified some abilities that were not anticipated in psychometric theories. Tests of these abilities need to be constructed and evaluated for their potential as pilot aptitude measures.

Ability Tests Are Too Narrow in Bandwidth

ECTs measure narrow aspects of human performance with high precision, and in recent years, there has been some effort to try out ECTs as pilot selection tests. The BAT, for example, includes encoding speed, mental rotation, and Sternberg short-term memory search tests. However, these did not contribute significantly to the prediction of pass/fail. Part of the problem here may lie in the criterion (more on that later), but researchers should keep in mind that rarely have ECTs correlated better than .3 with complex performances (Hunt, 1980), and so it is possible that a tremendous variety of ECTs would be needed to account for a complex criterion. It is also possible that ECTs correlate as well with broader cognitive abilities that are already measured by operational batteries as they do with the criterion of interest. For example, starting with the general notion of the modern pilot as an ''information manager,'' the original designers of the BAT included information-processing tests such as mental rotation, encoding speed, and short-term memory search. But these same constructs have also been considered components of broader cognitive abilities such as visualization (e.g., mental rotation) and verbal ability (encoding speed, short-term memory search), both of which are measured quite well by the AFOQT. It is likely that any new ability test considered for addition to an existing battery will be relatively narrow in scope (Cronbach, 1970), and perhaps what is needed as a safeguard is a means of assessing a proposed test's validity (stand-alone and incremental) in the lab prior to the expensive step of operational validation with real pilots and aircraft (again, more on that later).

Tests Chosen to Indicate Abilities Have Inadequate Stability

Measurements used for personnel decisions must show stability; that is, the rank order of individuals must not change substantially over time—otherwise, we would not be selecting people on the basis of persistent characteristics (Thorndike, 1949). Certain types of tests used in pilot selection such as elementary cognitive tasks and psychomotor tests generally show only modest stability over time. For example, information-processing speed tests had test-retest correlations ranging from .01 to .66 with a time lag of 10 days on a sample of navy enlisted personnel (Sacuzzo & Larson, 1987). Roznowski (1993) found test-retest correlations of .23 to .87 (mean .59, time lag 14 days) for a range of latency measures from ECTs varying in complexity. The more complex tasks tended to have higher stability. The extent to which stability is a problem for ECTs in the BAT is not yet known.[4] We do have estimates of stability for BAT psychomotor tests and the summary composite score. Stability estimates for psychomotor tests ranged from .16 to .46, with a time lag of two to three weeks between administrations (Mercatante, 1988). Overall, the BAT composite score had a test-retest correlation of .56, with a time lag of only 24 hours between administrations (Carretta, 1992), so it is likely that stability is a problem with at least this implementation of computer-based testing. Compare the BAT estimate of .56 to a .81 obtained on the AFOQT Pilot composite score (Berger, Gupta, Berger, & Skinner, 1990), in which the time lag varied from 1 to 18 months or more. In fairness, it is difficult to make meaningful comparisons between studies because samples varied in range of ability, time between testing, and time available to test, among other things.

Tests Were Constructed without Adequate Attention to Theory

A failing that appears to be almost universally true is that personnel selection tests have not been constructed with a facet structure or experimental design in mind. A facet is a structural feature of a test item that determines item difficulty. Tests with a faceted design basically have a built-in experimental design. For example, consider the standard sentence-picture verification or grammatical reasoning task (e.g., Baddeley, 1968). Subjects are presented simple sentences and are asked to decide whether they are true or false in describing a simple picture:

A is not followed by B

A   B.

There are 32 items formed using the following five facets: precedes versus follows, passive versus active voice, positive versus negative, A first versus B first, and true versus false. Passive versus active voice is a particularly effective determinant of item difficulty, as is positive versus negative sentence. When facets can be identified and used in test construction, item difficulties can be anticipated, and parallel forms of tests can be easily constructed (Irvine, Dann, & Anderson, 1990).

The idea of a faceted test originated with Guttman (1959), and the main proponents of such tests have been Guttman and his colleagues (e.g., Guttman, Epstein, Amir, & Guttman, 1990; Guttman & Levy, 1991). I believe that test construction can benefit from this and related approaches without the constructor embracing facet theory in its entirety. By employing a facet approach, researchers can determine what aspects of a test correlated with piloting success if not all aspects. But without a theory underlying the test, test improvement is a haphazard process. For related approaches, see Kyllonen (1991) and Irvine, Dann, and Anderson (1990). Other investigators have been interested in task facets as a means of identifying or manipulating examinees' choice of solution strategies (e.g., Kyllonen, Lohman, & Snow, 1984).

PROBLEMS WITH THE LEARNING SAMPLE APPROACH

The learning sample approach as implemented in CAPSS (Spinner, 1991) appears to be quite successful, but I have at least three concerns about this approach:

- Transfer of training from real or simulated flight hours
- Interpretability of training scores
- Lack of theoretical base for summarizing performance data

Transfer of Training from Real or Simulated Flight Hours

There is reason to be concerned about how transfer from previous experience might affect validity. Both experience in piloting aircraft and operating flight simulators (even inexpensive PC-based systems) might be expected to transfer to CAPSS, and whether this would increase or decrease validity depends on the nature of the flying tasks represented in the simulation. If the flying task has a consistent mapping of responses to stimuli across trials, the flying task can become an automated skill such that with practice performance becomes less erratic and draws fewer attentional resources (Ackerman, 1988, 1990, 1992). Consistently mapped tasks also demonstrate decreasing individual variation with practice. Thus, we might expect that some relatively simple flying tasks—for example, straight-and-level cruise, constant speed climb or descent, constant speed, and shallow bank turns—would become less predictive of primary flight training outcomes if pilot candidates practiced these prior to testing. Another possibility, raised by Embretson (1992), is that complex tasks can become more predictive with experience if individuals have had the opportunity to work out effective solution strategies either on their own or with instruction. Posttraining or practice scores on such tasks reflect both initial ability and what Embretson called "cognitive modifiability." It is the latter construct that might provide incremental validity. Thus, it might be found that if pilot candidates have acquired strategies for dealing with the complex demands of some flying tasks such as climbing and descending turns, slow flight, and landings, that performance of these tasks becomes more predictive of primary flight training outcomes.

Interpretability of Test Scores

A related problem concerns the interpretability of test scores on measurement systems such as CAPSS. Which is the better candidate, a novice with no flight hours who is a low pass on CAPSS or a relative expert with a private pilot's license who is a high pass? A score adjustment based on prior flying experience (e.g., number of flight hours, highest rating held) might be possible, but this would not work for experience that its not publicly verifiable such as simulator hours.

Lack of a Theoretical Basis for Summarizing Performance Data

Spinner (1991) was aware of the problems associated with using stepwise statistical procedures in developing prediction equations. However, CAPSS yielded 20,700 summary measures designed to depict candidates' performance in the simulator over brief time periods that had to be combined somehow. Spinner employed a bottom-up, empirical approach to develop his equation, taking steps to avoid capitalization on chance. Nonetheless, it is highly preferable to have a theory guiding the derivation of performance scores, so that the scoring procedure can be generalized to new simulation systems, new training syllabi, or new criterion measures in the aircraft (Spinner, 1991).

PROBLEM SHARED BY THE APPROACHES: THE CRITERION

A problem shared by the approaches is that traditional criterion measures are ill-suited for research. In their meta-analysis of pilot selection research, Hunter and Burke (1995b) reported that 391 of 468 validity coefficients (85 percent) used pass/fail as the criterion. Pass/fail is problematic for three reasons. First, a dichotomous criterion mathematically constrains correlations (Cohen, 1983; Nunnally, 1967), and significant predictor-criterion relationships can be obscured. Second, the proportion passing USAF/UPT is driven by policy decisions in addition to quality of student performance. The USAF can raise or lower the proportion passing according to the perceived need for new pilots. Third, pass/ fail decisions are made on the basis of flight instructors' ratings of student performance in check flights. Flight instructors are fallible observers subject to the same lapses in attention, errors, and biases common to all humans. Adding to the problem, student pilots are not rated by the same flight instructors; thus, the flight instructor becomes a significant and possibly overshadowing source of variance in check flight scores. Delaney (1992) found that three training squadrons varied significantly among themselves in mean check flight scores even though the squadrons did not differ in aptitude. Delaney's solution was to standardize within squadron prior to correlational analyses.

The problems outlined above point to the need for objective, automated measures of pilot performance. Perception of this need was also voiced by the USAF Scientific Advisory Board (SAB) Panel on Training and Human Factors (SAB, 1994).

PROPOSAL FOR IMPROVED PILOT SELECTION RESEARCH

My proposal for an improved pilot selection battery calls for five steps that combine the best of the basic attributes and learning sample approaches. The five steps are:

- Specify the pilot aptitude domain through task and componential analyses.
- Conduct basic research to broaden the sampling of abilities beyond traditional psychometrics.
- Construct battery-utilizing multiple indicators of each proposed ability.
- Validate battery against meaningful criteria in laboratory.
- Validate battery against objective criteria obtained in training aircraft.

In what follows, I discuss each of these in further detail. My starting assumption is that the proposed test battery would be hosted on a personal computer equipped with a large 17-inch, high-resolution color monitor, flight sticks and rudder pedals, and other peripherals as needed. With the exception of recovery from spatial disorientation, every testing idea mentioned below is feasible, given a Pentium computer and a fast graphics card. However, spatial disorientation testing might require some advances in graphics and virtual reality technology before it becomes feasible.

Ability Requirements and Componential Analyses of Piloting Tasks

The pilot aptitude domain has never been adequately specified, with most battery developers relying on armchair analyses of the piloting task or job analyses with expert pilots as the basis for selecting tests. Systematic job analyses with expert pilots could be quite useful in specifying hypotheses for the ability requirements for piloting. Fleishman and Quaintance (1984), for example, have developed rating scales to evaluate ability requirements in the cognitive, perceptual/spatial, physical, and psychomotor domains. Typically, a sample of experts is asked to rate clusters of piloting tasks on ability requirements, and ratings are analyzed for consistency. Outcomes of this type of study are described in Hunter and Burke (1995a). The challenge to this approach to ability requirement specification is making the ability description comprehensible to the subject matter expert, who is unlikely to have a background in psychology. If the rating task is not meaningful to the rater, the resulting data are going to be worthless. Interrater consistency is a partial safeguard. But rather than rely on verbal descriptions alone, I would prefer to demonstrate ability requirements with automated tests. So, for example, when asking an expert pilot how important working memory is for performing an instrument approach, we would explain what working memory is, then demonstrate the requirement with a few items from working memory tests.

As mentioned earlier, a type of componential analysis might be used to identify the major components of cockpit skills. Abilities requirement analyses of the type described above assist in developing hypotheses about what abilities are involved in piloting. With experimental methods modeled after part-task training, we might be able to do more than hypothesize. Piloting is a complex task requiring the coordination of numerous subtasks. Simulation systems sometimes employ a part-task training approach that isolates components of the whole task and permits practice on the components until skill is attained. There are three types of part-task approaches commonly used—segmentation, fractionation, and simplification (Wightman & Lintern, 1985). Segmentation partitions a task on temporal or spatial dimensions and can be applied to tasks that are composed of a series of subtasks with discernible end points. Backward-chaining, for example, might be used to teach flare and touch down, the final tasks in landing, with prior segments being added successively in training. Fractionation applies to complex tasks in which two or more components are executed simultaneously. Straight and level flight in a crosswind make simultaneous demands on both pitch and roll control. A fractionation approach would give independent practice on pitch and roll, then combine the two. The third approach, simplification, adjusts one or more characteristics of the task to make it easier. For example, if the lag between control input and stimulus display in a tracking task is reduced, task difficulty can be reduced to permit learning of the skill. Following fractionation and segmentation part-task training, the components are reintegrated using either a pure-part, repetitive-part, or progressive-part training schedule. However, the present interest lies in application of task partitioning to componential analysis. These approaches to task partitioning might be used to discover how piloting subtasks are related to fundamental cognitive, perceptual, and psychomotor abilities. Part-tasks could be presented to pilots participating in laboratory experiments along with tests assessing more elementary abilities. Regression or structural model equations could be used to relate part-task performance variables to ability variables. The part-tasks themselves might be used as selector tests, but they are likely to involve practiced skills or specialized pilot knowledge and might not be appropriate for the flight-naive pilot candidate. The part-task or componential approach described here might be useful in determining how and when various abilities are evoked during piloting an aircraft.

Basic Research on Human Abilities

Independent of any effort to better specify the abilities required for piloting aircraft, we need to conduct basic research on human abilities to better understand the abilities we can already measure and to discover new abilities that our batteries do not currently measure. Kyllonen (1993, 1994) has proposed a taxonomy for the cognitive domain. Kyllonen and his colleagues have been examining the cognitive psychology literature for new sources of individual differences in the parameters of models concerned with learning, problem solving, working memory, basic information processing, knowledge representation, and most recently, motor behavior. The six rows of the taxonomy reflect the major abilities suggested by cognitive psychology—declarative knowledge, procedural knowledge, working memory, processing speed, declarative (associative) learning, and procedural (skill) learning. The columns reflect three information domains suggested by psychometric analyses—verbal, quantitative, and spatial. Within each cell are three or four minor rows that correspond to task paradigms or item types. These are repeated across columns.

The Kyllonen et al. Cognitive Abilities Measurement (CAM 4.1) battery of 59 computer-administered tests, in some instances, measures cognitive abilities that were not assessable with printed tests. This is important, since we can imagine that piloting requires such abilities. Recent efforts of this Armstrong Laboratory team have been to develop a battery of 18 psychomotor tests to assess four factors that appear to be related to piloting aircraft: multilimb coordination, control precision, rate control, and response orientation (Tirre, 1995). Each of these was identified in the Fleishman and Quaintance (1984) taxonomy. Future research is being directed toward determining whether the CAM categories can be meaningfully extended to the psychomotor domain. For example, can a test of psychomotor working memory be constructed? Working memory is a limited capacity system designed to simultaneously store and process information. Is there a working memory system dedicated to psychomotor programs? We suspect that there is such a system and that the closest we currently have to a test of such a system would be a test of the multilimb coordination factor, which requires the person to coordinate the movements of hands and feet in responding to complex visual stimuli.

In addition to psychomotor abilities, which may or may not map on the CAM abilities framework, I believe that further research on pilot aptitudes should be directed toward discovering the major factors in attention, dynamic visual perception, recovery from spatial disorientation, and situation awareness. These factors do not easily fit into the existing CAM taxonomy and, in some cases, might be viewed as more specialized abilities.

Attentional abilities suspected to be important to piloting include the ability to minimize interference between competing tasks (or time-share), the ability to scan visual displays and integrate information, the ability to focus attention on a subset of a visual display, the ability to inhibit irrelevant distraction, and the ability to switch attention, to name a few (Tham & Kramer, 1994). Despite considerable research on individual differences in attention (e.g., Braune & Wickens, 1986; Hunt & Lansman, 1982; Stankov, 1983), a truly comprehensive factor analytic study has not yet been performed. Research has not been reported that examines relationships among indices of the various forms of attentional control. Studies have generally focused on one aspect of attention, for example, attention switching (Gopher, 1982), or dual task performance (Hunt & Lansman, 1982). Concerning the latter, research has not consistently found evidence for a general time-sharing factor (Braune & Wickens, 1986; Keele & Hawkins, 1982), but I hope to see further work in this area in our lab (Ikomi & Tirre, 1994). Research employing a distinct mental coordination paradigm was successful in demonstrating a general multitasking ability (Yee, Hunt, & Pellegrino, 1991).

Dynamic visual perception has been studied under various guises by Scialfa, Garvey, Gish, Deering, Leibowitz, and Goebel (1988) and by Kennedy, Ritter, Dunlap, Lane, and Berbaum (1993), among others. Scialfa et al. found that dynamic visual acuity was factorially distinguishable from static acuity but that the factors were correlated .6. Kennedy et al. developed a battery of temporal acuity tests, which he defined as the ability to accurately and quickly perceive events as they occur serially over time. Distinctions between spatial and temporal acuity are supported by research evaluating neurophysiological aspects of visual processing (Livingstone & Hubel, 1988; Regan, 1982). Kennedy's battery included measures of phi phenomenon (apparent motion), perception of simultaneity, dynamic visual acuity, bistable stroboscopic motion, masking, and critical flicker fusion. Stability coefficients varied from .54 to .91, indicating that, for the most part, enduring abilities were being measured. For the most part, correlations with conventional aptitudes were nonsignificant. In terms of predictive validity, some preliminary evidence suggests that temporal acuity or dynamic visual perception is related to performance in a simulated aircraft landing task.

Spatial disorientation (SD) refers to "an erroneous orientational percept, that is, an erroneous sense of one's position and motion with respect to the plane of the earth's surface" (Gillingham, 1992, p. 297). My interest concerns whether we can measure recovery from SD in pilot candidates and whether this is a stable attribute of the person. A test of spatial disorientation recovery would likely involve a flight simulation program and some flight task that novices can learn quickly. Illusions that can result in SD originate in either the visual or vestibular systems (Gillingham, 1992). Since our proposed testing system would not be motion based (this would be quite expensive), we cannot simulate SD that originates in the vestibular system. There are two types of visual illusions that we have a reasonable chance to simulate—those involving the ambient visual system and those involving the focal visual system—and both might require advances in virtual reality technology before they become feasible. Examples of the former are erroneous perceptions of pitch and bank attitude caused by false horizons such as shorelines and sloping surface planes as in cloud formations. The absence of ambient visual orientation cues can also lead to SD. For example, landing approaches on exceptionally dark nights and over snowy terrain can result in misjudged flight parameters. Illusions involving the central visual or focal field include misjudging height above ground because local structures, vegetation, and other features are different in size from what the pilot is familiar with (size constancy) and misjudging approach slope because the landing strip is located on an incline and presents an image shape different from what the pilot would expect (shape constancy). Absence of focal visual orientation cues can be problematic, too. This occurs in featureless terrain or over glassy water, sometimes leading to overestimations of height above surface.

The term *situation awareness* (or SA) has been used to describe an important component of real-time operator tasks such as piloting an aircraft (Adams, Tenney, & Pew, 1995). Situation awareness in the context of piloting can be defined as the pilot's mental model of the aircraft's status, considered both internally (e.g., fuel remaining, position of flaps, engine condition) and externally (e.g., position relative to ground and other aircraft). Endsley (1988) elaborates on this idea by defining SA as the perception of elements in a volume of space and time, comprehension of their meaning, and projection of their status into the future. Cargo, transport, and combat pilots in fighter, attack, and bomber aircraft each require SA for their unique missions. My working hypothesis is that there is a core process of attaining and maintaining SA that is common to all missions and that pilots acquire skills in SA with experience and vary in asymptotic skill level.

The concept of situation awareness originated within the pilot community and only recently have psychologists become interested in it. Consequently, there is yet to be a consensual theoretical definition of SA. Some investigators appear to want to limit SA to the contents of the pilot's working memory (Endsley, 1988). Others broaden the scope of SA to include any information that can be activated to assist in assessing a situation, thus allowing preattentively processed information to influence SA (Sarter & Woods, 1991). Adams et al. (1995) proposed that SA also includes the process of planning actions. Expert pilots sometimes utilize strategies that facilitate SA, such as preplanning for emergencies and letting go of high workload strategies during emergencies. As a developer of pilot aptitude measures, I am interested in the basic perceptual and cognitive correlates of SA. Will tests of these correlates predict which pilots will attain the highest levels of SA? In particular, is it possible to measure SA aptitude in the context of some operator task that is familiar to all pilot candidates?

To answer my own question, I think that it is possible to capture some of the relevant variance in the context of performance in a driving simulation. It is hard to imagine a pilot candidate who has not driven an automobile, and so the driving context is likely to be useful in measuring SA aptitude. Gugerty (1995) reported his plans for research in our laboratory for measuring SA in a driving simulator called the PC DriveSim. Following Adams et al. (1995), Gugerty distinguishes between situation assessment, that is, the processes an operator goes through to gather and interpret information needed for performing a real-time task, and the situation model, which is the knowledge produced by these processes. The situation model is composed of a dynamic model of the current situation, models of situations likely to occur in the future, and plans for responding to them. Gugerty assumes that the situation model is active in working memory, and because much of the driver's task is processing spatial information, spatial memory is especially important.

So far, focus has been on one important aspect of driving SA; that is, knowledge of the locations of nearby "traffic" vehicles, and studies have used both explicit and implicit methods of assessing this knowledge. One problem with explicit SA measures is that they assess only conscious knowledge. However, automatic processes involving preattentively processed information are very important in real-time tasks like driving. Gugerty and Tirre (1995b) employed both implicit and explicit SA measures and presented data on these measures' reliabilities and intercorrelations.

Implicit probes involve having subjects watch an animated 3D display of a highway driving scene from the driver's viewpoint. Left-, rear-, and side-view mirrors show cars to the rear. The subject's car maintains speed and lane position without driver inputs ("autopilot"), but subjects must override the autopilot in emergency situations by using the arrow keys to accelerate, decelerate, and change lanes. Data are recorded on the following two implicit measures of SA: (1) sensitivity at detecting emergency situations (based on how often subjects attempt to avoid an emergency by making any driving response [hit rate] and how often they make unnecessary driving responses [false alarm rate] and (2) awareness of vehicles in the right and left blindspots (based on how often subjects crash into blindspot vehicles during emergency maneuvers). These implicit measures were chosen to reflect SA, not decision and response processes; that is, they are not measures of overall performance on the implicit probes.

Explicit probes involve having subjects watch a 3D driving scene, either in the mode described above (overriding autopilot) or in "passenger" mode, where they make no driving control actions. In either case, when the 3D scene ends, the subjects see a top-down, 2D view of the road and use the mouse to indicate the positions of traffic cars. The two main explicit measures of SA are (1) the percentage of cars recalled by the subject on each trial and (2) the average location error for recalled cars. The task includes scenarios that vary the number of cars on a road and their relative location as a type of workload manipulation.

The explicit measures of SA were highly reliable, with split-half reliabilities of .96 for percentage of cars recalled and .95 for average location error. Reliabilities for the implicit variables were at acceptable levels, .88 for sensitivity to emergency situations and .73 for awareness of cars in the blindspot. Figure 11.1 shows how the SA measures were intercorrelated and predicted global driving performance indexed by success in avoiding crashes.

Gugerty and Tirre (1995a) reported a preliminary cognitive correlates study of SA conducted as part of a larger factor analytic study of cognitive and perceptual-motor abilities. The abilities under consideration were working memory (WM, which was equated with fluid ability, Gf), multilimb coordination, visual search, and temporal processing (the ability to estimate time intervals and make discriminations concerning them). Table 11.1 shows how these abilities were correlated with the SA measures from PC DriveSim. These data suggest three

Figure 11.1
Relationships among Measures of Situation Awareness and Crash Avoidance in PC DriveSim

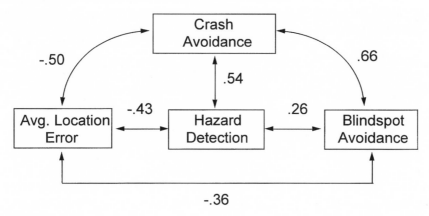

$N = 108$.

tentative inferences. The first is that Gf/WM is the best predictor of the implicit measures of SA. The second is that only temporal processing is ruled out as a predictor of our explicit measure of SA. And the third is that global performance (crash avoidance) is predicted by either Gf/WM or multilimb coordination. I performed two multiple regression analyses with these four predictors and crash avoidance as the dependent variable. In one case, Gf/WM came out as the sole significant predictor, and in another case, multilimb coordination came out as the sole significant predictor. These results are consistent with the hypothesis that SA depends critically on the working memory system. The degree of correlation with working memory was quite high, but we might expect this to decrease somewhat for a more selected population such as pilot candidates. Another concern is the correlation of SA with spatial orientation, because in piloting aircraft, spatial orientation might be a component of SA. In our studies, it might be possible to assess these two constructs separately.[5]

Multiple Indicator Test Battery

In this step, we actually assemble a prototype battery composed of the cognitive, psychomotor, attentional, perceptual, and specialized abilities investigated in the basic research phase. Construction of a prototype pilot aptitude battery could use the CAM 4.1 test battery as a starting point. CAM 4.1 is an excellent example of a multiple indicator approach to test battery design. The multiple indicator approach starts with the assumption that no single test adequately measures a given construct and that at least three tests are needed to identify a latent trait or factor. Humphreys's notion of systematic heterogeneity takes this

Table 11.1
Correlations of Situation Awareness Measures with Abilities

| | SA Measure | | | Global Performance |
| | Location Error (N = 46) | Hazard Detection (N = 88) | Blindspot Avoidance (N = 88) | Crash Avoidance (N = 134) |
Predictor				
Gf/Working Memory	-.46	.44*	.32*	.46**
Multilimb Coordination	-.50*	.31	.20 NS	.50**
Visual Search	-.49	.25	.23	.29
Temporal Processing	-.20 NS	.36	.16 NS	.38

*Only significant predictor in multiple regression analysis.
**Probably equally predictive.
NS = Not significant.

idea one step further. Humphreys (1976, 1985) suggests that by deliberately varying the item type or measurement method, one reduces the role of unwanted systematic nonattribute (method) error and emphasizes the role of the attribute of interest. Roznowski (1993) suggested that elementary cognitive tasks (ECTs) might be best likened to individual items in a factorially complex test that contain large amounts of specific, nonattribute, and error variance. If we can identify ECTs that load a common factor in our basic research, a score with decent psychometric properties (e.g., stability and predictive validity) would be found in the composite of those ECTs because the specific and method variance become minimized. Of course, the potential price to pay is that we increase the amount of overlap between the ECT composites and ability test scores such as the AFOQT that we already have. Roznowski (1993) found that a combination of similar ECTs correlated .63 with a test battery similar to the AFOQT.

Systematic heterogeneity in a test battery will buy a certain amount of predictive validity even when we do not know what the criterion is. Employing a facet design for each test and conducting a preliminary validation of the battery against a facsimile of the real-life criterion will enable us to tune the test battery to the particular criterion of interest. It is possible that some facet combinations yield more validity than others in predicting flight training performance. Examining correlations of facet combinations with the criterion should suggest how the test can be improved.

Validation of Battery against Laboratory Criteria

The next step is to obtain a preliminary validation of the prototype battery as a predictor of pilot training outcomes. To accomplish this, we contracted with Technology Systems Inc. to develop an inexpensive flight simulator for laboratory research that records detailed measurements of simulated flight performance. In laboratory studies, we train flight-naive students how to fly a high wing, single fixed-pitch propeller type of aircraft using this training system. The Basic Flight Instruction Tutoring System (BFITS) is a desktop PC-based tutorial and procedural flight training system hosted on a 486DX computer with joysticks and rudder pedals (Benton, Corriveau, Koonce, & Tirre, 1992). It consists of 31 lessons designed for the completely flight-naive student. The first 9 lessons present declarative knowledge about flight using text, graphics, and animation. Each lesson is followed by a multiple choice quiz. The remainder of BFITS is dedicated to training or testing particular flight maneuvers in a simulated Cessna 152 type of aircraft. Each lesson teaches knowledge required by the maneuver (e.g., level, medium banked turns), demonstrates the maneuver, and then allows the student to practice the maneuver with performance feedback until it is mastered. Data recorded for each flight include performance accuracy and variability (see Figure 11.2). Trials-to-mastery is recorded for every maneuver.

Is BFITS an effective training device? If BFITS training transfers to real flight performance, we can more confidently generalize from studies with BFITS to the behavior of student pilots in real training aircraft. Evidence for the transfer utility of BFITS was recently obtained in a study by Koonce, Moore, and Benton (1995). Koonce et al. formed experimental and control groups with students at a commercial flight school. The experimental group received training on BFITS prior to flight instruction, and the control group did not. Results demonstrated statistically significant transfer on both dependent variables considered. There was a savings of 29 percent in flight hours to solo flight and a savings of 36 percent in number of attempted landings before solo flight. This study needs to be replicated and extended using the automated flight performance measurement system, which I will describe in the next section. This will enable us to determine specifically which flight maneuvers show the most transfer.

In many respects, BFITS is similar to CAPSS (Spinner, 1991). BFITS records much the same performance data on practice flights as CAPSS and so faces the same challenge of data summarization. We are still exploring our options on this issue. However, for our preliminary studies, we have been using log trials-to-mastery on each lesson segment (maneuver) as dependent variables. There are tremendous individual differences and substantial correlations among these scores. It may turn out that this overall trials-to-mastery score is superior to any combination of performance measures—the whole may be greater than the sum of the parts!

Figure 11.2
Performance Feedback Graph from the Basic Flight Instruction Tutoring System

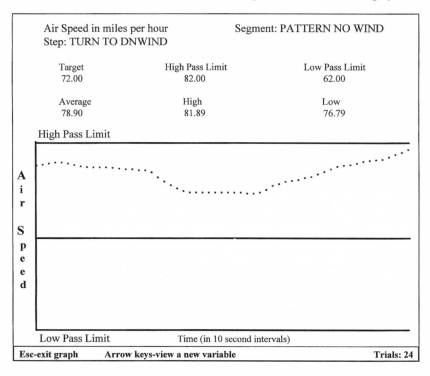

Validate Battery against Objective Criteria Obtained in Training Aircraft

Our preliminary test validation studies are conducted with BFITS, but we are aware that BFITS is imperfectly correlated with real flight performance. As a low-cost simulator, BFITS can represent some but not all aspects of flight with sufficient fidelity. We think it represents the cognitive demands of beginning flight quite well. Of course, there are visual and vestibular aspects of flight that BFITS cannot represent, and so the ultimate validation of a pilot aptitude battery must be in a real airplane. The Semi-Automated Flight Evaluation System, or SAFES, is a system being developed by Technology Systems to record in a real airplane the same flight performance data as BFITS records in a simulator (Benton, Baldwin, & Koonce, 1995). Performance evaluation is part of the normal teaching process in Undergraduate Pilot Training, and formal examinations occur six times in UPT. SAFES would be used to augment these evaluations with objective data on the precision with which the student pilot can handle his or her aircraft.

SAFES provides the following features: detailed objective measurements on a number of flight parameters, in-flight performance feedback via earphones, and flight playback capability in a BFITS-like simulator for debriefing and review. SAFES equipment includes a PC with computer-generated voice, a hand-held interface for the flight instructor, and a set of dedicated flight instruments (e.g., global positioning system [GPS] gyroscope), some of which are connected to the aircraft's pilot-static system.

Another criterion that could be recorded reflects the student's rate of flying skill acquisition. SAFES records trials-to-mastery on several flight maneuvers just like BFITS. Duke and Ree (1996) found that a combination of the AFOQT Pilot composite and BAT scores predicted the number of flying hours needed to achieve various training milestones in UPT. Keep in mind that in USAF/ UPT, flight hours are limited by design. In pilot training in the private sector, students are allowed to learn at their own pace (and expense, of course), and so these data would have less restriction of range than would be found in military pilot training. Less detailed time-to-learn criteria are also available routinely in private flight training, for example, flight hours to solo.

My emphasis on objectively recorded performance data does not imply that the flight instructor's evaluation is without merit. Quite the contrary, the flight instructor is likely to have significant insight into the student pilot's flying skills, which no electronic device could ever provide. Prior to any full-scale validation study, I would urge the development of a rating scale or other instrument that attempts to capture and quantify the flight instructor's assessment of the student's flying skills and his or her evaluation of the student's potential as a professional pilot. Ideally, the criterion for a validation study of a pilot selection test battery would actually be the common factor underlying a set of criteria, for example, precision of flight, learning rate, and instructor's assessment of student potential. I believe it is a safe assumption that these reflect a common factor, but if I am wrong, the individual criteria can be examined independently.

PRELIMINARY STUDY WITH BFITS AND CAM TESTS

At this point, I will describe our first study with BFITS and a subset of our cognitive and perceptual-motor battery. This will give an idea of how well our approach is working. In this study our interest was in the following questions:

- Do cognitive and perceptual-motor factors both contribute to the prediction of flying skill acquisition?
- Do lesson comprehension and trials-to-mastery on basic flight procedures have similar prediction equations?

Our sample consisted of 158 flight-naive students, 18 to 30 years of age, primarily men (80 percent) with a wide variety of educational backgrounds. We applied a 1-hour screening battery of cognitive and perceptual-motor tests to select the upper half of the ability distribution. We administered 26 computerized tests in two sessions of 3 hours each, then administered about 54 hours of BFITS in 4-hour sessions.

Regression Analysis Relating BFITS to Cognitive and Perceptual-Motor Factors

Because I was primarily interested in how latent abilities or factors were related to BFITS performance rather than any single test, I performed factor analyses of the 21 cognitive and 12 perceptual-motor ability measures obtained on the participants. The two domains were analyzed separately because of the low subject-to-variable ratios and then intercorrelated (see Table 11.2). In both factor analyses the number of factors was decided by the maximum likelihood test, and the factors were rotated using the Quartimax procedure—an orthogonal rotation that emphasizes the amount of variance explained by the first factor. Thus, if there is a general factor in the data, the first factor resulting from this rotation method will have high to moderate loadings on most variables.

For the cognitive test data, a five-factor solution accounting for 59.7 percent of the variance yielded a nonsignificant chi-square (chi-square $= 129.87$, $p = .16$, $df = 115$, chi-square/$df = 1.13$). I interpreted the factors as general cognitive ability g), information-processing speed (PS), dynamic visual perception (DVP), reading span (RS), and verbal comprehension (VC). Each of these factors was readily interpretable. As noted in previous research, working memory and skill learning tasks were among the highest g-loaded tasks (Kyllonen, 1993; Kyllonen & Stephens, 1990). The PS factor loaded response times to the physical/name identity, number comparison, and figure comparison tasks, and loaded reading and response time to sentences in the reading span test. The dynamic visual perception (DVP) factor loaded tasks requiring the participant to interpret moving or briefly exposed visual stimuli including the time to contact, inspection time, and the rapid serial classification tasks. A similar factor has been researched by Scialfa et al. (1988). The fourth factor loaded three measures from the reading span task, that is, sentence verification accuracy, word recall, and sentence verification time. It also loaded word recall from the running memory span task, which suggests a verbal working memory interpretation. The fifth factor (VC) primarily loaded two tests that had in common a verbal comprehension requirement—aviation knowledge and the Wonderlic Personnel Test (much of the content required comprehension of words and sentences).

I applied the same factor analytic procedure as before to the perceptual-motor tests. A four-factor solution resulted in a nonsignificant chi-square (chi-square $= 28.93$, $p = .22$, $df = 24$, chi-square/$df = 1.21$). I interpreted the four factors as being general perceptual-motor ability (g_{PM}, or alternatively, multilimb coordination), multilevel targeting (MLT), target interception and tracking (TI&T), and laser shoot (aiming) efficiency (LSE) (see Figures 11.3–11.6 for descriptions of some of the tests). As expected, the g_{PM} factor most strongly loaded the

Table 11.2
Correlations between Cognitive and Perceptual-Motor Factors

| | Perceptual-Motor Factors | | | |
Cognitive Factors	gPM	MLT	TI&T	LSE
General Cognitive Ability (g)	.444**	.158	-.195*	.021
Information Processing Speed	.023	.070	.221*	-.102
Dynamic Visual Perception	.420**	.125	.128	-.042
Reading Span	-.027	-.027	-.059	.029
Verbal Comprehension	.166	.011	-.040	.118

Two-tailed probability: *.05; **.002.
g_{PM} = General perceptual-motor.
MLT = Multilevel targeting.
TI&T = Target interception and tracking.
LSE = Laser shoot efficiency.
$N = 158$.

complex perceptual-motor tasks such as center the ball, target interception and tracking, and balloon popping. These were all multilimb coordination tasks requiring both flightstick and pedal inputs; thus, an alternative interpretation of the factor is multilimb coordination. The MLT and TI&T factors loaded primarily the parameters from the laser shoot II and helicopter target tasks, respectively. The fourth factor, LSE, loaded the hits per shots ratios from the two laser shoot tasks. The TI&T factor appears to correspond to the control precision factor, which was measured best by the rotary pursuit test. The other factors, MLT and LSE, should be investigated further in a battery that includes indicators of several known perceptual-motor factors.

As Table 11.2 shows, there was some variance shared between general cognitive ability/working memory and multilimb coordination, and between dynamic visual perception and multilimb coordination. After factor analysis of the aptitude variables, I regressed two dependent variables available from BFITS on the aptitude factor score estimates. The two dependent variables were percent correct on BFITS lesson examinations and log trials-to-mastery on BFITS flight lessons 10 to 13. The two dependent variables were correlated −.48, indicating that students who comprehended more of the declarative (academic) instruction tended to learn basic flight maneuvers in fewer trials.

Looking at the regression equation for lesson comprehension first (see Table 11.3), we see that it is predicted quite well ($R = .80$, $p < .0001$) with contributions by the working memory (general cognitive ability), verbal comprehension, and reading span factors. These results confirm the usual finding about

Figure 11.3
Center the Ball Test

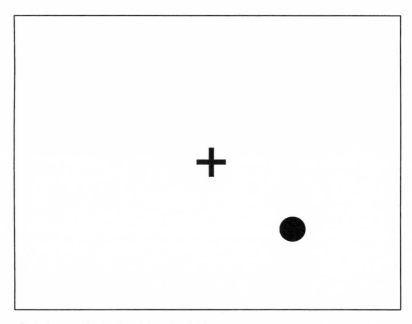

Keep the ball centered using joystick and pedal input.

academic learning: Working memory/general ability and verbal ability account for the variance, with general ability taking the lion's share.

In recent years an old debate has once again heated up between two groups that might be called the *g*-advocates and the multiple abilities advocates. The *g*-advocates (see Ree & Earles, 1991, for representative article) marvel at the consistency of *g* in predicting training outcomes and job performance. The multiple abilities advocates vary in their response to the evidence for the ubiquitous predictiveness of *g*. I believe the most sensible response is acceptance of *g* as a consistently potent predictor of training outcomes, especially training that is primarily declarative in nature. As for criteria that are more procedural in nature, that is, measurement tasks that require the examinee to demonstrate some skilled action, the level of prediction has been less impressive. This suggests that the search for predictors in addition to *g* will be fruitful, and supportive evidence is beginning to accrue (see, e.g., Collis, Tapsfield, Irvine, Dann, & Wright, 1995).

For the analysis of procedural learning, I decided to look at two criteria. The first was the logarithm of trials-to-mastery, and the second was a purified criterion obtained by partialing lesson comprehension out of log trials-to-mastery. Procedural learning (log trials-to-mastery) was predicted well (see Table 11.4; $R = .72$, $p < .0001$). In this case the significant contributions came from both

Figure 11.4
Target Interception and Tracking Test

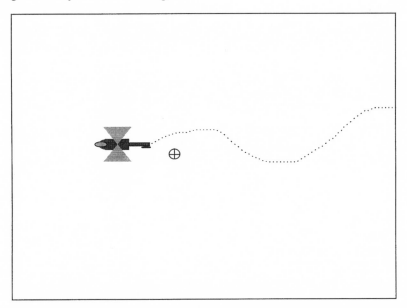

Intercept the helicopter using joystick and pedal input and press trigger to destroy target. The harder tracking task required holding crosshairs on target for three seconds before firing.

cognitive and perceptual-motor factors, that is, general cognitive ability (g), dynamic visual perception, and general perceptual-motor. Note that the only predictor shared by the declarative and procedural criteria is g.

Of course, one criticism that might be made against this analysis of procedural learning is that trials-to-mastery in basic flight maneuvers does not purely reflect procedural learning. There is reason to believe that declarative learning also contributes to learning basic flight maneuvers. As noted earlier, percent correct in lesson comprehension and trials-to-mastery were correlated—.48. The question arises whether g would play as strong a role in predicting procedural learning if declarative learning was partialed out of the criterion. If g has its effect on procedural learning indirectly through declarative learning, then we would expect g's contribution to be reduced to nothing in predicting the residualized criterion.

The purified procedural learning variable (Table 11.5) was predicted ($R = .56$, $p < .0001$) by three factors: dynamic visual perception, multilimb coordination, and a psychomotor task–specific factor. Dynamic visual perception refers to the ability to make discriminations about moving and briefly exposed visual stimuli (Scialfa et al., 1988). Multilimb coordination refers to the ability to coordinate hand and foot motions, one of the factors in Fleishman's taxonomy.

Figure 11.5
Laser Shoot I and II Tests

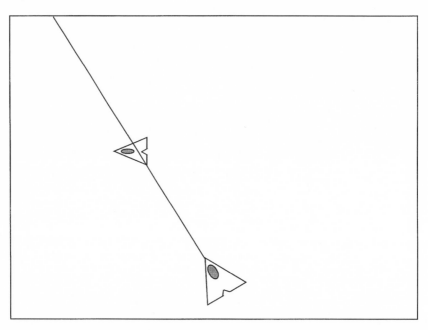

Aim at targets passing overhead with pedals (yaw), match size of target with joystick (pitch), and
press trigger to fire. Laser Shoot I required only aiming and firing.

The third significant predictor, multilevel targeting, involved aiming at targets
using pedals and matching the firing aircraft to the target aircraft in size with
pitch control. This factor merits closer examination in subsequent studies.

These findings are important in demonstrating the independent contributions
of perception and psychomotor control in predicting the acquisition of basic
flight skills. The finding that g's effect on procedural learning is indirect through
declarative learning merits further study.

FUTURE ACTIVITIES

As I mentioned earlier, we are primarily concerned with technologies for
selecting pilot candidates for ab initio training programs but foresee that we will
become involved in technologies for selecting pilots for advanced training. There
are two aspects to this problem. One is the general requirement for Air Force
pilots to be adaptable such that they can switch to new aircraft systems with
relative ease. Air Force pilots typically switch to new aircraft systems every
three or four years, and so adaptability is important. The second is the specific
requirement for situation awareness in combat pilots. As a pilot's career pro-

Figure 11.6
Balloon-Popping Test

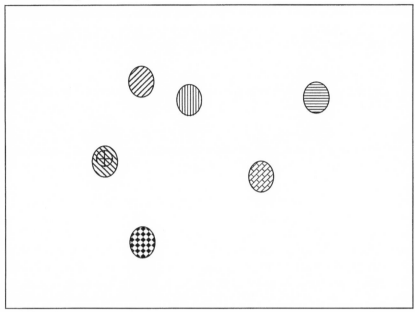

Place crosshairs on floating balloons of various colors and press trigger to pop. Balloons can be
    popped only in the order specified on the previous screen.

gresses and she or he moves up to increasingly complex aircraft systems, the
nature of the criterion should change also. Situation awareness is receiving the
lion's share of the attention in the aviation community today. With that in mind,
we have initiated a program of research and development concerned with the
measurement of SA in simulated F-16 combat operations. Like BFITS, we plan
to host the simulation on an inexpensive microcomputer. Work on the proposed
system, Situation Awareness Flight Trainer and Evaluator (SAFTE) (O'Donnell,
Eddy, Cardenas, Trafton, & Campbell, 1995), is actually under way, and so I
will describe our plans with it first.

SAFTE will need to be validated as a measure of situation awareness. Validation can take several forms, for example, criterion related, content, and construct (Messick, 1981). To establish a test's criterion-related validity, we
demonstrate that the test successfully discriminates between criterion groups or
significantly predicts criterion behaviors (e.g., a test of hypnotic susceptibility
predicts who can be hypnotized). Test validation of this type is an empirical
process. Content validity refers to the perception that the test samples the type
of tasks and behaviors implied by its name. To establish the content validity of
a test, one might compare the content of a test with a taxonomy of behaviors

Table 11.3
Regression Equation Predicting BFITS Declarative Learning Criterion

Variable	Beta	r	Part r	T	p
Verbal Comprehension	.282	.273	.281	5.779	.0000
General Cognitive Ability (g)	.738	.731	.737	15.141	.0000
Information Processing Speed	-.093	-.113	-.092	-1.898	.0596
Reading Span	.123	.143	.123	2.525	.0126

Note: Dependent variable was percent correct score on multiple choice examinations on lessons 1 to 9.
$R = .803$.
$F (4, 150) = 67.99$.
$p < .0001$.

or a job analysis. Construct validation refers to the process of testing hypotheses about the psychological attributes accounting for test score variance. To establish the construct validity of a test, one attempts to find evidence that (1) there is convergence of indicators intended to measure the same attribute despite surface dissimilarities and (2) there is divergence of indicators intended to measure different attributes. Construct validity can also be supported by (3) demonstrating that the test correlates with certain practical criteria or with tests of other distinct but related constructs (this is sometimes referred to as nomological validity). Construct validation can be conducted through several research strategies. The goal is to defend the intended interpretation of test scores.

As part of the SAFTE research and development effort, we hope to establish this measurement device's construct validity. We are planning on one experiment that incorporates the approaches described above. The key questions are: Do explicit measures of SA and implicit measures of SA indicate one underlying ability or two, or do they represent two highly related abilities driven by a general SA ability? Are the SA factors distinguishable from abilities that are theoretically unrelated? and Do the SA factors discriminate between groups that should demonstrate different levels of SA (e.g., experienced fighter pilots versus novice fighter pilots)? These questions can be addressed with the structural equation modeling approach (e.g., Bentler, 1993). Figure 11.7 represents two models that could be tested using the structural equation method. Model A is a hierarchical model in which a general SA factor (SAg) drives explicit and implicit SA factors. SAg is affected by two sources, that is, air combat experience and domain-specific attentional resources (i.e., residual capacity), which is affected by air combat experience and general attentional resources. Model B simplifies matters by positing domain-specific attentional resources as another SA primary factor.

To approach the issue of adaptability, we propose to investigate the transfer of skill from real aircraft to flight simulator. The analogous situation in the

Table 11.4
Regression Equation Predicting BFITS Procedural Learning Criterion

Variable	Beta	r	Part r	T	p
Dynamic Visual Perception	-.250	-.445	-.206	-3.142	.0021
Multilevel Targeting	-.118	-.261	-.110	-1.682	.0954
General Cognitive Ability (g)	-.403	-.581	-.333	-5.075	.0000
General Perceptual-Motor	-.245	-.568	-.179	-2.734	.0073

Note: Dependent variable was log of mean trials-to-mastery over first four flight lessons.
$R = .718$.
$F (4, 113) = 29.99$.
$p < .0001$.

operational world occurs when a pilot must retrain on a new aircraft (e.g., an F-16 pilot is transferred to an A-10). We will investigate two classes of variables as possible mediators of skill transfer: experience and performance abilities. The basic questions we pose are: (1) Do amount of experience (e.g., flight hours in aircraft and simulator hours) and diversity of experience (e.g., number and variety of aircraft flown, number and variety of simulators operated) reduce the required time to learn to operate a flight simulator? (2) Does recency of flight experience (e.g., number of flight hours in last three months) affect retraining time and does this variable interact with flight hours? And (3) which performance abilities measured by our pilot aptitude battery predict training time? Do these variables interact with experience, diversity, or recency in explaining variance in retraining time?

It is apparent that some of the variables described above have counterparts in

Table 11.5
Regression Equation Predicting Purified BFITS Procedural Learning Criterion

Variable	Beta	r	Part r	T	p
Dynamic Visual Perception	-.356	-.501	-.304	-3.891	.0002
General Perceptual-Motor	-.242	-.416	-.209	-2.678	.0085
Multilevel Targeting	.159	-.209	-.156	-2.005	.0474

Note: Dependent variable was log of mean trials-to-mastery over first four flight lessons with declarative learning score (percent correct lesson comprehension) partialed out.
$R = .559$.
$F (3, 113) = 17.13$.
$p < .0001$.

Figure 11.7
Measurement and Causal Models of Situation Awareness

Model A

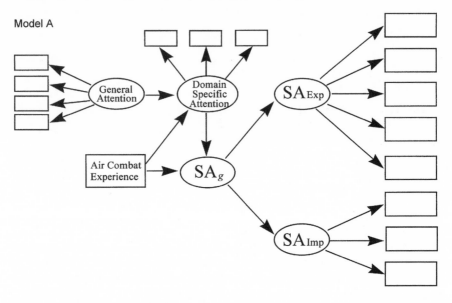

Model B

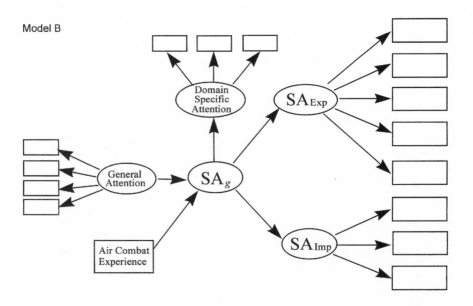

the experimental literature on learning and memory. For example, amount of experience (e.g., total number of flight hours) corresponds to degree of learning in the learning and memory literature; and recency corresponds somewhat to frequency and correlates inversely with time lag between training and perform-ance. But certain variables, for example, diversity of experience, have no readily identifiable counterparts in the experimental literature. Indeed, an experiment designed to address the interaction of these variables would be quite compli-cated. In my opinion, it would be to our advantage to first study these variables' effects on transfer/retraining in a correlational study, generally consistent with the perspective of Ulric Neisser (1982), who urged more naturalistic study of learning and memory phenomena. Questionnaires will be designed to measure the variables discussed above, and these would be administered along with pilot aptitude battery to a sample of pilots who vary in experience. A shortened version of BFITS will be administered that focuses on the flight skills identified as most critical by expert pilots.

FINAL COMMENTS

In summary, I believe that progress in pilot selection research depends on developments in several areas with special emphasis on (1) basic research on human abilities, particularly identifying new abilities suggested by the experi-mental literature on cognition, attention, perception, and perceptual-motor abil-ities; (2) construction of a test battery that employs multiple indicators and systematic heterogeneity, and (3) development of objective, automated measures of pilot performance as criteria in validation studies. What I have described here is an ambitious program of research and development, and by necessity, I have glossed over significant technical challenges that will have to be met. It is in-teresting to note that nearly every area of research mentioned in this chapter is being addressed by some unit within the air force's Armstrong Laboratory, and so a next-generation pilot selection test battery of the type described here is within our reach. Of course, one criticism that could be made of this proposal is that the test battery would be rather lengthy, possibly requiring two four-hour administrations. My response is that personnel selection effort in general, and test length in specific, should be weighed against job training costs and espe-cially the importance of the job. Pilots play immensely important roles in na-tional defense and transportation, and pilot selection merits more careful procedures that increased research attention would provide.

NOTES

The author's research described in this report was conducted as part of the Learning Abilities Measurement Program (LAMP), which was sponsored by the Air Force Office of Scientific Research (AFOSR) and the Armstrong Laboratory (AL). The opinions ex-pressed here are the author's and do not necessarily reflect those of the United States

Air Force. Many individuals have contributed significantly to the LAMP research described in this chapter. Thanks are due to John Tangney (AFOSR) and William Alley (AL/Human Resources) for their enthusiastic support for several years. Thanks are also due to my colleagues in LAMP, Patrick Kyllonen, Scott Chaiken, and Lee Gugerty, who have worked most closely with me in this research; and to my colleagues in the Aircrew Selection Research Branch, Joseph Weeks, Thomas Carretta, Malcolm Ree, Warren Zelenski, and Rick Siem, who have discussed many issues with me. I am also thankful for the many contributions of Rich Walker, Karen Raouf, Janice Hereford, Trace Cribbs, Henry Clark, Cindy Garcia, Brent Townsend, JoAnn Hall, Terri Simons, David Hartman, Brendan Underwood, Wayne Crone, Roger Dubbs, and Jamie Burns, who provided services in programming, data analysis, and data collection.

1. It is important to note that the Hunter and Burke meta-analysis did not attempt to adjust validities for range restriction and measurement error. In many cases, the needed statistics were simply not available.

2. This points out an inherent problem with the meta-analysis of validity studies—classification of predictor variables. The category of general ability might include tests as diverse as vocabulary and Raven's Progressive Matrices. One is hardly substitutable for the other, but a case could be made for either as an indicator of general ability.

3. Bartram (1995) summarized the development and validation of the Micropat battery sponsored by the British Royal Navy. The Micropat can be viewed as a hybrid of the basic attributes and learning sample approaches. It includes basic information-processing tasks as well as flight simulation tasks designed for the novice (e.g., landing). Predictive validity is comparable to the BAT with R hovering around .3 for samples at varying stages of training. The criterion again was pass/fail (pass rate was .73).

4. Comparable estimates are not yet available for ECTs in the BAT such as mental rotation, encoding speed, and short-term memory search. The only test-retest stability estimates available involved a time lag of 24 hours: .69, .62, and .79, respectively.

5. Recent developments in SA theory are described in a special issue of *Human Factors* edited by R. D. Gilson (1995).

REFERENCES

Ackerman, P. L. (1987). Individual differences in skill learning: An integration of psychometric and information processing perspectives. *Psychological Bulletin, 21*, 3–27.

Ackerman, P. L. (1988). Determinants of individual differences during skill acquisition: Cognitive abilities and information processing. *Journal of Experimental Psychology: General, 117*, 288–318.

Ackerman, P. L. (1990). A correlational analysis of skill specificity: Learning, abilities, and individual differences. *Journal of Experimental Psychology—Learning, Memory, and Cognition, 16*, 883–901.

Ackerman, P. L. (1992). Predicting individual differences in complex skill acquisition: Dynamics of ability determinants. *Journal of Applied Psychology, 77*, 598–614.

Adams, M. J., Tenney, Y. J., & Pew, R. W. (1995). Situation awareness and the cognitive management of complex systems. *Human Factors, 37*, 85–104.

Baddeley, A. D. (1968). A three-minute reasoning test based on grammatical transformation. *Psychonomic Science, 10*, 341–342.

Bartram, D. (1995). Validation of the Micropat Battery. *International Journal of Selection and Assessment, 3*, 84–95.

Bentler, P. M. (1993). *EQS: Structural Equations Program manual*. Los Angeles, CA: BMDP Statistical Software.

Benton, C., Baldwin, T., & Koonce, J. (1995). *Implementation of a Semi-Automated Flight Evaluation System (SAFES) phase 2* (Annual Technical Report). Brooks Air Force Base, TX: Armstrong Laboratory—Human Resources Directorate.

Benton, C., Corriveau, P., Koonce, J. M., & Tirre, W. C. (1992). *Development of the Basic Flight Instruction Tutoring System (BFITS)* (AL-TP-1991–0060). Brooks Air Force Base, TX: Armstrong Laboratory—Human Resources Directorate.

Berger, F. R., Gupta, W. B., Berger, R. M., & Skinner, J. (1990). *Air Force Officer Qualifying Test (AFOQT) Form P: Test manual* (AFHRL-TR-89–56). Brooks Air Force Base, TX: Air Force Human Resources Laboratory.

Braune, R., & Wickens, C. D. (1986). Time-sharing revisited: Test of a componential model for the assessment of individual differences. *Ergonomics, 29*, 1399–1414.

Carretta, T. R. (1989). USAF pilot selection and classification systems. *Aviation, Space, Environmental Medicine, 60*, 46–49.

Carretta, T. R. (1992). Short-term retest reliability of an experimental U.S. Air Force pilot candidate selection test battery. *International Journal of Aviation Psychology, 2*, 161–173.

Carretta, T. R., & Ree, M. (1994). Pilot candidate selection method: Sources of validity. *International Journal of Aviation Psychology, 4*, 104–117.

Cohen, J. (1983). The cost of dichotomization. *Applied Psychological Measurement, 7*, 249–253.

Collis, J. M., Tapsfield, P. G. C., Irvine, S. H., Dann, P. L., & Wright, D. (1995). The British Army Recruit Battery goes operational: From theory to practice in computer-based testing using item generation techniques. *International Journal of Selection and Assessment, 3*, 96–104.

Cronbach, L. J. (1970). *Essentials of psychological testing* (3rd ed.). New York: Harper & Row.

Delaney, H. D. (1992). Dichotic listening and psychomotor task performance as predictors of naval primary flight-training criteria. *International Journal of Aviation Psychology, 2*, 107–120.

Duke, A. P., & Ree, M. J. (1996). Better candidates fly fewer training hours: Another time testing pays off. *International Journal of Selection and Assessment, 4*, 115–121.

Embretson, S. (1992). Measuring and validating cognitive modifiability as an ability: A study in the spatial domain. *Journal of Educational Measurement, 29*, 25–50.

Endsley, M. (1988). *Situation awareness global assessment technique (SAGAT)*. Paper presented at the National Aerospace and Electronics Conference (NAECON), Dayton, OH.

Fleishman, E. A., & Quaintance, M. K. (1984). *Taxonomies of human performance: The description of human tasks*. Orlando, FL: Academic Press.

Frederiksen, J. R. (1981). Sources of process interactions in reading. In A. M. Lesgold & C. A. Perfetti (Eds.), *Interactive processes in reading*. Hillsdale, NJ: Erlbaum.

Gernsbacher, M. A., Varner, K. R., & Faust, M. E. (1990). Investigating differences in general comprehension skill. *Journal of Experimental Psychology: Learning, Memory, and Cognition, 16,* 430–445.

Gillingham, K. (1992). The spatial disorientation problem in the United States Air Force. *Journal of Vestibular Research, 2,* 297–306.

Gilson, R. D. (1995). Situation awareness [Special issue]. *Human Factors, 37* (1).

Gopher, D. (1982). A selective attention test as a predictor of success in flight training. *Human Factors, 24,* 174–183.

Gugerty, L. (1995, March). *Research on situation awareness in driving.* Paper presented at the Learning Abilities Measurement Program Mini-Conference on Human Perceptual-Motor Abilities, San Antonio, TX.

Gugerty, L., & Tirre, W. C. (1995a). Cognitive correlates of explicit and implicit measures of situation awareness. In D. J. Garland & M. R. Endsley (Eds.), *Experimental analysis and measurement of situation awareness: Proceedings of an international conference* (pp. 267–274). Daytona Beach, FL: Embry-Riddle Aeronautical University Press.

Gugerty, L., & Tirre, W. C. (1995b). Comparing explicit and implicit measures of situation awareness. In D. J. Garland & M. R. Endsley (Eds.), *Experimental analysis and measurement of situation awareness: Proceedings of an international conference* (pp. 259–266). Daytona Beach, FL: Embry-Riddle Aeronautical University Press.

Guilford, J. P., & Hoepfner, R. (1971). *Analysis of intelligence.* New York: McGraw-Hill.

Guilford, J. P., & Lacey, J. I. (1947). *Printed classification tests (Report No. 5).* Army Air Forces' Aviation Psychology Program Research Reports (Series). Washington DC: U.S. Government Printing Office.

Guttman, L. (1959). Introduction to facet design and analysis. In *Proceedings of the 15th International Congress of Psychology, Brussels, 1957.* Amsterdam: New Holland.

Guttman, R., Epstein, E. E., Amir, M., & Guttman, L. (1990). A structural theory of spatial abilities. *Applied Psychological Measurement, 14,* 217–236.

Guttman, L., & C. Levy, S. (1991). Two structural laws for intelligence tests. *Intelligence, 15,* 79–103.

Hilton, T. F., & Dolgin, D. L. (1991). Pilot selection in the military of the free world. In R. Gal & A. D. Mangelsdorff (Eds.), *Handbook of military psychology* (pp. 81–101). New York: John Wiley.

Humphreys, L. G.(1976). A factor model for research on intelligence and problem solving. In L. Resnick (Ed.), *The nature of intelligence* (pp. 329–340). Hillsdale, NJ: Lawrence Erlbaum.

Humphreys, L. G. (1985). General intelligence: An integration of factor, test, and simplex theory. In B. B. Wolman (Ed.), *Handbook of intelligence: Theories, measurement, and applications* (pp. 201–224). New York: Wiley.

Hunt, E. B. (1978). The mechanics of verbal ability. *Psychological Review, 85,* 109–130.

Hunt, E. B. (1987). The next word on verbal ability. In P. A. Vernon (Ed.), *Speed of information processing and intelligence.* Norwood, NJ: Ablex.

Hunt, E. B. (1980). Intelligence as an information processing concept. *British Journal of Psychology, 71*, 449–474.

Hunt, E. B., & Lansman, M. (1982). Individual differences in attention. In R. J. Sternberg (Ed.), *Advances in the psychology of human intelligence*. Hillsdale, NJ: Lawrence Erlbaum.

Hunter, D. R. (1989). Aviatior selection. In M. F. Wiskoff & G. M. Hampton (Eds.), *Military personnel measurement: Testing, assignment, evaluation*. New York: Praeger.

Hunter, D. R., & Burke, E. F. (1995a). *Handbook of pilot selection*. Brookfield, VT: Ashgate Publishing Co.

Hunter, D. R., & Burke, E. F. (1995b). Predicting aircraft pilot-training success: A meta-analysis of published research. *International Journal of Aviation Psychology, 4*, 297–313.

Ikomi, P. A., & Tirre, W. C. (1994). *A realistic multi-task assessment of pilot aptitudes* (Summer Faculty Research Program Final Report). Bolling Air Force Base, DC: Air Force Office of Scientific Research.

Irvine, S. H., Dann, P. L., & Anderson, J. D. (1990). Toward a theory of algorithm-determined cognitive test construction. *British Journal of Psychology, 81*, 173–195.

Keele, S. W., & Hawkins, H. L. (1982). Explorations of individual differences relevant to high level skill. *Journal of Motor Behavior, 14*, 3–23.

Kennedy, R. S., Ritter, A. D., Dunlap, W. P., Lane, N. E., & Berbaum, K. S. (1993). *Augmentation of the Basic Attributes Test Battery with tests of temporal acuity*. Orlando, FL: Essex Corp.

Koonce, J. M., Moore, S. L., & Benton, C. J. (1995, April). *Initial validation of a Basic Flight Instruction Tutoring System (BFITS)*. Paper presented at the 8th International Symposium on Aviation Psychology, Columbus, OH.

Kyllonen, P. C. (1991). Principles for creating a computerized test battery. *Intelligence, 15*, 1–15.

Kyllonen, P. C. (1993). Aptitude testing inspired by information processing: A test of the four-sources model. *Journal of General Psychology, 120*, 375–405.

Kyllonen, P. C. (1994). CAM: A theoretical framework for cognitive abilities measurement. In D. Detterman (Ed.), *Current topics in human intelligence: Volume IV, Theories of intelligence* (pp. 307–359). Norwood, NJ: Ablex.

Kyllonen, P. C., Lohman, D. F., & Snow, R. E. (1984). Effects of aptitudes, strategy training, and task facets on spatial task performance. *Journal of Educational Psychology, 76*, 130–145.

Kyllonen, P. C., & Stephens, D. (1990). Cognitive abilities as determinants of success in acquiring logic skills. *Learning and Individual Differences, 2*(2), 129–160.

Livingstone, M., & Hubel, D. (1988). Segregation of form, color, movement, and depth: Anatomy, physiology, and perception. *Science, 240*, 740–749.

Long, G. E., & Varney, N. C. (1975). *Automated pilot aptitude measurement system* (AFHRL-TR-75-58). Lackland Air Force Base, TX: Personnel Research Division, Air Force Human Resources Laboratory.

Melton, A. W. (Ed.). (1947). *Army Air Force Aviation Psychology Research Reports: Apparatus tests (Report No. 4)*. Washington, DC: U.S. Government Printing Office.

Mercatante, T. A. (1988). *The reliability and validity of psychomotor aptitude for pilot selection.* Unpublished master's thesis, St. Mary's University.

Messick, S. (1981). Constructs and their vicissitudes in educational and psychological measurement. *Psychological Bulletin, 89,* 575–588.

Neisser, U. (1982). *Memory observed.* San Francisco: Freeman.

Nunnally, J. C. (1967). *Psychometric theory.* New York: McGraw-Hill.

O'Donnell, R. D., Eddy, D., Cardenas, R., Trafton, G., & Campbell, J. (1995). *Development of the situation awareness flight training and simulation evaluation system: I—Definition of situation awareness measures and initial development of the flight simulator* (Draft Technical Report). Brooks Air Force Base, TX: Armstrong Laboratory, Human Resources Directorate.

Ree, M. J., & Earles, J. A. (1991). Predicting training success: Not much more than g. *Personnel Psychology, 44,* 321–332.

Regan, D. (1982). Visual information channeling in normal and disordered vision. *Psychological Review, 89,* 407–444.

Roznowski, M. (1993). Measures of cognitive processes: Their stability and other psychometric and measurement properties. *Intelligence, 17,* 361–388.

Sacuzzo, D. P., & Larson, G. E. (1987). *Analysis of test-retest reliability of cognitive speed tests* (NPRDC Technical Report No. 88-10). San Diego: Navy Personnel Research and Development Center.

Sarter, N. B., & Woods, D. D. (1991). Situation awareness: A critical but ill-defined phenomenon. *International Journal of Aviation Psychology, 1,* 45–57.

Scialfa, C. T., Garvey, P. M., Gish, K. W., Deering, L. M., Leibowitz, H. W., & Goebel, C. C. (1988). Relationships among measures of static and dynamic visual sensitivity. *Human Factors, 30,* 677–687.

Scientific Advisory Board Training & Human Factors Panel. (1994). *1994 SAB summer study: Life extension and capability enhancement of air force aircraft* (Vol. 2). Washington, DC: United States Air Force.

Spinner, B. (1991). Predicting success in primary flying school from the Canadian Automated Pilot Selection System: Derivation and cross-validation. *International Journal of Aviation Psychology, 1,* 163–180.

Stankov, L. (1983). Attention and intelligence. *Journal of Educational Psychology, 75,* 471–490.

Sternberg, R. J. (1977). *Intelligence, information processing, and analogical reasoning: The componential analysis of human abilities.* Hillsdale, NJ: Lawrence Erlbaum.

Tham, M., & Kramer, A. (1994). Attentional control and piloting experience. In *Proceedings of the Human Factors and Ergonomics Society 38th Annual Meeting* (pp. 31–35). Santa Monica, CA: Human Factors and Ergonomics Society.

Thorndike, R. L. (1949). *Personnel selection.* New York: Wiley.

Tirre, W. C. (1995, March). *Dimensions and correlates of psychomotor abilities.* Paper presented at the Learning Abilities Measurement Program Mini-Conference on Human Perceptual-Motor Abilities, San Antonio, TX.

Tirre, W. C., & Raouf, K. K. (1994). Gender differences in perceptual-motor performance. *Aviation, Space, & Environmental Medicine, 65(A),* A49–A53.

Wiener, S (1989). *Military flight aptitude tests.* New York: Arco Publishing Inc.

Wightman, D. C., & Lintern, G. (1985). Part-task training for tracking and manual control. *Human Factors, 27,* 267–283.

Yee, P. L., Hunt, E., & Pellegrino, J. W. (1991). Coordinating cognitive information: Task effects and individual differences in integrating information from several sources. *Cognitive Psychology, 23*, 615–680.

12

Criterion Development in Project A

Lawrence M. Hanser

BACKGROUND AND EARLY PLANNING

Other authors have reviewed the history of the misnorming of the Armed Services Vocational Aptitude Battery (ASVAB) that occurred in the late 1970s. One outgrowth of the misnorming was a requirement for the military services to demonstrate the validity of ASVAB as a device for screening service applicants. Do those who perform better on ASVAB actually make better soldiers, sailors, and airmen?

Rather than seeing this as a burden of proof required to justify then-current practices, the U.S. Army's deputy chief of staff for personnel and the leadership at the U.S. Army Research Institute (U.S. ARI) for the Behavioral and Social Sciences saw it as an opportunity to undertake research that would advance the army's techniques for selecting and assigning young men and women. This was the fall of 1980. The research program that encompassed the army-sponsored efforts to validate and expand military personnel selection and classification techniques came to be called simply "Project A."

I joined the Army Research Institute in January 1981. During a brief previous visit in fall 1980, I had the occasion to attend a briefing given by Milt Maier on the misnorming of the ASVAB. At that time, I did not realize that the focus of my eight years at ARI would be on validating and extending ASVAB.

My first assignment was to travel to Panama on a little-known and largely undocumented pilot project for Project A. During that trip, we administered surveys to a number of combat soldiers and pored over personnel records to uncover any information about their performance that could be reasonably used as a criterion against which to validate ASVAB. The results of that trip were largely undocumented, except for a paper presented by Captain Ed Williams at a regional psychology conference, because almost immediately upon our return we began to draft the Statement of Work (SOW) for Project A.

The SOW was loosely structured around ideas from a brief paper that Robert Sadacca had written earlier under an army contract with Battelle Laboratories. Led by Joyce Shields, a team of writers, including Hilda Wing, Beverly Popelka, this author, and later Kent Eaton, worked for over eight months under the watchful gaze of Cecil Johnson, the director of the Organizational and Systems Research Laboratory, and Joe Zeidner, the director of ARI, to create the final Statement of Work that was ultimately released near the end of 1981.

We organized the project around six "tasks." A monitor from within ARI and a task leader from the contractor's staff were assigned responsibility for each of these tasks. Because of the size and complexity of the project, one task was devoted to the overall management of the project (Task 6). The remaining five were research-oriented tasks. Three of the research tasks were devoted to criterion development (Tasks 3, 4, and 5), one was devoted to developing new predictor measures (Task 2), and one was devoted to data management and analysis (Task 1).

At the same time that we began writing the SOW, we published a "sources sought" announcement in the *Commerce Business Daily* to identify potential bidders. We received responses from fewer than six consortia expressing interest in the project. Ultimately, we received only three proposals that together stacked up to over five feet of paper.

Overall Design for Criteria in Project A

It has always been clear in the industrial psychology and test development and validation literature that far too little emphasis has been placed on criterion development. How many researchers have ended their reports with caveats, if not apologies, because they had settled for an existing criterion rather than constructing one more appropriate for their specific research project? To validate ASVAB as a predictor of military job performance, we had to feel comfortable that we had a comprehensive set of measures of performance. Furthermore, we expected an avalanche of professional scrutiny and did not desire to have the entire project criticized or discounted for lack of acceptable criteria.

Traditionally, military validation projects had relied on measures of performance in training as the criteria. One easy criticism of measures of training performance is that they are typically paper-and-pencil measures of job knowledge rather than realistic hands-on measures of performance. In fact, previous military validation efforts were criticized precisely because they had used training performance as the criterion. Although we expected performance in training to be an important criterion measure, at no time in planning Project A did we intend to use performance in training as the only criterion, or even as the primary criterion. We believed that success in training was necessary, but not sufficient, to ensure later successful performance as a soldier.

Our early thinking of how to structure the predictor/criterion relationships was clear, though not eloquent, in our notion of a "rolling predictor." This meant that as more information was obtained about a soldier over time, it would be "rolled into" previous information and used to predict later performance—what was a criterion at one point in time would serve as a predictor at a later point in time. Thus, ASVAB would be used to predict training performance, ASVAB and training performance together would be used to predict job performance for soldiers in their first tour of duty, and performance during a soldier's second tour of duty would be predicted by his or her performance during the first tour.

What I have not spoken about thus far, and what is an important factor to keep in mind, is that knowing we were undertaking an expensive validation effort, we didn't want to "just" validate ASVAB. How could we pass the opportunity to examine other potential predictor measures in the process? At all times we strove to be comprehensive, and to their credit, the army was supportive all along the way. Thus, it became even more important to do the best job we could to capture a comprehensive vision of what it meant for a soldier to "perform" in the army. What if we developed a useful predictor measure and didn't have an appropriate criterion that would allow us to discover the predictor's utility?

Coincident with the concept of a rolling predictor, we developed three sampling frames for the project (see Figure 12.1). These came to be called (1) the predictor development sample, (2) the concurrent validation sample, and (3) the longitudinal validation sample. Each was designed to serve as a test bed and proving ground for instruments developed up to that point in time and as a potential source of early and regular results that we could report to our sponsors. The choice of samples and the testing design for each sample was driven by the logic of how the project would proceed temporally—timing was a critical variable throughout the conduct of the project.

Because we intended to include a longitudinal validation component and timing was short, we would have to begin early to develop any new predictor measures (to supplement ASVAB) that were envisioned as having potential utility for selecting and classifying recruits. The sooner these were ready for administration to our longitudinal sample, the sooner our longitudinal sample could begin to mature. But before administering the predictors to our longitudinal sample, we would need to test them. Hence, we designated a cohort of soldiers as our predictor development sample on which we would test our preliminary predictor battery. This allowed for one iteration of modifications to the preliminary predictor battery prior to testing it against our newly developed criterion measures.

Our concurrent validation sample was the first point at which we would be able to test both our new predictor measures and our new criterion measures.

Figure 12.1
Project A Sampling Frames

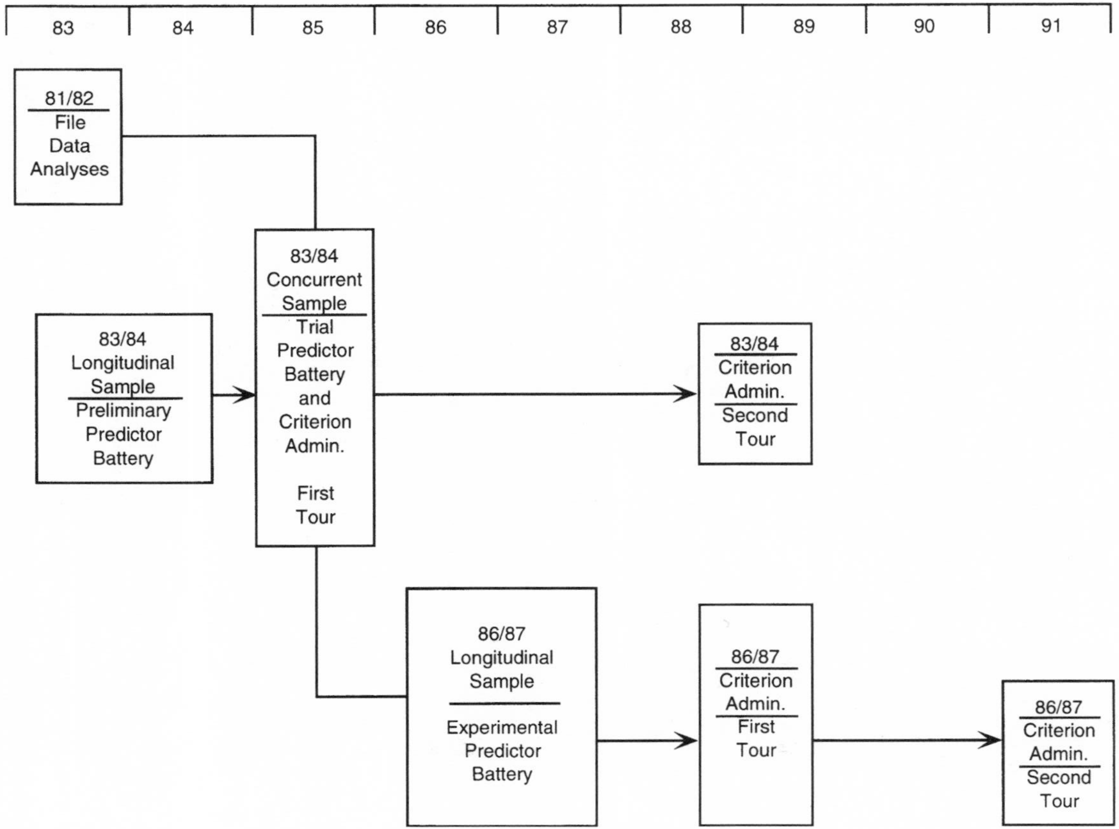

Our intention was to administer concurrently our trial predictor battery and criterion measures and to analyze the results in that sample in enough time to make modifications to the trial predictor battery prior to administration to the longitudinal sample.

We also knew that the support for Project A could diminish or disappear at any point in time and that early measures of performance, even if imperfect, would provide useful results we could share with our army sponsors to bolster what might become flagging support for the project. We characterized this as the "war in eighty-four" attitude—meaning 1984. Measures of performance in training became the first criterion measure required in Project A. The development of measures of performance in training was assigned to a team of researchers and designated simply as "Task 3."

As we further considered what it meant to be a successful soldier, in addition to successfully completing training, we knew that there were some tasks that all soldiers were required to perform (e.g., administering first aid; defending against nuclear, biological, and chemical attacks) and some that were a function of a soldier's military occupational specialty (MOS) (e.g., truck mechanics repair brakes, and cannon crewmen aim and fire howitzers). The researchers in Task 4 were directed to develop measures of the former, what we called "Army-wide" performance. Task 5 researchers developed measures for the latter, MOS-specific performance.

This is, of course, a great oversimplification of the final set of criterion measures that were developed and used and ignores the long processes of job analysis and test construction that were required to develop them.

SAMPLING REPRESENTATIVE OCCUPATIONS

In addition to the need to develop an overall plan for the timing of the research tasks and the need to organize our thoughts about the criterion space, a major concern was how to sample occupations. The task of validating ASVAB is enormous in scope, if only because the army enlists soldiers into 35 broad career fields representing several hundred distinct occupational specialties. Clearly, a means for sampling career fields and occupations was needed. After much debate over issues such as the size of cohorts in each specialty, importance to the army's mission, and representativeness of the kinds of skills, knowledges, and abilities required across the army, we settled on 19 MOSs (see Table 12.1).

These 19 MOSs were divided into what we referred to as "Batch A" and "Batch Z." (We already had a Project A and Project B and wished not to further confuse what we were doing!) The primary distinction was to be that we did not develop hands-on tests of performance for Batch Z MOSs. This decision was cost driven. Hands-on tests were simply too expensive to develop, field test, and administer for all 19 MOSs in our sample, even for the U.S. Army.

Table 12.2 summarizes the specific criterion instruments developed in Project A matched with the Batch A or Batch Z occupations (see Table 12.1) to

Table 12.1
MOSs in Project A

Batch A		Batch Z	
11B	Infantryman	12B	Combat Engineer
13B	Cannon Crewman	16S	MANPADS Crewman
19E	Armor Crewman	27E	TOW/Dragon Repairer
31C	Single Channel Radio Operator	51B	Carpentry/Masonry Specialist
63B	Light Wheel Vehicle Mechanic	54E	Chemical Operations Specialist
64C	Motor Transport Operator	55B	Ammunition Specialist
71L	Administration Specialist	67N	Utility Helicopter Repairer
91A	Medical Specialist	76W	Petroleum Supply Specialist
95B	Military Police	76Y	Unit Supply Specialist
		94B	Food Service Specialist

which they were administered during the testing of the concurrent validation sample in summer of 1985.

During the summer of 1985, these measures were administered to a total of 9,430 soldiers in the 19 Batch A and Z MOSs who were stationed in the United States and Europe. This was the concurrent validation sample. Sample sizes by MOS are listed in Table 12.3.

When one considers the comprehensive nature of the set of criterion measures, the large number of distinct occupations, and the sheer numbers of soldiers tested, the scope of effort and amount of data collected during the concurrent validation phase of Project A was staggering. Clearly, we had amassed a large amount of data to analyze and had created a complex analytic task for ourselves.

ANALYZING AN EMBARRASSMENT OF CRITERION RICHES

The number and variety of criterion measures that we had constructed served to greatly complicate the task of trying to make sense of the data that were collected. We had, in effect, succeeded in constructing a huge multitrait, multimeasure matrix and now had to seek ways to understand it. Would our data support our theories? Even our simple theory that some tasks were "Army-wide" and some were "MOS-specific"? We also carried around in our heads the well-known distinction between typical and maximal performance and that our rating measures tapped soldiers' "typical" performance, while the hands-on and knowledge tests tapped their "maximal" performance. With so many different measures, how could we sort out the validity of these ideas, let alone the validity of predictors such as ASVAB for predicting performance? At the time we were field testing our criterion measures, we drew a picture of what

Table 12.2
Summary of Criterion Measures Used in Batch A and Batch Z Concurrent Validation Samples

Performance Measures Common to Batch A and Batch Z

- Army-wide rating scales (all obtained from both supervisors and peers).
  —Ten behaviorally anchored rating scales (BARS) designed to measure factors of non-job-specific performance.
  —Single scale rating of overall effectiveness.
  —Single scale rating of noncommissioned officer (NCO) potential.
- Combat prediction scale containing 40 items.
- Paper-and-pencil tests of training achievement developed for each MOS (130–210 items each).
- Personnel File Information form developed to gather objective archival records data (awards and letters, rifle marksmanship scores, physical training scores, etc.).

Performance Measures for Batch A Only

- Job sample (hands-on) tests of MOS-specific task proficiency.
  —Individual is tested on each of 15 major job tasks in an MOS.
- Paper-and-pencil job knowledge tests designed to measure task-specific job knowledge.
  —Individual is scored on 150 to 200 multiple choice items representing 30 major job tasks. Ten to 15 of the tasks were also measured hands-on.
- Rating scale measures of specific task performance on the 15 tasks also measured with the knowledge tests. Most of the rated tasks were also included in the hands-on measures.
- MOS-specific behaviorally anchored rating scales (BARS). From six to 12 BARS were developed for each MOS to represent the major factors that constitute job-specific technical and task proficiency.

Performance Measures for Batch Z Only

- Additional Army-wide rating scales (all obtained from both supervisors and peers).
  —Ratings of performance on 11 common tasks (e.g., basic first aid).
  —Single scale rating on performance of specific job duties.

Auxiliary Measures Included in Criterion Battery

- A Job History Questionnaire, which asks for information about frequency and recency of performance of the MOS-specific tasks.
- Army Work Environment Questionnaire—53 items assessing situational/environmental characteristics, plus 46 items dealing with leadership.
- Measurement Method rating obtained from all participants at the end of the final testing session.

Source: J. P. Campbell (1988, table 2.4).

Table 12.3
Sample Sizes by MOS

MOS	N's
Batch A MOS	
11B Infantryman	702
13B Cannon Crewman	667
19E Armor Crewman	503
31C Single Channel Radio Operator	366
63B Light Wheel Vehicle Mechanic	637
64C Motor Transport Operator	686
71L Administration Specialist	514
91A Medical Specialist	501
95B Military Police	692
Batch Z MOS	
12B Combat Engineer	704
16S MANPADS Crewman	470
27E TOW/Dragon Repairer	147
51B Carpentry/Masonry Specialist	108
54E Chemical Operations Specialist	434
55B Ammunition Specialist	291
67N Utility Helicopter Repairer	276
76W Petroleum Supply Specialist	490
76Y Unit Supply Specialist	630
94B Food Service Specialist	612

we thought might reflect a model of performance for army occupations. This picture appears as Figure 12.2.

The analyses that the Project A staff of scientists undertook were quite substantial and are well beyond the scope of this chapter to describe. My intent here is to highlight what are some of the most important details of the analyses and of the results we obtained.

We began with a belief that performance is multidimensional—a simple sum of scores across all of the tests and rating scales was unacceptable to us (and, we hope, to others). At the other extreme, there were simply too many scores from the different criteria to use without further reducing them to a smaller set of meaningful scores (i.e., 15 hands-on task scores, 30 job knowledge task test scores, a school knowledge test score, and 30 rating scales for each of two or more raters).

Figure 12.2
A Preliminary Model of Performance in Military Occupations

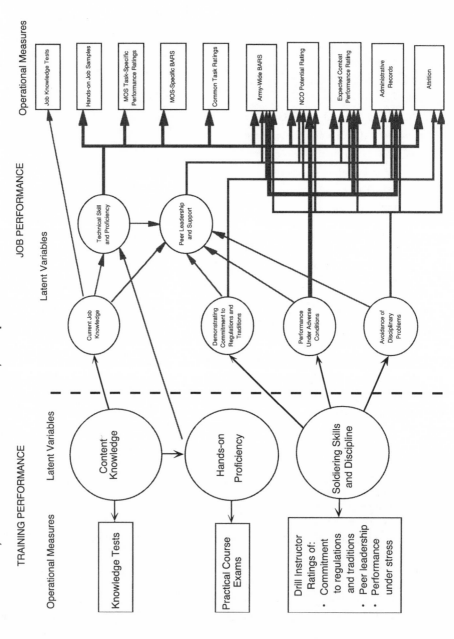

We needed to understand the latent structure of performance. If performance is not unidimensional, then what are its dimensions? As was noted in J. P. Campbell (1988, p. 124), "For personnel psychologists it is almost second nature to talk about predictors in terms of theories and constructs. However, on the performance side, the textbooks are virtually silent." We had little from the literature to guide us. Nevertheless, the first steps we planned to take were to work within each of the broad measurement methods represented by our criteria—hands-on tests, written tests, and ratings. How would we assign scores within each of these domains that would represent meaningful aspects of soldiers' performance?

In the following sections, I will spend little time on the details of the scoring procedures themselves, or how we developed them. We applied relatively straightforward and well-known judgmental and statistical methods to aid us; it is not important to spend time in this chapter discussing these—in-depth digressions of our analyses and detailed decisions are available elsewhere (cf., J. P. Campbell, 1988; J. P. Campbell, McHenry, & Wise, 1990). I focus instead on the outcomes of our analyses and their meaning.

Scoring the Hands-on Tasks and Knowledge Tests

For each of our nine Batch A MOSs, we had a hands-on test consisting of approximately 15 tasks, a job knowledge test that was constructed to be parallel to the hands-on test with an additional number of tasks included, and a training knowledge test focused on what soldiers were taught during formal training. Soldiers' responses to these tests formed the grist for our analyses.

We started by taking the army's task lists for the MOSs in our sample and defining 34 functional categories that represented all of the functions performed by newly trained soldiers in these occupations. Ten of these functional categories were common across all the MOSs in our sample, and the remaining were each specific to an individual MOS (see J. P. Campbell, 1988, for a complete list of these categories).

Two examples will serve to clarify further what we meant by a functional category. One category we defined as common to all MOSs in our sample was labeled "first aid." We defined this category thusly:

Consists of items whose primary purpose is to indicate knowledge about how to sustain life, prevent health complications caused by trauma or environmentally induced illness, including the practice of personal hygiene. Includes all related diagnostic, transportation, and treatment items except those items normally performed in a patient care facility. Includes items related to safety and safety hazards. (J. P. Campbell, 1988, p. 80)

The following is our definition of the functional category labeled "Operate howitzer sights and alignment devices." This category is specific to cannon crewmen (MOS 13B):

Consists of items whose primary purpose is to indicate knowledge required to orient, lay a howitzer on an azimuth of fire using the howitzer sights, position aiming posts and the collimator, boresight, and engage direct fire targets from the assistant gunner's position. (p. 82)

After these functional categories were defined, staff who had developed and administered the hands-on tests and the job and school knowledge tests independently sorted tasks and items into these 34 categories. There was over 90 percent agreement within each occupation on the sorting of tasks and items into these categories.

In addition to functional categories, we thought that it might prove worthwhile to differentiate soldiers based on a criteria scoring method that organized tasks and items in terms of their level of cognitive and psychomotor complexity. We developed a categorization scheme along these lines that focused on behavioral requirements of the tasks and items rather than their functional characteristics. We defined four categories of knowledge requirements and two categories of performance requirements for tasks or items:

1. Recognition and recall of facts
2. Recall of procedures
3. Interpretation and application
4. Inference from principle
5. Simple motor
6. Complex motor

Similar project staff members sorted hands-on tasks and job knowledge items into each of these categories. Agreement on sorting into these categories averaged about 80 percent. The reduction of scores using the behavioral requirements categorization scheme ultimately yielded scores with low reliability that were deemed unuseful, and this path of inquiry was abandoned.

Through a series of principal components analyses computed separately for each of the Batch A MOSs, the 10 common functional category scores and 24 MOS-specific functional category scores (i.e., 2 to 5 MOS-specific functional categories for each Batch A MOS) were reduced to the six factors shown in Table 12.4. We labeled these collectively as CVBITS (communications, vehicles, basic soldiering, identify targets, technical, safety/survival; the military's penchant for acronyms had clearly infected us).

These six dimensions were sufficient to describe the hands-on tasks, job knowledge test items, and school knowledge test items for soldiers in all of our Batch A MOSs. Thus, we now had a means for generating scores on these measures for each soldier.

At this point, it is important to remember that each of the tests represented in these analyses was constructed for a specific and distinctive MOS. That is, a

Table 12.4
Summary of Hands-on and Knowledge Test Dimensions

Communications

Vehicles

Basic Soldiering

Identify Targets

Technical

Safety/Survival

separate job analysis had been used for each MOS in the development of these measures. Yet our analyses showed substantial commonality of performance factors across MOSs—the distinction among MOSs was retained in only one factor that we labeled "technical." All MOSs shared in common the other performance factors. These results provided for us a glimmer of proof that our hypothesis that performance in jobs consists of many common aspects that all jobs share and a few aspects that are unique to each job was correct.

Scoring the Rating Scales

The behaviorally anchored rating scales that we gathered on soldiers in our concurrent validation sample included 10 army-wide performance rating scales (e.g., Technical Knowledge/Skill, Effort, Following Regulations and Orders, and Leadership), rating scales for each specific MOS (containing 6 to 12 scales per MOS), a combat performance prediction rating scale, a single-item NCO potential rating, and a single item overall effectiveness rating.

Factor analyses were used to reduce these scales to a more manageable set (see J. P. Campbell, 1988, for a complete discussion of these analyses). The factors, as we labeled them, and the scales they were derived from, are shown in Table 12.5. Our rating scales reduced to seven dimensions plus two individual single-item scales.

From these results, it is clear that the rating scales added dimensionality to our criteria that had not been captured by our hands-on and knowledge tests. But perhaps as important is that the converse is also true: Hands-on and knowledge tests capture variance in performance that is not captured by ratings. Keep in mind that our rating scales included dimensions of task performance, so that one might have thought that the rating scales themselves were all-inclusive in measuring performance.

These results, which become even more clear when these criteria are put together, provide an important lesson for practicing personnel researchers. It may not be sufficient to use only rating scales when conducting validity research,

Table 12.5
Summary of Factor Results for Rating Scales

Army-wide Performance Rating Scales Factors
   Job-Relevant Skills and Motivation
   Personal Discipline
   Physical Fitness and Military Bearing
MOS-specific Rating Scales Factors
   Core Responsibilities
   Other Responsibilities
Combat Rating Scales Factors
   Performing Under Adverse Conditions
   Avoiding Mistakes

because rating scales alone probably do not encompass all of the important elements of performance that one desires to measure in job incumbents.

Scoring the Administrative Records

We collected several pieces of information from soldiers' official personnel files to round out our criteria. These included a count of awards and certificates, M16 rifle qualification, reenlistment eligibility, promotion rate, physical readiness, and administrative punishments (Articles 15 and flag actions). All were hand collected from field personnel records except for promotion rate, which was calculated from official computerized personnel records.

After examining the distributional statistics of these measures and the correlations among them, it was decided that five indices would be retained. These are listed in Table 12.6.

PUTTING THE CRITERIA TOGETHER—WHAT DOES IT ALL MEAN?

To our knowledge, no team of researchers had ever had available for analyses as complete an array of criterion measures on as wide a sample of occupations as we had at the end of the concurrent validation phase of Project A. Certainly, we had not reached that point without attracting some criticism, and I would be remiss if I did not point out the major aspects of it before progressing further with the story. Bear in mind that I speak for myself and did not consult with other members of the Project A research team prior to or after writing the following few paragraphs.

Project A did not occur in a vacuum. Each of the other military services was

Table 12.6
Administrative Measures Indices

Awards/Certificates
Physical Readiness
M16 Rifle Qualification
Articles 15/Flag Actions
Promotion Rate (deviation from the mean)

undertaking its own version of Project A, and representatives from all of the services as well as the Department of Defense met regularly to discuss the totality of these projects. A committee from the National Research Council (NRC; Committee on the Performance of Military Personnel) was also looking over our collective shoulders and meeting with us on occasion.

There were two major areas in which the opinion of the Project A research team disagreed with the others. The first of these had to do with the meaning and importance to be attached to hands-on tests. In jargon adopted by members of the NRC committee, hands-on tests were to be the "benchmark" measure of performance against which all other measures of performance were to be judged. Our perspective was that performance was multidimensional and could not be captured by hands-on tests alone.

The other difference of opinion arose over our procedure for sampling tasks to be included in our hands-on measures. Our approach included elements of feasibility of testing and judgments of the relative importance and representativeness of tasks to overall job performance. Our final decisions in task selection were all approved by military representatives who were experts in the occupations we were testing. Some members of the NRC committee believed that we should have randomly sampled tasks from the domain of tasks in order to be able to make inferences about a soldier's performance. A similar concern was raised over our choice to use military personnel as scorers for the hands-on tasks.

Each of these topics was discussed at length with Project A's own scientific advisory committee that consisted of well-known and -respected experts in the fields of industrial psychology, test theory, and statistics. We proceeded on the advice and guidance of our advisory committee and did not modify either of our opinions as stated above.

Modeling Performance

At this point, we were interested in determining whether a single model of performance could be developed that would suitably fit all of the MOSs in our sample and, by extension, all MOSs in the army. The final set of reduced cri-

Table 12.7
Reduced Set of Criterion Measures

6   hands-on CVBITS scores

6   job knowledge CVBITS scores

6   training knowledge CVBITS scores

3   Army-wide rating scores

2   job-specific rating scores

2   combat performance prediction rating scores

1   NCO potential rating score

1   overall effectiveness rating score

5   administrative index scores

terion measures that we worked with on this issue are listed in Table 12.7. A correlation matrix of these scores was calculated and factor analyzed separately for each of the nine Batch A MOSs. These exploratory factor analyses were used to develop a single model of performance against which all nine occupations could be tested using the LISREL confirmatory factor analysis program (Jöreskog & Sorbom, 1981). The model that emerged from these analyses included the five job performance constructs labeled and defined in Table 12.8 (after figure 7.3 in J. P. Campbell, 1988). When this model was tested jointly for the set of nine MOSs as a group, it fit very well. That is, the five constructs in Table 12.8 are a good description of performance in the nine Batch A MOSs. There are several additional details that were considered in developing this model, but the reader is directed to the more in-depth treatment of these analyses offered in J. P. Campbell (1988) or J. P. Campbell et al. (1990).

VALIDITY OF ASVAB

It seems unfair to begin our final discussion of the importance of the criterion development work carried out within Project A without providing the reader with the slightest hint as to whether ASVAB is a valid predictor of performance in military occupations. In this regard, we offer a brief summary of validities. It is clearly valid as a predictor of several of the five Project A performance constructs.

Table 12.9 shows validity coefficients using a general four-factor cognitive composite score from ASVAB to predict five job performance constructs. These coefficients have been corrected for range restriction and shrinkage.

CONCLUSIONS

The criterion measures developed in Project A clearly were comprehensive in scope and have great value for understanding what it means to be a soldier

Table 12.8
Job Performance Constructs Derived in Project A

Core Technical Proficiency
This performance construct represents the proficiency with which the soldier performs the tasks that are "central" to the MOS. The tasks represent the core of the job, and they are the primary definers of the MOS. For example, the first-tour Armor Crewman starts and stops the tank engines; prepares the loader's station; loads and unloads the main gun; boresights the M60A3; engages targets with the main gun; and performs misfire procedures. This performance construct does not include the individual's willingness to perform the task or the degree to which the individual can coordinate efforts with others. It refers to how well the individual can execute the core technical tasks the job requires, given a willingness to do so.

General Soldiering Proficiency
In addition to the core technical content specific to an MOS, individuals in every MOS also are responsible for being able to perform a variety of general soldiering tasks—for example, determines grid coordinates on military maps; puts on, wears, and removes M17 series protective mask with hood; determines a magnetic azimuth using a compass; collects/reports information—SALUTE; and recognizes and identifies friendly and threat aircraft. Performance on this construct represents overall proficiency on these general soldiering tasks. Again, it refers to how well the individual can execute general soldiering tasks, given a willingness to do so.

Effort and Leadership
This performance construct reflects the degree to which the individual exerts effort over the full range of job tasks, perseveres under adverse or dangerous conditions, and demonstrates leadership and support toward peers. That is, can the individual be counted on to carry out assigned tasks, even under adverse conditions, to exercise good judgment, and to be generally dependable and proficient? While appropriate knowledges and skills are necessary for successful performance, this construct is meant only to reflect the individual's willingness to do the job required and to be cooperative and supportive with other soldiers.

Personal Discipline
This performance construct reflects the degree to which the individual adheres to army regulations and traditions, exercises personal self-control, demonstrates integrity in day-to-day behavior, and does not create disciplinary problems. People who rank high on this construct show a commitment to high standards of personal conduct.

Physical Fitness and Military Bearing
This performance construct represents the degree to which the individual maintains an appropriate military appearance and bearing and stays in good physical condition.

in the U.S. Army. Although our data confirmed a single multidimensional model of performance for the military occupations included in Batch A, and perhaps for all U.S. Army enlisted occupations, a more important question is whether such a model has wider applicability to jobs in general. This is perhaps the most

Table 12.9
Validity of ASVAB for Predicting Military Performance

Job Performance Construct	ASVAB Cognitive Composite
Core Technical Proficiency	.63
General Soldiering Proficiency	.65
Effort and Leadership	.31
Personal Discipline	.16
Physical Fitness and Military Bearing	.20

important and intriguing outcome of the careful development and analysis of criterion measures carried out in Project A.

Core Technical Proficiency, Effort and Leadership, and Personal Discipline seem clearly relevant in the universe of occupations. However, two of the constructs, General Soldiering Proficiency and Physical Fitness and Military Bearing, at first glance may not appear to have much meaning outside of a military context. Yet consider the notion that all jobs or families of jobs share common performance requirements. For example, perhaps all engineering jobs share a common core of mathematical skills even though electrical engineers perform specific core technical work that is quite different from civil engineers. Similarly, it is hard to imagine an occupation that doesn't require some level of communication skill. As for Physical Fitness and Military Bearing, it also strikes us as obvious that most every occupation has codes for suitable attire and acceptable levels of personal hygiene.

Perhaps the distinction among occupations is not whether these constructs are relevant but rather the level of each construct that represents acceptable performance. For example, though all jobs may require communication skill, certainly not all jobs require the same level of communication proficiency for the incumbent to be considered successful. Thus, we might envision job families that share similar profiles of required levels of each of the constructs.

I believe that the single most important outcome of the criterion work accomplished in Project A is that it provides us with an empirically based comprehensive framework for thinking about the nature of occupations and how we select and train individuals for them.

REFERENCES

Borman, W. C., Motowidlo, S. J., Rose, S. R., & Hanser, L. M. (1985). *Development of a model of soldier effectiveness* (ARI Technical Report 741). Alexandria, VA: U.S. Army Research Institute for the Behavioral and Social Sciences.

Campbell, C. H., Campbell, R. C., Rumsey, M. G., & Edwards, D. C. (1986). *Development and field test of task-based MOS-specific criterion measures* (ARI Technical Report 717). Alexandria, VA: U.S. Army Research Institute for the Behavioral and Social Sciences.

Campbell, C. H., Ford, P., Rumsey, M. G., Pulakos, E. D., Borman, W. C., Felker, D. B., de Vera, M. V., & Riegelhaupt, B. J. (1990). Development of multiple job performance measures in a representative sample of jobs. *Personnel Psychology, 43*, 277–300.

Campbell, J. P. (Ed.). (1988). *Improving the selection, classification, and utilization of army enlisted personnel: Annual report, 1986 fiscal year* (ARI Technical Report 792). Alexandria, VA: U.S. Army Research Institute for the Behavioral and Social Sciences.

Campbell, J. P., & Harris, J. H. (1985). *Criterion reduction and combination via a participation decision-making panel.* Paper presented at the annual meeting of the American Psychological Association, Los Angeles.

Campbell, J. P., McHenry, J. J., & Wise, L. L. (1990). Modeling job performance in a population of jobs. *Personnel Psychology, 43*, 313–333.

Davis, R. H., Davis, G. A., Joyner, J. N., & de Vera, M. V. (1987). *Development and field test of job-relevant knowledge tests for selected MOS* (ARI Technical Report 757). Alexandria, VA: U.S. Army Research Institute for the Behavioral and Social Sciences.

Jöreskog, K. C., & Sorbom, D. (1981). *LISREL VI: Analysis of linear squares methods.* Uppsala, Sweden: University of Uppsala.

Pulakos, E. D., & Borman, W. C. (1986). *Development and field test of army-wide rating scales and the rater orientation and training program* (ARI Technical Report 716). Alexandria, VA: U.S. Army Research Institute for the Behavioral and Social Sciences.

Riegelhaupt, B. J., Harris, C. D., & Sadacca, R. (1987). *The development of administrative measures as indicators of soldier effectiveness* (ARI Technical Report 754). Alexandria, VA: U.S. Army Research Institute for the Behavioral and Social Sciences.

Toquam, J. L., McHenry, J. J., Corpe, V. A., Rose, S. R., Lammlein, S. E., Kemery, E., Borman, W. C., Mendel, R., & Bosshardt, M. J. (1988). *Development and field test of behaviorally anchored scales for nine MOS* (ARI Technical Report 776). Alexandria, VA: U.S. Army Research Institute for the Behavioral and Social Sciences.

Wallace, S. R. (1965). Criteria for what? *American Psychologist, 20*, 411–418.

Wise, L. L., Campbell, J. P., McHenry, J. J., & Hanser, L. M. (1986). *A latent structure model of job performance factors.* Paper presented at the annual meeting of the American Psychological Association, Washington, DC.

13

Medical School Admissions Testing

Judith A. Koenig and Andrew Wiley

BACKGROUND

Early in the 1980s, a pattern of course-taking behavior began to emerge among premedical students. This pattern, which came to be called the "premedical syndrome," was characterized by a narrow focusing of coursework and extracurricular activities on the sciences, to the exclusion of advanced study in the humanities and social sciences. Students' perception that such preparation increased the likelihood of acceptance to medical school was thought to be the motivation behind this behavior.

Changes in medical school curricula, which were driven by changes in the field of medicine, made this type of undergraduate preparation particularly undesirable. More than ever, physicians needed the skills to deal with the social and ethical issues of the profession. New demands in the medical profession required that physicians be trained to gather and assess data; to apply basic concepts and principles in solving scientific and clinical problems; and to communicate effectively with patients, colleagues, and the public. To meet the demands of the profession, medical schools altered instructional approaches and increased the emphasis placed on problem solving.[1] They called for candidates to pursue a wide variety of course offerings to be ready to face the challenges of medical education and medical practice (Muller, 1984; Swanson & Mitchell, 1989).

The Medical College Admission Test (MCAT), which is typically taken during the junior or senior year of a premedical student's undergraduate program, is considered by many students to be the gatekeeping exam for individuals aspiring to practice medicine. While medical school admissions offices report that MCAT scores are only one of many sources of information considered when evaluating the credentials of their applicants, premedical students view MCAT scores as capable of "making or breaking" their chances for admission. The MCAT administered during the 1980s was seen as contributing to premedical students' perceptions that knowledge acquisition in the sciences was more important than study in the social sciences and humanities (Review Committee, 1986). This exam reported six scores, four of which were science scores: Biology, Chemistry, Physics, and Science Problems. Moreover, the two nonscience sections (Skills Analysis: Reading and Skills Analysis: Quantitative) presented questions in passage formats with passages drawn from medical and behavioral science settings. While the exam's psychometric properties were very respectable and its predictive value well established (Association of American Medical College [AAMC], 1987; Jones & Thomae-Forgues, 1984; Mitchell, 1990), its content and format were regarded as contributing to the premedical syndrome (Review Committee, 1986).

As sponsor of the MCAT, the Association of American Medical Colleges (AAMC) must concern itself with the plethora of issues that typically face a testing program. Prospective test takers, as well as undergraduate college faculty members, must be kept informed of tested content and skills. Test score users must be supplied with interpretive information and their test use practices monitored. The exam's psychometric properties must be investigated. Of equal importance is the exam's impact on the groups of individuals required to take it.

Given the concerns about the MCAT's influence on premedical students' course selection, the AAMC embarked on a project to review the format and content of the examination. This chapter describes the revisions made to the exam and the research efforts designed to evaluate the validity of the new test battery.

REVISING THE MCAT

Efforts to revise the exam began in 1983 with the formation of an "Essay Committee" charged with determining the utility and feasibility of including a direct writing assessment on the MCAT. This eight-member group, consisting of medical school admissions officers, undergraduate advisers, and a consultant experienced in large-scale writing assessment, designed a series of studies to explore alternative assessment formats, skill domains, and scoring procedures. They conducted research using data from several pilot administrations of essay questions to evaluate the reliability of scoring procedures, the utility of writing assessment scores for admissions decision making, and the impact of writing assessment on various population groups. Their work was finalized in a set of recommendations laying out guidelines for the writing assessment (for discussions of results of studies, see Koenig, 1995; Koenig & Mitchell, 1988; MCAT Evaluation Panel, 1989).

Revision of the test battery's multiple choice sections was initiated in 1987 and guided by the MCAT Evaluation Panel. This 15-member group—consisting of medical school deans, admissions officers, basic and clinical science faculty members, a practicing physician, a medical student, and an undergraduate adviser—established goals for MCAT revision and identified a series of studies to be conducted. These studies included (1) a survey of MCAT examinees on ways in which they used test score data in making application and retesting decisions; (2) comparison of medical school performance for individuals with broad and science-focused premedical preparation;[2] (3) simulation of various models for revised test formats and estimation of their predictive value; and (4) review of the content and concepts assessed. Detailed information on the results of these studies can be found in AAMC (1992), Koenig (1992), Koenig, Li, and Haynes (1990), MCAT Evaluation Panel (1989), and Mitchell and Haynes (1990).

The two committees concluded their work by submitting a single set of recommendations for test revisions to be operationalized in 1991. Within their recommendations, the committees set forth the conceptual framework that would underlie the format of the revised test battery. These recommendations reinforced the medical community's view that physicians must be more than holders of vast amounts of scientific information. They emphasized the need for physicians able to apply the principles of scientific problem solving, to critically evaluate situations, and to arrive at logical solutions. Mastery of basic concepts in biology, chemistry, and physics, while still considered prerequisite, was not judged to be a sufficient indicator of success in medical school (Swanson & Mitchell, 1989).

The revised MCAT was designed to reinforce medical education's call for candidates with balanced undergraduate preparation and who possessed knowledge of basic science concepts as well as the ability to think critically. Its three multiple choice sections (Verbal Reasoning, Physical Sciences, and Biological Sciences) and direct writing assessment (the Writing Sample) were developed to assess (1) mastery of basic concepts in biology, chemistry, and physics; (2) facility with scientific problem solving and critical thinking; and (3) communication/writing skills. To discourage premedical students from loading up on science courses, science content coverage was restricted to the content typically covered in first-year biology, chemistry, and physics courses.

In their recommendations, the committees established several intended outcomes to be associated with the 1991 revisions. First was the reduction in the length of the test day, accomplished by shortening the exam by approximately 80 minutes. A second goal was to communicate the medical communities' desire for physicians broadly prepared to deal with the human and social issues of medicine as well as the technological problems of the profession. It was hoped that the balance of science and nonscience test sections would convey the message that exposure to nonscience areas was as important as knowledge acquisition in the sciences. The extent to which this goal is accomplished is being evaluated by several studies that track changes in premedical preparation patterns over time.

Also stated as goals were the formation of an exam that assesses knowledge of prerequisite entry-level science concepts, facility with science problem solving and critical analytical thinking, and communication and writing skills; the promotion of fair and reasoned use of MCAT data by those using scores in decision making; and the development of an exam that would meet or exceed the previous version's usefulness in identifying those apt to succeed in medical school.

These latter three goals form the basis for an extensive research effort designed to accumulate validity evidence for the revised exam. This effort consists of a variety of studies directed at assessing attainment of the goals. Work is guided through the assistance of the MCAT Validity Studies Advisory Group, a 10-member panel consisting of representatives from medical school admissions and undergraduate advising settings. This group provides advice regarding design of studies, collection of data, and interpretation of results.

CONCEPTUAL FRAMEWORK FOR VALIDITY STUDIES

Given that a primary purpose of the MCAT is to select applicants likely to be successful in medical school, validity assessment must begin with examination of the relationships between test scores and subsequent performance in medical school. However, a review of recent literature on validity assessment makes clear that validation efforts must consist of more than gathering criterion-related evidence. Contemporary validity theorists advise that construct validity must be viewed as central to all validation effort (Cronbach, 1989; Kane, 1992; Moss, 1995; Shepard, 1993). Studies should be organized around the question, Does the test measure the content and skills it intends to measure?

Researchers emphasize that a test needs to be evaluated in relation to its relevance, values, and social consequences as well as in relation to its applied purpose (Messick, 1989; Shepard, 1993). Of particular importance is consideration of the values implied by the examination and the impact of test score use on those required to take it. The decision context within which the test is used must also be a factor in validity assessment. If a test is being used within an admissions setting, it should be evaluated on the extent to which it increases the ability of the decision makers to select applicants who will be most successful in this setting.

Cronbach (1988, 1989) and Angoff (1988) additionally stress that validity evidence should rely on more than correlations between the test and miscellaneous criteria. A unifying theory must tie the observed relationships together. Rational argument and empirical verification should guide development of plans for integrated studies of test score meaning, utility, and use as well as of the social consequences of the test battery.

Review of Kane's (1992) argument-based approach to validation was particularly useful in developing an organizing theory for planned research on the MCAT. Kane encouraged development of an ''interpretive argument as the framework for collecting and presenting validity evidence . . . to provide convincing evidence for its inferences and assumptions, especially its most questionable assumptions'' (Kane, 1992, p. 527). To do so, Kane made three suggestions: (1) The argument should be coherent and stated clearly; (2) the conclusions must follow reasonably from assumptions; and (3) the assumptions made must be plausible or verifiable by empirical evidence.

Using Kane's approach, a series of hypotheses was generated to serve as a guide for the design of validity research. Studies were then identified that would provide an accumulation of empirical evidence upon which to test each hypothesis. These hypotheses are stated below:

1. MCAT scores are accurate representations of the skills the exam purports to measure.

2. MCAT scores are generalizable across samples of items and forms of the test.

3. The tested science concepts and facility with scientific problem solving, critical thinking, and communication skills are predictive of successful performance in the medical school curriculum.

4. MCAT scores are used appropriately by those making admissions decisions.

The various studies designed to evaluate the validity of the MCAT are discussed below in the context of the posed hypotheses. The next portion of this chapter presents each hypothesis followed by the evidence being collected to evaluate the tenability of the hypothesis.

VALIDITY EVIDENCE FOR THE MCAT

Hypothesis 1: MCAT Scores Are Accurate Representations of the Skills the Exam Purports to Measure

The following sections describe efforts to accumulate data regarding the content and construct validity of MCAT. Two different strategies are discussed. The first considers procedures used to identify the content and cognitive skills to be assessed. The second involves collecting empirical evidence examining the relationships between MCAT and relevant concurrent measures as well as analysis of the test battery's factor structure.

Developing Content Specifications. Messick has argued that concerns about the validity of a test should always be tied to the meanings of scores; he supported the use of the term *content relevance* because he saw it as distinguishing between concerns about the validity of the test (i.e., how the score is used) and concerns about the development of the test (Messick, 1975, 1980). Others argue that content validity is fundamental to the validity of a test (Sireci, 1995; Yalow

& Popham, 1983). All argue that content validity, because of its focus on the tested content and not on test scores, is essential in understanding what the test scores mean. Evaluation of the MCAT's content validity must begin with a review of research conducted to define the domain of concepts and skills to be covered by the exam.

As mentioned previously, a content review was undertaken as part of the MCAT Evaluation Panel's research efforts to determine the character of the revised exam. To accomplish this review, content outlines were developed for each of four science disciplines (Biology, General Chemistry, Organic Chemistry, and Physics). Included topics were those posited to represent the domain of material prerequisite for mastery of concepts taught in medical school.

Content outlines were distributed to samples from two populations: those who instruct *medical* students and those who instruct *premedical* students. Medical school faculty respondents evaluated topics on the extent to which they were prerequisite for the medical school curriculum. Undergraduate faculty members rated topics on the extent to which they were covered during the first-year course sequences typically taken by premedical candidates.

Analysis was completed by cross-tabulating results from both surveys. The final content domain defined for MCAT's science sections consisted of the topics that met two criteria. Included topics were (1) judged by medical school reviewers to be prerequisite for medical school and (2) indicated by premedical faculty as covered during first-year course sequences at the vast majority of undergraduate institutions. The Evaluation Panel decided that biology content should be tested in a Biological Sciences section and physics in a Physical Sciences section. Rather than include a separate chemistry section, they determined that chemistry content should be split between the two science sections, with organic chemistry material tested in Biological Sciences and general chemistry content tested in Physical Sciences (AAMC, 1988). This decision maintained the balance of science and nonscience sections (Physical Sciences and Biological Sciences versus Verbal Reasoning and Writing Sample) and, since including a third test section would increase administration time, reduced the length of the test day.

The panel initially pursued development of a Verbal Reasoning test that assessed humanities and social sciences subject matter. After reviewing several prototypes for such an exam, they agreed that while prospective physicians should be familiar with nonscience-oriented material, the subject matter of humanities and social science courses was not appropriate to be tested on the MCAT. Further, because the content coverage of social science and humanities courses differs vastly from institution to institution, defining the content domain would be difficult. To reinforce their view that well-rounded preparation was important, the panel decided that Verbal Reasoning passages should be drawn from texts in humanities, social sciences, and natural science areas not tested by the science sections, but the associated questions should not require knowledge of specific subject matter. The panel believed that inclusion of texts from these disciplines would emphasize the importance of exposure to a wide range of reading materials.

Developing Cognitive Specifications. In response to the increasing numbers of medical school programs that include independent learning and problem-solving components, the Evaluation Panel recommended that multiple choice test sections assess critical and analytical thinking. To identify more clearly the cognitive domains for each test section, advice was sought from a number of cognitive psychologists. This group discussed various methods for defining critical thinking and concluded by establishing four cognitive specifications for the Verbal Reasoning test: comprehension, evaluation, application, and incorporation of new information. Seven cognitive skills were identified for the science sections: evaluation, flexibility in scientific reasoning, hypothesis testing, identifying components and relationships, identifying main ideas, reasoning using quantitative data, and seeking clarification.

Specification of the cognitive domain for the Writing Sample was similarly accomplished. The Essay Committee desired that this section of the test assess examinees' ability to (1) develop a central idea; (2) synthesize concepts and ideas; (3) present ideas cohesively and logically; and (4) write clearly, following accepted practices of grammar, syntax, and punctuation consistent with timed, first-draft composition. Clarification of the model for Writing Sample prompts and further specification of "synthesis of concepts" required the advice of several experts in the area of cognition and topic development. With the experts' assistance, the committee decided that Writing Sample prompts should stimulate examinees to use synthesis in the context of reconciling opposing viewpoints. The prompt model identified to elicit these skills begins with a brief general statement intended to be accessible to the majority of examinees. The writing tasks involve explaining the statement, describing circumstances in which the statement might be contradicted or judged not applicable, and discussing ways in which the conflict between the initial statement and its opposition might be resolved.

Empirical Evidence. The first set of empirical evidence upon which to evaluate the MCAT's construct validity is based on the relationships between MCAT section scores and a number of concurrent criteria. These concurrent measures include self-appraisal of academic skills, undergraduate grade-point average (GPA) in the sciences (biology, chemistry, physics, and mathematics courses), and GPA in the nonsciences (all other courses). Through a survey completed at the time of test registration, MCAT examinees are routinely requested to appraise their skill levels in a number of academic areas. Self-appraisals of skills are collected using a four-point rating scale that ranges from "poor" to "excellent." Undergraduate GPA data are available only for individuals who apply to medical school and are collected when the application is submitted, typically several months subsequent to taking the MCAT. To determine the relationships with these concurrent measures, simple correlations were computed. For these

Table 13.1
Spearman's Rho Correlation Coefficients between MCAT Scores and Examinees'
Self-Appraisals of Academic Skills

	MCAT Section			
Academic Area	**Verbal Reasoning**	**Physical Sciences**	**Biological Sciences**	**Writing Sample**
Physical Sciences	.14	.37	.26	.04
Biological Sciences	.16	.20	.30	.07
English Composition	.20	-.04	.02	.20
English Literature	.13	-.08	-.02	.13

Note: $N = 3,390$.
Data based on a random sample of 1994 MCAT examinees.

analyses, the patterns of relationships were examined to discern evidence of convergent and discriminant validity.

Table 13.1 presents Spearman correlations computed between MCAT scores and self-appraisal of skills in the physical sciences, the biological sciences, English composition, and English literature for the 1994 group of test takers. Examination of these data reveals that the correlations between a given test section and self-appraisal of skills in the relevant area are higher than correlations between the test section and self-ratings in irrelevant areas. For example, self-ratings in the physical sciences are most highly related to performance on the Physical Sciences section (.37), whereas self-ratings in the biological sciences are most strongly related to performance on the Biological Sciences section (.30). Self-appraisal of English composition skills is more highly related to Verbal Reasoning and Writing Sample (.20 each) performance than to scores on the science sections. Although these correlations tend to be somewhat low, the patterns of relationships are supportive of construct validity.

Intercorrelations among MCAT scores and correlations between MCAT scores and undergraduate GPA are presented in Table 13.2. Here it can be seen that the expected patterns of relationships are evident. The Physical and Biological Sciences sections have stronger correlations with each other (.74) than with the Verbal Reasoning (.60 and .62, respectively) and the Writing Sample sections (.28 and .29, respectively). The Writing Sample section shows a stronger relationship with Verbal Reasoning (.39) than with the science sections. The Physical and Biological Sciences sections show stronger correlations with undergraduate science GPA (.41) than do the Verbal Reasoning and Writing Sample (.28 and .16, respectively) sections. Correlations with nonscience GPA are similar across the four test sections, a result most likely due to the wide mix of courses grouped into the nonscience category.

While these data confirm that hypothesized relationships appear to exist, they

Table 13.2
Pearson Correlation Coefficients among MCAT Scores and Undergraduate Grade-Point Averages for All 1993 Applicants to U.S. Medical Schools

	Physical Sciences	*Writing Sample*	*Biological Sciences*	*Science GPA*	*Nonscience GPA*
Verbal Reasoning	.60	.39	.62	.28	.25
Physical Sciences	--	.28	.74	.41	.23
Writing Sample		--	.29	.16	.18
Biological Sciences			--	.41	.25
Science GPA				--	.64

Note: N = 42,508.

alone do not provide sufficient evidence to confirm that MCAT measures the skills it purports to measure. Examination of the factor structure of the test battery is also necessary. Toward this end, initial exploratory factor analysis studies have been completed (Li & Mitchell, 1992). Although results generally supported the factor structure hypothesized for MCAT, some questions were raised regarding the factor structure of the two science sections. Whereas the uniqueness of the Verbal Reasoning and Writing Sample sections was supported, organic chemistry items, which are part of the Biological Sciences section, appeared to have strong cross loadings with the Physical Sciences section. Further investigation of these results is planned using confirmatory factor analysis. To avoid a ''confirmationist bias'' that would lead to seeking only support for the proposed MCAT factor structure, alternative factor structures will be hypothesized and tested.

Hypothesis 2: MCAT Scores Are Generalizable across Samples of Test Items

Each test section is developed according to a standard blueprint designed by the two advisory committees. Three types of specifications form the basis for this blueprint: content specifications, cognitive specifications, and item difficulty levels. Application of these specifications is discussed separately for the multiple choice sections and the Writing Sample.

Multiple Choice Sections. Based on the results of the content review, science material was categorized into groupings called "content frames." Using the MCAT Evaluation Panel's perceptions of the relative importance of various subject matter, the number of items to be drawn from each content frame was determined. Also determined by the MCAT Evaluation Panel was the number of items per test form to be drawn from each of the cognitive areas, as specified in the previous section. The number of items from each content frame and from each cognitive area remains constant across test forms.

Science item writers are recruited from the population of undergraduate faculty members who teach courses in the four tested science disciplines as well as medical school faculty members who teach basic science courses. Writers are given assignments to prepare units (a unit is a passage along with its associated questions) that meet certain content and cognitive skills. All units undergo a technical review for accuracy as well as a sensitivity review for racial/ethnic or gender bias before being administered. Units that pass the reviews are field-tested prior to their use as scored items. From the field testing, estimates of difficulty level, discrimination level, and Differential Item Functioning (DIF) are obtained. A target frequency distribution and mean value for difficulty levels are set; each test form must meet this specification.

Form construction for the Verbal Reasoning section is handled similarly. Specified numbers of items from each cognitive area must be included on each form of the test. Although Verbal Reasoning questions do not test subject matter, the test specifications designate the numbers of passages to be drawn from each of three disciplines (humanities, social sciences, and natural sciences). Undergraduate faculty members in the relevant disciplines are recruited to prepare Verbal Reasoning units. Generally, Verbal Reasoning passages are adapted from published materials; the writers prepare questions intended to assess the various cognitive skills. After items have been developed and screened for accuracy and sensitivity, they are field-tested in the same manner as science items, and similar item statistics are computed. Using the estimates of difficulty obtained from the field testing, a target mean level of difficulty and frequency distribution for difficulty values are met for each form.

Multiple forms of the test are administered on each testing occasion and equated to the April 1991 base population using equipercentile equating. Raw scores are converted to scaled scores ranging from 1 to 15 for each multiple choice test section. Reliability levels are determined using internal consistency methods (coefficient alpha) and over the past five years have consistently been between .85 and .88. Given that internal consistency estimates have been stable across numerous forms of the test, it is reasonable to conclude that the internal structure is similar from one form of the test to another.

Writing Sample. A somewhat different approach is used to assemble and evaluate the generalizability of Writing Sample forms. Because all Writing Sample prompts were designed to measure similar writing and cognitive skills and knowledge of specific subject matter is not being assessed, assembly of forms primarily relies on estimated difficulty levels. It is relevant to note here that a Writing Sample form consists of two prompts; examinees must respond to both and are allowed 30 minutes to write each composition. Prompts are administered to all examinees in the same sequence; the first prompt is seen only during the first 30-minute period and the second prompt only during the final 30 minutes.

Using data collected from pilot testings conducted in conjunction with operational administrations, prompt means and standard deviations were estimated. Target mean and standard deviation ranges were set for Writing Sample forms, and prompts are selected for inclusion on forms so that the resulting forms meet these specifications. During form assembly, attention is paid to the subject matter of prompts to ensure that cuing from the first prompt to the second does not occur.

Each essay is scored blindly on a six-point scale by two trained readers. The two scores are summed to create a total score for each essay. When the two scores are more than a point apart, a third, more experienced reader scores the essay and determines the total. The two total scores are combined to create a final numeric score that is converted to a letter score for reporting.[3]

Reliability levels for the Writing Sample were derived using two methods. First, a measure of internal consistency was calculated using the Spearman-Brown Prophecy Formula (Crocker & Algina, 1986). Using this method, the two total scores were correlated and corrected for test length. Reliability estimates ranged from .77 to .80 for the 1992 through 1994 administrations.

The second method used generalizability analysis (Brennan, 1983). Here, a person by rater nested within prompt design was used allowing estimates of variance components for three main effects (persons, prompts, and raters within prompts) and two interaction effects (person by prompt; and person by rater within prompt). The generalizability coefficients ranged from .76 to .82 for the 1992–1994 test administrations. In each case, the variance attributable to prompt was negligible (Koenig, 1995).

Hypothesis 3: The Tested Science Concepts and Facility with Scientific Problem Solving, Critical Thinking, and Communication Skills Are Predictive of Successful Performance in the Medical School Curriculum

In 1991, agreements to participate with predictive validity research were developed with 16 medical schools. These schools, which were chosen to be representative of the 125 U.S. medical schools, were selected based on factors such as size, type of curricula, geographic region, and characteristics of the student population. Schools agreed to submit a number of student performance measures including course grades in years one through four, course contact hours, and indicators of academic difficulty. Preadmission data obtained for each student (in addition to MCAT) included undergraduate GPA, the selectivity of the student's undergraduate institution as measured by the Astin Index,[4] and any institution-specific measures used when evaluating applicants (i.e., interview ratings, estimates of maturity or leadership qualities, and health-related work experience). Collection of these preadmission data allowed for evaluation of MCAT's predictive value within the context of other data typically used during decision making. As part of the agreement with schools, the AAMC prepares reports discussing the results of analyses and allowing evaluation of the adequacy of institutional selection procedures.

The study follows two cohorts, students who first entered medical school in the fall of 1992 and those who first entered medical school in the fall of 1993. To date, year one and two performance data for the 1992 entering class and year one data for the 1993 entering class have been collected for the majority of schools in the sample. Performance was summarized by computing end-of-year grade-point averages, weighted by course contact hours, for both cohorts as well as year two cumulative grade-point averages for the 1992 entrants.

In addition to medical school grades, an indicator of the incidence of academic difficulty is also being collected. Incidents of academic difficulty are recorded when a student withdraws, is dismissed, or delays graduation for academic reasons. Although not yet available, these data will be analyzed using logistic regression to examine the likelihood of encountering difficulty at various MCAT score levels.

Also being collected from study schools are performance ratings in six clerkship rotations required during the third and fourth years of medical school (Family Practice, Medicine, Obstetrics/Gynecology, Pediatrics, Psychiatry, and Surgery). Ratings are being obtained in six skill areas: overall clinical knowledge; overall clinical competence; clinical judgment; communication with patients and patients' families; communication with peers and supervisors; and use of information resources. For each area, the extent to which MCAT scores are related to these areas of clerkship performance will be examined.

Another type of criterion measure available for analysis is performance on licensing examinations. Subsequent to the second year of medical school, students are required to take Step 1 of the United States Medical Licensing Examination (USMLE). Step 2 and Step 3 of the USMLE are taken after the fourth year of medical school and the first year of residency, respectively. Attainment of a passing score on the three Step exams is required for medical licensure. At this writing, Step 1 scores were available for the 1992 cohort.

The relationships among MCAT, GPA, institutional selectivity, and available criterion measures were investigated using multiple regression analysis. Regressions were run separately for each school and correlation matrices corrected for restriction in range using the procedure developed by Lawley and described in Lord and Novick (1968). Restriction in range corrections were based on MCAT, GPA, and selectivity data for each school's applicant pool. Multiple correlation coefficients were obtained for five unique predictor sets and results summarized across schools. The five predictor sets are described below.

Set	Variables
1	Undergraduate science GPA + Undergraduate nonscience GPA (UGPAs)
2	Verbal Reasoning + Physical Sciences + Writing Sample + Biological Sciences (MCTs)
3	UGPAs + selectivity
4	UGPAs + MCATs
5	UGPAs + selectivity + MCATs

For each regression, all variables were entered simultaneously. An MCAT composite score[5] was formed for several schools at which the sample size was too small to enter variables individually. Because institution-specific preadmission data are not consistent across schools, they were not included in these summary analyses, although they are included in analyses conducted to prepare institutional reports on the validity of school-level selection procedures.

Table 13.3 reports the ranges and median values for the multiple correlation coefficients obtained for the five sets of predictors. As is evident in Table 13.3, MCAT scores appear to have slightly higher correlations with medical school grades and USMLE scores than do UGPA data. However, prediction of performance was improved when the two sets of predictors were considered jointly. When interpreting multiple correlation coefficients, it is often useful to consider R^2 values, or percent of variance explained. The percent of variance accounted for by using GPAs and MCATs in combination ranged from a low of 41 percent ($.64^2$) when the criterion was year one GPA to a high of 58 percent ($.76^2$) when predicting cumulative GPA.

MCAT's utility within the context of the admissions process becomes evident when values obtained for predictor set 3 are compared with those obtained for predictor set 5. The increase in median values observed when comparing these predictor sets ranged from a low of .08 for the 1993 cohort's Year 1 GPA to a high of .22 for the 1992 cohort's USMLE Step 1. Adding selectivity to the predictor set, which already included UGPAs and MCATs, did not substantially increase predictive values. These data point toward a significant relationship between MCAT scores and subsequent medical school performance. A more complete description of this work can be found in Mitchell, Haynes, and Koenig (1994).

Using these data, it is also possible to examine correlations between MCAT and grades in individual medical school courses. Simple correlations were computed within school and corrected for univariate range restriction (Linn, Harnisch, & Dunbar, 1981) based on characteristics of the school's applicant pool; results were summarized across schools using ranges and median values.

Table 13.4 presents median corrected correlations between MCAT, science GPA (SGPA), nonscience GPA (NSGPA), and first-year grades. While this analysis would traditionally fall under the rubric of criterion-related validity, it also

Table 13.3
Median Values and Ranges of Corrected Multiple Correlations[1] between Preadmission Data and Medical School Performance Measures for 1992 and 1993 Entering Classes at Medical Schools Participating in MCAT Predictive Validity Research Studies

				Medical School Performance Measures		
Predictor Sets	Year 1 GPA Class of 1992	Year 1 GPA Class of 1993	Year 2 GPA Class of 1992	Cumulative Year 1-2 GPA Class of 1992	USMLE Step 1 Class of 1992
Undergraduate GPA (UGPA):					
Median	.54	.50	.55	.55	.48
Range	.40 - .74	.32 - .79	.20 - .74	.36 - .73	.35 - .64
MCAT Scores (MCAT):					
Median	.67	.57	.62	.64	.72
Range	.38 - .78	.36 - .66	.23 - .70	.43 - .78	.58 - .79
UGPA, Institutional Selectivity(Select):					
Median	.60	.60	.60	.63	.53
Range	.50 - .80	.32 - .82	.23 - .79	.43 - .82	.40 - .73
UGPA, MCAT:					
Median	.75	.64	.71	.76	.75
Range	.48 - .80	.50 - .85	.31 - .77	.49 - .81	.62 - .81
UGPA, MCAT, Select:					
Median	.75	.68	.72	.76	.75
Range	.53 - .82	.50 - .85	.32 - .81	.51 - .84	.62 - .82
Number of Schools	13	8	10	9	14

[1]Note: Multiple correlations corrected for restriction in range.

Table 13.4
Corrected Pearson Correlations between Preadmission Data and First-Year Grades for 1992 and 1993 Entering Classes at Medical Schools Participating in the MCAT Predictive Validity Research Studies

First-Year Course	Undergraduate GPA		MCAT Section				Number of Classes
	Science GPA	Nonscience GPA	Verbal Reasoning	Physical Sciences	Writing Sample	Biological Sciences	
Gross Anatomy:							19
Median	.36	.19	.12	.32	.05	.41	
Range	.25 to .66	-.04 to .56	.00 to .49	.09 to .56	-.16 to .26	.15 to .59	
Microscopic Anatomy:							13
Median	.38	.19	.28	.28	-.06	.40	
Range	.15 to .67	-.01 to .56	.04 to .52	-.06 to .47	-.20 to .22	.16 to .56	
Microbiology:							8
Median	.39	.20	.28	.40	.14	.53	
Range	.25 to .65	.02 to .43	.01 to .48	.40 to .51	-.11 to .26	.19 to .68	
Biochemistry:							19
Median	.44	.18	.21	.42	.03	.54	
Range	.25 to .68	.02 to .51	-.09 to .52	.08 to .57	-.13 to .25	.14 to .66	
Physiology:							19
Median	.39	.17	.25	.43	.11	.51	
Range	.23 to .61	-.01 to .35	.00 to .45	.29 to .57	.00 to .22	.05 to .64	
Neuroscience:							18
Median	.39	.25	.21	.32	.11	.36	
Range	.16 to .74	.07 to .45	-.18 to .39	-.05 to .49	-.10 to .25	-.10 to .63	
Psych/Human Behavior:							12
Median	.26	.14	.32	.22	.16	.24	
Range	-.01 to .56	.02 to .56	.16 to .71	-.17 to .55	-.02 to .22	-.07 to .62	
Patient/Clinical Care:							11
Median	.29	.13	.18	.20	.04	.18	
Range	-.04 to .49	-.02 to .45	.05 to .60	-.30 to .53	-.01 to .10	-.28 to .40	

Note: Correlations corrected for restriction in range. Writing Sample correlations are for the 1993 cohort only.

provides evidence of construct validity. For example, MCAT science sections and SGPA consistently related strongly with grades in science areas (i.e., Microbiology, Physiology) but showed weaker relationships with grades in non-science-oriented courses (Behavioral Sciences, Patient Care). Verbal Reasoning showed a strong relationship with grades in Behavioral Sciences and a weaker relationship with grades in basic science areas. Writing Sample scores did not show relationships with first-year coursework. This finding was expected, given that the content and methods of evaluation for first-year courses are quite different from the skills assessed by the Writing Sample. Separate studies of the Writing Sample are planned in which data will be collected from institutions having courses that include writing components.

Further analyses will examine the relationship between MCAT scores and clerkship ratings, third- and fourth-year grades, scores on USMLE Steps 2 and 3, and the incidence of academic difficulty and distinction.

Examination of Differential Prediction. Validity theorists note that validity assessment often ends once the theorized relationships are confirmed (Cronbach, 1989; Kane, 1992; Shepard, 1993). They caution researchers not to assume a "confirmationist bias" and thereby neglect to seek out data that might refute findings. Researchers are further advised to listen to a testing program's critics as well as its supporters. Often, a program's harshest critics pose the questions most in need of investigation. Common criticisms leveled against standardized examinations are that they are biased against women and racial/ethnic minorities; that higher scores can be obtained by enrolling in costly commercial coaching courses; and that performance gains, attributable to increased familiarity with the test but not to improved knowledge and skills, are associated with repeated testings.

Analyses that attend to these criticisms have been designed in order to examine MCAT's differential prediction. The first of these studies examines differential prediction for examinees who retest and for those who enroll in commercial preparation courses. For each of these studies, examinees will be divided into mutually exclusive groups (i.e., repeat test takers versus first-time test takers; examinees who took a coaching course versus those who did not). By comparing the regression lines across groups, an accurate assessment of the criterion-related validity for each of these subgroups will be assessed.

The second of these studies involves comparisons for examinees grouped by gender and racial/ethnic status. Using first- and second-year grades provided by the study schools, the differential prediction for groups defined by race and gender will be investigated. Because within-school sample size is not problematic for gender groups, a direct comparison of within-school prediction equations is feasible. For race groups, within-school sample sizes are very small. Since the knowledge and skills represented by course grades are not necessarily similar from school to school, aggregating data across schools is not straightforward. As a remedy, a plan to conduct a validity generalization study is currently being considered. If results indicate that validity generalizes across settings (schools), methods for collapsing data will be explored with the goal of sufficiently increasing sample sizes to yield stable results.

Group differences will also be examined for prediction of academic difficulty. Work done on the pre-1991 version of the MCAT showed that the probability of encountering academic difficulty increased as MCAT scores dropped below eight (Jones & Vanyur, 1983). Some differences in these patterns were noted for African-American students (Jones & Mitchell, 1986). Similar analyses will be conducted for the 1991 version of the MCAT.

A third set of criterion data available for analysis is USMLE scores. Since the various steps of the USMLE are administered to all medical students, sample size is not a concern for analyses with this criterion measure. Comparison of prediction equations will enable further examination of differential predictive validity.

Plans are also under way to examine the factor structure of the MCAT across different examinee population groups using confirmatory factor analysis. The exploratory work by Li and Mitchell (1992) found that for female, Asian, and African-American groups the two science sections appeared to collapse into one omnibus science factor; for the white male group, the science sections appeared to form two factors similar to the factor structure hypothesized for the examination.

Finally, before leaving the topic of prediction for women and minorities, the precautions employed during form assembly to ensure the fairness of the MCAT should be described. Extra effort is made to recruit minority and women item writers for all multiple choice sections. Once items are developed but before they are field-tested, sensitivity reviews are conducted during which minority and women reviewers from various regions of the country evaluate whether item content might be differentially accessible to examinees. Care is also taken to avoid any items that may provoke an emotional response. Items that survive sensitivity reviews are field-tested; DIF analyses are performed on field test data using the Mantel-Hanzel statistic (Dorans & Holland, 1993). Items flagged as functioning differentially are reviewed and revised before administration as scored items.

Hypothesis 4: MCAT Scores Are Used Appropriately by Those Making Admissions Decisions

A primary concern for a testing program must be the consequences of making decisions based on scores. With this concern in mind, the Evaluation Panel established promotion of fair and reasoned use of test data as an intended outcome for the revised battery. One way to address this concern is to make interpretive materials readily available; another is to gather data on test use.

Two surveys have been conducted to solicit information on the ways in which scores are incorporated into admissions decisions; the first focused on score use for all test sections (Mitchell et al., 1994); the second on Writing Sample score use (Koenig & Mitchell, 1993). Of particular importance in these questionnaires was collection of information on the types of inferences admissions committees make from score data. Test scores should not be considered as infallible measures that can be relied upon to the exclusion of other indicators of qualifications. When making decisions, test score users should remember to consider scores within the reported confidence intervals. These survey results indicated that appropriate types of inferences were being made from score data and that MCAT scores were among many criteria being considered by admissions committees.

In addition to evaluating test score usage, Mitchell's survey sought to assess the social consequences of the revised version of the MCAT. The new MCAT was designed to send a message to prospective medical students that developing a broad base of knowledge was important and that focusing preparatory efforts entirely on the sciences was not acceptable. The survey asked for respondents' perceptions of the 1992 entering class in terms of breadth of premedical preparation. In relation to the previous five entering classes, admissions committee members described the students as more broadly prepared and as demonstrating greater ranges of interests. This perception can be substantiated with empirical data. Comparison from 1990 to 1993 of percentages of examinees by type of preparation reveals that the percentage who can be described as having a broad preparation has increased from 14.5 percent to 18.6 percent (Validity Studies Advisory Group [VSAG], 1994). This finding, although encouraging, needs to be investigated further. Studies involving collection of data from undergraduate health professions advisers on changes in preparation patterns are planned.

SUMMARY

Kane (1992) suggested that an assessment of the validity of a test should be approached in the same manner as one approaches a rational argument. Arguments must be clearly presented, and assumptions must be inherently plausible or supported by empirical evidence. Four hypotheses were identified for investigation as part of the MCAT validity studies. The first hypothesis requires evaluation of content and construct validity. Here, the methods by which content and cognitive domains were defined were presented as initial evidence. Ongoing studies collect data on relationships of scores with concurrent measures and on the factor structure of the test battery. The first sets of findings demonstrate that the expected patterns of relationships exist.

The second hypothesis requires investigation of the comparability of test forms. Item development and form assembly procedures were described. Score reliability estimates were presented as empirical evidence that the internal structure has remained constant across test forms.

Evidence of criterion-related validity is being collected to test the tenability of the third hypothesis, that scores on the test battery are predictive of performance in medical school. Based on the initial sets of results, MCAT scores demonstrated strong relationships with grades in years one and two of medical school and performance on the USMLE Step 1. Efforts are ongoing to further analyze these relationships as additional criterion data are collected.

The final hypothesis addresses score use by decision makers. Data collection efforts have involved the conduct of surveys to evaluate score use practices. To date, results are favorable. Additional studies will further investigate the impact of the test battery on the premedical preparation of prospective physicians.

FUTURE DIRECTIONS

Ongoing evaluation of MCAT's use in selection and its relevance to current medical education curricula is crucial to maintaining a valid admissions test. The overall research plan presented in this chapter presents only a portion of the work conducted to maintain the MCAT. In addition to validation efforts, score use and test preparation practices must be monitored continually. Toward this end, numerous publications are produced and services offered to assist medical schools in their use of MCAT data and examinees in their efforts to prepare for the test (AAMC, 1990, 1992, 1995, 1996).

The research plan presented here, while still in the early stages of implementation, is regularly evaluated and updated as events warrant. A continuous stream of new issues presents alternative concerns to be investigated. While work on the confirmatory factor analysis is just beginning, plans are already being laid to expand criterion-related validity studies to include more systematic collection of data on noncognitive predictors, such as motivation and maturity. A content review of current undergraduate curricula always remains in the background to be considered as well. Examination of the extent to which MCAT scores are predictive of performance in nontraditional settings (such as problem-based curricula) is also under way. Because of the many potential issues that may arise, the research plan presented here cannot be viewed as static. Rather, the plan must be allowed to evolve, as critics and supporters of the test bring new issues to the forefront.

NOTES

The authors are indebted to Karen J. Mitchell for her critique of an earlier version of this chapter and for her work on developing the current version of the MCAT and designing and conducting much of the validity research discussed. Special thanks are due to the members of the MCAT Validity Studies Advisory Group (Shirley Nickols Fahey, Clarice Fooks, Debra Gillers, Robert Lee, Fernando S. Mendoza, Lewis H. Nelson III, George Nowacek, Martin A. Pops, Robert F. Sabalis, Gerry R. Schermerhorn, and Marliss Strange), whose contributions to the validity research project have been invaluable. The authors are also grateful to Patricia Cooleen for her assistance in preparing this document and to Robert L. Beran, Allen E. Doolittle, John L. Hackett, Scott H. Oppler, Stephen G. Sireci, and Deborah L. Whetzel for their many helpful comments and suggestions.

1. During the 1980s and continuing into the present, schools began introducing "prob-

lem-based learning'' courses and curricula. Problem-based learning refers to curricula or courses in which instruction is based on case studies using small group tutorials that emphasize independent, self-directed learning.

2. It is important here to note that the purpose of this study was to determine if individuals who pursued broad preparations would be handicapped when they encountered the medical school curriculum. Results demonstrated that while performance in the first two years was slightly lower for broadly prepared individuals than for those who focused on the sciences, by the third year, performance was similar across the two groups.

3. The Essay Committee selected the alphabetic reporting scale for the Writing Sample in order to convey a message to admissions committees that the Writing Sample assesses a unique set of skills and should be considered differently than multiple choice scores.

4. An institution's Astin Index is the mean total SAT (Scholastic Aptitude Test) score for all students admitted in a given year.

5. The MCAT composite consisted of the simple sum of the four scores, with Writing Sample scores converted to numbers.

REFERENCES

Angoff, W. H. (1988). Validity: An evolving concept. In H. Wainer & H. Braun (Eds.), *Test validity* (pp. 19–32). Hillsdale, NJ: Erlbaum.

Association of American Medical Colleges. (1987). *Use of MCAT data in admissions: A guide for medical school admissions officers and faculty.* Washington, DC: Author.

Association of American Medical Colleges. (1988). *Review of science content specifications for the Medical College Admission Test.* Unpublished manuscript, Author.

Association of American Medical Colleges. (1990). *MCAT student manual.* Washington, DC: Author.

Association of American Medical Colleges. (1992). *Use of Medical College Admission Tests data in 1993 student selections: A guide for medical school admissions officers and faculty.* Washington, DC: Author.

Association of American Medical Colleges. (1995). *Scoring the MCAT Writing Sample.* Washington, DC: Author.

Association of American Medical Colleges. (1996). *Characteristics of MCAT examinees 1994–1995.* Washington, DC: Author.

Brennan, R. L. (1983). *Elements of generalizability theory.* Iowa City: American College Testing Program.

Crocker, L., & Algina, J. (1986). *Introduction to classical and modern test theory.* New York: Harcourt Brace Jovanovich.

Cronbach, L. J. (1988). Five perspectives on validity argument. In H. Wainer & H. Braun (Eds.), *Test validity* (pp. 3–17). Hillsdale, NJ: Erlbaum.

Cronbach, L. J. (1989). Construct validation after thirty years. In R. L. Linn (Ed.), *Intelligence: Measurement, theory and public policy* (pp. 147–171). Urbana: University of Illinois Press.

Dorans, N. J., & Holland, P. W. (1993). DIF detection and description: Mantel-Haenszel and standardization. In P. W. Holland and H. Wainer (Eds.), *Differential item functioning* (pp. 35–66). Hillsdale, NJ: Lawrence Erlbaum.

Jones, R. F., & Mitchell, K. (1986). *Racial/ethnic differences in the predictive validity of MCAT scores*. Paper presented at the annual meeting of the American Educational Research Association, San Francisco, CA.

Jones, R. F., & Vanyur, S. (1983). MCAT scores and student progress in medical school. *Journal of Medical Education, 59*, 527–531.

Jones, R. F., & Thomae-Forgues, M. (1984). *Validity of the MCAT for predicting performance in the first two years of medical school* (Medical College Admission Test Interpretive Studies Series Report # 84–1). Washington, DC: Association of American Medical Colleges.

Kane, M. (1992). An argument-based approach to validity. *Psychological Bulletin, 112*, 527–535.

Koenig, J. A. (1992). Comparison of medical school performances and career plans of students with broad and with science-focused premedical preparation. *Academic Medicine, 67*, 191–196.

Koenig, J. A. (1995). *Examination of the comparability of MCAT Writing Sample test forms*. Paper presented at the annual meeting of the American Educational Research Association, San Francisco, CA.

Koenig, J. A., Li, W., & Haynes, R. A. (1990). *Estimation of the validity of the 1991 MCAT for predicting medical school grades, NBME performance, and academic difficulty*. Unpublished manuscript, Association of American Medical Colleges.

Koenig, J. A., & Mitchell, K. J. (1988). An interim report on the MCAT essay pilot project. *Journal of Medical Education, 63*, 21–29.

Koenig, J. A., & Mitchell, K. J. (1993). Use of Medical College Admissions Test Writing Sample data in medical school admissions decisions. *The Advisor, 13*, 13–15.

Li, W., & Mitchell, K. J. (1992). *Preliminary investigation of the 1991 Medical College Admission Test factor structure*. Paper presented at the annual meeting of the American Educational Research Association, San Francisco, CA.

Linn, R. L., Harnisch, D., & Dunbar, S. (1981). Corrections for range restriction: An empirical investigation of conditions resulting in conservative correction. *Journal of Applied Psychology, 66*, 655–663.

Lord, F. M., & Novick, M. R. (1968). *Statistical theories of mental test scores*. Reading, MA: Addison-Wesley.

MCAT Evaluation Panel. (1989). *Final reports of the MCAT Format and Content Review and the MCAT Essay Pilot Project*. Unpublished manuscript, Association of American Medical Colleges.

Messick, S. (1975). The standard problem: Meaning and values in measurement and evaluation. *American Psychologist, 30*, 955–966.

Messick, S. (1980). Test validity and the ethics of assessment. *American Psychologist, 35*, 1012–1027.

Messick, S. (1989). Validity. In R. L. Linn (Ed.), *Educational measurement* (3rd ed., pp. 13–103). Washington, DC: American Council on Education & National Council on Measurement in Education.

Mitchell, K. J. (1990). Traditional predictors of performance in medical school. *Academic Medicine, 65*, 149–158.

Mitchell, K. J., & Haynes, R. (1990). Score reporting for the 1991 Medical College Admission Test. *Academic Medicine, 65*, 719–723.

Mitchell, K., Haynes, R., & Koenig, J. (1994). Assessing the validity of the updated Medical College Admission Test. *Academic Medicine, 69* (5), 394–401.

Moss, P. A. (1995). Themes and variations in validity theory. *Educational Measurement: Issues and Practices, 14* (2), 5–13.

Muller, S. [Chairman]. (1984). Physicians for the twenty-first century: Report of the Project Panel on the general professional education of the physician and college preparation for medicine. *Journal of Medical Education, 59*, Part 2.

Review Committee. (1986). *Report of the Ad Hoc MCAT Review Committee.* Unpublished manuscript, Association of American Medical Colleges.

Shepard, L. A. (1993). Evaluating test validity. *Review of Research in Education, 19*, 405–450.

Sireci, S. G. (1995). *The central role of content representation in test validity.* Paper presented at the annual meeting of the National Council on Measurement in Education, San Francisco, CA.

Swanson, A., & Mitchell, K. J. (1989). MCAT responds to changes in medical education and physician practice. *Journal of the American Medical Association, 262*, 261–263.

Validity Studies Advisory Group. (1994). *Hot topics in admission: Update on the MCAT Validity Studies.* Paper presented at the annual meeting of the Association of American Medical Colleges, Boston, MA.

Yalow, E. S., & Popham, W. J. (1983). Content validity at the crossroads. *Educational Researcher, 12*, 10–14.

14

Assessment of Individuals with Disabilities: Educational Utility or Social Futility?

Sidney R. Miller and Pamela F. Miller

RECENT ISSUES AND DEBATE

The use of standardized tests to categorize individuals and groups has been challenged since the inception of testing (Jensen, 1980). Jensen notes that such tests have been criticized for inappropriate test items and the contamination of test scores by extraneous factors. These criticisms have led to charges that standardized tests are invalid, unreliable, and ultimately culturally biased.

Beginning in the 1950s a series of federal court cases began that centered around the Fourteenth Amendment and its "equal protection" clause (Turnbull, 1986). In *Hobsen v. Hansen* (1969) plaintiffs successfully challenged the tracking, that is, separation, of African-American students in the Washington, D.C. school system. The court was convinced that standardized tests that purported to determine an individual's future educational, social and employment opportunities were biased toward white middle-class students. The court ruled that such tests were not fair in assessing the abilities of nonwhite students.

Subsequent legal action was brought on behalf of individuals with disabilities. The courts found that the practice of using standardized tests as the sole criterion for identifying and making placement decisions about individuals with learning, behavioral, and social skill deficits had led to the placement of many children, youths, and adults in restrictive and sometimes debilitating environments. This had in turn prevented children and youths with identified disabilities from interacting with children and youths without disabilities. The courts found that such placements could deny students with disabilities access to specific educational services, resulting in inadequate and inappropriate training and instruction (*Larry P. v. Riles*, 1984; and *Diana v. State Board of Education*, 1973).

In the 1970s the Congress of the United States noted at numerous court decisions favored plaintiffs with disabilities. To codify all the preceding litigation and legislation addressing the education of individuals with disabilities, the Congress passed in 1974 the Education for All Handicapped Children's Act (Public Law 94–142). The act called for specific steps to be followed in assessing an individual's current level of school performance, including the use of at least two sources of data before decisions could be reached about a specific educational disability label and the type of educational services that should be provided.

The legislation required that the data collected, and the procedure used to collect the data, should be conducted in a professionally fair manner. The act did require that children whose primary language is not English should be evaluated in their native tongue. It did not spell out in detail safeguards to ensure fairness, equality, and unbiased procedures and instruments. The concern among many was that the assessment process was producing culturally, experientially, and economically influenced test results that in turn produced biased educational and career opportunities. The Congress sought to remedy this problem through general admonishments. But the lack of specifics in the legislation did not correct the misuses and abuses of tests and prompted new litigation challenges to the instruments and the testing procedures. The legal challenges have frequently been upheld, compelling the testing and instructional community to reevaluate the assumptions about the test instruments and the tests' utility. This has led educators to explore alternatives to current testing procedures, test data utilization and interpretation, and the types of data collected and their use.

CURRENT TEST LIMITATIONS

Salvia and Ysseldyke (1985) noted that the debate over testing questions a number of assumptions about the entire assessment process, including beliefs that (a) the person using the instrument is competent to administer the test(s), (b) errors are an ever present phenomenon of the process, (c) the students being tested are comparable across experiences and opportunities, (d) the behavior sampling procedures used are adequate and unbiased, and (e) observed behavior is a predictor of future behavior(s). Salvia and Ysseldyke further observed that individuals with learning, behavioral, social, physical, and sensory impairments have often been excluded from the test standardization process.

While the debate since the 1950s has focused on constitutional guarantees, only within the past two decades has the debate begun to shift to the educational limitations of standardized inferential measurement with students with disabilities. Cantor (1991) and Brandon (1988) have questioned the assessment process used for all students in the public schools, and each has called for increased data-based decision making based on actual school performance.

Shinn and McConnell (1994) have suggested that school psychologists and other school-oriented professional personnel have identified the wrong methodology, environment, and instructional models as their operational core. Others have called for valid inquiries into the essence of school-based assessment, instruction, and learning in the education milieu (Moss, 1992; Moss et al., 1991). Shinn and McConnell (1994) noted that the discussion needs to be more inclusive, including issues of gender, program emphasis, and curricular content.

In response to researchers like Shinn and McConnell (1994), Cantor (1991), and Brandon (1988), professional disciplines such as school psychology and special education are challenging the standardized inferential measurement tools because their educational utility in the classroom is marginal. Decisions relating to language, mathematics, social studies, and science instruction based on intelligence and aptitude quotients have not yielded positive performance changes. Programming and instruction based on these same measures in the areas of social behavior and vocational performance have yielded equally disappointing outcomes in special and general education.

The inclusion of diverse student populations in the regular and special education classroom requires more appropriate and functionally useful data for both the regular and special education teacher. Phillips, Hamlett, Fuchs, and Fuchs (1993) concluded that most special and regular classrooms are not effectively measuring and monitoring student programs and that alternative strategies need to be employed. The investigators concluded that standardized school and classroom testing has limited instructional relevancy and, as a result, yielded unsystematic teacher-constructed tests and classroom observations. Such criticisms have escalated the debate and challenged traditional standardized measurement.

Besides the questionable validity, reliability, and utility of standardized testing, such tests can also be challenged on economic factors. The time and cost of administering individualized, standardized tests constitute a major practical and financial issue raised by legislators, school administrators, and policy analysts. While a curriculum- or criterion-based test can be developed and administered by the regular classroom teacher within days for a nominal cost, standardized measures must be administered by highly paid professionals. It may take days or weeks to obtain results. Such delays hinder a teacher's ability to make needed modifications or changes in instruction, behavior management, and vocational and transitional programming and training.

Questions of test efficacy coupled with the concerns for timeliness and cost effectiveness have cast doubt on the current use, interpretation, and application of standardized tests. Concerns such as these cannot be beneficial to the field of special education at a time when the nation is rethinking its educational priorities, individual and group civil rights, personal responsibilities, family values, and economic realignment.

One of the larger federal expenditures of education funds is for special education—in excess of $2.5 billion annually. This level of expenditure makes the field of special education a large target and its associated services a major focus for legislators intent on demonstrating fiscal frugality and social responsibility. Ineffective and costly services and programs place the practices in special education in jeopardy. Both the political realities and the issues of test efficacy and instructional utility provide ample rationale for the development of improved assessment procedures and instruments that lead and contribute to enhanced learning and performance.

The collective responsibility of the regular and special educator is to respond more effectively to a diverse population of students with disabilities, estimated at approximately 10 percent of the school population. The traditional data from inferential test instruments appear to be less effective than content-specific assessment packages (Marston, 1989). Traditional diagnostic procedures have not provided educators adequate guidelines for decision making relative to school placement, instructional level, and performance outcomes. The information yielded has not always been appropriate or germane to the local school's goals and objectives.

The assessment focus in regular education has tended to converge on the generic academic areas of mathematics, social studies, science, and language. The measurement procedures have generally focused on achievement through the administration of individual or group tests. Such tests provide norm-referenced outcomes that are often unrelated to actual community and school curriculum, instructional intent, and life experiences. Too often the outcomes of such tests have been found to be the result of an individual's social and economic background and experiences and not a measure of actual school learning and performance. In addition, standardized tests are typically administered either at the beginning or end of the school year. As a result, teachers are not provided with the type of information that would enable them to monitor student progress and change or modify instruction and placement during the school year.

Recognizing the limitations of existing procedures and instrumentation, clinical and school psychologists, special educators, and school administrators have pursued the development of more relevant and cost-effective instrumentation. The goal has been to develop procedures and instruments that (a) are easier to use; (b) provide information that can be understood by administrators, teachers, parents, students, and the general public; (c) provide educationally useful information; (d) facilitate the continuous monitoring of student performance in the learning environment; (e) provide functional information about school and community performance; and (f) enable educators to monitor and adjust individual student placement, instructional strategies, and instructional materials.

While such goals are admirable and should be supported, the special education population presents some formidable problems in the area of assessment. A student with a disability may exhibit an inconsistent pattern of ability ranging from high to low cognitive functioning, from efficient to inefficient sensory-motor functioning, and from appropriate to inappropriate social development and interaction. Such a range of ability is not easily detected and monitored through portfolio and work sample analysis. Further, legal and ethical considerations require consideration of the effect of age and gender bias on outcomes, as well as the cultural fairness of the procedures and instrumentation used. Each of these factors complicates the assessment process and clouds any outcomes that result.

SPECIAL EDUCATION CONSIDERATIONS

In designing any special education assessment process and battery of instruments, one must first ensure that the package provides increased precision; is timely and disability sensitive; and is sensitive to issues of race, primary language, culture, gender, and age. Special education's pursuit of an assessment process that provides increased precision must also consider the following factors:

1. The need to monitor and revise daily instruction to meet individual student needs.
2. The influence of culture on learning values and behaviors in the classroom.
3. The influence of discrete disabilities on the learner's attitudes and performance.
4. The influence of language and experience on placement, curriculum, and social integration.
5. The role of legal advocacy on behalf of the student.
6. The potential economic impact of the adversarial legal process on the school's ability to deliver effective services.
7. The influence of the courts in the program delivery process, including the implied legal threat to intrude into the administration and instructional decision-making process.

These factors are among the reasons there is an effort in the field of special education to develop and implement alternative school-sensitive systems that provide instructional entry-level data that reflect individual school curriculum and content; enable classroom teachers and other school personnel to monitor instructional efficacy on a daily basis; provide performance data based on the student's actual achievement and mastery of each day's assignment; and enable the school's staff to document that the learning is achieved, maintained, and generalized.

Where the assessment responsibilities previously rested almost wholly with licensed clinical and school psychologists, the effort to empower the teacher in the assessment process offers the possibility of increased and more accurate daily academic, social, vocation, and functionally based monitoring at a lower per student cost. Such classroom- and teacher-based findings will yield timely and on-site instructional decisions. The data will yield educationally, socially, and vocationally relevant programming. This programming will then interface with ongoing placement, instruction, and curriculum modifications.

The use of curricular and behaviorally oriented, school-sensitive instrumentation enables schools to make change decisions throughout the school year rather than waiting until the end of the academic year. The use of the standardized, norm-referenced instrumentation, administered by specialized personnel, limits the frequency of the administration of the tests because of per test booklet charges, the necessity of using specialized testers, and the obligation to use complex scoring protocols. These factors impede the transfer of information to the classroom teacher. Finally, standardized testing involves increased financial costs to the school system at a time when shrinking educational budgets are commonplace.

Greenwood and Rieth (1994) note that there is an increasing reliance on data to make decisions, using a variety of assessment procedures. Mercer and Mercer (1989) added that data-based management can enable teachers to reach a variety of decisions that will influence the planning and implementation of instruction and, eventually, the student's school-based achievement and mastery. Like the student, the teacher has a professional investment in the data yielded and the student's performance. The teacher, unlike the clinical or school psychologist, is held accountable for the student's academic, social, and vocational achievement and subsequent program and placement decisions.

The assessment process for the teacher combines the barometric needs of the meteorologist, the microcalibrations of the precision machinist, the confidence of the physician performing orthoscopic surgery, and the intuitive capacity of the data analyst for the National Security Agency. The assessment process ranges from measurement of a student's academic achievement as he or she is preparing to enter college to detecting of cognitive activity that will enable an individual with severe and profound disabilities to sort gaskets manufactured in a variety of colors and shapes.

Many of the skills and content areas observed in individual programs for individuals with disabilities either are not addressed or are not addressed adequately in standardized individual group assessment measures.

CURRICULUM-BASED ASSESSMENT

More recently, discussion has centered around the failure of standardized tests to actually measure the effectiveness of instruction in the classroom. One perceived solution to the crisis in testing and identification appears to revolve around the goal to produce more environmentally pertinent data—data that can be used to identify and program for children and youths with disabilities in the schools. Among the approaches now being investigated in special education is the use of curriculum-based assessment (CBA). CBA is perceived by some (Ferguson & Fuchs, 1991; Fuchs, Fuchs, Hamlett, & Ferguson, 1992; Jones & Krouse, 1988) as an effective ecologically based procedure.

Blankenship (1985) underscored the critical dimension of CBA when she observed that assessment, curriculum, and instruction are interdependent. She noted that when they become isolated, they become dysfunctional, and then, like threads in a tapestry, they must be reunited for educators and psychologists to recognize the relevant patterns and develop appropriate programming. Blankenship contended the interest and use of CBA would grow with the recognition that the three threads must be joined but warned that the process of joining the threads and the application of the principle would be time-consuming and challenging.

McLoughlin and Lewis (1990) noted that there is a growing interest in the use of CBA and a growing body of research supporting the use of CBA in the classroom. McLoughlin and Lewis found that CBA is particularly useful for observing and regulating performance and progress and modifying curricular steps, instructional materials, and instructional strategies and approaches in the classroom. These authors note that for CBA to be effective it must measure instruction directly, and measurement intervals must be constant and of a relatively short duration. CBA can consist of informal inventories and quizzes that assess performance in specific school-targeted areas.

According to Luftig (1989), CBA reflects four inclusive aspects of the school environment: First, it is curriculum based; second, it is behaviorally defined; third, it seeks to measure well-defined domains; and, fourth, it assesses minimal levels of proficiency in the school. Luftig notes that the process requires that the curriculum be structured and sequential. The process can be adapted to either a development or a functional curriculum focus. Luftig indicates that modern application of the term *curriculum* relates to what is specifically taught—and not to the sum total of a student's experiences. He, along with Howell and Morehead (1987), identifies a series of guidelines associated with the development of a CBA instrument. The guidelines establish that the CBA process must (a) be based on clear behavioral tasks, (b) relate precisely to the components of the curriculum being taught, (c) focus on the student's current level of performance, and (d) begin instruction where the student lacks the requisite skills.

A variety of data-based approaches have been used to demonstrate the efficacy and validity of CBA procedures. Among the correlation and validity studies that have been conducted using disabled populations are Deno, Mirkin, and Chiang (1982), Fuchs, Fuchs, and Maxwell (1988), and Marston and Deno (1982). These studies demonstrated that CBA results correlated with standardized group-administered instruments at levels ranging from .59 to .91. The studies used such measures as Stanford Achievement Test reading subtest, Science Research Associates reading subtest, and the California Achievement Test to obtain reliability coefficients and criterion-related validity. Bain and Garlock (1992) conducted a cross validation study, evaluating the locally developed CBA procedures across curriculum and standardized achievement measures. The results yield positive correlations at the .05 level of significance across two schools and three grade levels.

Such reliability and validity scores have prompted investigators to explore the application of CBA instrumentation as tools to integrate and reintegrate populations with disabilities in the general population. Past efforts at placing students with disabilities into the normalized environment have yielded disappointing outcomes and have generated caution and reluctance on the part of teachers and school administrators. During the 1980s and early 1990s, investigators (Deno, Marston, Shinn, & Tindal, 1983; Shinn & Marston, 1985; Shinn, Tindal, Spira, & Marston, 1985) sought to establish standards by which they could assess the school readiness of a student with disabilities. The original argument suggested that students with disabilities who achieved at the 50th percentile of the general school population could function satisfactorily in the regular inclusive classroom. Others have challenged the 50th percentile assumption, questioning why students with disabilities must achieve at or above the level of one half of the local school population. Others have indicated (Shinn, Habedank, Rodden-Nord, & Knutson, 1993) that the CBA tests standardized on local populations could be used to place students with disabilities who are functioning at a ''satisfactory'' level. The objective criterion for ''satisfactory'' has remained undefined by both investigators and the courts (*Board of Education v. Rowley*, 1992) but appears to suggest a level that is lower than average, or below the 50th percentile. Allen (1989) suggests that the placement and reintegration could be based on minimal skill levels.

Shinn et al. (1993) conducted two studies to determine whether special education children at the elementary level could qualify for general education placement based on the criterion of ''satisfactory'' performance. The investigators found at the ideographic (individual student) performance level that 36 to 40 percent of the students in grades 1–5 met the criteria at or better than at least one student in the general education program. These data were supported by a nomothetic (group) analysis that yielded similar results. The data indicate that a large portion of the special education population could potentially function successfully in the general education environment with low-performing peers.

One major argument for CBA is the phenomenon that one characteristic students with disabilities share is their inability to progress through the school curriculum (Ysseldyke, Thurlow, Graden, Wesson, Algozzine, & Deno, 1983). Howell and Caros (1992) concluded that the population also exhibits deficits in prior knowledge and skills to perform adequately. One means of resolving the problem is to realign the students' knowledge and skills with the school's curriculum (Howell & Caros, 1992). These authors noted that the essential criterion of any assessment process is the amount of change that results from the findings and subsequent intervention and find that CBA fulfills that promise. Fuchs, Fuchs, Bishop, and Hamlett (1992) concurred with Howell and Caros, finding that CBA is an assessment method for helping educators build more efficacious instructional programs.

To rectify what Fuchs, Fuchs, Bishop, and Hamlett (1992) perceived as deficiencies in the literature, the authors sought to identify and synthesize the findings of studies conducted in general education environments. In this analysis, they noted that studies using primary-level classrooms were investigated using CBA as the assessment tool of choice to assess the level of student performance within a specific curriculum and then to develop appropriate instructional intervention. According to the investigators, general educators were able to implement the CBA process in the classroom, and use of the process yielded growth among the students. Fuchs and coworkers cautioned that general educators require information, explanation, and training in the use and conduct of CBA. Specifically, the investigators reported that general educators required specific assistance in developing appropriate interventions once they had obtained the description of actual curriculum-based student performance.

CBA'S LIMITATIONS

While CBA offers the pragmatic classroom educator and the school administrator a number of benefits, CBA can also be misused. Luftig (1989) cautions educators to consider the following:

First, most CBA tests are not supported by reliability and validity data. Most such tests are constructed by classroom teachers who wish to obtain here-and-now information about a student's current level of performance. Nonstandardized CBA tests are not designed to predict a student's future academic, social, and vocational performance. Thus, nonstandardized CBA tests cannot provide information on the student's level of performance relative to same-age and -grade peers outside the present educational setting.

Second, CBA does involve the expenditure of teacher time to develop, administer, and score a test. A CBA test is usually administered to one student at a time, not a whole group of students who are at approximately the same place at the same time. In comparison to the administration of a standardized test, CBA, at least from the teacher's point of view, can be a labor-intensive process.

Finally, with CBA, when results are obtained the performance of each student must be correlated with a singular set of curriculum materials. To be effective the CBA test must reflect each of the critical learning steps addressed by the curriculum materials. The student is not expected to move on until he or she has mastered each of the steps and their subcomponents. This adds to the time required to test, instruct, and evaluate the learner and his or her progress.

Each of these factors suggests that CBA and standardized tests can be used to realize legitimate social policy and educational objectives. No one approach can be all things to the educational community. This concept must be accepted by the professional educational leadership community if effective and appropriate assessment is to occur consistently. The following recommendations are designed to bring about this change in perspective and practice:

First, we need to modify the mind-set of school personnel and policy makers who believe that the primary purpose of assessment is to rank students in relationship to one another in order to illustrate the quality of schooling, instruction, and placement of students.

Second, we need to overcome the reluctance of school psychologists, administrators, teachers, and other support personnel to learn how to employ new tools and skills in the areas of assessment and instructional development.

Third, we must persuade all participants in the educational process to evaluate students based on the skills they have mastered rather than a student's class ranking or grades.

Fourth, we need to focus on the daily performance of each student as well as his or her long-term potential.

Fifth, we must recognize that the information obtained via continuous assessment by school personnel is just as relevant and germane to the student's placement and instruction as the annual year-end measure of student achievement and school performance.

These five recommendations will take time and resources to implement successfully. Training, demonstration, and leadership will promote more appropriate assessment and instruction and ultimately improve student performance.

The inappropriate use of standardized tests and CBA will undermine services and support for children and youths with disabilities. It is time to become more knowledgeable about the benefits and drawbacks of each assessment procedure. Students, families, and policy makers must be assured that the assessment of choice effectively interfaces with classroom materials, instructional strategies, and student performance within and outside the school's perimeter.

REFERENCES

Allen, D. (1989). Periodic and annual reviews and decisions to terminate special education services. In M. R. Shinn (Ed.), *Curriculum based measurement: Assessing special children* (pp. 184–203). New York: Guilford.

Bain, S. K., & Garlock, J. W. (1992). Cross-validation of Criterion-Related Validity for CBM reading passages. *Diagnostique, 17,* 202–208.

Blankenship, C. S. (1985). Linking assessment to curriculum and instruction. In J. F. Cawley (Ed.), *Practical mathematics: Appraisal of the learning disabled* (pp. 59–79). Rockville, MD: Aspen Systems Corporation.

Board of Education v. Rowley, 458 U.S. 176 (1982).

Brandon, J. I. (1988). Alternative educational delivery approaches: Implications for school psychology. In J. L. Graden, J. E. Zins, & M. C. Curtis (Eds.), *Alternative educational delivery systems: Enhancing instructional options for all students* (pp. 563–571). Washington, DC: National Association of School Psychologists.

Cantor, A. (1991). Effective psychological services for all students: A data based model of service delivery. In G. Stoner & M. R. Walker (Eds.), *Interventions for achievement and behavior problems* (pp. 49–78). Silver Springs, MD: National Association of School Psychologists.

Deno, S. L., Marston, D., Shinn, M. R., & Tindal, G. (1983). Oral reading fluency: A simple datum for scaling reading disabilities. *Topics in Learning and Learning Disabilities, 2,* 53–59.

Deno, S. L., Mirkin, P. K., & Chiang, B. (1982). Identifying validity measures of reading. *Exceptional Children, 49*, 36–45.

Diana v. State Board of Education, Civ. Act. No. C-70–37 (N.D. Cal. 1970, further order, 1973).

Ferguson, C., & Fuchs, L. S. (1991). Scoring accuracy within curriculum-based measurement: A comparison of teachers and microcomputers. *Journal of Special Education Technology, 11*(1), 26–32.

Fuchs, L. S., Fuchs, D., Bishop, N., & Hamlett, C. L. (1992). Classwide decision-making strategies with curriculum-based measurement. *Diagnostique, 18*(1), 39–52.

Fuchs, L. S., Fuchs, D., Hamlett, C. L., & Ferguson, C. (1992). Effects of expert system consultation within curriculum-based measurement using a reading maze task. *Exceptional Children, 58*, 436–450.

Fuchs, L. S., Fuchs, D., & Maxwell, S. (1988). The validity of informal reading comprehension measures. *Remedial and Special Education, 9*(2), 20–28.

Greenwood, C. R., & Rieth, H. J. (1994). Current dimensions of technology-based assessment in special education. *Exceptional Children, 16*(2), 105–113.

Hobson v. Hansen, 269 F. Supp. 401, 514 (D.D.C. 1967), aff'd. sub nom. Smuck v. Hobson, 408, F.2d 175 (D.C. Cir. 1969).

Howell, K. W., & Caros, J. S. (1992). The application of curriculum-based evaluation to social skills. *Diagnostique, 18*(1), 53–68.

Howell, K. W., & Morehead, M. K. (1987). *Curriculum based evaluation for special and remedial education.* Columbus, OH: Charles E. Merrill.

Jenkins, J. R., Jewell, M., Leceister, N., Jenkins, L., & Troutner, N. (1990). *Development of a school building model for educationally handicapped and at risk students in regular education classrooms.* Paper presented at the American Educational Research Association, Boston.

Jensen, A. R. (1980). *Bias in mental testing.* New York: Free Press.

Jones, E. D., & Krouse, J. P. (1988). The effectiveness of data-based instruction by student teachers in the classroom for pupils with mild handicaps. *Teacher Education and Special Education, 11*(1), 9–19.

Larry P. v. Riles, 343, F. Supp. 1306, aff'd., 502 F.2d 963, further proceedings, 495 F. Supp. 926, aff'd., 502, F.2d 693 (9th Cir. 1984).

Luftig, R. L. (1989). *Assessment of learners with special needs.* Boston, MA: Allyn and Bacon.

Marston, D. (1989). A curriculum-based measurement approach to assessing academic performance: What it is and why do it. In M. Shinn (Ed.), *Curriculum-based measurement: Assessing special children* (pp. 18–78). New York: Guilford Press.

Marston, D., & Deno, S. L. (1982). *Implementation of direct and repeated measurement in the school setting* (Research Report No. 106). Minneapolis: University of Minnesota Institute for Research on Learning Disabilities.

McLoughlin, J. A., & Lewis, R. B. (1990). *Assessing special students* (3rd ed.). Columbus, OH: Merrill Publishing Company.

Mercer, C. D., & Mercer, A. R. (1989). *Teaching students with learning problems* (3rd ed.) New York: Macmillan.

Moss, P. A. (1992). Shifting conceptions in educational measurement: Implications for performance assessment. *Review of Educational Research, 62*(3), 229–258.

Moss, P. A., Beck, J. S., Ebbs, C., Herter, R., Matson, B., Muchmore, J., Steele, D., & Taylor, C. (1991). *Further enlarging the assessment dialogue: Using portfolio to communicate beyond the classroom.* Paper presented at the annual meeting of the American Educational Research Association, Chicago.

Phillips, N. B., Hamlett, C. L., Fuchs, L. S., and Fuchs, D. (1993). Combining classroom curriculum-based measurement and peer tutoring to help general educators provide adaptive education. *Learning Disabilities Research and Practice, 8*(3), 148–156.

Salvia, J., & Ysseldyke, J. E. (1985). *Assessment: In special and remedial education* (3rd ed.). Boston, MA: Houghton Mifflin.

Shinn, M. R., Habedank, L., Rodden-Nord, K., & Knutson, N. (1993). Using curriculum-based measurement to identify potential candidates for reintegration into general education. *Journal of Special Education, 27*(2), 202–221.

Shinn, M. R., & Marston, D. (1985). Differentiating mildly handicapped, low achieving, and regular education students: A curriculum based approach. *Remedial and Special Education, 6,* 31–38.

Shinn, M. R., & McConnell, S. (1994). Improving general education instruction: Relevance to school psychologists. *School Psychology Review, 23*(3), 351–353.

Shinn, M. R., Tindal, G., Spira, D., & Marston, D. (1987). Learning disabilities as a social policy. *Learning Disabilities Quarterly, 10,* 17–28.

Turnbull III, H. R. (1986). *Free appropriate education: The law and children with disabilities.* Denver, CO: Love Publishing Company.

Ysseldyke, J. E., Thurlow, M., Graden, J., Wesson, C., Algozzine, B., & Deno, S. (1983). Generalization from five years of research on assessment and decision making: The University of Minnesota Institute. *Exceptional Education Quarterly, 1,* 75–93.

15

Employment Testing in Private Industry

Wanda J. Campbell and David J. Kleinke

ASSESSING CLIENT NEEDS

One of the first lessons that you learn when you make the transition from academe to testing in the private sector is that tests are tools. Organizations want tests that identify competent people, don't have adverse impact, don't offend anyone, look like tests should look, don't cost a lot of money, and can be developed quickly. The job of a corporate psychologist is to find a comfortable balance in meeting these goals, which may at times be in conflict. Personal allegiances to any particular selection tool quickly fall by the wayside if the test cannot meet many of these criteria.

In this chapter, we are going to describe some of the ways corporate psychologists have been performing these balancing acts. We will describe some of what we and our colleagues have learned along the way.

What Kind of Test Is Best for the Particular Need?

When you are faced with a need for a selection instrument, the first issue is what type of test should be used. Resolving this issue is not about reliability and validity. Certainly, reliability and validity are important in evaluating selection instruments; however, there are a number of different testing technologies that can produce reliable and valid tests. Your responsibility is to find the technology that will best meet the needs of your client.

Therefore, your first job is to find out what the client's needs are. What are the problems? Are the people selected unable to complete the training program?

If so, is the problem lack of specialized knowledge, such as knowledge of electrical principles, or is the problem lack of basic skills? These kinds of problems could be addressed with job knowledge or cognitive ability tests, respectively. Another problem may be that the candidates are bright enough, but their interpersonal skills are atrocious, and the company is losing business because of it. In this case, the answer might be some type of work sample, perhaps role-play exercises. Still another problem could be that the employees are having too many job-related injuries. People are dropping equipment or hurting themselves lifting. The solution may be some type of physical ability test to ensure that those selected have the strength to perform the required tasks.

As you listen to your client describe his or her needs, try to get a feel for the demands placed on the client. Try to understand exactly what the problem is that you are trying to solve and what consequences are likely to result from different courses of action. If the client needs to hire large numbers of people in the next four to six weeks and you don't already have a testing process in place, you need to find a way to meet the deadline. Doing a full-blown job analysis and developing your own customized test battery is not a viable alternative. One solution is to observe incumbents performing the job; read the job descriptions, specifications, and training material; and interview job incumbents and supervisors about job requirements. Depending on your other job commitments, you may or may not be able to put together a task inventory for supervisors and incumbents to complete. Based on the information available, you then could review off-the-shelf tests and choose the best one for your purposes. It is quite possible that the test you buy will not be as good as the one you could construct yourself. That is immaterial. If the client truly needs to have the hiring done in six weeks, then a perfect test delivered in six months is useless. An off-the-shelf test is a viable, if less-than-perfect, alternative.

This scenario illustrates a rite of passage for corporate psychologists. Businesses seldom need the best product possible. They need a product that will work within the prescribed parameters. Factors such as time and money are often more critical factors in the decision process than a potential marginal increase in validity or elegance.

As you learn about your clients' needs, you should also be paying attention to their preferences. Does this client prefer computer-administered tests as opposed to paper-and-pencil tests? Does that client want a videotape format? You may not always be able to meet their needs and wants, but you increase the odds dramatically if you begin by talking to the client. It's also a lot easier to maintain the testing function if you get the reputation for trying to meet your clients' needs.

Another factor to consider when selecting among various employment tests is the organization's history and culture regarding testing. We are all limited by what came before us, both positive and negative. If the organization discontinued using a particular personality inventory because it asked about sexual orientation or religious beliefs, you will probably find it difficult to introduce another personality inventory, even if the instrument you want to introduce avoids these types of items. By the same token, if one of your clients has had a great deal of success with a work sample, don't be surprised if you get more requests for work samples. Your clients are your best protectors and most vocal opponents in your struggle for survival in the changing work environment.

The section that follows describes some of the selection instruments that are used in private industry. The primary focus will be on describing the advantages and disadvantages of the approaches while also providing practical advice in developing and using the instruments.

SURVEY OF POPULAR SELECTION TECHNIQUES

Cognitive Ability Test

By far, the most popular type of valid selection technique is the cognitive ability test. Although the components change as a function of the results of the job analysis, this type of test is used more widely within and across organizations employing industrial psychologists than any other assessment tool.

Cognitive ability tests have much to recommend them. They are relatively easy to develop and validate. The constructs typically measured by cognitive ability tests (e.g., reading comprehension, mathematical ability) are well established, and the technology for developing these types of tests is well developed. Hunter and Hunter (1984) indicate that for entry-level jobs no other predictor can equal the validity of these tests.

Paper-and-pencil cognitive ability tests are cost-effective in that large numbers of candidates may be tested simultaneously. There are few other selection techniques that may be administered with a ratio of 15 or more candidates to 1 test administrator.

Still another benefit of cognitive tests is the case of maintaining standardization. Everyone takes the same test; everyone has the same amount of time; and there is no room for rater bias in the scoring. Using optical scanners and computer scoring reduces the possibility of scoring errors and enables the user to scan and score tests within hours of administration.

Cognitive ability tests are not without their detractors. The biggest concern is probably the adverse impact of these batteries. Most cognitive batteries have adverse impact against some minorities, and some tests have adverse impact against women. While psychologists are as eager as anyone else to eliminate adverse impact, the popularity of cognitive ability tests is a testament to their effectiveness. Psychologists understand the difference between adverse impact and illegal discrimination. As long as the cognitive ability tests are valid for all groups of people, it is likely that they will remain popular, despite their adverse impact.

Another criticism of cognitive ability tests is that they generally have less acceptability, or "face validity," than work samples. This criticism is true to varying degrees, depending on the job and test batteries. One option for increasing the face validity of some types of cognitive ability tests is to engineer job components into the testing environment. For example, tests of reading ability could use job-relevant terminology in the reading passages. An even better solution would be to extract reading material from training or work manuals for the passages in reading tests. In general, the greater the face validity, the easier it is to sell the test to the relevant parties—management, labor unions, and job candidates.

Computer-Administered Tests. The newest refinement to the cognitive ability tests has been their conversion from paper to computer. Some of the benefits of this transition have been increased assurance that test administration procedures are standardized, enhanced test security, and instantaneous and error-free computation and storage of test scores. A practical benefit of computer-administered tests is that the technology causes the test to be viewed by many relevant parties as "state of the art," even if the only difference is the method of administration.

Another, less obvious, benefit of computerized testing is that candidates are able to take as much time as necessary to read the instructions. Therefore, candidates who previously may have been too embarrassed to slow down the rest of the group with questions are now able to take the additional time required to ensure understanding of the directions. Understanding the directions should not be part of the test.

Computer-administered tests have their own set of challenges. First, not all candidates have experience with computers. Therefore, some personal computer training must be made available for candidates who wish it. Providing time for training candidates on computers takes away from the time available to test the candidates, thereby reducing the reliability estimates (Dyer, Desmarais, Midkiff, Colihan, & Olson, 1992). Another problem cited by Dyer et al. is that it takes longer to read from a screen than a paper.

A logistical problem associated with computer-administered tests is that there may be more candidates to test than there are computers. This can happen when a line manager decides to send someone in for testing, and the message never gets delivered to the test administrator. Even when things go as planned, computerized testing can take more administrative time. It takes eight hours to administer a one-hour test to 16 candidates on two computers; by contrast, all of the candidates could be administered a paper-and-pencil test at the same time. Purchasing additional computers and software may be hampered by budget constraints, particularly in this age of downsizing, and borrowing a computer brings with it a whole new set of problems.

Logistics also can be a problem for companies who administer tests at multiple locations. For most companies, multiple locations means purchasing duplicate sets of computers and software. Once again, budget considerations rear their ugly heads. Some companies have tried to cut corners by using the personal computers for other purposes. One problem associated with a multiple-use personal computer is that various users may load up the memory with an assortment of software programs and files that may interfere with the functioning of the test. Other potential problems with not dedicating a computer to employment testing are software interaction effects and test security (Dyer, Desmarais, & Midkiff, 1993). One company solved its hardware problem during validation by the creation of a Mobile Testing Unit, a 40-foot coach equipped with 19 computer workstations and a spare (Midkiff, Dyer, Desmarais, Rogg, & McCusker, 1992).

Administering a test on a computer rather than on paper also opens the door to hardware and software problems. These eventualities dictate the need for a test administrator to be readily available to correct difficulties with dispatch. The testing situation is stressful enough for candidates without introducing a computer troubleshooting component. The candidate is not the only one who is distressed by computer difficulties during test administration. Test administrators can also become frustrated when the software does not seem to operate properly. A solution found by one company is to have an 800 hotline number for dealing with software problems. The person charged with accepting these calls needs an abundance of patience and tact in addition to problem-solving and computer skills. These characteristics often do not come in the same person.

A final issue is the determination of the comparability of paper-and-pencil tests and their computer-administered counterparts. This is particularly difficult when components of the test battery are speeded. One company sidestepped the problem by considering the computer-administered test as a new test, with its own validity, norms, and cutoffs. Equivalency was not attempted. All tests administered prior to an established date were given by paper, and those after the prescribed date were administered on a computer.

Computer-Adaptive Tests. Whereas computer-administered tests simply replicate the paper-and-pencil form of the test, others called ''computer-adaptive tests'' administer test questions based on the candidate's response to the previous question. Questions are calibrated to various difficulty levels, and the software randomly selects questions from prescribed difficulty levels according to the decision rules established. For example, a candidate who correctly responds to a question may be presented with a question from the next-most-difficult level of questions, while a candidate who responds incorrectly might move to a less difficult set of questions.

Very few organizations have implemented computer adaptive testing. A primary benefit for those who have is the enhanced security associated with the random selection of calibrated items. Although the technology permits the use of different numbers of test questions for different candidates, depending on the number of questions required to determine knowledge or ability level, many organizations have decided to give everyone an equal number of test questions. This decision is influenced by the perceived difficulty in explaining the technology to laymen in the event that the test is challenged in court or in an arbitration.

Administering an equal number of test questions to all candidates eliminates the time-savings advantage associated with computer adaptive tests. Thus far, experience in the field has shown that computer adaptive testing has actually increased the test administration time without any attendant gains in reliability and validity.

Computer adaptive tests are expensive to develop and, like all computerized tests, pose a host of logistical problems for companies. It is too early to tell whether the initial expenditure for test development and implementation will pay off in test security and efficiency in the scoring and storage of test data.

Keyboarding Tests

Keyboarding tests differ from those presented in the previous section in that these tests are skills tests. Many companies are now providing typing tests on a personal computer, although some companies have retained their typewriters and give candidates the choice of taking the test on a typewriter or a personal computer.

The introduction of a computer-based typing test has been dictated by content and face validity issues. There aren't many jobs today where an individual spends very much time typing on a typewriter. Some employers have encountered recent high school graduates who were perplexed about the operation of a typewriter since they were trained on computers.

A difficulty in equating typewriters and computers for keyboarding skills tests is that differences in the equipment may be reflected in the response speed. Would someone be able to type equally fast on both machines? An additional problem is accuracy. It is a lot easier to correct a problem on a computer than it is to correct it on a typewriter.

A related problem is differences in the computer equipment used for testing. Many newer generations of computers are faster than earlier models, and this lack of standardization could affect test results. Similarly, all candidates should be tested using the same type of keyboard. In particular, keyboards for portable computers should be avoided because of differences in the size and spacing of the keys.

A natural progression from the typing test on a computer is a word processing test. This type of test is currently being used by fewer companies than the keyboarding test. These tests tend to come in two forms: those associated with a particular word processing software and those with a generic word processing program. In the generic version, candidates complete a brief training program and practice session to learn the new software before taking the test. The advantage of the generic type of test is that it is not tied to any software program and therefore does not become obsolete with the introduction of new software versions. The disadvantage of the generic type is that candidates skilled in a particular word processing package may experience negative transfer. In addition, some particularly skilled word processors may not pay sufficient attention to the instructions in the generic program, resulting in a low score. Attempts have been made to avoid this last problem by warning candidates of the fact that this software may use different commands than the software with which they are familiar.

Structured Interviews

Next to cognitive ability tests and skills tests, the structured interview is probably the next most popular selection tool. The prevalence of the structured interview is most likely a concession to managers who want an interview before making the hiring decision. Since managers insist on the interview process, despite the long history of poor validity (Hunter & Hunter, 1984; Mayfield, 1964; Ulrich & Trumbo, 1965), steps are taken by psychologists in many organizations to make the process more valid by adding structure (Huffcutt & Arthur, 1994; McDaniel, Whetzel, Schmidt, & Maurer, 1994).

The amount and nature of structure provided to the interviews vary by company. Some of the least formal programs provide guidance on job-related topics to be covered by the interviewer. The more formal structured interviews generally ask candidates to describe a time when they experienced a certain type of situation, the manner in which they handled it, and the result. By dealing with general types of work-related situations, candidates without a great deal of work experience are able to respond to questions. For instance, a candidate with no retail experience may have difficulty describing the handling of an irate customer but could respond to questions concerning the handling of a disagreement or experience dealing with angry people.

Structured interviews have the advantage of being able to tap interpersonal skills that may not be measured in the cognitive ability tests. In addition, the interviews can cover a broad range of experiences. More important, structured interviews help keep the interviewers on track with job-related questions. Providing a guide of questions to follow introduces a higher level of standardization to the process. Because of the guide, interviewers can be confident that they really did ask the same questions of each candidate.

One criticism of the structured interview from the perspective of managers is the diminishment of control. Managers may see themselves as being tied to the process, and the guidelines may be perceived as limitations. One way to avoid this problem is to include influential managers in the process of establishing the parameters and subject of the interview questions. You have to include managers in the process anyway in order to assure job relatedness. Making sure that the most powerful managers are part of the process helps ensure their acceptance as well as the acceptance of their peers.

When building the structured interview, it is necessary to build some room for the manager to follow up on candidate responses that provide valuable insight and information. Neither psychologists nor managers are able to anticipate every line of response. In order to make the system flexible, you have to build in some room to maneuver within the established parameters. This provision is also likely to reduce managerial complaints and ensure that they use the process. Procedures that increase the validity of a test are of no value if they are not used.

Obtaining accurate ratings is never easy, and interviewer ratings from structured interviews are no exception. One option is to include space on the interview guide for interviewer notes on candidate responses and provide a place for the rater to indicate the constructs demonstrated in these responses. Behaviorally anchored rating scales are great if you have the time to develop them. At a minimum, steps should be taken to add behavioral examples for some of the anchors. It is critical that the interviewers be able to conceptualize differences among the various levels of each scale and that they agree on the values.

Situational Judgment Inventories

These paper-and-pencil inventories seem to be used most often for white-collar exempt positions. Situational judgment inventories are particularly relevant for positions involving customer contact but would be useful for any positions that involve human interaction.

Situational judgment inventories possess many of the benefits of cognitive ability tests and structured interviews. In fact, many organizations have based their structured interviews on situations that could constitute a situational judgment inventory. Both techniques collect critical incidents to develop the scenarios and typical responses. Like cognitive ability tests, and unlike situational interviews, situational judgment inventories are inexpensive and efficient to administer (Motowidlo, Dunnette, & Carter, 1990). These inventories are a logical supplement to cognitive ability tests in that they test whether the candidate knows how to behave in a particular situation. They might be viewed as measures of practical intelligence (Motowidlo et al., 1990).

Well-constructed situational judgment inventories can provide insight into the candidate's work ethic, judgment, and a host of other job-related constructs not measured by the cognitive ability tests. It is, therefore, not surprising that many psychologists have found these instruments to add incremental validity to the cognitive ability tests. In addition, some organizations suggest that these inventories may have somewhat less adverse impact than the cognitive ability tests. Research by Motowidlo et al. (1990) indicated that the inventories were valid for whites, blacks, males, and females.

Situational judgment inventories have a great deal of face validity. As such, they have the added benefit of providing a realistic job preview. This enables candidates who are not desperate for a job to self-select out of the selection process if the situations encountered are not appealing. Another definite benefit of the inventories is that the format keeps candidates interested, and they like it. These are very real advantages for those companies where candidates are also customers.

Situational judgment inventories are more tedious and expensive to develop than cognitive ability tests. You need a lot of critical incidents, and each one needs to have a range of responses. In order to reduce problems of social desirability, some psychologists develop options that represent minor distinctions in behavior. The less desirable options should not be overtly so.

Even when attempts have been made to reduce the effect of social desirability, a major concern associated with situational judgment inventories is that the candidates will not actually behave in the same way as indicated in the inventory. At least one company has overcome this problem by pairing the situational job inventory with role-playing exercises. The situational judgment inventory identifies the candidates who know what to do, and the subsequent role-plays determine whether the candidate's behavior reflects this knowledge. Since role-play exercises are very labor-intensive, the less expensive situational judgment inventory serves as a valuable screen.

Another limitation of situational judgment inventories is that the responses to the problem are limited by the response options provided. The instrument does not measure particularly creative responses. This is one more reason to supplement these inventories with structured interviews, role-plays, or both.

The next section will deal with assessment centers, which provided much of the knowledge that we have acquired concerning role-plays and other work samples.

Assessment Centers

Assessment centers have traditionally been used for the selection of managers and sales staff. Increasingly, assessment centers are being used for developmental purposes. There are a number of explanations for this transition. One explanation is that many organizations promote current employees into management positions. Current employees and their supervisors can become quite hostile when told that the assessment center results indicate that the employee is not currently a good candidate for promotion. Often, the supervisor has publicly praised the employee sent for assessment. If the assessment center subsequently pronounces the employee unfit for promotion, the supervisor's judgment comes into question. If the supervisor has political power, questions are predictably raised concerning the accuracy and value of assessment center evaluations. Even if the balance of power is such that the assessment center is able to survive repeated attacks by supervisors, the assessment center often operates under a cloud of suspicion.

Those companies that continue to use assessment centers for selection as well as developmental purposes generally have substantial managerial support. An ideal situation is when the managers within the company have been promoted to their positions as a result of their performance in the assessment center. This tends to reduce their questions about the validity of the process. Obviously, the assessment center must operate for some time to reach this stage. A strategy to get to this point is to use influential managers as assessors.

Many organizations who have continued using assessment centers for selection have reduced the number of exercises. This reduction, like the elimination of many assessment centers, has probably been prompted by cost considerations. By carefully evaluating the exercises and retaining only those that measure constructs that cannot be measured less expensively, some companies have improved the cost efficiency of their selection procedures. The exercises most likely to be included are role-plays and in-baskets.

Group exercises are less popular for selection purposes because of the inability to provide a standardized testing environment. The composition of the group influences the behavior exhibited and the evaluation. One costly solution is to have assessors function in prescribed roles as members of the group. Another alternative is to simply use group exercises for developmental purposes.

One newcomer to the exercises is the multimedia or video exercise. Candidates watch a videotape that is stopped at prescribed spots. The candidate then is asked to read material, write a response, or in some other way respond to the situation portrayed in the videotape.

Despite the changes made to the particular form of the assessment center, one enduring characteristic of this approach is that it measures actual candidate behavior and it predicts subsequent job performance (Hunter & Hunter, 1984; Schmitt, Gooding, Noe, & Kirsch, 1984). You don't have to guess what the candidate will do. Another advantage of assessment centers is that they have a great deal of face validity. The exercises look like the jobs, which makes the job of selling the technique to managers and candidates a bit easier.

The operation of an assessment center requires a great deal of work as well as money. A lot of time and money goes into the training and supervision of the assessors. Training assessors for a single exercise may be accomplished in a day, but training for a one-day assessment center normally takes three to five days. The assessors must become so familiar with the exercises and the scripts of prescribed behaviors that they can behave in a consistent manner across candidates. Assessors need to know what they can and cannot do, and they need to know it so well that they can convincingly assume the prescribed role. In addition to the exercises, the candidates must learn the constructs and be able to distinguish among different levels of the constructs.

It is important to remember that when assessors are being trained, retrained, or performing assessments, they are not performing their regular jobs. This commitment of time poses a particular problem if most of the assessments are performed by a small group of "expert" assessors. Many departments within organizations are unwilling to part with their best people for extended periods of time. By contrast, there are some less capable individuals whose services would be made readily available, and assessment center managers must keep alert to the quality of the proposed assessors. Organizers of assessment centers need to decide whether the centers will operate full-time or on an as-needed basis. If the assessment centers are operated sporadically at regional locations, the loss of management time to the assessor role becomes less troublesome, but the concern of maintaining the skill level of the assessor arises. Optimally, assessors need to perform their role often enough to remain proficient but infrequently enough to avoid interfering with their regular responsibilities. One organization suggested that four assessments a year was a good balance. Many of the companies who have retained the assessment center as a selection tool have moved to conducting assessments periodically.

The location of the assessment center also influences the cost. A central location for the operation of the assessment center often means that the location has limited use for other purposes since the facilities are frequently used for assessment. This may mean that food and lodging must be provided for assessors and candidates. If the assessments are conducted in regional centers, they are probably operated less frequently, and it may be possible for the assessment suite to double as a conference center. The operation of regional assessment centers also reduces costs associated with housing and feeding candidates and assessors.

All of these problems are greatly simplified when the assessment is reduced to one or two exercises. This reduction in exercises means that assessors need less training, each assessor can evaluate more candidates in a short period of time, and assessors have an easier time maintaining their expertise.

One of the most damaging criticisms of assessment centers is that the consensus ratings are based on assessors' reports concerning what happened during the exercises. Having a group of assessors agree on ratings on an exercise after they all hear the same report is not the same thing as the group reaching agreement after all assessors have viewed the candidate in the exercise. This criticism is also apt for ratings made across exercises. A related concern is that each assessor's report may be influenced by the assessor's role in the exercise. The perception of assessors may be affected by the assessor's role as observer versus participant. These problems can be reduced by creating audiotapes of each exercise and randomly checking tapes to ensure quality control.

Biodata

Biodata inventories are a natural progression from the job application blank. The rationale is that one's life experiences can predict subsequent job performance and that a multiple choice questionnaire covering life experiences related to job performance could be used as a supplement to or alternative to cognitive ability tests.

Biodata inventories have a long history of successful use as a selection device for insurance agents (Brown, 1978; Dalessio & Silverhart, 1994; Thayer, 1977). The technique has been widely recognized as a valid technique for employee selection (Hunter & Hunter, 1984; Reilly & Chao, 1982; Schmitt et al., 1984). A number of organizations have achieved a great deal of success using the technique to predict productivity and turnover.

Some of the companies that have been particularly pleased with their biodata inventories developed them using an empirical approach and then performed factor analyses to gain a better understanding of the underlying constructs responsible for success. Increasingly, the trend seems to be to try to combine the best of the empirical and rational approaches.

Advantages associated with biodata inventories are that they are easy to administer, may be used to measure constructs not tapped by cognitive ability tests, and tend to have less adverse impact than cognitive tests. The fact that usage is not more widespread may be attributable to the discovery of other techniques with similar advantages (e.g., situational judgment inventories) or to some of the difficulties that are discussed in the following paragraphs.

One substantial problem with biodata inventories is that very large samples are required to develop the questionnaires. Hunter and Hunter (1984) suggest 400 to 1,000 participants, and these estimates have been confirmed by some current users. In addition, those inventories that are empirically developed need to be rekeyed every few years (Hunter & Hunter, 1984; Reilly & Chao, 1982). Thus, the use of biodata instruments entails a recurring developmental expense.

A second problem encountered with biodata inventories is that candidates are not always forthright in their responses. Goldstein (1971) and Weiss and Dawis (1960) reported substantial response bias, while Cascio (1975) and Mosel and Cozan (1952) found little response bias. The question for practitioners is, When can we trust what the candidates tell us?

Kluger, Reilly, and Russell (1991) suggested that some candidates' tendency toward response bias may be thwarted by keying each response option for each item. Candidates inclined toward a social desirability bias chose more extreme responses, which may not receive the most weight with this system.

Stokes, Hogan, and Snell (1993) found substantial differences in the biodata keys developed for incumbents and applicants. The largest difference between applicants and incumbents was the significantly higher level of socially desirable responses by applicants. Examination of the content of items disclosed few differences between applicants and incumbents on categories of items that were more objective and verifiable.

These findings fit with many experiences of psychologists in the field. As a group, applicants often have higher biodata scores than the job incumbents when items are not verifiable. Thus, incumbent samples are not always optimal for developing biodata instruments for applicant populations. To reduce problems with social desirability bias, Gandy (personal communication, January 18, 1996) has recommended writing items to enhance the appearance of verifiability and using option level analyses for keying.

Another solution for dealing with social desirability bias is to incorporate scales designed to detect such responses. While such scales may provide insight for purposes of selection, it poses a problem when feedback is given. Gandy (personal communication, January 18, 1996) has suggested that the problem may be dealt with by advising the candidate of ''difficulties associated with some of the responses'' and suggesting that the candidate retake the inventory. When the candidate is a displaced union employee, the feedback problem is magnified. One company has ceased using a "social desirability scale" as a settlement of a union grievance.

A final problem with biodata inventories that are less objective is that some candidates dislike the questions and view them as an invasion of their privacy. The questions often lack face validity, and it is sometimes difficult to provide a satisfactory explanation without giving clues concerning the most desirable response. Once again, items that have the appearance of being job related and verifiable (in addition to being empirically job related) may provide a solution.

Many of the issues that have been covered with respect to biodata inventories also apply to personality tests.

Personality Tests

Some organizations employing industrial psychologists have been reluctant to employ personality tests outside of situations involving safety considerations. The exceptions are the assessment of candidates for positions involving teamwork and the individual assessment of high-level managers. Much of this reluctance probably has been fueled by early unfavorable reviews (Guion & Gottier, 1965; Schmitt et al., 1984). Recent research, particularly that focusing on the "Big Five" personality factors (Norman, 1963), has been more optimistic about the value of personality testing (Barrick & Mount, 1991; Hough, 1991; Hough, Eaton, Dunnette, Kamp, & McCloy, 1990; Ones, Mount, Barrick, & Hunter, 1994; Tett, Jackson, & Rothstein, 1991; Tett, Jackson, Rothstein, & Reddon, 1994). The construct Conscientiousness appears to have consistent success in predicting job and training proficiency for a range of occupations (Barrick & Mount, 1991). Personality measures have also been used to predict counterproductive behavior such as turnover and shrinkage (Paajanen, 1986, 1988).

Personality tests have the advantage of measuring constructs that are not typically measured by cognitive ability tests (McCrae & Costa, 1987). As such, they should add incremental validity and have the benefit of reduced adverse impact. These tests are typically administered as paper-and-pencil tests, which means that they are efficient and inexpensive to administer to large groups of candidates.

A major concern with personality tests is the lack of face validity. At least one psychologist has told me that a personality test was found to be effective, but it was impossible to convince the management to implement it. Tests that lack face validity may be more susceptible to legal and union challenges than those that look like the job.

Personality tests may be problematic when it comes to feedback. People are not readily expected to be able to make drastic changes in their personality, so feedback is likely to be of little developmental value in terms of the particular job sought. Feedback may be useful in making suggestions regarding alternative career paths. Feedback for career planning makes sense when the candidates tested are current employees displaced by reorganization. Most organizations would not be willing to devote the time and expense necessary to provide substantial feedback to outside candidates.

Another concern of many practitioners is that some applicants may distort their responses to enhance their chances of gaining employment. Research indicates that individuals are able to distort their responses in the desired direction (Hough et al., 1990; Schwab, 1971) and that scales may be developed to detect such bias (Hough et al., 1990). Such scales may be employed with greater ease when dealing with outside applicants who are provided with minimal feedback. Current employees interested in promotion or movement across job families generally require much more feedback. Many employees and union officials are able to translate "Social Desirability" scales into the less attractive, more easily understood "Lie" scale. If you are going to deny a displaced employee a job because of the results of a "Social Desirability" scale, you need very good evidence that the scale works.

Other legal concerns with some personality tests are questions of invasion of privacy and the interpretation of personality tests as medical exams. Concerns regarding invasion of privacy may be minimized to the extent that the personality instrument appears to be job related. If the questions asked appear reasonable to the job candidates, they may be less likely to seek redress. Research by Rosse, Miller, and Stecher (1994) suggest that applicants react more positively to personality testing when it is used in conjunction with cognitive ability tests.

Another argument in favor of designing items in personality tests that appear to be job related is that it may reduce the chance that the test battery is viewed as a medical exam. The identification of certain scales as measuring constructs typically associated with clinical evaluation could be unfortunate if you are faced with a charge of discrimination under the Americans with Disabilities Act (ADA). Another category of tests that has been greatly affected by the passage of the ADA is that of physical ability tests.

Physical Ability Tests

The passage of the Americans with Disabilities Act and the elimination of group norms in the amendments to the Civil Rights Act caused many companies to eliminate their physical ability tests. Prior to this legislation, many companies employed physical ability tests to measure strength and stamina for blue-collar jobs. Some who have continued using the tests have moved the placement of the tests from preoffer to postoffer. The advantage of administering the test postoffer is that it can be administered after the candidate has been provided with a physical, thereby reducing the chance of injury during the administration of the physical ability test.

Other companies have continued to administer the physical ability test preoffer but have had candidates sign waivers relieving the company of responsibility in the event of injury. Another option to reduce liability is to have the candidate have his or her physician provide a note indicating the conditions under which the physical ability test may be administered. One concern with this latter alternative is that physicians may not be well informed on aspects of labor law and may provide information that goes beyond that requested. Not having an awareness of the existence of a disability is advantageous for employers if no accommodations are required during employment testing. If you don't know about the existence of the disability, you can't use it as a basis for an adverse employment decision.

CONSTRUCTION OF A SELECTION PROCESS

Choosing among Selection Techniques

Developing a selection process is a bit like a judgmental regression process. The criteria determining whether a selection technique enters the selection equation and stays there are the acceptability to the organization and the validity. Acceptability to the organization includes face validity, cost, ease of administration, and whether the technique meets perceived needs.

The first selection tool to enter the process is the interview. The presence of an interview is nonnegotiable and supersedes even cognitive ability tests in the weight organizations attach to its value. Typically, the second technique to enter the process is the cognitive ability test. Cognitive ability tests have wide generalizability and are cost-effective. Many organizations end the process here. In order for another technique to enter the process, it must be organizationally acceptable and add enough incremental validity to justify the investment of time and money. It is at this point that the trade-offs are made among techniques.

After selecting the components of a selection process, the next step is to determine the order. Cognitive ability tests are probably the most defensible and cost-effective selection technique available. These tests are used early in the process because organizations need to have an inexpensive technique for reducing the number of candidates considered. The importance of the defensibility is that the highest percentage of candidates are rejected at this stage. Biodata inventories are often used in conjunction with cognitive ability tests, although some organizations have introduced them as weighted applications blanks, thereby preceding even the cognitive ability tests.

Situational judgment inventories typically follow cognitive ability tests and precede more interactive selection techniques. The reason that such inventories would tend to follow cognitive ability tests is that there is greater room for speculation concerning the correct response. Also, there is no reason to waste the time and money administering a situational judgment inventory to candidates who do not possess sufficient ability to successfully complete the cognitive component.

After traditional paper-and-pencil tests are administered (either via paper or computer), interactive techniques tend to be introduced. Interactive tests include interviews, role-plays, or assessment centers. In all of these cases, the cost of administration is high, as the ratio of interviewer/rater/administer to candidate is 1 to 1 or more. Within this group of techniques, the interview typically occurs last, and sometimes there is more than one. This provides a final opportunity for each side to take the measure of the other before making a commitment.

Internal versus External Development of Test Batteries

Once decisions have been made regarding the types of tests to be used, decisions must be made regarding whether the tests will be custom-made or off-the-shelf and who will provide the tests.

Off-the-shelf tests have the advantage of quick and relatively inexpensive implementation but will not be tailored to the particular needs of the organization. A less obvious problem with off-the-shelf tests is that the more popular tests may provide security and legal risks. The more companies that use a particular test, the greater the risk that a copy of the test will find its way into the hands of a potential candidate. Another problem is that the more companies that use a test, the greater the exposure to challenges by government agencies, plaintiffs in lawsuits, and labor unions. An adverse court decision involving a test will probably result in a higher number of challenges, even when the basis for the action is something other than test characteristics. Candidates are more likely to recall the result than the particular facts that led to the adverse decision.

If an organization chooses to develop customized tests, the next question is whether the test should be developed internally or externally. This decision is largely determined by whether the organization possesses the expertise and manpower to perform the work internally. If the organization anticipates legal or union activity with respect to the implementation or use of a test, it may be wise to spend the extra money and have the test developed by a recognized expert in the field.

Some organizations prefer to develop the test internally. Tests that are developed internally typically are less expensive; provide greater control over the process; and provide greater flexibility to handle last-minute changes. The knowledge of internal staff of political realities and alliances also can expedite test development and implementation.

Developing tests internally also has some drawbacks. Internal development generally takes longer, because most organizations do not have staff that can be dedicated to a particular project. Most corporate psychologists have competing demands, and difficult decisions must be made regarding priorities. Two problems that are more difficult to overcome are the lack of objectivity of internal staff and heightened security concerns on the part of the participants in the validation research.

Increasingly, organizations are working in partnership with external consultants. Each side performs those functions for which they are best suited. Internal staff are often involved with the development of sampling plans and identification of individuals to be included in the validation research, while external consultants often serve as the destination for tests administered and criterion data. In these situations, it is generally advantageous to have internal staff review all material before it is distributed in the organization and attend all meetings between the consultants and the organizational representatives. Internal staff are in a better position to identify potential trouble spots specific to their organization. The attendance of internal staff at meetings serves as a sign of their support for the project and also ensures that misunderstandings are kept to a minimum.

When entering into a contract with an external consultant, you need to spell out in specific detail the products and services to be provided by each party; the time limits for each phase of the product development; charges for each aspect of the work; and consequences for missed deadlines. Some psychologists negotiate into their contracts cost reductions to accompany any missed deadlines. Partnerships with consultants are improved to the extent that clear two-way communication occurs on a regular basis.

Labor Union Considerations

When current, union-represented employees are given selection instruments as part of the bidding process, their local unions can become very interested. Typical collective bargaining agreements specify that jobs be given to the most senior qualified bidder. Determining seniority is generally a routine decision. The problems arise when the company wishes to use a formal selection procedure. "Qualified" then equates to "can pass the test." Local unions tend to see this as threatening the seniority system. They would substitute "has been rated 'acceptable' by supervisor" for "qualified."

This is not the forum for arguing the merits of current job performance appraisal, particularly for predicting performance in the next job. Our concern here is that using a selection procedure to identify a "qualified" bidder requires that there be a cutoff score. Setting that score must be responsive to the interpretation that it defines job qualification.

When the selection procedure is used for outside applicants as well as internal bidders, new considerations arise. The same cutoff score must be applied to both groups. Some managers have suggested that lower cutoffs be applied for internal candidates than for external ones. Their reasoning is that the employer has more knowledge of the internal candidate and that the employees have invested their time and efforts for the employer. However, any process that makes it more difficult for an external candidate than for an internal one almost certainly maintains or worsens gender or ethnic imbalance in the company's staff. Our experience is that most desirable jobs have disproportionately large numbers of men or whites. To make jobs less available for applicants from the general workforce perpetuates the situation.

Collective bargaining agreements sometimes refer to selection procedures. These may refer to end-of-training achievement or performance tests jointly produced by the union and company. If so, the union may wish to use this provision to gain access to secure materials. This only underscores the need for selection professionals to inform and involve labor relations management as procedures are being developed and implemented.

Test Security and Training of Test Administrators

Test security doesn't have the appeal to many corporate psychologists that development and validation possesses, but it is equally important. The value of a test diminishes rapidly when it becomes accessible to candidates outside of the testing environment. To ensure the security of the tests, many organizations number each test battery and keep a written record tracking the test battery from receipt to destruction. The test batteries are kept locked up, and access outside of the actual administration is limited to test administrators and corporate psychologists.

Organizations differ in whether test storage is centralized or decentralized, but there seems to be a trend for centralization in test scoring. One reason for this is that loss of a scoring key is even more devastating than the loss of a test, particularly for power tests. A second reason is that centralization of scoring may reduce the likelihood of errors in scoring, since the administrators in the central location regularly score tests. A third reason is that storing scored tests and test data in a centralized location is beneficial when responding to legal actions related to the test.

Limiting the access of the test poses some interesting problems for the corporate psychologist. It is not unusual for line managers and executives to request the opportunity to review the test. Organizations are divided on their responses. Some psychologists provide the tests in these circumstances, because they fear that refusal might jeopardize the use of the test in the organization. Others firmly refuse to make tests available to anyone who is not involved with the administration or who is not actually taking the test as part of the employment process.

One disadvantage of providing the test to line managers and executives is that the requesting manager or executive may self-administer the test to "see how well it works." Having to explain to an executive why a test that he or she has failed is a good predictor of job performance is an experience few of us would desire. Another disadvantage of providing the test to management is the concern that the manager may unwittingly provide some clues to candidates concerning how to improve their test performance. In addition to reducing the validity of the test for the candidate receiving the assistance, we also have a situation where other candidates have been treated less beneficially. This may pose equal employment difficulties as well as standardization problems.

Some organizations have prepared brochures describing the test battery and/ or testing process. These brochures may be given to managers and union officials to illustrate the types of questions that appear on the tests without compromising test security. These brochures also serve a good public relations function by providing the candidates with information on what to expect in the testing situation. Anything that can take the mystery out of the process is normally beneficial to all involved. These brochures are particularly beneficial when dealing with candidates who require accommodations under the American with Disabilities Act. The brochures are invaluable in explaining what is involved in the testing situation so that disabled candidates can make informed decisions about the types of accommodations that are required.

A security issue that does not receive a great deal of attention is the training of test administrators. At a minimum, most organizations have a new test administrator observe an experienced administrator, serve as a co-administrator, and then perform the administration under the supervision of the experienced administrator. This training program is supplemented in many organizations by the creation of a test administration manual that sets forth the instructions for test administration and provides guidance for handling various testing situations (e.g., candidate becomes ill during test). The organizations with the best training programs supplement the on-the-job training and testing manual with a full day of training, followed by a test administration test. Successful completion of the training is required before administrators are permitted to handle test materials, administer an employment test, or work with test scores or results. The goal in all of the training is to ensure standardization of test administration and to safeguard the privacy of candidates with respect to test scores and results.

Once the test administrators are trained, steps need to be taken to ensure that they maintain the standards learned during the initial training. A number of organizations have a manager in the testing area periodically observe a testing session to ensure that the test administrator is not deviating from established policy or modifying the prepared script.

Some innovative organizations with large testing programs conduct annual meetings for their test administrators. These meetings provide the testing manager with an opportunity to review important points, bring in relevant speakers, and provide roundtables for discussion of testing issues. In addition, these meetings can serve a team-building function, which is beneficial for individuals on the firing line of test administration.

FUTURE CHALLENGES AND OPPORTUNITIES

Among the challenges and opportunities faced by corporate psychologists are a changing work environment and a changing workforce.

Changing Work Environment

Organizations throughout the country seem to be undergoing reorganization. Many have undergone multiple reorganizations, and some appear to be in a constant state of flux. As a result of the reorganizations, jobs are changing. In order to be responsive to the needs of organizations, psychologists need to reduce the amount of time that is required to analyze jobs and develop valid selection instruments. In the most dynamic environments, the jobs don't last as long as the typical process to develop tests.

One effect of the reorganizations has been the expansion of many employees' jobs. Often jobs are combined, and individual employees now handle entire processes themselves. Sometimes, when varied expertise is required to meet goals, teams of employees from different departments are assembled to respond more efficiently to customer needs. The changing job responsibilities require ever-increasing skill levels, and it is likely that this trend will continue (Johnston, 1987).

In order to keep pace with this changing work environment, Cascio (1995) has suggested that industrial/organizational psychologists need to change their focus when analyzing jobs. Rather than the traditional task-based approach, we need to move to a process-based approach. Focusing on processes would seem to entail an aggregation of tasks into meaningful clusters, which are translated into skill requirements. Rather than analyzing jobs, we would be analyzing job clusters, which may or may not correspond to previous job families. It may be a matter of directing our attention to a greater extent on the commonalities among jobs.

The most obvious commonality among jobs is the effect of g on job performance (Hunter & Hunter, 1984; McHenry, Hough, Toquam, Hanson, & Ashworth, 1990; Olea & Ree, 1994; Schmidt, Gast-Rosenberg, & Hunter, 1980; Schmidt & Hunter, 1980). Based on this research, you could easily conclude that there was no need for even doing job analyses. The only real question often seems to be the degree of complexity and the extent to which g contributes to job performance. One would expect that intelligence levels would have a greater effect on the performance of a vice president than on the performance of the individual's secretary, even though both individuals were performing valuable work.

While many psychologists are impressed with the results of research on validity generalization, the legal community may not share our optimism. If we decide to pursue this approach, we need to be prepared for the daunting task of explaining validity generalization in an understandable fashion to judges and juries, not to mention our own managers.

Increasingly, the skills required to perform many of today's jobs are not merely technical. As employees work together in teams, interpersonal skills are gaining in importance. Borman and Motowidlo (1993) distinguish between task performance and contextual performance. Task performance refers to the job-specific tasks and attendant abilities. Contextual performance refers to those activities that support the organization. Examples of these activities include volunteering to assume additional responsibilities, assisting others who need help, and communicating effectively. Components of contextual performance are not job specific. Therefore, selection instruments designed to measure these constructs would be resilient to job changes.

Changes in the Workforce

Johnston (1987) got the attention of many corporate psychologists with the publication of *Workforce 2000*. One of the concerns raised is a disparity between the low education and skills level of the candidate population and the high skills demanded for the fastest-growing jobs.

One implication of this situation is that members of the corporate world will be competing with each other for the most highly skilled employees. Those psychologists responsible for developing and implementing selection instruments for positions requiring high levels of skills will find that face validity has become even more important. In addition to determining how well a selection tool works, it will become critical that the selection process not be aversive. Work has already begun on candidates' reactions to selection tools (Macan, Avedon, Paese, & Smith, 1994; Rosse et al., 1994; Smither, Reilly, Millsap, Pearlman, & Stoffey, 1993).

Not all of the jobs will require high levels of ability. Johnston (1987) suggested that there will be increases in the demand for employees in the service and retail industries, as well as an increased demand for administrative support. While these are not among the highly skilled occupations, successful job candidates will still need to be able to read, perform elementary mathematical calculations, and follow directions.

Successful performance in positions such as these, like their higher-skilled counterparts, requires personal characteristics in addition to those related to task performance. If employees are dealing with the public, they need to be courteous and be able to communicate. Sometimes, what the employees don't do can also be important. Paajanen (1986, 1988) has been successful in predicting counterproductive behavior. Counterproductive behavior ranges from taking unauthorized breaks to theft and vandalism. More recent work has focused on understanding the multidimensionality of General Work Behavior (Hunt, Hansen, & Paajanen, 1994) and understanding the constructs that distinguish reliable from counterproductive behavior (Hunt, Hansen, & Paajanen, 1995).

As we come to understand more of the factors that contribute to successful performance within and across skill levels, we enhance our ability to identify those characteristics that should be obtained through employment selection and those that can be developed through training.

REFERENCES

Barrick, M. R., & Mount, M. K (1991). The big five personality dimensions and job performance: A meta-analysis. *Personnel Psychology, 44*,1–26.

Borman, W. C., & Motowidlo, S. J. (1993). Expanding the criterion domain to include elements of contextual performance. In N. Schmitt & W. C. Borman (Eds.), *Personnel selection in organizations* (pp. 71–98). San Francisco: Jossey-Bass.

Brown, S. H. (1978). Long-term validity of a personal history item scoring procedure. *Journal of Applied Psychology, 63*, 673–676.

Cascio, W. F. (1975). Accuracy of verifiable biographical information blank responses. *Journal of Applied Psychology, 60*, 767–769.

Cascio, W. F. (1995). Whither industrial and organizational psychology in a changing world of work? *American Psychologist, 50*, 928–939.

Dalessio, A. T., & Silverhart, T. A. (1994). Combining biodata test and interview information: Predicting decisions and performance criteria. *Personnel Psychology, 47*, 303–315.

Dyer, P. J., Desmarais, L. B., & Midkiff, K. R. (1993). Multimedia employment testing in IBM: Preliminary results from employees. In J. J. McHenry (Chair), *Computer and multimedia testing for new skills and abilities: Practical issues*. Symposium conducted at the meeting of the Society for Industrial and Organizational Psychology, San Francisco, CA.

Dyer, P. J., Desmarais, L. B., Midkiff, K. R., Colihan, J. P., & Olson, J. B. (1992). Designing a multimedia test: Understanding the organizational charge, building the team, and making the basic research commitments. In P. J. Dyer (Chair), *Computer-based, multimedia testing: Merging technology, reality and scientific uncertainty*. Symposium conducted at the meeting of the Society for Industrial and Organizational Psychology, Montreal, Quebec.

Goldstein, I. L. (1971). The application blank: How honest are the responses? *Journal of Applied Psychology, 55*, 491–492.

Guion, R. M., & Gottier, R. F. (1965). Validity of personality measures in personnel selection. *Personnel Psychology, 18*, 135–164.

Hough, L. M., Eaton, N. K., Dunnette, M. D., Kamp, J. D., & McCloy, R. A. (1990). Criterion-related validities of personality constructs and the effect of response distortion on those validities. *Journal of Applied Psychology, 75*, 581–595.

Huffcutt, A. I., & Arthur, W., Jr., (1994). Hunter and Hunter (1984) revisited: Interview validity for entry-level jobs. *Journal of Applied Psychology, 79*, 184–190.

Hunt, S. T., Hansen, T. L., & Paajanen, G. E. (1994). Generic work behaviors: The components of non-job specific performance. In F. L. Schmidt (Chair), *The construct of job performance*. Symposium conducted at the meeting of the Society for Industrial and Organizational Psychology, Nashville, TN.

Hunt, S. T., Hansen, T. L., & Paajanen, G. E. (1995). The structure of the Personnel Decisions, Inc. Employment Inventory: An investigation into the anatomy of a valid predictor of reliable work behavior. In J. Hogan (Chair), *Research on employee deviance and unreliability*. Symposium conducted at the meeting of the Society for Industrial and Organizational Psychology, Orlando, FL.

Hunter, J. E., & Hunter, R. F. (1984). Validity and utility of alternative predictors of job performance. *Psychological Bulletin, 96*, 72–98.

Johnston, W. B. (1987). *Workforce 2000: Work and workers for the 21st century*. Indianapolis, IN: Hudson Institute.

Kluger, A. N., Reilly, R. R., Russell, C. J. (1991). Faking biodata tests: Are option-keyed instruments more resistant? *Journal of Applied Psychology, 76*, 889–896.

Macan, T. H., Avedon, M. J., Paese, M., & Smith, D. E. (1994). The effects of applicants' reactions to cognitive ability tests and an assessment center. *Personnel Psychology, 47,* 715–738.

Mayfield, E. C. (1964). The selection interview: A reevaluation of published research. *Personnel Psychology, 17,* 239–260.

McCrae, R. R., & Costa, P. T., Jr. (1987). Validation of the five-factor model of personality across instruments and observers. *Journal of Personality and Social Psychology, 52,* 81–90.

McDaniel, M. A., Whetzel, D. L., Schmidt, F. L., & Maurer, S. D. (1994). The validity of employment interview: A comprehensive review and meta-analysis. *Journal of Applied Psychology, 79,* 599–616.

McHenry, J. J., Hough, L. M., Toquam, J. L., Hanson, M., & Ashworth, S. (1990). Project A validity results: The relationship between predictor and criterion domains. *Personnel Psychology, 43,* 335–354.

Midkiff, K. R., Dyer, P. J., Desmarais, L. B., Rogg, K. L., & McCusker, C. R. (1992). The multimedia test: Friend or foe? In P. J. Dyer (Chair), *Computer-based, multimedia testing: Merging technology, reality and scientific uncertainty.* Symposium conducted at the meeting of the Society for Industrial and Organizational Psychology, Montreal, Quebec.

Mosel, J. L., & Cozan, L. W. (1952). The accuracy of application blank work histories. *Journal of Applied Psychology, 36,* 365–369.

Motowidlo, S. J., Dunnette, M. D., & Carter, G. W. (1990). An alternative selection procedure: The low-fidelity simulation. *Journal of Applied Psychology, 75,* 640–647.

Norman, W. T. (1963). Toward an adequate taxonomy of personality attributes: Replicated factor structure in peer nomination personality ratings. *Journal of Abnormal & Social Psychology, 66,* 574–583.

Olea, M. M., & Ree, M. J. (1994). Predicting pilot and navigator criteria: Not much more than g. *Journal of Applied Psychology, 79,* 845–851.

Ones, D. S., Mount, M. K., Barrick, M. R., & Hunter, J. E. (1994). Personality and job performance: A critique of the Tett, Jackson, and Rothstein (1991) meta-analysis. *Personnel Psychology, 47,* 147–156.

Paajanen, G. E. (1986). *Development and validation of the PDI Employment Inventory.* Paper presented at the annual meeting of the American Psychological Association, Washington, DC.

Paajanen, G. E. (1988). *The prediction of counterproductive behavior by individual and organizational variables.* Unpublished doctoral dissertation, University of Minnesota.

Reilly, R. R., & Chao, G. T. (1982). Validity and fairness of some alternative selection procedures. *Personnel Psychology, 35,* 1–62.

Rosse, J. G., Miller, J. L., & Stecher, M. D. (1994). A field study of job applicants' reactions to personality and cognitive ability testing. *Journal of Applied Psychology, 79,* 987–992.

Schmidt, F. L., Gast-Rosenberg, I., & Hunter, J. E. (1980). Validity generalization results for computer programmers. *Journal of Applied Psychology, 65,* 643–661.

Schmidt, F. L., & Hunter, J. E. (1980). The future of criterion-related validity. *Personnel Psychology, 33,* 41–60.

Schmitt, N., Gooding, R. Z., Noe, R. A., & Kirsch, M. (1984). Meta-analyses of validity studies published between 1964 and 1982 and the investigation of study characteristics. *Personnel Psychology, 37,* 407–422.

Schwab, D. P. (1971). Issues in response distortion studies of personality inventories: A critique and replicated study. *Personnel Psychology, 24*, 637–647.

Smither, J. W., Reilly, R. R., Millsap, R. E., Pearlman, K., & Stoffey, R. W. (1993). Applicant reactions to selection procedures. *Personnel Psychology, 46*, 49–76.

Stokes, G. S., Hogan, J. B., & Snell, A. F. (1993). Comparability of incumbent and applicant samples for the development of biodata keys: The influence of social desirability. *Personnel Psychology, 46*, 739–762.

Tett, R. P., Jackson, D. N., & Rothstein, M. (1991). Personality measures as predictors of job performance: A meta-analytic review. *Personnel Psychology, 44*, 703–742.

Tett, R. P., Jackson, D. N., Rothstein, M., & Reddon, J. R. (1994). Meta-analysis of personality-job performance relations: A reply to Ones, Mount, Barrick, & Hunter (1994). *Personnel Psychology, 47*, 157–172.

Thayer, P. W. (1977). "Somethings old, somethings new." *Personnel Psychology, 30*, 513–524.

Ulrich, L., & Trumbo, D. (1965). The selection interview since 1949. *Psychological Bulletin, 63*, 110–116.

Weiss, D. J., & Dawis, R. V. (1960). An objective validation of factual interview data. *Journal of Applied Psychology, 44*, 381–385.

16

Using Tests to Promote Classroom Learning

Frank N. Dempster

In this chapter, I argue that traditional uses of classroom tests should be supplemented by an approach that fully recognizes the role of tests in the learning process. At the present time, the available evidence suggests that few teachers make optimal use of tests for learning (e.g., Guza & McLaughlin, 1987; Kuhs, Porter, Floden, Freeman, Schmidt, & Schwille, 1985). For example, textbooks and syllabi used in teacher education courses convey the strong impression that students receive little or no instruction on how to use tests to promote learning. In a recent sampling of educational psychology texts and tests and measurement texts, I found absolutely no mention of the extensive literature on tests and learning (Âirasian, 1991; Biehler & Snowman, 1990; Dembo, 1991; Good & Brophy, 1990; Gronlund & Linn, 1990; Slavin, 1991).

To some extent then, the burden of responsibility for this state of affairs appears to rest upon those whose responsibility it is to design and articulate models of effective instruction. Although many models of instructional design have been developed over the past two decades (Dick & Carey, 1990; Dick & Reiser, 1989; Gagne & Briggs, 1979; Kemp, 1985; Seels & Glasgow, 1990), none explicitly recognize the role of tests in the learning process. To be sure, an evaluation component is a common feature of instructional design models (Gibbons, 1981; Hannum & Hansen, 1989; Seels & Glasgow, 1990), but learning and evaluation are never effectively integrated. Evaluation is viewed as a means of determining the effectiveness of the instructional plan so that modifications can be made if necessary. Thus, tests are viewed as tools to determine if learning has occurred. What is missing in these models, as well as classroom practice, is the understanding that instruction and evaluation are inextricably linked by the fact that tests, in and of themselves, promote learning.

In the section to follow, I review representative research on tests and learning. After that, theoretical issues and practical implications associated with this research are discussed. I conclude the chapter by suggesting several directions for future research.

RESEARCH ON TESTS AND LEARNING

One of the complexities of research is that the act of measurement often has an effect on what is measured. In physics, for example, procedures designed to pinpoint the location of a single quantum of light may actually alter its behavior. Memory is no exception: It is affected not only by additional study opportunities but also by tests—even though they may be designed simply to assess the individual's state of knowledge about a subject. As Lachman and Laughery (1968) put it, "Test[s] . . . though they be designed to measure changes in the state of the human memory system have profound and perhaps residual effects on the state of that system" (p. 40).

Research on the effects of tests on learning has made it abundantly clear that tests do more than simply test; they also promote learning, even when no corrective feedback is provided and when there are no further study opportunities (e.g., Allen, Mahler, & Estes, 1969; Anderson & Biddle, 1975; Donaldson, 1970; Gates, 1917; Hogan & Kintsch, 1971; Izawa, 1971; Jones, 1923–1924; Lachman & Laughery, 1968; Nungester & Duchastel, 1982; Petros & Hoving, 1980; Raffel, 1934; Rea & Modigliani, 1985; Rothkopf, 1966; Runquist, 1983, 1986; Slamecka & Katsaiti, 1988; Spitzer, 1939; Wheeler & Roediger, 1992). This effect is also truly remarkable in the scope of its application. It has been found with all sorts of tests (e.g., multiple choice, short-answer, essay) and with all sorts of learning material ranging from traditional laboratory learning lists (e.g., unrelated word lists) to more ecologically valid material such as prose passages and arithmetic facts. In many cases, the effect has been strong. For example, Jones (1923–1924) found that the retention test scores of previously tested students were twice that of untested students. In other words, taking a test can confer substantial benefits on the retention of the same material tested on a later date, even when no corrective feedback is provided and when there are no further study opportunities. In addition, the beneficial effects of tests on later retention are not simply due to the fact that retrieval may provide an additional presentation of the target material (Carrier & Pashler, 1992). Thus, the effectiveness of tests cannot be explained in terms of an additional study opportunity.

The "test-spacing effect" refers to the fact that spaced tests (tests that are spread out over time) are more effective than massed tests (tests that occur relatively close together in time), especially if the intertest intervals are of an expanding nature (Landauer & Bjork, 1978; Modigliani, 1976; Rea & Modigliani, 1985; Whitten & Bjork, 1977). In a study of name learning, for example, a pattern of increasing intervals between successive tests, in which subjects attempted to write the last names of fictitious characters in response to their first names, was superior to a pattern of uniform spacing (Landauer & Bjork, 1978).

In a related study, Rea and Modigliani (1985) investigated the effects of tests on the retention of grade-appropriate multiplication facts and spelling lists. In the massed uniform condition, the subjects received four evenly spaced tests occurring relatively close together in time; whereas, in the expanded condition, the interval between each of the successive tests increased by roughly 50 percent. Following the fourth test, a final test was administered. For multiplication facts, retention in the expanded condition was almost twice that in the massed condition. For spelling lists, a more modest, but still significant, difference in the same direction was obtained. Furthermore, expanded testing was equally beneficial for children of all ability levels.

Research on testing has revealed a number of other conditions that either diminish or heighten the effects of tests, whether massed or spaced. First, tests are normally most effective if the material to be learned is first tested relatively soon but not immediately after its presentation (Anderson & Biddle, 1975; Modigliani, 1976; Spitzer, 1939). This phenomenon is nicely illustrated in a study by Spitzer (1939), who tested the entire sixth-grade population of 91 elementary schools in Iowa. Each child read a highly factual article and then was tested one or more times at various intervals following reading. An especially significant outcome, from a practical perspective, was that students whose initial test had occurred 1 and 7 days after reading scored 15 to 30 percent higher on a final test two weeks later than did students whose initial test had occurred 14 or 21 days following reading.

Second, information tested but not recalled at the first opportunity is not as likely to be recalled later as is information that was tested and remembered (e.g., Anderson & Biddle, 1975; Jones, 1923–1924; Modigliani, 1976; Runquist, 1986). Thus, the so-called potentiating effect of test trials applies mainly to test questions with successful outcomes. Nevertheless, even items that were not recalled on an earlier test may be recalled on a later test, a phenomenon known as "reminiscence" (e.g., Wheeler & Roediger, 1992). Finally, tests do not just slow the rate of forgetting from test to test. Remarkably, tests may also result in net improvements in recall across tests, a phenomenon first reported by Ballard (1913) and now known as "hypermnesia." Hypermnesia has been reported in many situations, particularly those in which overall levels of performance are fairly high (see Payne, 1987, for a review). Although most studies of hypermnesia have used simple learning materials taught in the laboratory, there have been several demonstrations of the phenomenon using more realistic materials acquired in naturalistic settings (Bahrick & Hall, 1993; Brown, 1923; Hermann, Buschke, & Gall, 1987). In the study by Bahrick & Hall (1993), for example, robust hypermnesia effects were obtained for three types of educationally relevant content—namely, foreign language vocabulary, general knowledge, and names of portraits of famous individuals.

Third, the facilitating effects of tests are greater for repeated questions than for new items (Anderson & Biddle, 1975; Nungester & Duchastel, 1982; Roth-kopf, 1966; Runquist, 1986; Sones & Stroud, 1940). For instance, Rothkopf (1966) had college students study a lengthy selection from a book on marine biology, followed by questions on the passage. On a later test, these students performed substantially better than a control group on repeated items and mod-estly better on new items (an indirect effect), even though knowing the answer to one question should not have given the answer to another. As Anderson and Biddle (1975) noted, however, the aggregate indirect benefit is likely to be greater than the direct benefit. ''Only the points of information about which . . . questions are asked could be directly affected, whereas presumably every point in the text could be indirectly influenced'' (p. 92).

THEORETICAL ISSUES

The effects of tests on learning have received a great deal of theoretical at-tention, particularly in recent years. Nevertheless, relatively few studies have been conducted to determine why a test given between an initial learning episode and a final test enhances a subject's memory. Unlike the effects of reviews (i.e., additional study opportunities) on learning, which have spawned a number of clearly distinguishable hypotheses, testing has inspired only two—namely, the amount of processing hypothesis and the retrieval hypothesis.

Amount of Processing Hypothesis

The simplest explanation for the effects of intervening tests is that tests im-prove memory performance by increasing the amount of processing devoted to particular items. An intervening test merely causes subjects to process infor-mation for an additional time prior to a final test, thereby improving final test performance. In short, test trials act primarily as additional study trials.

There are, however, at least four problems with this hypothesis. First, retriev-ing an item from memory when tested has beneficial effects for later retention above and beyond the effects due merely to studying the item (Carrier & Pashler, 1992). Second, there is some evidence that experimental conditions affect rep-etitions in the form of presentations and tests differently, suggesting that they have differential effects on learning. For example, Sones and Stroud (1940) provided seventh graders with either a test or a review at various intervals fol-lowing the reading of an article. Forty-two days after the reading, a multiple choice retention test was administered. For subjects who had received a prior test, performance on the final retention test decreased as the interval between the original reading and the prior test increased. By contrast, the effect of the review on final retention was independent of the interval between the original reading and the review.

A third difficulty with the amount of processing hypothesis is that once some to-be-learned information is stored in memory, as indicated by a correct response to a test, further test trials tend to enhance performance more than further study trials (Brainerd, Kingma, & Howe, 1985; Halff, 1977; Nungester & Duchastel, 1982), even when the test questions and review statements contain the same content (Bruning, 1968). This is especially likely if the subject has achieved a high level of initial learning (Nungester & Duchastel, 1982). Finally, test-spacing effects seem to call for a more sophisticated explanation than that afforded by the amount of processing hypothesis. As it now stands, this hypothesis seems to lead to the straightforward prediction that massed tests should be just as effective as spaced tests.

Retrieval Hypothesis

In broad terms, the retrieval hypothesis suggests that it is the processing engendered by acts of retrieval that accounts for the effects of intervening tests, not merely the amount of processing. Intuitively, this notion is appealing because tests normally afford fewer retrieval cues than additional study opportunities. Furthermore, Glover (1989) found that an intervening free recall test had a more facilitative influence on a final test than an intervening cued recall test and that an intervening cued recall test had a larger effect on the final test than an intervening recognition test. This pattern of results was obtained whether the final test was free recall, cued recall, or recognition. Thus, the effectiveness of an intervening test was an inverse function of the availability of retrieval cues, just as the retrieval hypothesis would predict. According to Glover (1989), these findings suggest that it is the number and completeness of retrieval events that set the parameters of testing effects.

The retrieval hypothesis also provides a better account of test-spacing effects than does the amount of processing hypothesis. The basic idea is that when presented with a test item, an attempt is made to retrieve some memory of the target information. If the spacing between tests is relatively short, the results of the previous encounter with that information will be more accessible than if the spacing between tests is relatively lengthy. Thus, the subject will need to devote more attention or processing effort to spaced repetitions than to massed repetitions (Dempster, 1996). Thus, full retrieval processes are more likely to occur on spaced tests than on massed tests (e.g., Glover, 1989).

The specifics of the retrieval hypothesis come in a variety of forms. Some have suggested that retrieval attempts may provide general practice or create a retrieval context that will be similar to that during later retrieval attempts and thus boost the likelihood of correct retrieval at a later date (Landauer & Bjork, 1978; Runquist, 1983). This account is difficult to reconcile with the fact that the beneficial effects of prior testing apply mainly to items that were successfully retrieved on that test. On the other hand, this account helps to explain the indirect effects of tests as well as reminiscence and hypermnesia. Indeed, indirect effects are most likely to obtain when the to-be-remembered material is related topically or semantically (Anderson & Biddle, 1975; Runquist, 1986). Under these circumstances, the benefits of general retrieval practice might be expected to extend to items that were not previously tested or tested but not successfully retrieved.

Other accounts assume that the beneficial effect of retrieval occurs not at a global level but rather at the level of individual items. The act of retrieval may either strengthen existing "retrieval routes" to the representation of the item in memory (Birnbaum & Eichner, 1971; Bjork, 1975) or result in the creation of new routes (Bjork, 1975). It is assumed that these new routes will increase the total number of retrieval routes to the representation of an item in memory and, thus, raise the probability of correct recall on a later test.

Each of these versions of the retrieval hypothesis can be directly extended to account for the superiority of test trials over study trials (cf. Carrier & Pashler, 1992). In the former case, retrieval routes that will prove useful later are more likely to be strengthened by an earlier retrieval than by an earlier study opportunity. In the latter case, the creation of new retrieval routes should be more likely to occur during retrieval than during study. The problem with this hypothesis is that there is little evidence that multiple retrieval routes are a sufficient condition of improved recall (e.g., Postman & Knecht, 1983).

In addition to the retrieval routes versions of the retrieval hypothesis, it has been proposed that intervening tests have their effect on subsequent retrieval by "unitizing" the set of items retrieved (Glover, 1989). According to this hypothesis, the activation pathways among retrieved items are strengthened (cf. Anderson, 1990). On subsequent tests, then, the set of items previously retrieved have stronger links to one another, and the retrieval of any one member of the set increases the likelihood of retrieving any other member of the set. Although the unitizing version of the retrieval hypothesis focuses on the relations between items, rather than on individual items per se, it—like the retrieval route versions—applies only to previously retrieved items. In fact, each of these versions is seriously challenged by indirect effects, reminiscence, and hypermnesia.

There are, however, a number of models of retrieval that suggest potential explanations of reminiscence, and thus hypermnesia, although as Roediger and Wheeler (1993) note, reminiscence is still largely a puzzle some 80 years after it was first discovered. These include models that describe memory search in terms of sampling with replacement (e.g., Rundus, 1973) or in terms of a recursive sampling from a pool of responses (Estes, 1955). Both models provide a general account of how items not retrieved on an earlier test may "recover" over time. One way of adding specificity to these models is to assume that recall tests cause output interference. As a consequence, some items are blocked at retrieval by the successful retrieval of other items. As time passes, new items are sampled from memory, including some that were interfered with earlier (cf. Madigan, 1976; Smith & Vela, 1991).

PRACTICAL IMPLICATIONS

Given the long and eventful history of research on tests and learning, one might assume that their implications for classroom practice would already be well known. However, this does not appear to be the case. Tests are regarded mainly as instruments for making decisions about grading and pacing, not as a means of improving learning (cf. Dempster & Perkins, 1993). Furthermore, there is little evidence of any serious effort to disseminate the results of research on tests and learning to the educational community.

These considerations raise the question of how best to put into practice the results of research on tests and learning. Fortunately, research has identified strategies for strengthening the effects of testing on learning. In this section, each of these strategies is discussed in terms of their implications for making more effective use of tests for learning purposes in the classroom.

Material Should Be Tested Soon after It Is Introduced

This point is nicely illustrated in the study by Spitzer (1939) discussed in an earlier section. The explanation for his finding is simple: A test administered soon after the material is introduced is likely to result in high performance levels and engender feelings of success and accomplishment. The importance of these outcomes cannot be exaggerated. Self-efficacy, which refers to students' perceptions of their capability to perform certain tasks, is one of the best predictors of school achievement (Thomas, Iventosch, & Rohwer, 1987), and the main mechanism for building self-efficacy in a given domain appears to be experiencing repeated success on tasks in that domain (Schunk, 1984).

Tests Should Be Frequent

In a recent meta-analysis of the frequency of testing literature, Bangert-Drowns, Kulik, and Kulik (1988) reported on overall effect size (difference in mean scores divided by the standard deviation of the less frequently tested group) of .25 favoring the more frequently tested group on final summative tests taken by all groups. Moreover, groups that received a relatively large number of tests did considerably better on the final exam than groups that received an intermediate number of tests. Of course, more frequent testing beyond a certain number may result in diminishing returns on learning if test performance is already high.

There are at least two explanations for test frequency effects. First, frequent testing would tend to encourage continuous study and discourage the deleterious but common practice of cramming—"a heavy burst of studying immediately before the exam which followed a long period of neglect" (Sommer, 1968, p. 105). Second, frequent tests are likely to result in less test anxiety than less frequent tests, because fewer tests usually means that each test "counts more."

This may explain, at least in part, why research has consistently found that students favor more frequent testing. In four studies reporting student attitudes toward testing, all favored more frequent testing, with an average effect size of .59, a large effect (Bangert-Drowns et al., 1988).

These findings are especially noteworthy inasmuch as many courses of instruction do not include frequent tests. It is not unusual, for example, for postsecondary classes to have only two (a midterm and a final) or three tests in a term. Tests also are not an integral part of teachers' regular instruction at the elementary level, even though a particular subject may be taught three to five times a week. In one survey, fourth- and sixth-grade mathematics teachers reported having administered an average of about 18 curriculum-embedded tests per year or approximately 1 test every two weeks (Burry, Catteral, Choppin, & Dorr-Bremme, 1982). Worse, it appears that teachers test more frequently in mathematics than in reading and that grade level and amount of testing are inversely related (Yeh, 1978).

Some Tests Should Be Cumulative

Although there have been few investigations of cumulative testing in ongoing classrooms, basic laboratory research as well as the more applied research that is available suggests that cumulative tests will result in higher levels of learning than tests related only to content presented since the last test (Burns, 1970; MacDonald, 1984). What's more, Rohm, Sparzo, and Bennett (1986) found that if students had an opportunity to retake tests given weekly, cumulative testing promoted better end-of-course achievement than noncumulative testing. This finding suggests that cumulative testing will be especially helpful if tests are frequent and retakeable.

In most courses of instruction, the topics covered are either moderately interrelated or hierarchical, so that later material draws heavily on earlier material. Thus, the clever use of cumulative questions is likely to enhance the indirect effects of testing. Indirect effects, as I noted earlier, occur when taking a test on a subject helps the student learn material that is not directly tested. For example, a test item about direct current electricity is likely to facilitate the student's understanding of alternating current. Although the direct effects of testing are stronger than indirect effects (e.g., Anderson & Biddle, 1975; Rothkopf, 1966), indirect effects are likely to be substantial if the student must continually review old material that is conceptually related to new material.

Cumulative tests are especially beneficial if they are frequent. For example, Fitch, Drucker, and Norton (1951) found that students who received weekly quizzes followed by cumulative monthly quizzes had significantly higher final exam scores than did students who had only the monthly quizzes. Similarly, fifth graders tested daily performed better on cumulative weekly spelling tests than did students who received only the weekly tests (Reith, Axelrod, Anderson, Hathaway, Wood, & Fitzgerald, 1974). Furthermore, even quizzes that contain just one or two questions covering previously tested material can be helpful, so long as the quizzes are frequent (Burns, 1970; MacDonald, 1984).

Cumulative Tests Should Provide Distributed Practice

As decades of psychological research have shown, distributed practice, whether in the form of reviews or tests, is much more effective than massed practice, especially if the intervals between each successive test expands (e.g., Dempster, 1988; Landauer & Bjork, 1978; Rea & Modigliani, 1985). This means that the most effective way of spacing cumulative tests is to ensure that there is a progressive increase in the interval between each of the successive tests (e.g., one week, three weeks, six weeks).

As might be expected, spaced tests, because they hold the student responsible for the material to be remembered over a relatively lengthy period of time, are especially helpful in promoting long-term retention (Dempster, 1989). In addition, cumulative spaced tests can help prevent unnecessary testing, which might occur if the intervals between successive tests are short and a high level of mastery is reached fairly quickly.

Test Feedback Should Be Immediate Rather Than Delayed

Although tests can be expected to promote learning even without feedback, studies show that immediate feedback promotes learning even further and that immediate feedback is usually more effective than delayed feedback. Immediate feedback can be accomplished, of course, by making an answer key available to students immediately following the test. In many classrooms, however, it appears that students must wait a day or two or even a week before receiving feedback.

One mode of instruction that lends itself to immediate feedback is computer-based instruction. Among the advantages that computers offer the testing process is that they can be programmed to provide immediate feedback via a variety of feedback strategies such as answer until correct (AUC), knowledge of response (KOR), and knowledge of correct response (KCR) (Clariana, Ross, & Morrison, 1991).

One example of just how computers can be programmed to make effective use of tests and feedback was reported by Siegel and Misselt (1984), who conducted a study in which students were taught foreign language vocabulary. When a student made an error, he or she received immediate corrective feedback, and the missed work was programmed to reappear according to an expanded ratio practice schedule. For example, the first retesting of a missed word might occur after an interval of three intervening items; if that test had a successful outcome, the third test would occur after an interval of six intervening items, and so forth. If at any time during practice an item was missed, the entire procedure was reset.

Posttest performance revealed that this procedure was successful, resulting in substantial gains in vocabulary learning. Unfortunately, computer-based instruction is often modeled after traditional flashcard drills (McDermott & Watkins, 1983) and fails to incorporate optimal testing and feedback procedures (Clariana et al., 1991). Clearly, Siegel and Misselt's (1984) technique could be expanded to guide instruction in a variety of curricular domains, including spelling, arithmetic, science, history, and language arts.

FUTURE RESEARCH DIRECTIONS

The absence of a detailed specification of just how tests promote learning is the major theoretical shortcoming associated with research on tests and learning. Nevertheless, there are reasons to believe that retrieval processes play a major role. The retrieval hypothesis is at least consistent with the fact that once some to-be-learned information is stored in memory as indicated by a correct response to a test, further test trials tend to enhance performance more than study trials (e.g., Halff, 1977; Nungester & Duchastel, 1982). This suggests that acquisition and forgetting obey different laws (Brainerd et al., 1985) and that further study increases the number of immediately accessible items, whereas testing, because of its greater demands on retrieval operations, increases their resistance to forgetting (Runquist, 1986). Thus, testing may be a unique resource for improving classroom learning; testing may provide benefits—possible in long-term retention—that reviews and additional study opportunities do not provide. However, if further progress is to be made relative to this issue, the effects of testing on retrieval need to be depicted in greater detail.

A more detailed depiction of testing effects should also include an explanation of indirect effects. At the present time, research suggests that, at least to some extent, a quiz may cause the learner to review mentally the material covered by the quiz, including material not directly tested (McGaw & Grotelueschen, 1972). However, it might also be the case that indirect effects are due to specific associations to the test questions themselves. In either case, it is not clear whether the critical variable in indirect effects is spaciotemporal or topical-semantic similarity (Anderson & Biddle, 1975). Obviously, indirect effects have a great deal of educational significance; if teachers knew their cause, they could structure their tests in such a way so as to maximize their overall effect.

Finally, future research should evaluate the effects of different types of classroom tests (e.g., multiple choice, short-answer, essay) on learning. While previous research has shown that a variety of different types of tests promote learning, that research does not enable us to draw conclusions about what types of tests are most beneficial. Furthermore, different kinds of tests may tend to promote different kinds of learning. For example, multiple choice tests may promote mainly fact learning (e.g.: During the American Civil War, the economy of the Confederacy was largely agrarian), whereas essay tests may more effectively enhance the students' understanding of relations among facts (e.g.: The American Civil War was a clash between two very different economies). Knowing which type of test will best promote any given learning objective would provide clues as to the mechanisms responsible for testing effects and would be of considerable value to educators.

SUMMARY

In this chapter, I review research that demonstrates, beyond any reasonable doubt, that tests promote learning. Furthermore, this research has identified a number of strategies that should enable classroom teachers to optimize their use of tests for that purpose. Two explanations for the effects of tests on learning are also discussed, the amount of processing hypothesis and the retrieval hypothesis. Of the two, the retrieval hypothesis provides a better account of the data. However, future research that is focused on specifying the exact nature of the retrieval process during testing, the indirect effects of tests on learning, and the relative effects of different types of tests on learning would likely contribute to a better understanding of this phenomenon. Although classroom tests are underutilized in terms of their potential for improving learning, they have clear and verifiable implications for helping students learn and retain information over a relatively lengthy period of time.

REFERENCES

Åirasian, P. W. (1991). *Classroom assessment*. New York: McGraw-Hill.

Allen, G. A., Mahler, W. A., & Estes, W. K. (1969). Effects of recall tests on long-term retention of paired associates. *Journal of Verbal Learning and Verbal Behavior, 8*, 463–470.

Anderson, J. R. (1990). *Cognitive psychology and its implications* (3rd ed.). New York: Freeman.

Anderson, R. C., & Biddle, W. B. (1975). On asking people questions about what they are reading. In G. H. Bower (Ed.), *The psychology of language and motivation* (Vol. 9, pp. 90–132). New York: Academic Press.

Bahrick, H. P., & Hall, L. K. (1993). Long intervals between tests can yield hypermnesia: Comments on Wheeler and Roediger. *Psychological Science, 4*, 206–207.

Ballard, P. B. (1913). Oblivescence and reminiscence. *British Journal of Psychology Monograph Supplement, 1*, 1–82.

Bangert-Drowns, R. L., Kulik, J. A., & Kulik, C. C. (1988). *Effects of frequent classroom testing*. Unpublished manuscript, University of Michigan.

Biehler, R. F., & Snowman, J. (1990). *Psychology applied to teaching* (6th ed.). Boston: Houghton Mifflin.

Birnbaum, I. M., & Eichner, J. T. (1971). Study versus test trials and long-term retention in free-recall learning. *Journal of Verbal Learning and Verbal Behavior, 10*, 516–521.

Bjork, R. A. (1975). Retrieval as a memory modifier: An interpretation of negative recency and related phenomena. In R. L. Solso (Ed.), *Information processing and cognition: The Loyola symposium* (pp. 123–144). Hillsdale, NJ: Erlbaum.

Brainerd, C. J., Kingma, J., & Howe, M. L. (1985). On the development of forgetting. *Child Development, 56*, 1103–1119.

Brown, W. (1923). To what extent is memory measured by a single recall trial? *Journal of Experimental Psychology, 6*, 377–382.

Bruning, R. H. (1968). Effects of review and testlike events within the learning of prose material. *Journal of Educational Psychology, 59*, 16–19.

Burns, P. C., (1970). Intensive review as a procedure in teaching arithmetic. *Elementary School Journal, 60*, 205–211.

Burry, J., Catteral, J., Choppin, B., & Dorr-Bremme, D. (1982). *Testing in the nation's schools and districts: How much? What kinds? To what ends? At what costs?* (CSE Report No. 194). Los Angeles: Center for the Study of Evaluation, University of California.

Carrier, M., & Pashler, H. (1992). The influence of retrieval on retention. *Memory & Cognition, 20*, 633–642.

Clariana, R. B., Ross, S. M., & Morrison, G. R. (1991). The effects of different feedback strategies using computer-administered multiple-choice questions as instruction. *Educational Training, Research, and Development, 39*, 5–17.

Dembo, M. H. (1991). *Applying educational psychology in the classroom* (4th ed.). New York: Longman.

Dempster, F. N. (1988). The spacing effect: A case study in the failure to apply the results of psychological research. *American Psychologist, 43*, 627–634.

Dempster, F. N. (1989). Spacing effects and their implications for theory and practice. *Educational Psychology Review, 1*, 309–330.

Dempster, F. N. (1996). Distributing and managing the conditions of encoding and practice. In E. L. Bjork & R. A. Bjork (Eds.), *Handbook of perception and cognition* (Vol. 10: *Memory*, pp. 317–344). San Diego, CA: Academic Press.

Dempster, F. N., & Perkins, P. G. (1993). Revitalizing classroom assessment: Using tests to promote learning. *Journal of Instructional Psychology, 20*, 197–203.

Dick, W., & Carey, L. (1990). *The systematic design of instruction* (3rd ed.). Glenview, IL: Scott, Foresman and Company.

Dick, W., & Reiser, R. A. (1989). *Planning effective instruction*. Englewood Cliffs, NJ: Prentice-Hall.

Donaldson, W. (1970). Output effects in multitrial free recall. *Journal of Verbal Learning and Verbal Behavior, 10*, 577–585.

Estes, W. K. (1955). Statistical theory of spontaneous recovery and regression. *Psychological Review, 62*, 145–154.

Fitch, M. L., Drucker, A. J., & Norton, J. A., Jr. (1951). Frequent testing as a motivating factor in large lecture courses. *Journal of Educational Psychology, 42*, 1–20.

Gagne, R. M., & Briggs, L. J. (1979). *Principles of instructional design* (2nd ed.). New York: Holt, Rinehart and Winston.

Gates, A. I. (1917). Recitation as a factor in memorizing. *Archives of Psychology, 6*, 1–104.

Gibbons, A. S. (1981). The contribution of science to instructional development. *National Society for Performance & Instruction Journal, 20*.

Glover, J. A. (1989). The "testing" phenomenon: Not gone but nearly forgotten. *Journal of Educational Psychology, 81*, 392–399.

Good, T. L., & Brophy, J. E. (1990). *Educational psychology: A realistic approach* (4th ed.). New York: Longman.

Gronlund, N. E., & Linn, R. L. (1990). *Measurement and evaluation in teaching* (6th ed.). New York: Macmillan.

Guza, D. S., & McLaughlin, T. F. (1987). A comparison of daily and weekly testing on student spelling performance. *Journal of Educational Research, 80*, 373–376.

Halff, H. M. (1977). The role of opportunities for recall in learning to retrieve. *American Journal of Psychology, 90*, 383–406.

Hannum, W. H., & Hansen, C. (1989). *Instructional systems development in large organizations*. Englewood Cliffs, NJ: Educational Technology Publications.

Hermann, D. J., Buschke, H., & Gall, M. B. (1987). Improving retrieval. *Applied Cognitive Psychology, 1*, 27–33.

Hogan, R. M., & Kintsch, W. (1971). Differential effects of study and test trials on long-term recognition and recall. *Journal of Verbal Learning and Verbal Behavior, 10*, 562–567.

Izawa, C. (1971). The test trial potentiating model. *Journal of Mathematical Psychology, 8*, 200–224.

Jones, H. E. (1923–1924). The effects of examination on permanence of learning. *Archives of Psychology, 10*, 21–70.

Kemp, J. E. (1985). *The instructional design process*. New York: Harper & Row.

Kuhs, T., Porter, A., Floden, R., Freeman, D., Schmidt, W., & Schwille, J. (1985). Differences among teachers in their use of curriculum-embedded tests. *Elementary School Journal, 86*, 141–153.

Lachman, R., & Laughery, K. L. (1968). Is a test trial a training trial in free recall learning? *Journal of Experimental Psychology, 76*, 40–50.

Landauer, T. K., & Bjork, R. A. (1978). Optimum rehearsal patterns and name learning. In M. M. Gruneberg, P. E. Morris, & R. N. Sykes (Eds.), *Practical aspects of memory* (pp. 625–632). New York: Academic Press.

MacDonald, C. J., II. (1984). A comparison of three methods of utilizing homework in a precalculus college algebra course (Doctoral dissertation, Ohio State University, 1984). *Dissertation Abstracts International, 45*, 1674-A.

Madigan, S. (1976). Reminiscence and item recovery in free recall. *Memory & Cognition, 4*, 233–236.

McDermott, P. A., & Watkins, M. W. (1983). Computerized vs. conventional remedial instruction for learning disabled pupils. *Journal of Special Education, 17*, 81–88.

McGaw, B., & Grotelueschen, A. (1972). Direction of the effect of questions in prose material. *Journal of Educational Psychology, 63*, 586–588.

Modigliani, V. (1976). Effects on a later recall by delaying initial recall. *Journal of Experimental Psychology: Human Learning and Memory, 2*, 609–622.

Nungester, R. J., & Duchastel, P. C. (1982). Testing versus review: Effects on retention. *Journal of Educational Psychology, 74*, 18–22.

Payne, D. G. (1987). Hypermnesia and reminiscence in recall: A historical and empirical review. *Psychological Bulletin, 101*, 5–27.

Petros, T., & Hoving, K. (1980). The effects of review on young children's memory for prose. *Journal of Experimental Child Psychology, 30*, 33–43.

Postman, L., & Knecht, K. (1983). Encoding variability and retention. *Journal of Verbal Learning and Verbal Behavior, 22,* 133–152.

Raffel, G. (1934). The effect of recall on forgetting. *Journal of Experimental Psychology, 17,* 828–838.

Rea, C. P., & Modigliani, V. (1985). The effect of expanded versus massed practice on the retention of multiplication facts and spelling lists. *Human Learning, 4,* 11–18.

Reith, H., Axelrod, S., Anderson, R., Hathaway, F., Wood, K., & Fitzgerald, C. (1974). Influence of distributed practice and daily testing on weekly spelling tests. *Journal of Educational Research, 68,* 73–77.

Roediger, H. L., III, & Wheeler, M. A. (1993). Hypermnesia in episodic and semantic memory: Response to Bahrick and Hall. *Psychological Science, 4,* 207–208.

Rohm, R. A., Sparzo, J., & Bennett, C. M. (1986). College student performance under repeated testing and cumulative testing conditions. Reports on five studies. *Journal of Educational Research, 80,* 99–104.

Rothkopf, E. Z. (1966). Learning from written instructive materials: An exploration of the control of inspection behavior by test-like events. *American Educational Research Journal, 3,* 241–249.

Rundus, D. (1973). Negative effects of using list items as recall cues. *Journal of Verbal Learning and Verbal Behavior, 12,* 43–50.

Runquist, W. N. (1983). Some effects of remembering on forgetting. *Memory & Cognition, 11,* 641–650.

Runquist, W. N. (1986). The effect of testing on the forgetting of related and unrelated associates. *Canadian Journal of Psychology, 40,* 65–76.

Schunk, D. (1984). Self-efficacy perspective on achievement behavior. *Educational Psychologist, 19,* 48–58.

Seels, B., & Glasgow, Z. (1990). *Exercises in instructional design.* Columbus, OH: Merrill.

Siegel, M. A., & Misselt, A. L. (1984). Adaptive feedback and review paradigm for computer-based drills. *Journal of Educational Psychology, 76,* 310–317.

Slamecka, N. J., & Katsaiti, L. T. (1988). Normal forgetting of verbal lists as a function of prior testing. *Journal of Experimental Psychology: Learning, Memory, and Cognition, 14,* 716–727.

Slavin, R. E. (1991). *Educational psychology: Theory into practice* (3rd ed.). Englewood Cliffs, NJ: Prentice-Hall.

Smith, S. M., & Vela, E. (1991). Incubated reminiscence effects. *Memory & Cognition, 19,* 168–176.

Sommer, R. (1968). The social psychology of cramming. *Personnel and Guidance Journal, 9,* 104–109.

Sones, A. M., & Stroud, J. B. (1940). Review with special reference to temporal position. *Journal of Educational Psychology, 31,* 665–676.

Spitzer, H. F. (1939). Studies in retention. *Journal of Educational Psychology, 30,* 641–656.

Thomas, J. W., Iventosch, L., & Rohwer, W. D., Jr. (1987). Relationships among student characteristics, study activities, and achievement as a function of course characteristics. *Contemporary Educational Psychology, 12,* 344–364.

Wheeler, M. A., & Roediger, H. L., III. (1992). Disparate effects of repeated testing:

Reconciling Ballard's (1913) and Bartlett's (1932) results. *Psychological Science, 3*, 240–245.

Whitten, W. B., II, & Bjork, R. A. (1977). Learning from tests: Effects of spacing. *Journal of Verbal Learning and Verbal Behavior, 16*, 456–478.

Yeh, J. P. (1978). *Test use in schools*. Washington, DC: National Institute of Education, U.S. Department of Health, Education, and Welfare.

17

Smart Testing

Patrick C. Kyllonen

INTRODUCTION

This chapter describes a prototype aptitude battery that incorporates all current significant technology associated with abilities measurement. This includes computer delivery, item-generation (generative) technology, multidimensional adaptive technology, comprehensive cognitive abilities measurement, time-parameterized testing, and a latent factor-centered design. Currently, different testing projects, particularly in the military, both in this country and abroad are engaged in components of this research. However, these activities are working independently, and until now, there has been no attempt or plan to integrate the diverse efforts. By integrating these activities, a concerted effort will result in a prototype for the next-generation computerized aptitude battery. Such a battery, incorporating the latest advances from the research front, would be capable of measuring a much wider variety of abilities than are measured by current systems, in a shorter amount of testing time. A key feature of the battery would be increased upgradability, both maintenance upgradability and design upgradability. Maintenance upgradability refers to the capability for keeping items current and invulnerable to compromise. Design upgradability refers to the capability for incorporating new tests, and new abilities composites, as research demonstrates the need for such upgrading.

The chapter is organized as a set of five problems associated with current aptitude testing systems, accompanied by solutions to those problems.

1. The first problem is that tests have been criticized as overly narrow and limited in the range of human abilities they are capable of measuring. The solution is to take

advantage of developments in cognitive psychology that suggest additional human abilities factors and to test those factors using computers.

2. Increasing the number of factors to test is going to be difficult because it is unlikely that additional testing time will be made available. The solution to this problem is to increase the efficiency of testing by using Computerized Adaptive Testing (CAT) methods, which promise to cut testing time by 66 percent.

3. New tests based on cognitive psychology and implemented as CATs may prove particularly difficult to secure, increasing the likelihood of test compromise problems. The solution here is to take advantage of the power of cognitive methods to enable the computer the capability to actually generate test items itself, "on the fly."

4. Controlling for the speed-accuracy trade-off is a problem in cognitive testing. Some examinees go fast at the expense of accuracy, and others are more careful but at the cost of slow performance. A solution proposed is to adaptively speed up the presentation of items as examinees demonstrate the ability to respond correctly at a given rate.

5. It is difficult to improve an operational test battery, even in the face of positive research evidence, because the operator community, those responsible for administering the test, is reluctant to change scoring and reporting procedures. The solution here is to change the focus of the scoring system from a "test-based" one to a "factor-based" one.

The remainder of the chapter is a more detailed discussion of these problems and solutions.

THE "LIMITATIONS OF TESTS" PROBLEM AND EXTENDED ABILITIES MEASUREMENT

Problem

For many years, there has been a widespread perception that aptitude test batteries are limited in the kinds of human abilities they measure. There is a belief that intelligence as measured by tests is a narrow kind of intelligence, that due to the inherent limitations of the paper-and-pencil, multiple choice formats, many important abilities are left unmeasured. This has led to the belief that there are some individuals who are "good test takers" who "test well" but are not necessarily going to prove to be the best students or the best performers on the job. The traditional view is that performance on the job, performance in training, and performance on aptitude tests all depend on the same and relatively small set of abilities factors. The alternative view is that tests miss important factors that are required for success in training and on the job.

Solution

During the 1980s, a number of projects were initiated to address this problem. The US Army's Project A, the Department of Defense's Enhanced Computer

Abilities Testing (ECAT) project, and the US Air Force's Learning Abilities Measurement Program (LAMP) all had as their goal the capability of measuring increased numbers of abilities. A somewhat related effort, an ambitious project by Carroll (1995) to summarize essentially all the literature on human abilities, also began during this time. There were two sources of optimism for these projects. One was that developments in cognitive psychology promised a new foundation for aptitude testing, a foundation based on improved conceptions of human information processing. The second was that rapid advances in micro-computer technology unleashed aptitude testers from the shackles of the paper-and-pencil test format and promised the capability for measuring a much broader range of thinking, learning, problem-solving, and decision-making skills. This increased capability was due to the computer being able to present a much richer array of information with precise control over how that information is presented and also to collect a wider variety of response data, such as reaction times, eye movements, continuous motion sequences, voice input, and so on.

All these projects were successful in some ways. The army's Project A demonstrated the power of the computer in its ability to measure reaction times and psychomotor abilities. The ECAT project demonstrated that new abilities tests, particularly ones measuring spatial ability, might add predictive efficiency to the currently operational aptitude battery, the Armed Services Vocational Aptitude Battery (ASVAB). As a result of that effort, a new test, the Assembling Objects test, is being added to the ASVAB. Carroll's review and reanalysis of aptitude tests provided a comprehensive picture of the range of human abilities, including both those that could be measured with paper-and-pencil tests and ones that required a computer. A particularly useful feature of Carroll's effort was the development of a comprehensive taxonomy of human abilities. The ASVAB can be analyzed with respect to this taxonomy, and this analysis can show what abilities are currently not measured by the ASVAB. That is, the analysis can identify gaps in the ASVAB, and future abilities research can be productively focused on filling in those gaps to yield an aptitude testing system more comprehensive than the ASVAB.

On the other hand, there were limitations to these previous efforts. Both Project A and the ECAT project relied on nomination procedures for generating new tests, and while this resulted in interesting suggestions, it provided no assurance that the particular tests nominated and evaluated were the best tests that could have been nominated. Redoing the two projects might very well have led to a completely different set of tests and perhaps to a different set of conclusions regarding the value of the concept of ''information-processing'' tests.

Carroll's project, because of its comprehensiveness (he evaluated almost all useful data available on aptitude tests of every kind), did not suffer the limitations of the nomination method. However, Carroll did not suggest, let alone create, an aptitude test battery based on his taxonomy, and thus no validity study was ever conducted based on his abilities framework. It is perhaps unfortunate that Carroll's taxonomy was published only after the two major validation projects, Project A and the ECAT, were already finished. Both certainly could have benefited from the taxonomy in guiding the test nomination process.

A second problem with the test nomination method is that they are test focused rather than construct or factor focused. Thus, the results of the validity studies depended directly on the strength of the particular tests chosen. The problem with this approach is that the source for negative results is difficult to identify. If a particular test, such as a reaction time test, shows no incremental validity over, for example, the ASVAB in predicting training success, then it is difficult to determine whether this lack of improvement is due to the fact that reaction time, as a construct, is not useful in predicting training success or whether simply the particular reaction time test nominated has problems.

The US Air Force's LAMP's Cognitive Abilities Measurement (CAM) project was from the outset construct focused. Rather than relying on a test nomination procedure for generating an aptitude test battery, the CAM project employed a kind of "top-down" approach in which the key components of the human cognitive system were identified, then a variety of tests to measure those components were developed. A "consensus information processing" model was used to identify the key components, a working memory, two long-term memories, declarative and procedural, and a system governing the rate at which information processing occurred. Also, the contents of information processing were partitioned into verbal, quantitative, and spatial domains. This analysis yielded a six process factor by three content factor taxonomy, where the process factors were working-memory capacity, information-processing, speed, declarative and procedural knowledge, and declarative and procedural learning. Within each cell of this taxonomy, various (three to four) paradigms were either developed or identified from the literature for measuring the particular ability identified in the taxon (e.g., verbal working-memory capacity, quantitative information-processing speed, spatial procedural-learning rate). Details of the CAM project are provided elsewhere (Kyllonen, 1991, 1994a, 1995). The key point here is that the CAM taxonomic framework has assisted in the development of an aptitude testing battery that has been shown to increase the breadth of abilities measured beyond those measured by the ASVAB. We have also demonstrated incremental validity of those abilities in predicting various training criteria and are now in the process of evaluating the utility of the CAM battery in predicting success in operational air force training (Searcy, Sawin, & Tiegs, 1996).

THE "LIMITED TIME PROBLEM" AND ADAPTIVE TESTING

Problem

Regardless of the source for new tests, the desire to measure more abilities collides with the essentially unavoidable practical constraint of time available for testing them. A standard amount of time allotted to aptitude testing, in a variety of contexts, seems to be about three hours. For example, many educational aptitude test batteries, such as the Scholastic Aptitude Test (SAT), the Graduate Record Exam (GRE), the American College Testing Service's Exam, and the Miller Analogies Test, take no longer than about three hours to administer, and aptitude batteries administered as part of military testing programs, such as the ASVAB and the British Army Recruit Battery, allow about three hours. These time-honored ceilings have led to institutional expectations that probably make the expansion of time set aside for aptitude testing extremely unlikely.

Solution

If the amount of time the personnel system allows for aptitude testing will not be expanded, but the number of abilities and the number of tests to be administered will be, there is a question of how that might be accomplished. CAT is a potential solution. An adaptive test decreases testing time without losing precision in estimating an examinee's ability level by selecting items that adaptively "zero in" on that examinee's ability level. Time spent administering items that are much too difficult or too easy for an examinee will be minimized, which reduces the total amount of time spent testing. What does this mean in the context of an actual aptitude test battery such as the ASVAB? It means that in addition to the 10 ASVAB subtests currently administered, several additional tests could be included without affecting the total duration of the testing session. It has been shown that a computerized adaptive version of ASVAB (CAT-ASVAB) reduces testing time by approximately 50 percent (Segall, 1995). Table 17.1 shows that the maximum number of items administered to an examinee in CAT-ASVAB is a little over half the number administered in the standard paper-and-pencil ASVAB. And most individuals receive less than the maximum number because the target precision level (one equivalent to the expected precision level for ASVAB) is reached before the maximum number of items is administered.

Further advances in psychometrics may lead to even more savings in the time needed to measure additional abilities. Traditional Computerized Adaptive Testing technology is unidimensional. CAT tests, at least ones currently implemented, such as the CAT-ASVAB, rely on unidimensional item response theory (IRT) models for item selection and scoring. Thus, CAT is designed to measure a single ability at a time. Because test batteries, such as the ASVAB, are usually multidimensional (i.e., they measure more than one ability), CAT technology is often implemented to measure multiple abilities one after another. For example, CAT can be used to measure verbal ability and, once finished, can then be used to measure quantitative ability, and so on, in a sequential test-by-test, or ability-by-ability, fashion. A limitation of this procedure is that it fails to recognize the correlation between abilities in producing ability estimates and consequently is

Table 17.1
Comparison of ASVAB and CAT Testing

Test	N ASVAB items	CAT Pool	CAT Test Length
General Science	25	110	15
Arithmetic Reasoning	30	209	15
Word Knowledge	35	228	15
Paragraph Comprehension	15	88	10
Auto Information	25*	104	10
Shop Information	25*	103	10
Math Knowledge	25	103	15
Mechanical Comprehension	20	103	15
Electronics Information	20	97	15
Total	195	1145	120

*Auto Information and Shop Information are combined in a single test, Auto and Shop Information, in the ASVAB. There are 25 items in that combined test.

inefficient. Recent work (Segall, 1996) has demonstrated the feasibility of a Multidimensional Adaptive Testing (MAT) approach. The primary benefit of MAT is that it has the potential for further reducing the amount of testing time required to obtain ability estimates at a constant level of precision.

Segall's MAT approach achieves additional savings in testing time in two ways. First, it takes advantage of the insight that every item response made by an examinee is relevant to ability estimates for every test (or factor) being measured. This is because tests (or abilities factors) are positively correlated. Thus, if an examinee responds correctly to a vocabulary item, that not only affects the system's estimate of the examinee's vocabulary ability, but it also affects the estimate of an examinee's "arithmetic reasoning" ability, their "mechanical comprehension ability," and every other ability being measured by the battery. Clearly, the more highly the two abilities are correlated, the greater the effect of a response to one ability item to another ability item, and if two abilities are not very highly correlated, a response to one ability item will not have much effect on the estimate of the other. But the key point is that because every ability estimate is affected in some way by every response, it will take less time to achieve an ability estimate at a given precision level when multiple abilities are assessed simultaneously.

The second way in which Segall's MAT system saves testing time is that it can incorporate expected item response time as a factor in selecting items. In traditional unidimensional CAT, the system selects items that simply yield the most information with respect to the ability being measured. These are items for which the result of whether the examinee passes or fails will yield the greatest effect on the system's estimate of the ability being measured. That is, if the examinee passes the item, the system's estimate of the examinee's ability will change relatively substantially, and if the examinee fails the item, the system's estimate will also change (technically, what is minimized through item selection is the variance of $\hat{\theta}$, the estimated ability). But the only consideration for item selection, typically, will be how much of an effect on the ability estimate the passing or failing result will have.

In contrast, what is minimized in MAT item selection is not the variance of the single ability variable, but what Segall refers to as the "volume of the credibility elipsoid," or Ck' (k' is a particular item), which is essentially the variability or dispersion of all the ability variables considered simultaneously. That is, the item k' selected for administration is that item of all the items available in the pool for all the abilities being tested that will have the greatest impact on all the ability estimates the battery is designed to measure taken together. Segall suggests the possibility of replacing Ck' with $pk' = Ck' / tk'$, where tk' is the amount of time a particular item takes to administer (e.g., the average response time for that item). That is, rather than selecting the item k' that provides the largest decrement in the volume of the credibility elipsoid, the system could select the item that does so per unit of time. Presumably, a similar substitution could be used in unidimensional item selection, but the greater heterogeneity in expected response times over items in a MAT item pool makes this index especially interesting in MAT. Segall notes that the rank ordering of candidate items can vary quite substantially, depending on whether the Ck' or tk' criterion is used for selection. For example, in the ASVAB, response times for vocabulary items are short, whereas those for paragraph comprehension are much longer, and so despite the fact that the two kinds of items provide similar information (they are highly correlated), vocabulary items will more likely be chosen using the tk' criterion.

Segall suggests that MAT can in principle shave an additional third off the time taken for testing over CAT. Thus, a MAT version of the three-hour ASVAB might take as little as one hour to administer. This would leave lots of time for measuring additional abilities during a three-hour testing session.

Caveats

Segall's analysis of the feasibility and time savings associated with an MAT approach was based on a computer simulation study. No actual MAT battery exists. As Segall notes, an actual MAT battery might raise problems that do not arise with a standard unidimensional CAT battery. In particular, because MAT considers all items from all tests simultaneously in item selection, it is possible for a test to begin with, for example, a vocabulary item, followed by an arithmetic reasoning item, followed by a mechanical comprehension item, and so on, in what might appear to the examinee to be an unpredictable and perhaps confusing pattern. This confusion might even be exacerbated because of the nature of adaptive testing, which tends to select items that are more difficult than examinees are typically used to (most examinees have an expectation of getting most of the items in a standard test correct, but adaptive tests tend to select items where the probability of passing is closer to half).

It may be that mixing item types is not really that great a problem. Extant tests such as the Wonderlich Personnel Inventory use a mixed item format without apparent problems, and there is some evidence that such mixing does not affect the validity of the test (Chastain, 1993). Still, the success of an MAT battery will probably depend even more than other kinds of batteries do on the examinee's understanding of item instructions. This will be a particular challenge with new kinds of test batteries, such as the CAM battery, because of the novelty of test types that appear in such batteries. Discussions of these issues and suggestions for improving computerized tests are available (Kyllonen, 1991). It may also prove useful to replace the standard item selection function used in adaptive testing with one that progressively increases the difficulty of items until an examinee can no longer reliably solve them. Although this strategy is certainly less efficient than the adaptive item selection strategy, it might relieve some user acceptance problems if MAT tests, for example, prove to be too discomforting due to the relentless administration of not only constantly changing types of items but fairly difficult ones at that.

TEST COMPROMISE PROBLEMS AND GENERATIVE TESTING

The Item Theft Problem

In 1993, the Educational Testing Service (ETS) released the first version of a CAT Graduate Record Exam. For the first time, examinees had a choice of taking the standard paper-and-pencil GRE or the CAT version. Stanley Kaplan, a test-coaching company, employed several very bright individuals to take the CAT version of the test and between them memorize the correct answers to the first few questions. Because of the nature of adaptive testing, knowing the correct answer to the first few questions enables the examinee to quickly advance to the top of the scoring range. Thus, while stealing the answers to many questions appearing on any one of several possible forms is a fruitless strategy with standard tests, it proved to be much easier with a CAT version of the test in that only a small subset of the pool of the items have to be memorized. Then, once in possession of this small subset of key questions, it is relatively easy to train examinees to memorize their answers and thereby achieve top scores. ETS quickly corrected the problem by inserting new items and changing the adaptive algorithm, but nevertheless the point had been clearly made: CAT tests compared to standard ones are potentially much more susceptible to item theft.

The Cat out of the Bag Problem

The development of the CAM battery is almost a textbook case of the Department of Defense's model for the development of a technology. The DoD proscribes the progression of research ("Program 6" money) from basic research (6.1) through exploratory (6.2) and then advanced development (6.3) and ending in fielded systems (6.5). The CAM project began as a basic research project (6.1) in cognitive psychology where the issue was how best to identify the components of the human information-processing system and to determine the nature and range of individual differences in those components. The project then advanced to exploratory development status (6.2) as the issue changed to how to develop an actual test battery (see, e.g., Kyllonen, 1995) and to determine the degree to which that battery predicted various training criteria in the laboratory as compared to the ASVAB (Christal, 1991; Shute & Kyllonen, 1990). With indications of success of the CAM battery concept, the project then moved out into the field. The battery was further tuned for mass testing, air force enlistees entering into select training programs were administered the battery, and their success in technical training was tracked (Searcy, Sawin, & Tiegs, 1996). At this point, the customers of the research, the Air Education and Training Command and the Air Staff's Deputy for Personnel, began preparations for administering the battery as part of the air force's personnel classification program. It is at this point that issues of test security begin to loom critical.

The test security problem is illustrated in Figure 17.1. At the basic research

Figure 17.1
Illustration of the Test Security Problem

"Cat out of the Bag" Problem

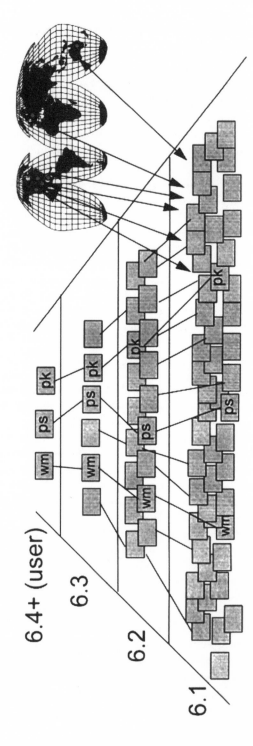

Note: Many test concepts are generated through free exchange at the basic research (6.1) stage; some of those concepts survive to the operational testing stage.

(6.1) stage, it is productive to exchange test concepts and actual tests with re-searchers at universities and other institutions throughout the country or, for that matter, throughout the world. This is done through scientist exchange programs, collaborative research projects, and other mechanisms. Most of these exchanges prove to be dead ends with respect to the development of a test battery (although they usually are meritorious in other respects), but a few concepts or even tests prove useful enough to be further refined and developed into the next phase (6.2) of research. The process continues here, with some test ideas continuing to bubble up through to the next phase, others falling by the wayside, and so on, until a final fielded test battery emerges in the hands of the using organi-zation. The test security problem at this point, of course, is that the tests in the soon-to-be operational battery have their roots in 6.1 research and are therefore publicly available. There is then a natural tension between the operators even-tually responsible for administering the battery and the researchers responsible for developing it. The operators wish to secure the product at each stage in its life cycle, but the researchers rightly believe that the best product depends on openness and active exchange. The situation appears to create inevitable conflict between the goals of test security and openness in development.

Solution

A solution to both the item theft problem associated with CAT and the ''cat out of the bag'' problem associated with the test development cycle is to flood the testing marketplace with so many items that a priori possession of answer keys is of essentially no value to the examinee. (Imagine an examinee attempting to memorize the answers to millions of items.) This may be accomplished through the use of generativity.

Current operational (or near-operational) Computer Adaptive Testing systems, such as CAT-ASVAB and ETS's Adaptive GRE, rely on a methodology of ''item banking'' in which the computer selects items for an examinee from a pool or bank of prestored items. For several years the United Kingdom's Min-istry of Defense has been employing an alternative to item banking involving the computer in *generating* items rather than simply *selecting* prestored items (Irvine, Dann, & Anderson, 1990). The principle behind item generation is to determine the information-processing steps people take to solve problems, then to develop an algorithm that systematically manipulates the processing required by an item. The computer then can generate items ''on the fly'' by applying the algorithm. This process takes the place of the traditional costly process of gen-erating items by hand, then field-testing them to determine which ones ''work'' and which ones do not. The primary benefit of generative testing is that test maintenance costs are reduced, and item theft becomes essentially impossible.

The CAM battery, for the most part, was designed to accommodate genera-tivity. Most CAM test items conform to a factorial or faceted design, in which the levels of the various facets can be manipulated so as to systematically alter item difficulty. Figure 17.2 illustrates how this is done. The three tests illustrated in the figure are verbal, quantitative, and spatial variants (i.e., three separate tests) of what in CAM terminology is called the "4-term order" paradigm, tests designed to measure working-memory capacity. An examinee is shown the four screens in succession, where the first three provide instructions on how to order the stimuli, and the fourth provides eight possible orders of the four stimuli from which the examinee is requested to choose one as the correct answer. In this paradigm the facets manipulated are whether the set information (e.g., "furniture comes before animals") is shown first or last, the presence of negation (e.g., in the spatial version, the batch running through the arrow indicates that the object should not be moved above the other), the markedness of the term linking the two objects (e.g., x comes before y versus x comes after y), and so on. Changing the levels of these facets changes the difficulty of the items. For example, items with set information first have been found to be easier than items with set information last, items with marked relations (e.g., comes after) are harder than others, and items with negation (e.g., does not come after) are harder than those without.

Tests constructed in this manner can be administered to groups of subjects, and the effects of facet manipulations on difficulty can be determined (see Figure 17.3). Then an evaluation of the degree to which the faceted model accounts for the item-to-item variability in difficulty can be conducted. Such an evaluation might show that the faceted model sufficiently accounts for difficulty, or it might suggest additional important facets to be included in the model. But once an adequate model of item difficulty is established, it is then possible to build items to target difficulty levels. If there are random factors in the faceted design (e.g., instances of furniture or animals in the verbal four-term ordering paradigm), those facets can be sampled from to provide numerous items at a given difficulty level. For example, the expression "dogs come before horses" could be replaced with "cats come before cows" or "lions come before elephants," and so on.

Clearly, there is empirical work to be done on faceted models to determine the effects of the various kinds of facets. Still, the power of this model-based approach is that once an adequate model is developed, it is not necessary to collect empirical data on every possible item that could be administered. This will have the effect of reducing the time and expense associated with forms development. Also, considerable model development has already been done in cognitive psychology on exactly the kinds of tests that appear in the CAM battery (Evans & Dennis, 1991) and similar information-processing-inspired batteries, such as the British Army Recruit Battery (BARB; Dann, 1995).

Figure 17.2
Example of Verbal, Quantitative, and Spatial Items of the Four-Term Ordering Test

Test Design Facets

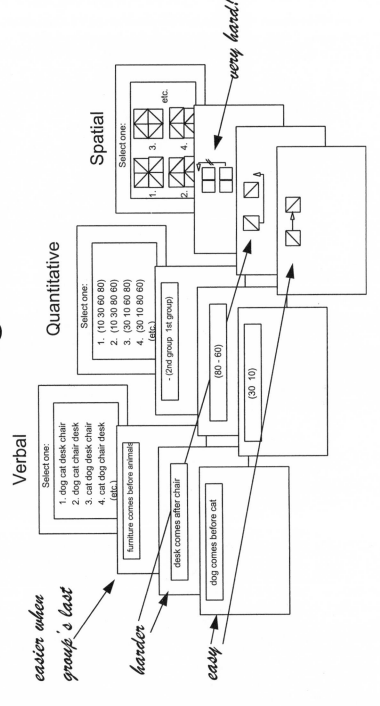

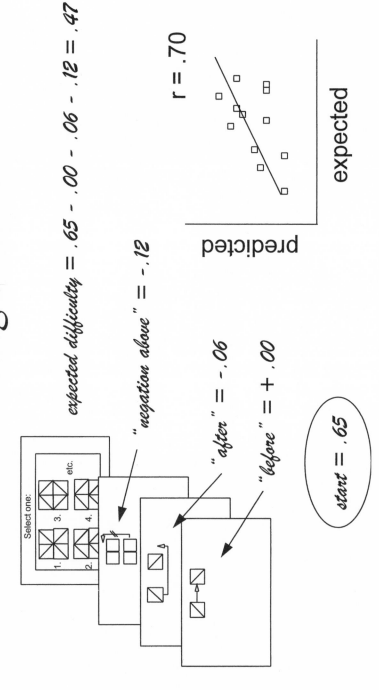

Test Design Facets

THE "SPEED-ACCURACY TRADE-OFF" PROBLEM AND
TIME-PARAMETERIZED TESTING

Problem

A perennial problem with computerized testing has been how to treat response time information. In paper-and-pencil testing, an examinee's score is based solely on the number of correct responses (perhaps corrected for guessing) obtained within a standard time limit for the test. Computerized tests allow for the recording of every response action by the examinee, and thus it is commonplace to record the amount of time an examinee spends on every item. What is unclear is whether to treat response time as a separate score (from number correct) or to adjust the correctness score by the response time value, or to combine the two scores (response time and accuracy) in some other way.

On most cognitive tests, it is possible to obtain a higher accuracy score by taking more time to solve items or, conversely, to minimize response time at the cost of less accurate performance. In cognitive psychology, there has been considerable research on this, the so-called speed-accuracy trade-off problem, but there has been no completely satisfactory resolution. Furthermore, a somewhat surprising, but nevertheless fairly consistent, result emerging from validity studies of cognitive tests has been that processing speed factors have proven to be unimportant in predicting the success of various learning outcomes. One possibility is that processing speed per sc is unimportant in determining the success of learning in various contexts. But another possibility is that we have not yet developed a fair method for measuring processing speed due to the problems created by speed-accuracy trade-offs that vary from one examinee to another.

Solution

There have been a variety of attempts to solve the speed-accuracy trade-off problem. A common practice is simply to record two scores for every test, an accuracy (e.g., percentage correct) and a latency (e.g., mean response time) score. The problem with this method is that the examinee does not know which score is more important and therefore cannot determine an optimal speed-accuracy trade-off. Another method is to set various response deadlines, then record the improvement in accuracy occurring as deadlines increase. Such improvements sometimes prove to be fairly regular, and it then becomes possible to model the growth in accuracy over time by as few as two parameters, such as slope and asymptote (e.g., Chaiken, 1993; Lohman, 1986). This method has the benefit of avoiding indeterminacy in what constitutes optimal behavior on the part of the examinee, in that he or she attempts simply to maximize accuracy for whatever duration is allowed by the response deadline.

Both these methods still suffer from a kind of scoring parsimony problem in that they require two scores to characterize performance on a single test. In many respects, it seems desirable to have a single score emerge from a single test performance, as is the case with paper-and-pencil tests. Just simply ignoring latency does not seem to be an adequate solution in that response time certainly says something about how adeptly an individual is able to solve test items. Thus, another solution has been to create test scores as the ratio of number of items correctly solved over the amount of time taken to correctly solve them (e.g., Kyllonen, 1993). Variants on this score include various rescalings of the two components in the score, such as using d' or the inverse of log (errors) to replace number or percentage correct, and using log (latency) to replace latency. A feature of this ratio score is that it is analogous to the score obtained with paper-and-pencil tests, although with paper-and-pencil tests, the denominator (response time), of course, is a constant (i.e., the time limit for the test). Unfortunately, this accuracy over response time score also has been shown to be problematic, particularly as speed increases at the cost of decreased accuracy (Dennis & Evans, 1996). If this is the case, then that suggests that the speed-accuracy trade-off decision still affects the score one receives on the test, and the problem of examinee indeterminacy with respect to how to calculate an optimal speed-accuracy trade-off reemerges.

A promising solution, suggested by Evans and Wright (1993), that combines the desirable examinee-determinacy feature of the deadline method with the single-score feature of the ratio methods is to simply include a deadline as another facet of difficulty. That is, items with shorter deadlines are treated simply as more difficult items of the same type. In an adaptive test, if an examinee was able to solve particular items correctly, then the system might deliver more difficult items to the examinee by simply decreasing the response deadline for those kinds of items. The deadline facet thus would be treated like any other difficulty facet associated with the test.

A concern with this method is that response time represents a facet of performance that is at least somewhat independent of other structural facets that affect item difficulty. In fact, Lohman's (1986) speed-accuracy model is based on the idea that at least in spatial information processing, speed of performing spatial operations is fairly independent of the difficulty of the spatial operation an examinee is able to perform. Nevertheless, some preliminary monte-carlo evaluations of the Evans-Wright deadline model have suggested that response time might appropriately be treated as another difficulty manipulation rather than as a feature that changes the nature of the task. Empirical analyses of both simple arithmetic computation items (Wright, Tapsfield, & Kyllonen, 1994) and progressive matrices reasoning items (Embretson, 1995) have also suggested that treating deadlines as simply difficulty-altering facets rather than as construct-altering facets might prove workable.

Considerable empirical research is probably necessary to establish the feasibility of treating response time (deadlines) as simply a difficulty-altering facet. It may be that for some kinds of tasks altering deadlines alters the ability being tapped by the task. For example, Embretson's study was motivated by the desire to analyze the degree to which short deadlines induce stress, and therefore her expectation was that a short deadline task would be a test of an individual's ability to cope with stress rather than a measure of the individual's reasoning ability per se. It could also turn out that over some intervals deadline manipulation is simply a difficulty-manipulating facet, but if time becomes too short, then it does change the nature of the task. Another factor that might prove important is whether the test is essentially a speeded or a power test, to use the terminology associated with paper-and-pencil tests (speeded tests consist of relatively simple items, and the time limits for the test are set so that few examinees complete the tests; consequently, one's score is determined primarily by how quickly one responds; power tests consist of relatively complex items with relaxed time limits, and one's score is determined primarily by how accurately one responds).

THE "TEST MAINTENANCE PROBLEM" AND LATENT FACTOR–CENTERED SCORING

Problem

The goal of an aptitude testing system typically is to estimate an individual's abilities, which are presumed to underlie performance both on the tests and in training (or in education or on the job, depending on what the tests are designed to predict performance on). For example, in the military services, general ability is presumed to underlie performance on both the ASVAB and in technical school training, which motivates the use of an estimate of general ability to predict an examinee's likelihood for successfully completing training. The various military services also use additional scores estimated from the ASVAB for classification purposes. For example, the air force classifies training schools into four categories (general, mechanical, administrative, and electronic), and scores corresponding to each of those four areas are computed from different combinations of the ASVAB subtests. An individual is eligible to enter training in those areas where his or her score, which in the air force is called an Aptitude Index, meets an entry standard. Here again, the principle behind this arrangement is that a particular ability, for example, mechanical ability, is assumed to underlie both performance on the particular subset of tests used to compute the Mechanical Aptitude Index and performance in the training schools in the mechanical specialty area.

Even though the goal of the testing system is to estimate an individual's underlying or latent ability, the estimation is imperfectly accomplished by computing a score based on that individual's observed test scores. For example, the air force classification system estimates the Mechanical Aptitude Index as the sum of two ASVAB subtest scores, the Mechanical Comprehension and the Auto and Shop Information subtests. Similarly, the other Aptitude Indexes used in the classification system are computed as simple linear combinations of subsets of ASVAB subtests.

Although this system works reasonably well, and has the advantage of allowing for simple computation of Aptitude Index scores from ASVAB subtest scores, there are some disadvantages. One is that the Aptitude Index scores are not necessarily the most valid scores that could be computed from the information available in the ASVAB. Greater differential classification and hence a more useful personnel assignment system could be achieved through the use of more complex mathematical systems for combining test score data (see, e.g., Muthén, 1994). But a more important limitation is that this kind of system leads to a focus on test scores per se rather than a focus on the abilities the tests are designed to measure. This in turn leads to undue conservatism in proving the test battery responsible for producing those scores.

There are many indications of a test focus, as opposed to an abilities focus, in the development of the ASVAB. As noted earlier in this chapter, the ECAT project relied on a test nomination procedure in the development of a new information-processing–inspired test battery. The initial developers of the ECAT battery surveyed the various services and solicited each service's ''most promising new tests.'' An abilities focus, in contrast, would have sought input primarily on what new abilities ought to be included in the ASVAB and then might have secondarily solicited suggestions for various tests of those abilities. Another example of the test focus is that the one tangible result from the ECAT project was simply to augment the ASVAB with a single new test, the Assembling Objects test, rather than to reconsider the larger issue of whether there might be additional abilities that ought to be measured by the ASVAB.

Because of the focus on tests rather than abilities, it has proven remarkably difficult to change the ASVAB. For example, there have been very few changes in the tests that go into the ASVAB over the last 30 years. There are probably a number of reasons for this. Systems for reporting scores and computing composites are developed and written into regulations to ease the burden on the operators who are responsible for the day-to-day personnel decisions involving those scores. With the focus on the mechanics of combining particular test scores to form the composites that are used for classification, there is institutional resistance to changing the components of that process, such as the tests themselves whose scores are combined.

Solution

Because the goal of the testing system is to estimate abilities rather than test scores per se, it makes sense that the testing system should be designed to produce latent factor scores, rather than test scores that are then combined in linear composites. A short-term implementation of this suggestion probably involves simply developing new, more psychometrically sophisticated algorithms for combining test score information to yield Aptitude Indexes that are used for classification. The availability of lightweight, inexpensive calculating machines makes it now technically feasible to combine test score information in much more sophisticated ways than has ever been done before in operational contexts. Indeed, with computerized testing, that technology is available in the testing machine itself and can be completely transparent to the operator responsible for actually using the scores in personnel decisions. The CAT stations could be programmed to yield Aptitude Indexes of significant mathematical sophistication without operator intervention.

But there is an even more important benefit to moving to a latent factor–centered testing system. That is, once the focus moves away from test scores toward ability or factor scores, the issues about which tests are used to actually produce the scores become less important. Once the focus on tests is replaced with a focus on factors, it should become much easier to change the tests that make up the battery. The advantage to this is that as better tests for measuring a particular factor are developed, they can more easily be added into the test battery. The factor being measured remains the same; only the means for measuring that factor changes. This gives the battery the desirable feature of design upgradability.

As an example, suppose that the CAM battery were to replace the ASVAB as the aptitude testing battery in the Department of Defense's personnel selection and classification system. Suppose also that the CAM factors, such as working-memory capacity and information-processing speed, became the new Aptitude Indexes, replacing the Mechanical, General, Administrative, and Electronic Aptitude Indexes currently in use. In the current CAM battery, there are four tests or testing paradigms for measuring working-memory capacity. However, these paradigms are only a small subset of the paradigms one can find in the literature for measuring working-memory capacity. The paradigms used in the CAM battery were chosen because of their particularly good construct validity. But future research could reveal new, even more valid ways of measuring working-memory capacity. These newer methods could be substituted for existing ones, without changing at all the nature of what was being measured by the CAM battery.

Another interesting feature of a latent factor as opposed to a test-centered focus is that it is compatible with the MAT testing scheme outlined by Segall (1996). As Segall points out, a benefit of MAT is that it can be used to balance content. He cites the example of a general science test in which items are taken from biology, the physical sciences, and chemistry. In standard CAT testing, content balancing might be implemented by selecting equal numbers of items in the three content areas. Segall points out that if items from these three areas vary in difficulty (e.g., chemistry items are typically more difficult than items from the other two areas), this procedure has the disadvantage of selecting items that are relatively uninformative (e.g., low-ability examinees' responses to the difficult chemistry items are relatively uninformative). An alternative procedure implemented in MAT would be to consider the three content areas as separate, albeit highly correlated dimensions, or factors, and to select maximally informative items based on the criterion of "reducing the volume of the credibility elipsoid." Thus, responses to chemistry items would have an effect on the testing system's estimate of one's knowledge in the other two domains. Therefore, an examinee would still produce scores on all three content dimensions, but different examinees would be administered different mixtures of content, depending on their ability level.

An analogous balancing could occur at the paradigm level in a MAT version of the CAM battery. It is the case that some paradigms for measuring, for example, working-memory capacity, are more difficult than others. Paradigm factors could be established and a MAT implementation would then select items from a particular paradigm according to which paradigm was most informative with respect to the examinee's working-memory capacity. More adept examinees would be more likely to be administered items from the more difficult paradigms.

SUMMARY

In this chapter, I have discussed diverse new research on the theory and methodology for delivering tests of cognitive abilities factors on computer. The chapter has a strong practical emphasis, an emphasis on what needs to be done to actually field an advanced testing system for the twenty-first century. The system must be broad (measure all the aptitude factors that can potentially make a difference in a personnel selection and classification system), precise (measure those factors reliably), quick (measure all those factors in the same amount of testing time as we have available for testing currently—about three hours), and ready (i.e., the emphasis is on actually building the system rather than thinking about what direction basic research might be going over the next decade). I argue that all the necessary pieces are in place. What's needed is for those pieces to be brought together for methodological and theoretical advances to be synthesized in an advanced system demonstration project.

REFERENCES

Carroll, J. B. (1995). *Human cognitive abilities: A survey of factor-analytic studies*. New York: Cambridge University Press.

Chaiken, S. R. (1993). Two models for an inspection time paradigm: Processing distraction and processing speed vs. processing speed and asymptotic strength. *Intelligence, 17*, 257–283.

Chastain, R. (1993). *The flexibility factor in problem solving: Effects of mixing item types on information processing*. Unpublished doctoral dissertation, School of Education, Stanford University.

Christal, R. E. (1991). *Comparative validities of ASVAB and LAMP tests for logic gates learning* (Technical Report No. AL-TP-1991-0031). Brooks Air Force Base, TX: Air Force Systems Command.

Collis, J. M., & Irvine, S. H. (1993). *The combined ABC battery for RN/WRNS non-*

technician ratings: Studies of concurrent and predictive validity (Senior Psychologist [Naval] Technical Report TR313). London: Ministry of Defense.

Collis, J. M., Tapsfield, P. G. C., Irvine, S. H., Dann, P. L., & Wright, D. (1995). The British Army Recruit Battery goes operational: From theory to practice in computer-based testing using item-generation techniques. *International Journal of Selection & Assessment, 3*, 96–104.

Dann, P. L. (1995). *The BARB computer-based testing system* (Vol. 1) (HAL Technical Report No. 1–1991 [APRE]) Plymouth, United Kingdom: Department of Psychology, University of Plymouth.

Dennis, I., & Evans, J. St. B. T. (1996). The speed-error trade-off problem in psychometric testing. *British Journal of Psychology, 87*, 105–129.

Embretson, S. E. (1995). The role of working memory capacity and general control processes in intelligence. *Intelligence, 20*, 169–189.

Evans, J. St. B. T., & Dennis, I. (1991). *The CAM-4 test battery: Cognitive theory and item generation* (HAL Technical Report No. 1–1991 [APRE]). Plymouth, United Kingdom: Department of Psychology, University of Plymouth.

Evans, J. St. B. T., & Wright, D. E. (1993). *The properties of fixed-time tests: A simulation study* (Report to the Army Personnel Research Establishment, 3–1993). Plymouth, United Kingdom: Department of Psychology, University of Plymouth.

Irvine, S. H., Dann, P. L., and Anderson, J. D. (1990). Towards a theory of algorithm-determined cognitive test construction. *British Journal of Psychology, 81*, 173–195.

Jacobson, R. L. (1993). New computer technique seen producing a revolution in educational testing. *Chronicle of Higher Education, 40* (4), A22–23, 26.

Kyllonen, P. C. (1991). Principles for creating a computerized test battery. *Intelligence, 15*, 1–15.

Kyllonen, P. C. (1993). Aptitude testing inspired by information processing: A test of the four-sources model. *Journal of General Psychology, 120*, 375–405.

Kyllonen, P. C. (1994a). Cognitive abilities testing: An agenda for the 1990s. In M. G. Rumsey, C. B. Walker, & J. H. Harris (Eds.), *Personnel selection and classification*. Hillsdale, NJ: Lawrence Erlbaum.

Kyllonen, P. C. (1994b). Information processing. In R. Sternberg (Ed.), *Encyclopedia of intelligence*. New York: Macmillan.

Kyllonen, P. C. (1995). CAM: A theoretical framework for cognitive abilities measurement. In D. Detterman (Ed.), *Current topics in human intelligence: Volume IV, Theories of intelligence*. Norwood, NJ: Ablex.

Lohman, D. F. (1986). The effect of speed-accuracy tradeoff on sex differences in mental rotation. *Perception & Psychophysics, 39*, 427–436.

Muthén, B. (1994). *A note on predictive validity from a latent variable perspective.* Unpublished manuscript. School of Education, University of California, Los Angeles.

Muthén, B. O., & Gustafsson, J. -E. (1994). *ASVAB-based job performance prediction and selection: Latent variable modeling versus regression analysis.* Unpublished manuscript. Graduate School of Education, University of California, Los Angeles.

Searcy, C. A., Sawin, L. L., & Tiegs, R. B. (1996). *Differential item functioning on a battery of information processing tests.* Paper presented at the 11th Annual Meeting of the Society for Industrial and Organizational Psychology, San Diego, CA.

Segall, D. O. (1995). *Multidimensional adaptive testing.* Paper presented to the Manpower Accession Policy Working Group (MAPWG), Brooks Air Force Base, San Antonio, TX.

Segall, D. O. (1996). Multidimensional adaptive testing. *Psychometrika, 61*, 331–354.

Shute, V. J., & Kyllonen, P. C. (1990). *Modeling programming skill acquisition* (Report No. AFHRL-TP-90-76). Brooks Air Force Base, TX: Air Force Systems Command.

Wright, D., Tapsfield, P., & Kyllonen, P. C. (1994). *Analysis of a time-limited arithmetic problem-solving test* (Report from the Technical Cooperation Program; TTCP). Brooks Air Force Base, TX: Armstrong Laboratory, Human Resources Directorate.

Selected Bibliography

Ackerman, P. L. (1988). Determinants of individual differences during skill acquisition: Cognitive abilities and information processing. *Journal of Experimental Psychology: General, 117*, 288–318.

Åirasian, P. W. (1991). *Classroom assessment*. New York: McGraw-Hill.

American Association for Counseling and Development/Association for Measurement and Evaluation in Counseling and Development. (1989). *Responsibilities of users of standardized tests*. Alexandria, VA: Author.

American Association of School Administrators, National Association of Elementary School Principals, National Association of Secondary School Principals, & National Council on Measurement in Education. (1994). Competency standards in student assessment for educational administrators. *Educational Measurement: Issues and Practice, 13* (1), 44–47.

American Council on Education, Credit by Examination Program. (1995). *Guidelines for computerized-adaptive test development and use in education*. Washington, DC: Author.

American Counseling Association. (1995). *Code of ethics and standards of practice*. Alexandria, VA: Author.

Anastasi, A. (1990). What is test misuse? Perspectives of a measurement expert. In *The uses of standardized tests in America*. Proceedings of the 1989 ETS Invitational Conference. Princeton, NJ: Educational Testing Service.

Berliner, D. C., & Calfee, R. C. (Eds.). *The handbook of educational psychology*. New York: Macmillan.

Bond, L. (1995). Unintended consequences of performance assessment: Issues of bias and fairness. *Educational Measurement: Issues and Practice, 14* (4), 21–24.

Borman, W. C., Hanson, M. A., Oppler, S. H., Pulakos, E. D., & White, L. A. (1993).

Role of early supervisory experience in supervisor performance. *Journal of Applied Psychology, 78*, 443–449.

Borman, W. C., & Motowidlo, S. J. (1993). Expanding the criterion domain to include elements of contextual performance. In N. Schmitt & W. C. Borman (Eds.), *Personnel selection in organizations* (pp. 71–98). San Francisco: Jossey-Bass.

Brody, N. (1992). *Intelligence* (2nd ed.). San Diego: Academic Press.

Campbell, J. P., McHenry, J. J., & Wise, L. L. (1990). Modeling job performance in a population of jobs. *Personnel Psychology, 43*, 313–333.

Carrier, M., & Pashler, H. (1992). The influence of retrieval on retention. *Memory & Cognition, 20*, 633–642.

Carroll, J. B. (1993). *Human cognitive abilities. A survey of factor-analytic studies*. Cambridge: Cambridge University Press.

Cascio, W. F. (1995). Whither industrial and organizational psychology in a changing world of work? *American Psychologist, 50*, 928–939.

Das, J. P., Naglieri, J. A, & Kirby, J. R. (1994). *Assessment of cognitive processes*. Needham Heights, MA: Allyn & Bacon.

Davison, M., & Sharma, A. R. (1990). Parametric statistics and levels of measurement: Factorial designs and multiple regression. *Psychological Bulletin, 107*, 394–400.

Dempster, F. N. (1996). Distributing and managing the conditions of encoding and practice. In E. L Bjork & R. A. Bjork (Eds.), *Handbook of perception and cognition* (Vol. 10). San Diego, CA: Academic Press.

Dempster, F. N., & Perkins, P. G. (1993). Revitalizing classroom assessment: Using tests to promote learning. *Journal of Instructional Psychology, 20*, 197–203.

Dillon, R. F., & Pellegrino, J. W. (1989). *Testing: Theoretical and applied perspectives*. New York: Praeger.

Duke, A. P., & Ree, M. J. (1996). Better candidates fly fewer training hours: Another time testing pays off. *International Journal of Selection and Assessment, 4*, 115–121.

Embretson, S. (1992). Measuring and validating cognitive modifiability as an ability: A study in the spatial domain. *Journal of Educational Measurement, 29*, 25–50.

Estes, W. K. (1955). Statistical theory of spontaneous recovery and regression. *Psychological Review, 62*, 145–154.

Fischer, G. (1995). Derivations of the Rasch model. In G. Fischer & I. Molenaar (Eds.), *Rasch models: Foundations, recent developments, and applications*. New York: Springer-Verlag.

Fleishman, E. A., & Quaintance, M. K. (1984). *Taxonomies of human performance: The description of human tasks*. Orlando, FL: Academic Press.

Gardner, H. (1983). *Frames of mind: The theory of multiple intelligences*. New York: Basic Books.

Gustafsson, J. -E., & Undheim, J. O. (1996). Individual differences in cognitive functions. In D. C. Berliner & R. C. Calfee (Eds.), *The handbook of educational psychology* (pp. 186–242). New York: Macmillan.

Guttman, L., & Levy, S. (1991). Two structural laws for intelligence tests. *Intelligence, 15*, 79–103.

Hetter, R. D., Segall, D. O., & Bloxom, B. M. (1994). A comparison of item calibration media in computerized adaptive testing. *Applied Psychological Measurement, 18*, 197–204.

Humphreys, L. G. (1976). General intelligence: An integration of factor, test, and simplex theory. In B. B. Wolman (Ed.), *Handbook of intelligence: Theories, measurement, and applications* (pp. 201–224). New York: Wiley.

Hunter, D. R., & Burke, E. F. (1995). *Handbook of pilot selection*. Brookfield, VT: Ashgate Publishing Co.

Koenig, J. A., & Mitchell, K. J. (1993). Use of Medical College Admissions Test Writing Sample data in medical school admissions decisions. *The Advisor, 13*, 13–15.

Kyllonen, P. C. (1993). Aptitude testing inspired by information processing: A test of the four-sources model. *Journal of General Psychology, 120*, 375–405.

Lohman, D. L. (1993). Teaching and testing to develop fluid abilities. *Educational Researcher, 22*, 12–23.

Martin, C. J. (1994). *Army alpha to navy theta*. Paper presented at the thirty-sixth annual conference of the International Military Testing Association, Rotterdam, The Netherlands.

Michel, J. (1990). *An introduction to the logic of psychological measurement*. Hillsdale, NJ: Erlbaum.

Mitchell, K. J., Haynes, R., & Koenig, J. (1994). Assessing the validity of the updated Medical College Admissions Test. *Academic Medicine, 69*, 394–401.

Moss, P. A. (1992). Shifting conceptions in educational measurement: Implications for performance assessment. *Review of Educational Research, 62* (3), 229–258.

Ree, M. J., & Earles, J. A. (1994). The ubiquitous predictiveness of *g*. In C. Walker, M. Rumsey, & J. Harris (Eds.), *Personnel selection and classification*. Hillsdale, NJ: Erlbaum.

Rosén, M. (1995). Gender differences in structure, means and variances of hierarchically ordered ability dimensions. *Learning and Instruction, 5* (1), 37–62.

Index

About the Editor and Contributors

RONNA F. DILLON is Professor of Educational Psychology and Professor of Psychology, Southern Illinois University, Carbondale, Illinois. Dillon was named Spencer Fellow in 1983 for outstanding research contributions. Dillon's other books include *Individual Differences in Cognition*—Volume 1 with R. R. Schmeck and Volume 2; *Cognition and Instruction*, with Robert J. Sternberg; and *Testing: Theoretical and Applied Perspectives* and *Instruction: Theoretical Perspectives*, both with James Pellegrino.

WANDA J. CAMPBELL is Manager of Employment Testing, Edison Electric Institute, Washington, D.C.

THOMAS R. CARRETTA is Research Scientist, Aircrew Selection Branch, Human Resources Directorate, Armstrong Laboratory, Brooks Air Force Base, Texas.

J. P. DAS is Professor of Educational Psychology and is affiliated with the Development Disabilities Centre at the University of Alberta, Edmonton, Canada.

FRANK N. DEMPSTER is Professor of Educational Psychology, University of Nevada, Las Vegas, Nevada.

RUTH B. EKSTROM is Principal Research Scientist, Education Policy Division, Educational Testing Service, Princeton, New Jersey.

PATRICIA B. ELMORE is Professor of Educational Psychology, Southern Illinois University at Carbondale, Carbondale, Illinois.

SUSAN E. EMBRETSON is Professor of Psychology, University of Kansas, Lawrence, Kansas.

JAN-ERIC GUSTAFSSON is Professor of Educational Psychology, Department of Education and Educational Research, University of Goteborg, Mölndal, Sweden.

LAWRENCE M. HANSER is Senior Research Psychologist, RAND, Santa Monica, California.

REBECCA D. HETTER is Research Scientist, Defense Manpower Data Center, DoD Center Monterey, Seaside, California.

DAVID J. KLEINKE is Director of Employment Testing, Edison Electric Institute, Washington, D.C.

JUDITH A. KOENIG is Senior Research Associate, Medical College Admission Test Program Association of American Medical Colleges, Washington, D.C.

PATRICK C. KYLLONEN is Technical Director, Manpower and Personnel Division, Human Resources Directorate, Armstrong Laboratory, Brooks Air Force Base, Texas.

DAVID F. LOHMAN is Professor of Educational Psychology, Chair of the Division of Psychological and Quantitative Foundations, University of Iowa, Iowa City, Iowa.

PAMELA F. MILLER is Senior Research Project Specialist, Office of Research Development and Administration, Southern Illinois University at Carbondale, Carbondale, Illinois.

SIDNEY R. MILLER is Professor of Special Education, Southern Illinois University at Carbondale, Carbondale, Illinois.

KATHLEEN E. MORENO is Research Scientist, Defense Manpower Data Center, DoD Center Monterey, Seaside, California.

JACK A. NAGLIERI is Professor of School Psychology and Psychology, Ohio State University, Columbus, Ohio. He also holds appointments as a Senior Researcher at the Devereux Foundation's Institute for Clinical Training and Research and the Ohio State University's Nisonger Center.

MALCOLM JAMES REE is Scientific Adviser, Aircrew Selection Research Branch, Manpower and Personnel Research Division, Human Resources Directorate, Armstrong Laboratory, Brooks Air Force Base, Texas.

WILLIAM D. SCHAFER is Professor of Educational Measurement and Statistics, University of Maryland, College Park, Maryland.

DANIEL O. SEGALL is Research Scientist, Defense Manpower Data Center, DoD Center Monterey, Seaside, California.

RICHARD E. SNOW is Howard H. and Jesse T. Watkins University Professor of Education and Psychology, Stanford University, Stanford, California.

WILLIAM C. TIRRE is Senior Scientist, Cognitive Technologies Branch, Manpower and Personnel Research Division, Human Resources Directorate, Armstrong Laboratory, Brooks Air Force Base, Texas.

BRIAN K. WATERS is Program Manager, Manpower Analysis Program, Human Resources Research Organization, Alexandria, Virginia.

ANDREW WILEY is Research Associate, Medical College Admission Test Program, Association of American Medical Colleges, Washington, D.C.

ISBN 0-313-28984-0

EAN

9 780313 289842

90000>